Quicken® 2010

THE OFFICIAL GUIDE

Quicken® 2010

THE OFFICIAL GUIDE

Maria LANGER

New York Chicago San Francisco
Lisbon London Madrid Mexico City Milan
New Delhi San Juan Seoul Singapore Sydney Toronto

The McGraw·Hill Companies

Cataloging-in-Publication Data is on file with the Library of Congress

McGraw-Hill books are available at special quantity discounts to use as premiums and sales promotions, or for use in corporate training programs. To contact a representative, please e-mail us at bulksales@mcgraw-hill.com.

Quicken® 2010 The Official Guide

1 2 3 4 5 6 7 8 9 0   FGR FGR   0 1 9

ISBN 978-0-07-163499-1
MHID   0-07-163499-1

Sponsoring Editor	**Proofreader**
Megg Morin	Teresa Barensfeld
Editorial Supervisor	**Indexer**
Patty Mon	Judy Davis
Project Manager	**Production Supervisor**
Patty Wallenburg	George Anderson
Acquisitions Coordinator	**Composition**
Meghan Riley	TypeWriting
Technical Editor	**Art Director, Cover**
Mary Higgins	Jeff Weeks
Copy Editor	
Lisa McCoy	

Contents at a Glance

Part Five   Planning

Part Six   Tax

Part Seven   Appendixes

Contents

Part Two   Banking

Part Three   Investing

Part Four   Net Worth

Part Five   Planning

Part Six   Tax

Part Seven   Appendixes

Acknowledgments

This book, like most others, is the end product of a lot of hard work by many people. Among them are:

- Megg Morin, acquisitions editor at McGraw-Hill.
- The folks at Intuit, including Eddy Wu and Dale Knievel for their technical expertise and willingness to answer questions. Thanks also to Todd LaFrentz, Kooper Frame, and Mary Lunnenborg.
- The editorial folks at McGraw-Hill, including Patty Mon, Patty Wallenburg, and Meghan Riley.
- The technical editor Mary Higgins, copyeditor Lisa McCoy, proofreader Teresa Barensfeld, and indexer Judy Davis.

Introduction

Choosing Quicken Personal Finance Software to organize your finances was a great decision. Quicken has all the tools you need to manage your personal finances. Its well-designed, intuitive interface makes it easy to use. And its online and automation features make entering transactions and paying bills a snap. But if that isn't enough, Quicken also offers features that can help you learn more about financial opportunities that can save you time and money—two things there never seems to be enough of.

This introduction tells you a little about the book, so you know what to expect in the chapters to come.

About This Book

This book tells you how to get the most out of Quicken. It starts by explaining the basics—the common, everyday tasks that you need to know just to use the program. It then goes beyond the basics to show you how to use Quicken to save time, save money, and make smart financial decisions. Along the way, it shows you most of Quicken's features, including many that you probably didn't even know existed. You'll find yourself using Quicken far more than you ever dreamed you would.

Assumptions

This book makes a few assumptions about your knowledge of your computer, Windows, Quicken, and financial management. These assumptions gives it a starting point, making it possible to skip over the things that are assumed you already know.

What You Should Know About Your Computer and Windows

To use this book (or Quicken 2010, for that matter), you should have a general understanding of how to use your computer and Windows. You don't need to be an expert. As you'll see, Quicken uses many standard and intuitive interface elements, making it easy to use—even if you're a complete computer novice.

At a bare minimum, you should know how to turn your computer on and off and how to use your mouse. You should also know how to perform basic

Windows tasks, such as starting and exiting programs, using menus and dialog boxes (called just *dialogs* in this book), and entering and editing text.

If you're not sure how to do these things or would like to brush up on them, get *Windows 7 QuickSteps* from McGraw-Hill. This resource will provide all the information you need to get started.

What You Should Know About Quicken and Financial Management

You don't need to know much about either Quicken or financial management to get the most out of this book; it assumes that both are new to you.

This doesn't mean that this book is just for raw beginners. It provides plenty of useful information for seasoned Quicken users—especially those of you who have used previous versions of Quicken—and for people who have been managing their finances with other tools, such as Microsoft Money (welcome to Quicken!) or pencil and paper (welcome to the new millennium!).

Because the book assumes that all this is new to you, it makes a special effort to explain Quicken procedures as well as the financial concepts and terms on which they depend. New concepts and terms first appear in italic type. By understanding these things, not only can you better understand how to use Quicken, but you also can communicate more effectively with finance professionals such as bankers, stock brokers, and financial advisors.

Organization

This book is logically organized into seven parts, each with at least two chapters. Each part covers either general Quicken setup information or one of Quicken's five financial centers. Within each part, the chapters start with the most basic concepts and procedures, most of which involve specific Quicken tasks, and then work their way up to more advanced topics, many of which are based on finance-related concepts that Quicken makes easy to master.

It is not necessary to read this book from beginning to end. Skip around as desired. Although the book is organized for cover-to-cover reading, not all of its information may apply to you. For example, if you're not the least bit interested in investing, skip the chapters in the Investing Center part. It's as simple as that. When you're ready for the information that you skipped, it'll be waiting for you.

Here's a brief summary of the book's organization and contents.

Part One: Quicken Setup and Basics

This part of the book introduces Quicken's interface and features and helps you set up Quicken for managing your finances. It also provides the information you need to set up and test Quicken's online features. If you're brand-new to

Quicken, I highly recommend reading at least the first three chapters in this part of the book.

Part One has four chapters:

- **Chapter 1:** Getting to Know Quicken
- **Chapter 2:** Using Setup Tab Screens
- **Chapter 3:** Setting Up Accounts, Categories, and Tags
- **Chapter 4:** Going Online with Quicken

Part Two: Banking

This part of the book explains how to use Quicken to record financial transactions in bank and credit card accounts. One chapter concentrates on the basics, while another goes beyond the basics to discuss online features available within Quicken and on Quicken.com. This part of the book also explains how to automate many transaction entry tasks, reconcile accounts, and use Quicken's revised reporting features.

There are five chapters in Part Two:

- **Chapter 5:** Recording Bank and Credit Card Transactions
- **Chapter 6:** Using Online Banking Features
- **Chapter 7:** Automating Transactions and Tasks
- **Chapter 8:** Reconciling Your Accounts
- **Chapter 9:** Examining Your Bank Activity

Part Three: Investing

This part of the book explains how you can use Quicken and Quicken.com to keep track of your investment portfolio and get information to help you make smart investment decisions. The first chapter covers the basics of Quicken's investment tracking features, while the other two chapters provide information about online investment tracking and research tools and the features within Quicken.com that help you evaluate your investment position.

There are three chapters in Part Three:

- **Chapter 10:** Entering Your Investment Transactions
- **Chapter 11:** Using Transaction Download and Research Tools
- **Chapter 12:** Evaluating Your Position

Part Four: Net Worth

This part of the book concentrates on assets and liabilities, including your home and car and related loans. It explains how you can track these items in Quicken and provides tips for minimizing related expenses.

There are two chapters in Part Four:

- **Chapter 13:** Monitoring Assets and Loans
- **Chapter 14:** Keeping Tabs on Your Net Worth

Part Five: Planning

This part of the book tells you how you can take advantage of Quicken's extensive, built-in planning tools to plan for your retirement and other major events in your life. As you'll learn in this part of the book, whether you want financial security in your retirement years or to save up for the down payment on a house or college education for your children, Quicken can help you. It covers Quicken's Planners as well as its financial calculators. It also provides a wealth of tips for saving money and reducing debt.

There are three chapters in Part Five:

- **Chapter 15:** Planning for the Future
- **Chapter 16:** Using Financial Calculators
- **Chapter 17:** Reducing Debt and Saving Money

Part Six: Tax

This part of the book explains how you can use Quicken's Tax features to simplify tax preparation, plan for tax time, and reduce your tax liability.

Part Six has two chapters:

- **Chapter 18:** Simplifying Tax Preparation
- **Chapter 19:** Planning for Tax Time

Part Seven: Appendixes

If nineteen chapters of information aren't enough for you, three appendixes offer additional information you might find useful when working with Quicken:

- **Appendix A:** Managing Quicken Files
- **Appendix B:** Customizing Quicken
- **Appendix C:** Converting from Microsoft Money

Conventions

All how-to books—especially computer books—have certain conventions for communicating information. Here's a brief summary of the conventions used throughout this book.

Menu Commands

Quicken, like most other Windows programs, makes commands accessible on the menu bar at the top of the application window. Throughout this book, you are told which menu commands to choose to open a window or dialog or to complete a task. The following format is used to indicate menu commands: Menu | Submenu (if applicable) | Command.

Keystrokes

Keystrokes are the keys you must press to complete a task. There are two kinds of keystrokes.

- **Keyboard shortcuts** are combinations of keys you press to complete a task more quickly. For example, the shortcut for "clicking" a Cancel button may be to press the ESC key. When instructing you to press a key, the name of the key is in small caps, like this: esc. If you must press two or more keys simultaneously, they are separated with a hyphen, like this: CTRL-P.
- **Literal text** is text that you must type in exactly as it appears in the book. Although this book doesn't contain many instances of literal text, there are a few. Literal text to be typed is in boldface type, like this: **Checking Acct**. If literal text includes a variable—text you must substitute when you type—the variable is included in bold-italic type, like this: ***Payee Name***.

Icons

Icons are used to flag specific types of information.

New in Quicken 2010 In addition to interface changes, the folks at Intuit made changes to Quicken's feature set. The New in Quicken 2010 icon identifies many new features.

Sidebars

This book also includes What Does This Mean to You? sidebars. These sidebars are my attempt to put a specific Quicken feature into perspective by either telling you how it is used or offering suggestions on how you can use it. You'll learn a lot from these sidebars, but like all sidebars, they're not required reading.

About the Author

Maria Langer graduated from Hofstra University with a BBA in Accounting and worked as an accountant, auditor, and financial analyst over the next eight years. She's written more than 70 computer books, many of which are about business and productivity software such as Word, Excel, and FileMaker Pro. In 1998, she wrote *Quicken 99: The Official Guide*, and has been revising the book for each update of Quicken.

About the Contributors

Bobbi Sandberg has long been involved with computers, accounting, and writing. Her extensive background, combined with her ability to explain complex concepts in plain language, has made her a popular instructor, speaker and consultant.

Carole and Marty Matthews are principals in Matthews Technology, a firm dedicated to making technology easy through books, articles, Web sites, and consulting. Over the last 25 years they have produced over 100 books selling over a million and a half copies. See their Web site at http://matthewstechnology.com.

About the Technical Editor

Mary Higgins is an electrical engineer by education and she works as a systems analyst in IT at a biotech company in the San Francisco Bay Area. She writes extensively for work—business process documents, FAQs, functional and technical specifications, etc. She is a long-time Quicken user, having used each version since 1999. She enjoys pushing the limits of what the software is intended to do—clicking every button, navigating every menu path, reading the help files, etc. She reads and posts on the Quicken forums as it's always interesting to see how others are using Quicken and the different approaches to resolving issues.

Quicken® 2010

THE OFFICIAL GUIDE

Quicken Setup and Basics

This part of the book introduces Quicken Personal Finance Software's interface and features. It begins by explaining how to install Quicken and showing you the elements of its user interface. It offers an entire chapter with instructions for setting up Quicken for the first time using Setup Overview screen options. Then it tells you all about Quicken's accounts, categories, and classes, and then it explains how you can modify the default setup to add your own. Finally, it explains why you should be interested in online account services and how you can set up Quicken to access the Internet and Quicken.com. The chapters are:

Part One

Getting to Know Quicken

In This Chapter:

- *An overview of Quicken*
- *Installing Quicken*
- *Starting Quicken*
- *The Quicken interface*
- *Onscreen Help*

If you're brand new to Quicken Personal Finance Software, get your relationship with Quicken off to a good start by properly installing it and learning a little more about how you can interact with it.

This chapter provides a brief overview of Quicken, explains how to install and start it, takes you on a tour of its interface, and shows you how to use its extensive Onscreen Help features. Although the information provided in this chapter is especially useful to new Quicken users, some of it also applies to users who are upgrading. If you are a former Microsoft Money user, see Appendix C for some Microsoft Money specific comparisons and explanations.

What Is Quicken?

On the surface, Quicken is a computerized checkbook. It enables you to balance your accounts and organize, manage, and generate reports for your finances. But as you explore Quicken, you'll learn that it's much more. It's a complete personal finance software package—a tool for taking control of your finances. Quicken makes it easy to know what you have, how you are doing financially, and what you should do to strengthen your financial situation.

What Quicken Can Help You Do

At the least, Quicken can help you manage your bank and credit card accounts. You can enter transactions and have Quicken generate reports and graphs that show where your money went and how much is left.

Quicken can help you manage investment accounts. You can enter transactions and have Quicken tell you the market value of your investments. Quicken can also help you organize other data, such as the purchase price of your possessions and the outstanding balances on your loans.

With all financial information stored in Quicken's data file, you can generate net worth reports to see where you stand today. You can also use a variety of financial planners to make financial decisions for the future. And Quicken's tax features, including export into TurboTax and the Deduction Finder, can make tax time easier on you and your bank accounts.

Quicken's online features can automate much of your data entry. Online banking enables you to keep track of bank account transactions and balances, and to pay bills without writing checks or sticking on stamps. Online investing enables you to download investment transactions. You can also read news and information about investment opportunities and advice offered by financial experts.

Now tell me, can the paper check register that came with your checks do all that?

Quicken Versions

Intuit offers several versions of Quicken 2010 for Windows for managing personal finances: Starter, Deluxe, Premier, Home & Business, and Quicken Rental Property Manager.

Quicken Starter is an entry-level product designed for people who are new to personal finance software. As its name suggests, it includes basic features to track bank accounts and credit cards. It also enables you to use online account services and payments, shop for insurance and mortgages, and download investment information for a brokerage account.

Quicken Deluxe is more robust. Designed for people who want to take a more active role in financial management, investments, and planning, it includes all the features in Quicken Starter plus the financial alerts feature, money-saving features for tax time and debt reduction, and free access to investment information.

Quicken Premier has all the features of Quicken Deluxe, plus additional features for investing and tax planning and preparation.

This book covers Quicken Premier. Although much of its information also applies to Quicken Starter and Deluxe, this book covers many features that are not included in the Starter version and a handful of features that are not included in the Deluxe version. (The Quicken Premier icon identifies those features that are available only in Quicken Premier.) If you're a Quicken Starter or Deluxe user, consider upgrading to Quicken Premier, so you can take advantage of the powerful features it has to offer. One more thing—Intuit also offers two special versions of Quicken. If you're a small-business owner, Quicken Home & Business can handle all of your personal and basic business financial needs, including the business expenses you need to track for your tax return's Schedule C. If you manage one or more rental properties, Quicken Rental Property Manager can handle transactions and other information for tenants, rent income, and related expenses that you need to track for your tax return's Schedule E. As you can see, Intuit has you covered with a Quicken product, no matter what activities are part of your financial life.

Getting Started

Ready to get started? This section explains how to install, start, and register Quicken.

The instructions in this section assume you're installing Quicken on a computer running Windows Vista. Although Quicken will run under Windows XP or Windows 7, the pathnames mentioned in this section may be different if you install on a computer running an operating system other than Windows Vista.

Installing Quicken

Quicken uses a standard Windows setup program that should be familiar to you if you've installed other Windows programs.

Insert the Quicken 2010 CD into your CD or DVD drive. A dialog should appear, asking if you want to install the program to your hard drive. If so, click Yes to start the Quicken installer.

If this dialog does not appear automatically, you can start the installer by double-clicking the Computer icon on your desktop and then double-clicking the icon for your optical drive in the window that appears.

The installer displays a series of dialogs with information and options for installing Quicken. Read the information in the Welcome screen and click Next to continue. When asked to agree to a software license agreement, select the I Agree To The Terms Of The License Agreement And Acknowledge Receipt Of The Quicken Privacy Statement option. (If you select the other option, you cannot click Next and cannot install the software.) You can click the Quicken Privacy Statement link to open this important document in a Web browser window and read it; close the browser window when you're finished to return to the installer. Click Next in the Install Wizard window.

In the Destination Folder screen, the installer tells you where Quicken will be installed—normally C:\Program Files\Quicken. You can click the Change button and use the screen that appears to change the installation location. To keep the default location—which is what I recommend—just click Next.

In the Ready To Install The Program screen, the installer displays a summary of what it will do. If this is a first-time Quicken installation, all it will do is install Quicken 2010 and any updates to the program. But if you're upgrading from a previous version, the installer will begin by uninstalling whatever version is currently installed. (You can have only one version of Quicken installed on your computer at a time.) Only the Quicken program files will be deleted; your data files will remain intact, so you can use them with Quicken 2010. Click Install.

Wait while the installer uninstalls the previous version of Quicken (if necessary), copies the Quicken 2010 files and any updates to your hard disk.

As part of the installation process, the installer uses your Internet connection to check for and download Quicken updates. This ensures that you have the most up-to-date version of Quicken installed. When the update is complete, the Installer displays an Installation Complete screen. Click Done.

Quicken should start automatically. Skip ahead to the section titled "Preparing a Data File," later in this chapter, to start using Quicken. If Quicken does not start, follow the instructions in the next section to start it.

Starting Quicken

You can start Quicken in several different ways. Here are the two most common methods.

Opening the Quicken Shortcut

The Quicken installer places a Quicken Premier 2010 shortcut icon on your Windows desktop. Double-clicking this shortcut opens Quicken Premier.

Opening Quicken from the Task Bar

You can also use the Windows task bar's Start button to start Quicken and other Quicken components. Choose Start | All Programs | Quicken 2010 | Quicken 2010 to start Quicken.

Preparing a Data File

Quicken stores all of your financial information in a Quicken data file. Before you can use Quicken, you must either create a data file or convert an existing data file for use with Quicken 2010.

New User Startup

If you're a brand-new Quicken user, a Welcome To Quicken 2010 dialog appears. You have three options.

I Am A New User.   When you select this option and click Get Started, Quicken creates a new data file called *yourname*'s Quicken Data in a Quicken folder in your Documents folder. It opens the file and displays the Main View screen of the Home tab. This screen includes information and buttons that help you set up your Quicken data file. If you're following along and would like to set up your data file now, skip ahead to Chapter 2 and follow the instructions there. Then, to learn more about how Quicken works, read the section titled "The Quicken Interface," later in this chapter.

I Am A Current Quicken User.   When you select this option and click Get Started, Quicken displays the Select Your Data File dialog. Continue following instructions in the section titled "Existing User Startup" next.

I Am A Current Microsoft Money User.   Use this option to import your Microsoft Money data files into Quicken. For additional information about this option, see Appendix C.

Existing User Startup

If you upgraded from a previous version of Quicken, when you first start Quicken, the Select Your Existing Data File To Get Started window appears. It offers three options for getting started:

- **Open A File Located On This Computer** displays the Open Quicken File dialog, which you can use to select a file on your hard disk. After selecting and opening a file, continue following the instructions in the section titled "Converting a Data File as Part of an Upgrade."
- **Restore A Quicken Data File I've Backed Up To CD Or Disk** enables you to open a backup file for use with Quicken 2010. (This option works only with files you created using Quicken's Backup command, which is discussed in Appendix A.) When you select this option and click Next, Quicken displays the Restore From Backup File dialog so you can select the type of backup file, locate it on disk, and open it. Along the way, it prompts you for a location in which to save the file; normally this will be in the Quicken folder inside your Documents folder. If a dialog appears telling you that you have to convert the data file, continue following the instructions in the section titled "Converting a Data File as Part of an Upgrade." When restoration is complete, Quicken opens the data file.

- **Start Over And Create A New Data File** displays the Create Quicken File dialog, which you can use to enter a name for your new Quicken data file. It then opens the file and displays the Main View screen of the Home tab. This screen includes information and buttons that help you set up your Quicken data file. If you're following along and would like to set up your data file now, skip ahead to Chapter 2 and follow the instructions there.

Converting a Data File as Part of an Upgrade

The Convert Your Data File dialog appears any time you indicate that you want to update an existing Quicken data file for use with Quicken 2010. Clicking the Convert It! button converts the data file named in the dialog to Quicken 2010 format and saves the original file in C:\Users*yourname*\Documents\Quicken\ Q09Files. The path for the saved copy of the original file may vary depending on which previous version you are upgrading from.

Registering Quicken

Sooner or later Quicken's Product Registration dialog will appear. It tells you about the benefits of registering Quicken and displays two buttons:

- **Register Later** lets you put off the registration process. Use this option if you don't have the few minutes it takes to register or your computer is not connected to the Internet. Keep in mind, however, that certain Quicken features will not function until you register.
- **Register Now** begins the registration process. You'll need Internet access to complete this process.

To start the registration process, click the Register Now button. Then follow the instructions that appear on screen. When the registration process is complete, you can continue working with Quicken.

The Quicken Interface

Quicken's interface, which has been reworked for Quicken 2010, is designed to be intuitive and easy to use. It puts the information and tools you need to manage your finances right within mouse pointer reach. You never have to dig through multiple dialogs and menus to get to the commands you need most.

This section tells you about the components of the Quicken interface and explains how you can use them to make your work with Quicken easy.

The Main Window

The main Quicken window gives you access to most of Quicken's features and your stored information. It's split into two parts: the Account Bar and the Tabs. Let's take a look at each section.

Tabs

Tabs occupy the main part of the Quicken program window. Some tabs, such as the Banking tab (see Figure 1-1) and Investing tab, provide information about your financial status, as well as links and buttons for accessing Quicken features. Other tabs, such as the Setup tab (Figure 1-2), enable you to view and customize Quicken settings for your financial situation. You can specify which tabs you want to appear or remove the ones you don't use. Chapter 2 explains how.

Figure 1-1 • The Banking tab's Cash Flow window displays the impact of transactions for the month.

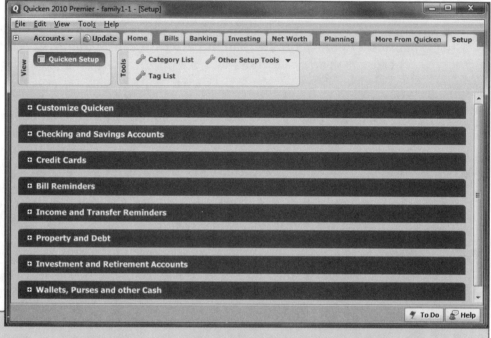

Figure 1-2 • Use options on subtabs within the Setup tab to set up Quicken for your financial information.

A tab exists for each major area of Quicken:

- **Home** displays customizable views of your Quicken data. (This feature was known as the Quicken Home page in previous versions of Quicken.) Learn how to add and customize the Home tab views in Appendix B.
- **Bills** provides information about your upcoming bills and offers tools for working with bills and reminders. Although the Bills tab is not new in Quicken, the corresponding Bills menu is. Chapter 7 discusses Bills tab options.
- **Banking** provides information about your cash, bank, and credit card accounts. If you have converted from earlier versions of Quicken, you may see other sections as well. Part Two discusses the Banking tab and its options in detail.
- **Investing** provides information about your investment and retirement accounts and any stocks or mutual funds you've asked Quicken to watch for you. Part Three covers investing and the Investing tab.

- **Net Worth** provides information about asset and debt accounts, including your home, car, related loans, and auto expenses. Part Four discusses the Net Worth tab and related features.

- **Planning** gives you access to Quicken's financial planners, as well as the assumptions you need to set up to use the planners effectively. Part Five discusses Quicken's financial planners and the Planning tab. In Quicken 2010, the Planning tab also includes tax-related options, such as projected taxes, a tax calendar, and your year-to-date income and tax-related expenses. (In previous versions of Quicken, these options appeared on the Tax tab, which has been removed in Quicken 2010.) Part Six covers Quicken's tax features.

In addition, Quicken offers other tabs you can use to set up Quicken and work with other features:

- **More From Quicken** displays information about additional Quicken services and special offers for online shopping deals. Learn more about this tab in Chapter 4.
- **Setup** offers tools for setting up Quicken for your financial situation. Chapter 2 discusses the Setup tab.

You can specify which tabs you want to appear or remove the ones you don't use. Learn how in Chapter 2.

At the top of each tab section are one or more buttons that indicate the current view (View) or displayed account (Acct). If there's more than one button or a menu in either of these areas, you can click a button or choose a menu command to switch to another view or account.

Account Bar

The Account Bar lists each of your Quicken accounts, organized by tab, on the left side of the main Quicken window (refer to Figure 1-1). If the Account Bar is not displayed (refer to Figure 1-2), you can display it by clicking the small plus sign (+) beside the Accounts button on the left end of the main window's tabs.

If you can't see all of the accounts in the Account Bar, you can click the arrow button at the top or bottom of the Account Bar to scroll its contents. You can also click the – or + button beside a section heading on the Account Bar to hide or display the list of accounts beneath it.

By default, account balances appear in the panel; however you can right-click the Account Bar and choose Hide Amounts from the context menu that appears to hide amounts from view. (This also makes the Account Bar narrower so more information appears in the window beside it.) This contextual menu offers additional options for the display of the Account Bar. You can also change the width of the Account Bar by dragging its right border.

The account names in the Account Bar are links, click an account name to view its register. You can customize the Account Bar to move accounts from one tab to another or to hide an account from the Account Bar totals; learn how in Chapter 3.

Other Windows

Quicken uses other windows to display information, depending on what you want to see or what task you are trying to perform.

List Windows

A list window (see Figure 1-3) shows a list of information about related things, such as accounts, categories, classes, or scheduled transactions. You can use a list window to perform tasks with items in the list.

Figure 1-3 • The Category List window displays a list of categories and transfer accounts.

Report Windows

Quicken's report windows (see Figure 1-4) enable you to create and access subreports based on a main report. A list of all reports appears in the left column of the window. Click a report link to view the report in the main window. To create a subreport, double-click a report line item amount. You can also use options and buttons at the top of the window to work with, customize, and save reports. Chapter 9 explains how to create and customize reports and graphs.

Features and Commands

Quicken offers a number of ways to access its features and commands, including standard Microsoft Windows elements, such as menus and dialogs, and Quicken elements, such as the toolbar, button bar, and links and buttons within Quicken windows.

Menus

Quicken displays five menus in a menu bar when you have chosen to display the recommended Standard menus as shown here. If you choose Classic menus, you

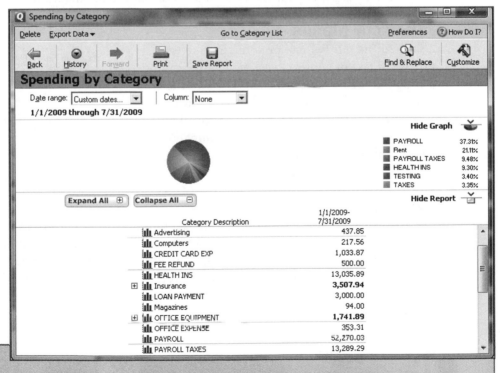

Figure 1-4 • The report window may include a report and a graph.

have an additional eight from which to choose. You can choose commands from the menus as follows:

- Click the menu name to display the menu. If necessary, click the name of the submenu you want, and then click the name of the command you want.
- Press the shortcut key combination for the menu command that you want. A command's shortcut key, if it has one, is displayed to the right of the command name on the menu.
- If your Windows program is set up to have keyboard access keys underlined, you can press ALT to activate the menu bar and press the keyboard key for the underlined letter in the menu that you want to open. If necessary, press the key for the underlined letter in the submenu that you want to open, and then press the key for the underlined letter in the command that you want.

Shortcut Menus

Shortcut menus (which are sometimes referred to as context or context-sensitive menus) can be displayed throughout Quicken. Point to the item for which you want to display a shortcut menu and click the right mouse button. The menu, which includes only those commands applicable to the item, appears at the mouse pointer, as shown here.

Dialogs

Like other Windows applications, Quicken uses dialogs to communicate with you. Some dialogs display a simple message, while others include text boxes, option buttons, check boxes, and drop-down lists you can use to enter information, similar to the one shown on top of the next page. Many dialogs also include a Help button that you can use to get additional information about options.

Toolbar

The toolbar is a row of buttons along the top of the application window, just beneath the menu bar as shown next, that gives you access to other navigation techniques and features. The Quicken toolbar does not appear by default, but can be turned on and customized. Learn how to customize it in Appendix B. Here's a quick look at the buttons that appear on the Quicken toolbar.

- **Back** (an arrow pointing left) displays the previously opened window.
- **Forward** (an arrow pointing right) displays the window you were looking at before you clicked the Back button. This button is only available if you clicked the Back button to view a previously viewed window.
- **Services** displays the Quicken Services window, which provides information about additional Quicken services.
- **Quicken.com** displays the Quicken.com home page in an Internet window. Chapter 4 introduces Quicken.com.

- **Calendar** displays the Calendar window, which shows scheduled calendar inflows and outflows.
- **One Step Update** opens the One Step Update dialog, so you can connect to the Internet and update all your online information at once. Clicking the triangle that's part of this button displays a menu of commands related to the One Step Update feature, including Update Settings, Manage My Passwords, Update Summary, and Schedule Updates. Chapter 7 discusses One Step Update.
- **Search** is a global search feature you can use to search for transactions entered into Quicken. Just enter the search criteria in the field and press ENTER.
- **Live** uses your Internet connection and default Web browser to connect to Intuit's Live Community feature. Learn more about this feature later in this chapter, in the section titled "Quicken Live Community."

Button Bar

The button bar is a row of textual buttons and menus that appears just above the contents of many Quicken windows (refer to Figure 1-4). Most items on the button bar, which vary from window to window, are buttons; simply click one to access its options. The items with triangles beside their names are menus that work just like the menu bar menus.

Keep in mind that Quicken's Onscreen Help may refer to the button bar as the toolbar. I refer to it as the button bar throughout this book to differentiate between it and the Quicken Tool Bar.

Links and Buttons in Tab Windows

Tab windows, such as the Banking tab window in Figure 1-1, include links, buttons, and menus you can use to get more information about using Quicken or to access its features.

Onscreen Help

In addition to the How Do I? menu in the button bar of many Quicken windows and the Help button in dialogs, Quicken includes an extensive Onscreen Help system to provide more information about using Quicken while you work. You can access most Help options from the Help menu, which is shown here.

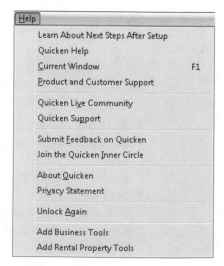

Here's a brief summary of some of the components of Quicken's Onscreen Help system.

Quicken Help

Quicken's Onscreen Help uses a familiar Windows Help interface. You can use it to browse or search Help topics or display Help information about a specific window.

Browsing or Searching Help

Start by choosing Help | Quicken Help. A Quicken Help window appears. The left side of the window has two tabs for browsing Help topics:

- **Contents** (see Figure 1-5) lists Help topics organized in "books." Clicking a book opens or closes the book. Clicking a topic link displays information and links for accessing additional information in the right side of the window.
- **Search Quicken Help** enables you to search for information about a topic. Enter a search word in the top of the tab, and then click the Ask button. Click the title of a topic in the search results list to display information about it in the right side of the window.

Getting Help for the Current Window

The Current Window command on Quicken's Help menu displays the Quicken Help window with information about the active window. This is probably the quickest and easiest way to get information about a specific topic or task with which you are working. You can also access this command by pressing F1.

What Does This Mean to You? Onscreen Help

These days, any decent software program offers onscreen help. So what's the big deal about Quicken's?

Quicken's Onscreen Help is especially ... well, *helpful*. It covers every program feature and provides step-by-step instructions for performing many tasks. Clickable links make it easy to jump right to a topic you want to learn more about. And as you'll discover while using Quicken, Help is available throughout the program—not just in the Quicken Help windows.

Onscreen Help also gives you, a Quicken user, the opportunity to help make Quicken a better software program. At the bottom of most Help windows, you'll find Yes and No buttons that you can use to tell Intuit whether the Help topic gave you the information you needed. Click the appropriate button as you use Onscreen Help to help the folks at Intuit make Onscreen Help more useful to you.

Figure 1-5 • The Contents tab of Quicken Help makes it easy to browse through Onscreen Help for specific information.

Product and Customer Support

The Product And Customer Support command on the Help menu opens the Quicken Product And Customer Support window, which offers links you can click to explore support options in Quicken Help or on the Intuit Web site.

Quicken Live Community

The Quicken Live Community command on the Help menu takes you online to Quicken's online user-to-user forum, where you can ask questions, get answers, and share information with other Quicken users. Click links or use the search feature to get the information you need to make the most of Quicken.

Quicken Support

Click Quicken Support on the help menu to open the Quicken support site on the Internet. Here you can look through frequently asked questions as well as find links to other Quicken resources.

Submit Feedback on Quicken

This link opens a Quicken feedback page on the Internet. While you may think that your idea or concern is not "important," it is to Quicken. It is partly through this feedback that Intuit designs its products

Join the Quicken Inner Circle

The Quicken Inner Circle is more than just a user feedback site. Intuit has created a collaborative community, one that works directly with product managers and others on the Quicken team.

About Quicken

This tells you which version of Quicken you are using as shown next. Along with the Privacy Statement menu option, this gives copyright information and credit to the many people who have made the program possible. The Privacy

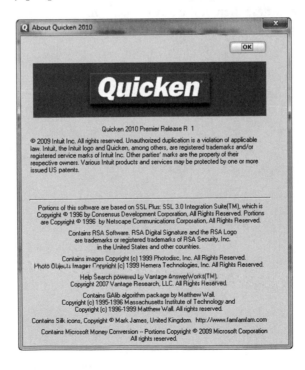

Statement tells Quicken's policies that ensure your privacy. Additional technical information about your Quicken file and system resources can be displayed by holding down CTRL and clicking Help | About Quicken. This can be useful in troubleshooting issues.

Upgrading Quicken

If you're wondering whether the version of Quicken installed on your computer is the best one for you, be sure to check out Help | Add Business Tools or Help | Add Rental Property Tools. These commands display a window that provides more information about features in Quicken Premier Home & Business or Quicken Rental Properties. These menu options window also includes links you can use to purchase unlock codes that will convert your version of Quicken to a more powerful version.

If you have already purchased an unlock code for Quicken, choose Help | Unlock Again to enter it into Quicken and upgrade immediately.

Exiting Quicken

When you're finished using Quicken, choose File | Exit. This saves your data file and closes the Quicken application.

Sometimes when you exit Quicken, you'll be asked whether you want to back up your Quicken data file. Learn how to back up data files in Appendix A.

Using Setup Tab Screens

Chapter 2

In This Chapter:

- *Overview of data files and accounts*
- *Quicken's Setup tab views*
- *Customizing Quicken*

To use Quicken Personal Finance Software, you must set up your Quicken data file for your financial situation. This means creating accounts and entering starting balance information.

Quicken's Setup tab offers a centralized location for setting up accounts, bills and deposits, categories, and tags. Rather than force you to use a wizard that requires you to set up certain parts of your Quicken data file before you can start using Quicken, the Setup tab enables you to set up any combination of Quicken's basic components. It also makes it possible to toggle off and on Quicken features to make its interface as simple or as complete as you need it to be.

This chapter explains how to use subtabs on the Setup tab to view and modify your Quicken setup. You are also shown how to set options in the Setup tab's View | Quicken Setup tab to fine-tune the display of data and Quicken features.

Before You Begin

Before you start the setup process, it's a good idea to understand how data files and accounts work. You should also gather together a few documents to help you set up your accounts properly.

Data Files

All of the transactions you record with Quicken are stored in a *data file* on your hard disk. This file includes all the information that makes up your Quicken accounting system.

Although it's possible to have more than one Quicken data file, it isn't usually necessary. One file can hold all of your transactions. In fact, it's difficult (if not downright impossible) to use more than one Quicken file to track a single account, such as a checking or credit card account. And splitting your financial records among multiple data files makes it impossible to generate reports that consolidate all of the information.

When would you want more than one data file? Well, you could use two data files if you wanted to use Quicken to organize your personal finances and the finances of your business, which has entirely separate bank, credit, and asset accounts, or if you're using Quicken to track the separate finances of multiple individuals.

Appendix A covers a number of data file management tasks, including creating additional data files and backing up your data files.

Accounts

An *account* is a record of what you either own or owe. For example, your checking account is a record of cash on deposit in the bank that is available for writing checks. A credit card account is a record of money you owe to the credit card company or bank for the use of your credit card. All transactions either increase or decrease the balance in one or more accounts.

The Setup tab subtabs help you create accounts within Quicken, so you can track the activity and balances in your bank, credit card, investment, and other accounts.

What You Need

To set up accounts properly, you should have balance information for the accounts that you want to monitor with Quicken. You can get this information from your most recent bank, investment, and credit card statements. It's a good idea to gather these documents before you start the setup process, so they're on hand when you need them.

If you plan to use Quicken to replace an existing accounting system—whether it's paper-based or prepared with a different computer program—you may also find it helpful to have a *chart of accounts* (a list of account names) or recent financial statements. This way, when you set up Quicken accounts, you can use familiar names.

The Setup Tab

Quicken's Setup tab offers easy access to features you can use to configure your Quicken data file. It includes several areas. The first subtab, Quicken Setup, offers the Customize Quicken area where you tell Quicken about yourself and how you want to work with Quicken. It also has several different account areas, as well as areas in which you can tell Quicken what you owe and what you earn.

This part of the chapter provides a tour of each area and explains how you can use it to set up a Quicken data file.

Customize Quicken

The Customize Quicken area of the Setup tab (see Figure 2-1) displays a complete overview of your Quicken setup. It is where you tell Quicken a bit about yourself, set some preferences and tell Quicken where you want to start each time you open the program and what you want to see.

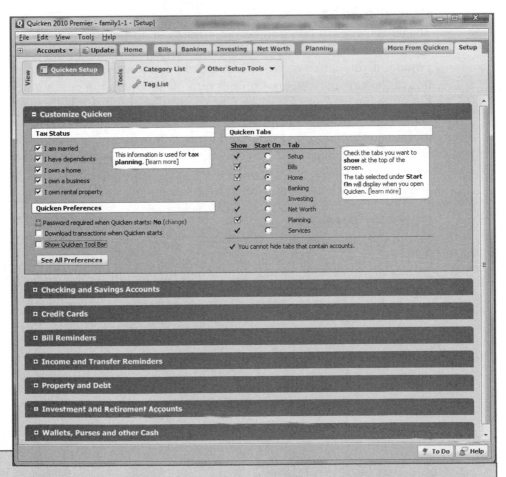

Figure 2-1 • The Customize Quicken area of the Setup tab helps you get started with Quicken.

The Customize Quicken area has three parts that work together to hide or display certain Quicken features:

Tax Status

Toggle check boxes in the Tax Status area to tell Quicken about you. The options you choose here will determine what categories Quicken automatically creates for you. For example, if you indicate that you're married, Quicken creates standard categories for income and expenses related to your spouse. If you indicate that you own a business, Quicken creates business-related categories. Keep in mind that this is just a starting point; you can add or remove categories as desired to meet your needs. Learn more about Categories in Chapter 3.

Quicken Tabs

Toggle Show check boxes and select a Start On option to determine which Quicken tabs and menus appear. This makes it possible to simplify the Quicken product if you don't need to access all of its features. For example, suppose you don't have any investments. You can turn off the Investing check box to remove the Investing tab from Quicken. The good thing about this is that you can always come back and toggle the check box back on if you need to. This feature is especially useful for new Quicken users with basic finances who just want to see the features they need. Keep in mind that you cannot hide the Setup or Banking tab or any tab that contain accounts. Setting the Start On option determines which tab appears each time you open Quicken.

Quicken Preferences

Quicken allows you to tell it your preferred way of doing things. For example, if you share your computer with someone else, you may want to protect it with a password. If so, click Change to open the Quicken File Password dialog as seen here. If you decide not to add a password now, you can add one later. To set a file password, from the menu bar, click File | Set Password For This Data File.

In the same area, you can tell Quicken to automatically download your transactions when you start Quicken. Learn about downloading in Chapters 4 and 6. You can also tell Quicken to show the Quicken Tool Bar as shown here.

If you want to see all the settings Quicken offers, click the See All Preferences button. Learn about Preferences in Appendix B

Checking and Savings Accounts

The Checking and Savings Accounts area, as seen in Figure 2-2, enables you to add checking or savings accounts to Quicken. Click the appropriate button and use the Account Setup dialog that appears to create the account. Learn more about setting up banking accounts in Chapters 3 and 5.

Once you have created checking or savings accounts, they appear in a list in this area. You must have at least one account to use Quicken.

Credit Cards

The Credit Cards area enables you to add credit card accounts to Quicken. Just click the Add Credit Card button and use the Account Setup dialog to create an

□ **Checking and Savings Accounts**

Add Checking and Savings accounts to track spending, reconcile statements, download bank activity and more.

Account Name	Type	Transaction Download ⑦	Online Bill Pay ⑦	
Brokerage (Cash)	Checking	—	No (Activate Bill Pay)	Edit
Casual Account	Checking	*Not Available*	No (Activate Bill Pay)	Edit
Checking	Checking	Yes (Direct Connect)	Yes (U.S. Bank - PFM Direc...	Edit
Checking 2	Checking	*Not Available*	No (Activate Bill Pay)	Edit
Checking 6789	Checking	Yes (Express Web Connect)	No (Activate Bill Pay)	Edit
Money Market	Checking	*Not Available*	No (Activate Bill Pay)	Edit
Savings	Checking	Yes (Express Web Connect)	No (Activate Bill Pay)	Edit
Vacation Savings	Savings	Yes (Express Web Connect)	—	Edit
Ckg - Misc	Checking	No (Activate Downloads)	No (Activate Bill Pay)	Edit
Single Mutual Fund (Cash)	Checking	—	No (Activate Bill Pay)	Edit
Work Funds	Checking	No (Activate Downloads)	No (Activate Bill Pay)	Edit

[Add Checking Account] [Add Savings Account]

Figure 2-2 • You can use the Setup tab's Checking and Savings Accounts area to quickly set up new accounts.

account. Learn more about setting up credit card accounts in Chapter 5. Once you have created one or more credit card accounts, they appear in a list in this area like the ones shown here.

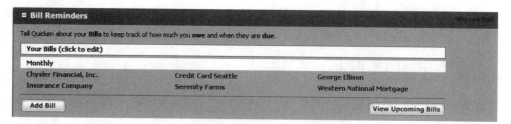

Bill Reminders

The Bill Reminders area, as shown next, enables you to add reminders for bills and other upcoming payment transactions. Click any displayed bill to edit it. Click the Add Bill button and the Add Bill Reminder dialog opens. Learn how to add bill reminders in Chapter 7. Once you've added bill reminders, they appear in this area. To see the bills that are due soon, click the View Upcoming Bills button.

Income and Transfer Reminders

The Income and Transfer Reminders area enables you to add paychecks, other income transactions, and account transfers. Click the appropriate button and use the dialog that appears to enter transaction information. I explain how to set up reminders for each of these items in Chapter 7. Once you've added these reminders, they appear in a list in this area as shown here.

Reminders are a terrific part of your Quicken program. You can access them from any account you have set up in the Banking, Investing, and Net Worth tabs as seen next.

| Download Transactions | **Bill and Income Reminders (2 Due)** |

However, if you have set up online banking, Quicken automatically downloads your transactions into your account register. To verify this default setting, click Edit | Preferences | Quicken Preferences | Downloaded Transactions. Note that to Automatically Add Downloaded Transactions To Registers is checked, as seen below. When this default preference is set, the Bill and Income Reminders tab appear only in the Investing tab and are absent from other account tabs.

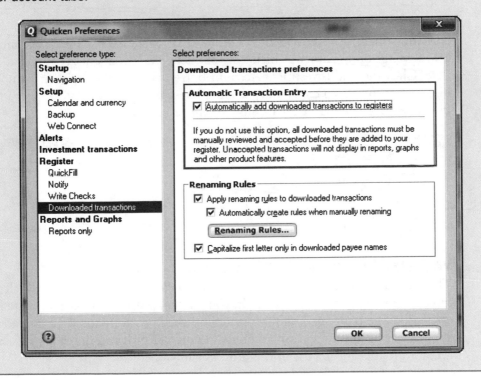

Property and Debt

The Property and Debt area enables you to create asset accounts, debt accounts, and loans associated with asset accounts. Click the appropriate button and use the dialog that appears to set up the account or loan. The items you add appear in this area of the Setup tab as seen on the top of the next page. Chapter 13 explains how to create asset and debt accounts and add loans.

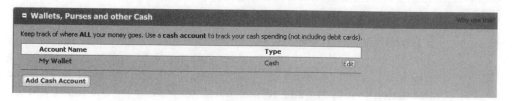

Investment and Retirement Accounts

The Investment and Retirement Accounts area enables you to create accounts for a wide range of investments, including tax-deferred retirement accounts, as seen here. Click the Add Investment Account button and use the Account Setup dialog that appears to create the account. The accounts you create appear in a list in this area. Chapter 10 explains how to create investment accounts.

Wallets, Purses and Other Cash

This final area of the Setup tab enables you to create a cash account, which you might want to use to track money in your wallet, purse, or other place you keep cash—like the jar of mad money on the top shelf of your pantry! Learn more about creating and using cash accounts in Chapter 5. If you do create a cash account, it appears in a list in this area, as shown here.

Category List

The Category List tool as seen below connects you to all the categories that have been set up in your data file. Quicken creates default categories based on check boxes you toggle on in the Customize Quicken snapshot of the Quicken Setup subtab (refer to Figure 2-1), but you can add or remove categories as necessary by clicking the New or Add Categories button or using one of the action buttons for a selected category. This subtab opens the Category List window, which is discussed in detail in Chapter 3.

Tags

The Tag List, as highlighted in the illustration, lists all of the tags that have been set up for your data file. You can click the New button to add a new tag or use buttons in the Action column for a selected tag to remove or modify a tag. Learn more about creating tags in Chapter 3.

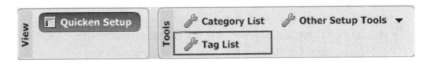

Other Setup Tools

Click Other Setup Tools to open a menu as seen next, from which you can add an account, recategorize any transaction, open the Renaming Rules dialog, view your Memorized and Online Payee lists and open the Password Vault.

Add Account

When you select the Add Account menu option, the Account Setup dialog appears. From this dialog you can enter eight different types of accounts as shown below. Chapter 3 discusses adding new accounts.

Recategorize

This menu option opens the Recategorize dialog as seen here, from which you can change the category for any transaction, memorized payee, or scheduled bill or deposit. See Chapter 5 for more about categories.

Renaming Rules

When you set up online banking to download transactions from your financial institution, your bank sometimes does not record a payee in the same way you might. For example, you might record a credit card transaction from Bill's Auto, while your bank shows the payee as ABB Automotive. Renaming rules help you and your bank to coordinate these payees. Learn more about downloaded transactions in Chapter 6.

Memorized and Online Payee Lists

These menu items open the lists of payees you have memorized or set up online. Chapter 5 and 6 discuss these lists.

Password Vault

If you have more than one or two accounts set up for online services, it can be a difficult task remembering all the passwords. Quicken offers a way to solve this problem with its Password Vault. You create a safe place for all of these passwords and Quicken protects them with a master password. You can then download your transactions all at the same time without having to enter individual passwords for each account. Learn more about the Password Vault in Chapter 7.

Setting Up Accounts, Categories, and Tags

Chapter 3

In This Chapter:

- *Overview of setting up accounts*
- *Working with the Account List window*
- *Setting up categories and subcategories*
- *Working with the Category List window*
- *Setting up tags*
- *Working with the Tag List window*

When you first set up your Quicken Personal Finance Software data file, it includes a number of default categories. Don't think you're stuck with just those categories. You can add and remove categories at any time. The same goes for accounts—you can add them as you see fit. Modifying the accounts and categories in your Quicken data file is a great way to customize Quicken to meet your needs.

In this chapter, I explain how to modify and work with the Quicken accounts and categories you'll use to organize your finances. I also explain how to set up an optional categorization feature: tags.

Accounts

To track your finances with Quicken, you must have created at least one account. While many of your expenditures may come from your checking account, you probably have more than one account that Quicken can track for you. By setting up all of your accounts in Quicken, you can keep track of balances and activity to get a complete picture of your financial situation.

This part of the chapter tells you a little more about Quicken's accounts and how you can use the Account List window to create and modify your accounts.

Types of Accounts

As discussed in Chapter 2, an *account* is a record of what you either own or owe. Quicken offers various kinds of accounts for different purposes. Table 3-1 summarizes the accounts and how they are organized within Quicken.

What You Own

In accounting jargon, what you own are *assets*. In Quicken, an asset is one type of account; several other types exist as well.

Spending Spending accounts, which are displayed in the Banking tab, are used primarily for expenditures. Quicken distinguishes between two types of spending accounts: checking and cash.

Account Type	Tab	Tab Group	Asset or Liability
Checking	Banking	Spending	Asset
Savings	Banking	Savings	Asset
Credit Card	Banking	Credit Card Accounts	Liability
Cash	Banking	Spending	Asset
Standard Brokerage	Investing	Investment	Asset
IRA or Keogh Plan	Investing	Retirement	Asset
401(k) or 403(b)	Investing	Retirement	Asset
529 Plan	Investing	Investment	Asset
House	Net Worth	Property (Asset)	Asset
Vehicle	Net Worth	Property (Asset)	Asset
Asset	Net Worth	Property (Asset)	Asset
Debt	Net Worth	Debt (Liabilities)	Liability

Table 3-1 • Overview of Quicken Account Types

Savings Savings accounts, which are displayed in the Banking tab, are used to record the transactions in savings accounts.

Investment Investment accounts, which are displayed in the Investing tab, are for tracking the stocks, bonds, and mutual funds in your portfolio that are not in retirement accounts. Quicken distinguishes among two types of investment accounts: Standard Brokerage (which may be used for one or more mutual funds) and 529 Plan.

Retirement Retirement accounts, which are also displayed in the Investing tab, are for tracking investments in retirement accounts. Quicken distinguishes between two types of retirement accounts. One type includes IRA or Keogh Plans, and the other combines 401(k) or 403(b) accounts. Retirement accounts should fall into either of these two broad categories.

Asset Asset accounts, which are displayed in the Net Worth tab, are used for tracking items that you own. Quicken distinguishes among three different types of asset accounts: House, Vehicle, and Other Asset. However, all the assets are displayed in the Property (Assets) section under the Net Worth tab.

What You Owe

The accounting term for what you owe, or your debts, is *liabilities*. Quicken offers two kinds of accounts for amounts you owe.

Credit Credit, which is displayed in the Banking tab as well, is for tracking credit card transactions and balances.

Liability or Debt Debt (Liabilities), which is displayed in the Net Worth tab, is for tracking loans and other liabilities.

Setting Up Accounts

You create new accounts with the Account Setup dialog. No matter what type of account you create, Quicken steps you through the creation process, prompting you to enter information about the account, such as its name and balance. In this section, I explain how to get started with the Account Setup dialog to set up new accounts.

Getting Started

Begin by opening the Account Setup dialog. There are several ways to do this; here are some of them:

- Choose Tools | Account List (or press CTRL-A) to display the Account List window (see Figure 3-1 later in this chapter). Click the Add Account button in the bottom-right corner of the window.
- Choose Banking | Banking Actions | Banking Accounts | Add Account.
- Click Investing | Actions | Investing Accounts | Add Account.
- Select Net Worth | Net Worth Actions | Property & Debt Accounts | Add Account.

The Account Setup dialog should begin by asking what type of account you want to create. From there, its options change, depending on the account type and whether you want to set it up for online account services, if available.

Entering Account Information

Follow the prompts in the Account Setup dialogs to enter required information for the account you are creating. Click the Next button to progress from one dialog to the next. You can click Back at any time to go back and change information. You know you're finished when the Next button is replaced with a Done button; click it to save the account information.

Account information includes the financial institution in which the account is held (if applicable), the account name, an optional description, the account balance, and the date of the account balance. Almost every type of Quicken account requires this information. If you don't know the balance of an account, you may set it to $0.00 and make adjustments later, either when you get a statement or when you reconcile the account. If the account can be accessed online by Quicken, Quicken will automatically download the account balance information, as well as many recent transactions, as part of the account creation process.

I provide details for creating specific types of accounts throughout this book:

- Banking accounts are covered in Chapter 5.
- Investing accounts are covered in Chapter 10.
- Net Worth accounts are covered in Chapter 13.

Finishing Up

When you've finished entering information for a new account, click the Done button. You may be prompted to enter more information about the account, depending on the type of account and the financial institution you selected for it. The detailed instructions in Chapters 5, 10, and 13 for creating specific account types review all of the additional information you may have to enter.

Working with the Account List Window

You can view a list of all of your accounts at any time. Choose Tools | Account List or press CTRL-A. The Account List window, which looks and works like the Accounts subtab in the Setup tab I discussed in Chapter 2, appears (see Figure 3-1). This window displays a list of all accounts organized by tab and group.

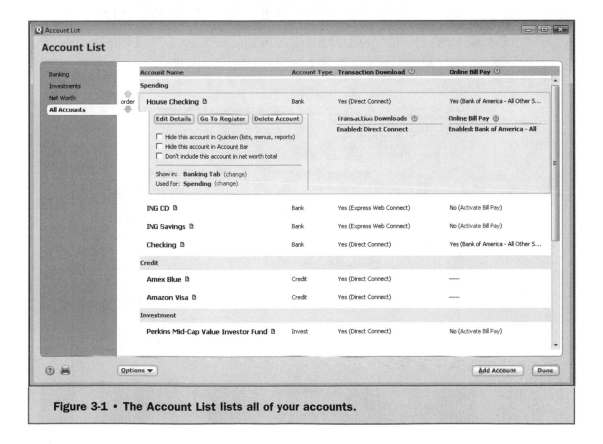

Figure 3-1 • The Account List lists all of your accounts.

Viewing Account Information

For each account in the Account List window (refer to Figure 3-1), Quicken displays the Account Name, Account Type, Transaction Download settings, and Online Bill Pay settings. You can add additional columns of information to the list by choosing commands from the bottom of the Options pop-up menu in the Account List window, shown next. Just select a command on the menu to toggle the display of some information on or off. This makes it possible to fully customize the appearance of the list and the information shown.

Working with Accounts

When you select an account, its display expands to show additional information and buttons. You can use these buttons to work with or modify an account.

Edit Details   The Edit Details button displays the General Information tab of the Account Details dialog for the account. As shown here, this dialog includes basic information about the account that you can view or edit. The Online Services tab, when available, tells you whether online services are available for the account and whether they are activated. It also lets you deactivate online services. (I tell you more about online account services in Chapters 6 and 11.)

Go To Register The Go To Register button opens the register for the account. I explain how to use the various types of account registers to enter and work with transactions throughout this book. (You can also open an account's register by double-clicking its name in the Account List window or by clicking it in the Account Bar.)

Delete Account The Delete Account button enables you to delete the account. It displays a dialog you can use to confirm that you want to delete the account. You must type **yes** into the dialog and click OK to delete the account. Remember that when you delete an account, you permanently remove all of its transactions from your Quicken data file. To get the account out of sight without actually deleting it and its data, consider hiding it instead. I explain how to do this next.

Hide This Account In Quicken This check box, when turned on, prevents the account from being displayed in lists, menus, and reports. This disables the two check boxes beneath it and removes the account from view in any list in which it would appear, except the Account List window. You may want to use this feature to remove accounts you no longer use or need to see—without removing the transactions they contain. Keep in mind that you cannot use a hidden account in a transaction; to do so, you must first unhide the account by turning off this check box for it. Just a side note: To truly hide an account in Quicken, select the Hide This Account In Quicken check box, and make sure the Show Hidden Accounts check box at the bottom-left corner of this Account List window is not selected.

Hide This Account In Account Bar To remove an account from the Account Bar, turn on this check box. Although the account remains visible in other lists and menus where it would normally appear, it no longer appears in the Account Bar. You may want to use this feature to keep the Account Bar short by excluding accounts you seldom access.

Don't Include This Account In Net Worth Total To exclude an account's balance from subtotal and total calculations, as well as the net worth displayed in the Account Bar, turn on this check box. This displays the balance for the account in gray in the Account Bar and omits the balance from any totals calculated in Quicken.

Activate Downloads or Activate Bill Pay These two options, which appear as links when available, display the Account Setup dialog. You can use this dialog to enable online account access features for the account. This option is available only for certain types of accounts and certain financial institutions. I explain how to use this dialog in Chapters 6 and 11.

Reorganizing Accounts

You can use options in the Account List window to reorganize accounts so they appear where you want them to.

Changing the Order of Accounts To change the order in which accounts appear in the Account List window and Account Bar, select an account and click the up or down Order button to move it. You can move an account to any position within its group.

Changing an Account's Group To change the group in which an account appears, select the account and click the Change link beside Show In or Used For. A Change Account Tab dialog like the one shown next appears. You can use drop-down lists in this dialog to change the Quicken tab in which the account appears, as well as the group within the tab. When you make changes and click OK, the account moves to that tab and group in the Account List window and the Account Bar. If you assign a group in a different tab, the account even moves the submenus of accounts for that tab—for example, choosing Net Worth Tab from the Show In drop-down list in the dialog moves the House Checking account to the Net Worth Accounts submenu under the Net Worth menu.

Categories

When you create a data file, Quicken automatically creates dozens of commonly used categories. Although these categories might completely meet your needs, at times you may want to add, remove, or modify a category to fine-tune Quicken for your use.

Types of Categories

There are basically two types of categories:

- **Income** is incoming money. It includes receipts such as your salary, commissions, interest income, dividend income, child support, gifts received, and tips.
- **Expense** is outgoing money. It includes insurance, groceries, rent, interest expense, bank fees, finance charges, charitable donations, and clothing.

Subcategories

A *subcategory* is a subset or part of a category. It must be the same type of category as its primary category. For example, you may use the Auto category to track

---

What Does This Mean to You? Categories

Categories? Subcategories? Sound confusing? Like a lot of work? Take it from me: it isn't. And it's worth the time you spend doing it.

Here's how it works. When you enter a transaction in Quicken, you'll categorize it using one of your predefined categories. (Sometimes Quicken can even guess the right category the first time you enter a transaction for a payee!) The next time you enter a transaction for the same payee, Quicken automatically assumes the transaction will use the same category, so Quicken enters it for you. I'm willing to bet that nine times out of ten, Quicken's assumption is right. So it really isn't that much work.

Worth the trouble? You bet! By properly categorizing transactions, you can get a true picture of where your money comes from and where it goes. You can create realistic budgets based on accurate spending patterns to help you save money. You can create tax reports that'll save you—or your tax preparer—time. You can even automate much of your tax preparation by exporting all those properly categorized transactions right into Intuit's TurboTax tax preparation software.

So don't leave category fields blank when you enter transactions. Take that extra step. It's worth it.

Besides, there's always the Misc category if you can't think of a more appropriate one.

---

expenses to operate your car. Within that category, however, you may want subcategories to record specific expenses, such as auto insurance, fuel, and repairs. Subcategories make it easy to keep income and expenses organized into manageable categories, while providing the transaction detail you might want or need.

Working with the Category List Window

You can view a list of all of your categories at any time. Choose Tools | Category List, or press SHIFT-CTRL-C. The Category List window appears (see Figure 3-2).

In this section, I explain how to use the Category List window to display, add, modify, delete, and perform other tasks with categories.

Changing the Category Display

The Category List window lists all categories and transfer accounts within up to eight broad headings, depending on check boxes you turned on in the Customize Quicken area of the Setup tab: Business Income, Business Expenses, Personal Income, Personal Expenses, Investment, Rental Expenses, Transfers, and All Categories. You can click a heading on the left side of the Category List window to display just those categories within it. Or, click All Categories to display all categories in your data file. You can also use the Show drop-down list at the top of the window to display categories that meet certain criteria, such as tax-related categories or unused categories.

In the main part of the window, category names appear in an outline view, with subcategories indented beneath them. You can turn on the Hide check box for a category to remove it from lists and menus without actually deleting it from your Quicken data file.

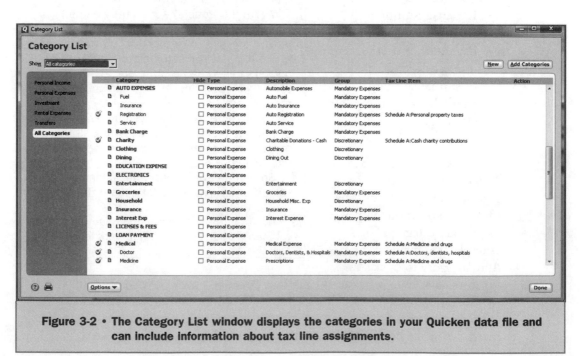

Figure 3-2 • The Category List window displays the categories in your Quicken data file and can include information about tax line assignments.

You can also choose commands from the Options menu at the bottom of the window to determine what information appears with the category names in the Category List window. Figure 3-2 includes category groups, types, and tax line item information. (I tell you more about assigning tax lines to categories in Chapter 18.) You can also show category descriptions and groups or any combination of all of this information.

Creating a New Category

To create a new category, click the New button at the top of the Category List window (refer to Figure 3-2). The Set Up Category dialog appears. Enter information about the category—this illustration shows an example—and click OK.

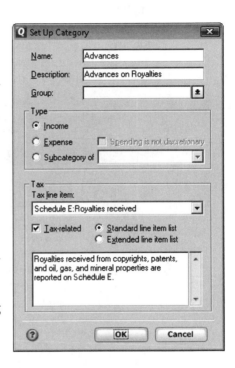

Here's a quick summary of the kind of information you should provide for each category.

Category Information The basic category information includes the category name, which is required, and the description and group, which are optional. Groups are used primarily for budgeting, which I discuss in Chapter 17. For now, you can either leave the Group box empty or choose an existing group from the drop-down list.

Type Use options in the Type area to select the type of category: Income, Expense, or Subcategory of. In addition to classifying income and expense items properly, the type of category you specify will determine where the category appears in reports and graphs. For example, income categories always appear before expense categories, and subcategories appear immediately below their parent categories. If you select Subcategory of, you must choose a category from the drop-down list beside it. If you do not have complete control over spending for an expense category, you can turn on the Spending Is Not Discretionary check box. This option, which is also used primarily for budgeting, applies to required fixed expenditures, such as rent, car insurance, and child care.

Tax   You can use the Tax area options to specify whether a category is tax-related and, if so, what tax form it appears on. This can be a real timesaver at tax time by enabling you to organize your income and expenditures as they appear on tax forms. I tell you more about using Quicken at tax time in Chapter 18. You are not required to enter anything in this area.

Adding Multiple Categories at Once

Quicken makes it easy to add multiple related categories all at once. For example, suppose you just bought your first home (congratulations!) and want to add categories for homeowners to your Quicken data file. Click the Add Categories button at the top of the Category List window (refer to Figure 3-2) to display the Add Categories dialog, which is shown here:

Choose a category group from the Available Categories drop-down list, and then click to add a green check mark beside each category you want to add. When you click Add, the selected categories appear in the Categories To Add list. Click OK to add the categories and dismiss the dialog.

Editing, Deleting, and Merging Categories

You can also use the Category List window (see Figure 3-2) to edit, delete, or merge categories. Select the name of the category you want to work with, and then click a button in the same row in the Action column on the right side of the window. Consider backing up your data before you edit, delete, or merge categories. Refer to Appendix A for more information about backing up in Quicken.

Edit The Edit button displays the Edit Category dialog, which looks and works just like the Set Up Category dialog (shown earlier) for the selected category. You can use this to make just about any change to a category. You can even "promote" a subcategory to a category by changing its type.

Delete The Delete button enables you to delete the selected category. Clicking the Delete button displays different dialogs, depending on the category that is selected. Quicken begins by warning you that the category and any subcategories beneath it will be deleted. Then:

- If you selected a category without transactions, when you click OK, the category is deleted.
- If you selected a category or subcategory with transactions, the Delete Category dialog, shown here, appears. You can use this dialog to replace the category with another category throughout your data file. Choose another category from the drop-down list and click OK. If you click OK without choosing a replacement category, any transactions that referenced the category you deleted will be marked as uncategorized. If the category you deleted has subcategories, this dialog appears for each subcategory that has transactions.

Merge The Merge button lets you merge transactions using the currently selected category with transactions using another category. This, in effect, recategorizes all of the transactions for the selected category. Clicking Merge displays the Merge Category dialog, shown next. Choose another category from the drop-down list. If you want to delete the category you selected, turn on the check box—this makes the dialog work the same way as the Delete Category dialog shown earlier. Click OK to perform the merge. One thing to keep in mind: If the category you selected is not used in any transactions, a dialog will tell you that there's nothing to merge.

Tags

A *tag* is an optional identifier for specifying what a transaction applies to. For example, if you have two vehicles for which you track expenses, you can create a tag for each vehicle, such as "Jeep" and "Chevy Truck." Then, when you record a transaction for one of the vehicles, you can include the appropriate tag with the category for the transaction. Because Quicken can produce reports based on categories, tags, or both, tags offer an additional dimension for tracking and reporting information.

I want to stress here that using tags is completely optional. It's not necessary to set them up or use them at all. In fact, many Quicken users—including a few I know at Intuit—don't take advantage of this feature. It's your decision.

Displaying the Tag List Window

Quicken maintains a list of all the tags you create. You can display the Tag List window by choosing Tools | Tag List, or by pressing CTRL-L. The illustration on the next page shows an example with some tags I created.

What Does This Mean to You? Tags

If you were doubtful about the benefit of using categories in transactions, tags will certainly be a hard sell. Fortunately, I don't have to sell it to you because you really don't have to use this feature at all.

That said, let me explain how I use tags. I write books for a living. I've written tons of them. And I use Quicken to track my income and expenses for each book.

Sure, I could use the category feature to set up a separate category for every book I've ever written or revised—there are currently 72 of them!—but why bother when the tag feature is available? I simply set up a separate tag for each book I've written. Then, when I record an income or expense transaction related to a specific title, I can use the same income and expense categories I always use for writing-related income and expenses. I just add, almost as an afterthought, the tag that corresponds to the book.

What's the benefit of doing this? Well, suppose I want to determine which of my titles earns the most money. I can create a Profit and Loss Report within Quicken, with separate columns for each tag—in this case, book title. Then, when it's time to revise a title, I know in advance whether it's going to be worth my while.

Maybe this example doesn't apply to you. But here's one that might.

Got kids? Try this. Create a separate tag for each child. Then, when you've got expenses for a specific family member, record the transaction with the appropriate tag name. (If you've got income related to a specific child, I'm impressed; be sure to include the tag name with those transactions, too.) Then, when that partially grown bundle of joy asks for $257.49 to buy a new cell phone, you can show him a report of how much he's cost you so far when you say no.

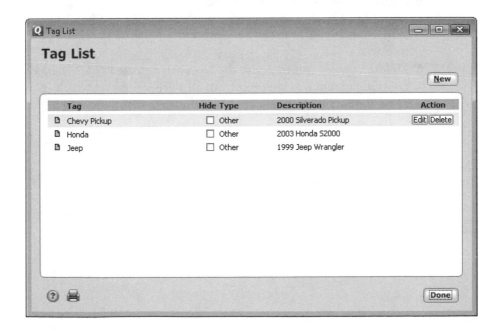

Creating a New Tag

Click the New button on the button bar in the Tag List window. The New Tag dialog, which is shown here, appears. Use it to enter information about the tag.

Only one piece of information is necessary: the tag name. You may want to make it short, so it's easy to remember and enter. The description can be used to provide additional information on the tag's use. The copy number enables you to associate tags with different but similar activities. For example, if you have two separate businesses for which you report activity on two Schedule Cs, you can assign Copy 1 to one business's tags and Copy 2 to the other business's tags.

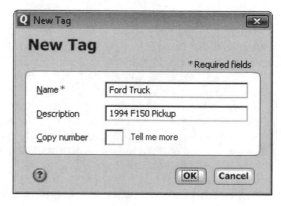

When you click OK, the tag is added to the list. You can create as many tags as you like.

Working with the Tag List Window

You can use buttons that appear beside a selected tag in the Tag List window to work with the tag list or a selected tag:

- **Edit** enables you to modify the currently selected tag name or other information.
- **Delete** enables you to delete the currently selected tag. When you delete a tag, the tag name is removed from all transactions in which it appeared. (The transaction remains properly categorized.)

Going Online with Quicken

Chapter 4

In This Chapter:

- *Benefits of going online with Quicken*
- *Getting connected to the Internet*
- *Setting up Quicken for an Internet connection*
- *Testing and troubleshooting your connection*
- *An introduction to Web surfing*
- *Accessing Quicken.com*
- *Exploring Quicken Picks*
- *Quicken financial partners*

Many of Quicken Personal Finance Software's features work seamlessly with the Internet. If you have access to the Internet, either through a connection to an Internet service provider (ISP) or through a connection to an online service such as America Online, you can take advantage of these online features to get up-to-date information, automate data entry, pay bills, and obtain Quicken maintenance updates automatically.

This chapter tells you why you might want to take advantage of Quicken's online features. Then it explains how to set up Quicken to go online. Finally, you'll learn a little about surfing the Web and are introduced to Quicken.com and Quicken Picks, two great sources of information and services for Quicken users.

Going Online

If you're already using your computer to access the features of the Internet or online services such as America Online, you probably already know a lot about it. This part of the chapter fills in any gaps in your knowledge by telling you about the benefits of going online with Quicken and addressing any security concerns you might have. Finally, for the folks who aren't already online, you will learn what you need to connect to the Internet to use Quicken's online features.

Why Go Online?

Before I go any further, I want to remind you that you don't *have* to go online to use Quicken. Quicken is a good financial management software package, even without its online features. But Quicken's online features make it a *great* financial management software package. As you'll see in this section and throughout this book, Quicken uses the Internet to help you make better financial decisions. How? By providing you with information and resources that are relevant to your personal financial situation.

The best way to explain the benefits of going online is to list a few of the features online users can take advantage of.

If You Have a Bank Account, You Can Benefit

Throughout the month, you write checks and mail them to individuals and organizations. You enter these transactions in your checking account register. At month's end, you reconcile the account. You can do all this without going online; learn how in Chapters 5 and 8.

But if you register for Transaction Download with your bank, you can download all bank account activity on a regular basis, so you know exactly when the transactions hit your account—even the ATM and debit card transactions you always forget to enter. If you register for Online Payment, you can pay your bills without licking another envelope or pasting on another stamp. Chapter 6 explains how all this works.

> ### What Does This Mean to You? Online Account Services
>
> Let me get something off my chest here. Transaction Download and Online Payment are the reasons I use Quicken to manage my finances.
>
> With five checking accounts, three savings accounts, and a handful of credit card accounts for my personal finances and the finances of two small businesses, I simply can't be bothered with manually entering transactions and writing checks. Heck, I'd be spending more time entering transactions than getting work done without Quicken online account services.
>
> I depend on Quicken's online features to automate transaction entry and bill payments. As you'll see throughout this book, Quicken has all kinds of timesaving features; in my opinion, the online features are the best of them.

If You Have Credit Cards, You Can Benefit

Do you have credit cards? If so, you can take advantage of Quicken's credit card tracking features, which is covered in Chapter 5, to keep track of your charges, payments, and balances. You don't need to go online.

But if you sign up for Transaction Download, all your credit card charges can be downloaded directly into Quicken, eliminating the need for time-consuming data entry, while giving you an up-to-date summary of your debt and how you spent your money. Learn more about this in Chapter 6.

If You Invest, You Can Benefit

Quicken can keep track of your investments, whether they are 401(k) accounts, mutual funds, or stocks. You can enter share, price, and transaction information into Quicken, and it will summarize portfolio value, gains, and losses. It'll even keep track of securities by lot. You don't need to go online to track your investments. Chapter 10 explains how.

But with online investment tracking features, Quicken can automatically obtain quotes on all the securities in your portfolio and update your portfolio's market value. Depending on your brokerage firm, you may also be able to download transactions, account balances, and holdings. Quicken can also alert you about news stories that affect your investments and automatically download the headlines, so you can learn more with just a click. You can also get valuable up-to-date research information about securities that interest you, so you can make informed investment decisions. Learn all about all this in Chapter 11.

If You Want to Save Money, You Can Benefit

If you're like most people, you spend money every day on the things you need or want to make your life better. Quicken can help you keep track of your spending by summarizing expenditures by category. It can also help you save money by enabling you to create a budget and keep your expenditures under control.

And with the help of Quicken's Internet-based Quicken Picks feature, you can shop for the deals online, without leaving the comfort of your desk. You can sign up to earn cash back on purchases you make with Quicken Picks deals. That'll put money back in the bank.

Enough Already!

If all this doesn't convince you that going online with Quicken can help you save time, save money, and get smarter, stop reading and skip ahead to Chapter 5. You'll probably never be convinced. I will say one more thing, however: after using Quicken's online features for more than 12 years now, I can't imagine using Quicken any other way.

Security Features

Perhaps you're already convinced that the online features can benefit you. Maybe you're worried about security, concerned that a stranger will be able to access your accounts or steal your credit card numbers.

You can stop worrying. The folks at Intuit and the participating banks, credit card companies, and brokerage firms have done all the worrying for you. They've come up with a secure system that protects your information and accounts.

PINs

A *PIN*, or *personal identification number*, is a secret password you must use to access your accounts online. If you have an ATM card or cash-advance capabilities through your credit card, you probably already have at least one PIN, so the idea shouldn't be new to you. It simply prevents anyone from accessing the account for any reason without first entering the correct PIN.

An account's PIN is initially assigned by the bank, credit card company, or brokerage firm. Some companies, such as American Express, require that your PIN consist of a mixture of letters and numbers for additional security. You can change your PINs to make them easier to remember—just don't use something obvious like your birthday or telephone number. And don't write it on a sticky note and attach it to your computer's monitor!

If you think someone might have guessed your PIN, you can change it. In fact, it's a good idea to change all your PINs and passwords regularly—not just the ones you use in Quicken.

Encryption

Once you're online and you've correctly entered your PIN, the instructions that flow from your computer to the bank, credit card company, or brokerage firm are *encrypted*. This means they are encoded in such a way that anyone able to "tap in" to the transmission would "hear" only gibberish. Quicken does the encryption using, at a minimum, the 56-bit single Data Encryption Standard (DES). Quicken is also capable of encrypting data with stronger methods, including the 128-bit RC4 or 168-bit triple DES. Once the encrypted information reaches the computer at the bank, credit card company, or brokerage firm, it is unencrypted, and then validated and processed.

Encryption makes it virtually impossible for any unauthorized party to "listen in" to your transmission. It also makes it impossible for someone to alter a transaction from the moment it leaves your computer to the moment it arrives at your bank, credit card company, or brokerage firm for processing.

Other Security Methods

Quicken also takes advantage of other security methods for online communications, including Secure Sockets Layer (SSL) encryption, digital signatures, and digital certificates. Together, these security methods make online financial transactions secure   even more secure than telephone banking, which you may already use!

Getting Connected

To take advantage of Quicken's online features, you need a connection to the Internet. You get that through an ISP, an organization that provides access to the Internet, usually for a monthly fee. These days, literally thousands of ISPs, including local phone and cable television companies, can provide the access you need for Quicken's online features.

If you don't already have an account with an ISP, you must set one up before you can configure Quicken to use its online features. Check your local phone book or newspaper to find an ISP near you. Your ISP can explain everything you need to get connected and help you set up your computer to go online.

Setting Up and Testing an Internet Connection

To use Quicken's online features, you may need to set up Quicken for your Internet connection. This part of the chapter explains how to set up, test, and troubleshoot a Quicken Internet connection.

If you went through the Setup process and created at least one account that utilizes Quicken's online features, chances are Quicken is already set up to work with your Internet connection. If that's the case, you can skip this section, unless you need to modify or troubleshoot your connection.

Internet Connection Setup

Choose Edit | Preferences | Internet Connection Setup. The Internet Connection Setup dialog, shown on the top of the following page, appears.

This dialog offers three options:

- **Use The Following Connection.** This option enables you to select from an existing list of Internet connections. This list is maintained by Windows, based on Internet connection profiles you create with the Internet Connection Wizard. If you have only one connection profile (like I do), the

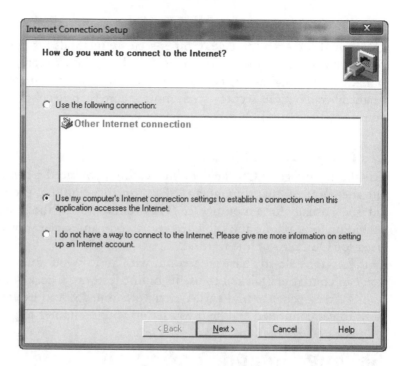

only item in this list will be Other Internet Connection. If you select this
option, when you click Next, the dialog explains what to do when you need
to connect to the Internet.

- **Use My Computer's Internet Connection Settings To Establish A
  Connection When This Application Accesses The Internet.** This option
  tells Quicken to use your active Internet connection profile to connect to the
  Internet from within Quicken. If you select this option, when you click Next,
  the dialog tells you a little about your connection. Quicken will automatically
  connect to the Internet using these settings any time it needs to.
- **I Do Not Have A Way To Connect To The Internet. Please Give Me More
  Information On Setting Up An Internet Account.** Select this option only if
  you do not already have an Internet connection set up within Windows.
  When you click Next, Quicken provides additional instructions for getting an
  ISP and using the Internet Connection Wizard to set up your connection.

Make your selections in the dialog and click Next and Done to get more
information or complete the setup process. If you need help setting up an
Internet connection, consult Windows Help.

You can change the options for an Internet connection profile at any time.
Just follow these instructions again.

Testing Your Connection with a Visit to Quicken.com

A good way to test your Internet connection is to visit Quicken.com, the official Quicken Web site. This site offers information about Intuit products, as well as special features for registered Quicken users. You'll learn more about Quicken.com later in this chapter and throughout this book. For now, connect to it to make sure your Internet connection works.

If it is not showing, click View and Show Tool Bar. Slide your mouse over the icons to determine the Quicken.com button. (It is the one with the house and the Q.) When you click the Quicken.com button, Quicken attempts to connect to the Internet using the settings in the Internet Connection Setup dialog.

What you see during the connection process will vary depending on your ISP. If you use an online service such as America Online, the service's access software may start automatically to make the connection. You may be prompted to enter a username or password. Other dialogs may appear. It may be necessary to switch from connection software back to Quicken by clicking the Quicken button on the Windows task bar.

When the connection is complete, Quicken requests the Quicken.com home page. It appears in a Quicken Internet window (see Figure 4-1).

If you were already connected to the Internet when you accessed one of Quicken's online features, or if you have a direct connection to the Internet, you won't see the connection happening. Instead, the Quicken.com page will simply appear in a Quicken Internet window (see Figure 4-1).

Troubleshooting Connection Problems

If you follow the instructions provided throughout this chapter, you shouldn't have any trouble connecting to the Internet with Quicken. But things aren't always as easy as they should be. Sometimes even the tiniest problems can prevent you from successfully connecting and exchanging data.

This section provides some troubleshooting advice to help you with connection problems you may experience. Check this section before you start pulling out your hair and cursing the day computers were invented.

Setup Problems

To determine whether the problem is a Quicken setup problem or a general Internet setup problem, exit Quicken and try connecting to the Internet from another program, such as your regular Web browser or e-mail program:

- If you can connect to the Internet from another program but not from Quicken, the problem may be with Quicken's Internet connection setup. Go

Figure 4-1 • The Quicken.com home page provides information about Quicken products and services, and links to features for registered users.

back to the section titled "Internet Connection Setup" earlier in this chapter, and repeat the setup process. You'll probably want to select the second option in the Internet Connection Setup dialog.

- If you can't connect to the Internet from any other program or with dial-up networking (for dial-up connections), the problem is with your Internet setup for Windows, your modem (for dial-up connections), your network (for direct connections), or your router (for direct connections). You must fix any problem you find before you can successfully set up and connect with Quicken. Consult Windows Help for assistance.

Modem Problems

Problems with a dial-up connection may be related to your modem. Try each of the following, attempting a connection after each one:

- Check all cables between your computer and your modem (if you have an external modem), and between your modem and the telephone outlet.
- Check the telephone line to make sure it has a dial tone and that it is not being used by someone else or another program.
- Turn off your modem, and then turn it back on. Or, if you have an internal modem, restart your computer. This resets the modem and may resolve the problem.

If you can connect but have trouble staying connected, try the following:

- Make sure no one is picking up an extension of the phone line while you are online.
- Make sure call-waiting is disabled by entering the appropriate codes for the dial-up connection.
- Have the phone company check the line for noise. If noise is detected, ask the phone company to fix the problem. (It shouldn't cost you anything if the line noise is the result of a problem outside your premises.)

Network or Router Problems

Problems with a direct connection may be related to your network or router. Try these things, attempting a connection after each one:

- Check all cables between your computer and the network hub or router.
- Check to make sure the correct proxy server information was entered into Windows Internet Connection Wizard.
- Restart your computer. Sometimes resetting your computer's system software can clear network problems.
- Ask your system administrator to check your network setup.
- Consult your ISP for additional assistance.

Exploring Quicken's Web-Based Features

You access Quicken's Web-based features from within Quicken software. In some cases, Quicken uses its built-in Web browser to display information; in other cases, it opens the default browser on your computer. This section tells new Internet users a little more about using the Web and then explains how you can access Quicken's Web-based features.

An Introduction to Web Surfing

Let me take a moment to explain exactly what you're doing when you connect to Quicken.com and the other Quicken features on the Web. If you're brand new to *Web surfing*—that is, exploring Web sites—be sure to read this section. But if you're a seasoned surfer, you probably already know all this stuff and can skip it.

One more thing: This section is not designed to explain everything you'll ever need to know about browsing the World Wide Web. It provides the basic information you need to use the Web to get the information you need.

Going Online

When you access Quicken's online features, you do so by connecting to the Internet through your ISP. It doesn't matter whether you connect via a modem or a network, or whether your ISP is America Online, your local cable company, or Joe's Internet Service. The main thing is having a connection or a conduit for information.

Think of an Internet connection as some PVC piping running from your computer to your ISP's computer, with a valve to control the flow of information. Once the valve is open (you're connected), any information can flow through the pipe in either direction. You can even exchange information through that pipe in both directions at the same time. This makes it possible to download (or retrieve) a Web page with your Web browser while you upload (or send) e-mail with your e-mail program.

Quicken's online features use the pipe (or connection) in two ways:

- The integrated Web browser enables you to request and receive the information you want. It's live and interactive—click a link, and a moment later your information starts to appear. Quicken can display Web pages in its built-in Internet window (see Figure 4-1) or your default browser's window.
- Transaction Download, Online Payment, and several other features work in the background to communicate with financial institutions with which you have accounts. Quicken sends information you prepared in advance and retrieves the information the financial institution has waiting for you.

This chapter concentrates on Web browsing with Quicken—using Quicken's integrated Web browser to access interactive features on Quicken.com. But it also provides some information to help you find financial institutions that work with Quicken for the Transaction Download and Online Payment features.

Navigating   The main thing to remember about the Web is that it's interactive. Every time a Web page appears on your screen, it'll offer a number of options for viewing other information. This is known as navigating the Web.

Hyperlinks and Forms   You can move from page to page on the Web in two ways:

- **Hyperlinks** (or links) are text or graphics that, when clicked, display another page. Hypertext links are usually underlined, colored text. Graphic links sometimes have a colored border around them. You can always identify a link by pointing to it—your mouse pointer will turn into a hand with a pointing finger, and a screen tip may appear to describe the link.
- **Forms** offer options for going to another page or searching for information. Options can appear in pop-up menus, text boxes that you fill in, check boxes that you turn on, or option buttons that you select. Multiple options often appear. You enter or select the options you want and click a button to send your request to the Web site. The information you requested appears a moment later.

Other Navigation Techniques   Several of the buttons on the Quicken browser's toolbar (refer to Figure 4-1) are navigation buttons:

- **Back** displays the previously viewed page.
- **Next** displays the page you viewed after the current page. This button is available only after you have used the Back button.
- **Stop** stops the loading of the current page. This may result in incomplete pages or error messages on the page. You might use this button if you click a link and then realize that you don't really want to view the information you requested.
- **Refresh** loads a new copy of the Web page from the Web site's server. This button is handy for updating stock quotes or news that appears on a page.
- **Print** enables you to print the currently displayed page.
- **Quicken.com** takes you to the Quicken.com home page (refer to Figure 4-1).
- **Full Browser** starts and switches to your default Web browser. Quicken continues to run in the background. You can switch back to Quicken at any time by clicking its icon on the Windows taskbar.

Accessing Quicken.com

Quicken.com, the official Quicken site, supports Quicken users in four different ways:

- Provides information about Quicken and Quicken-compatible software and services that can help you get the most out of Quicken.

- Enables registered Quicken users to store Quicken account balances, reminders, and transactions entered on the Web in a secure environment. These features can make Quicken.com an extremely useful tool, especially to Quicken users who spend much of their time away from home.
- Offers access to basic and advanced financial information, including stock quotes, loan rates, and insurance providers. This helps Quicken users find the financial information they need to make informed decisions.
- Provides access to Quicken support options, including online forums where Quicken users can get help for problems and answers to questions.

Quicken.com is a dynamic Web site that changes frequently. The screen illustration and features I tell you about will probably appear differently when you connect. In addition, brand-new features might be added after the publication of this book. That's why I won't go into too much detail. The best way to learn about the features of Quicken.com is to check them out for yourself.

Exploring Quicken Picks

Quicken Picks is a Web-based feature that helps you save time, save money, and shop smart by displaying special money-saving offers you can take advantage of when you shop online.

To get started, click the More From Quicken tab and then click the Quicken Picks button in the View area. The initial screen explains a little about what the feature does. To access the feature, click the Get Deals button.

Your computer will retrieve some information from the Internet before using your default Web browser to display a selection of top special offers by well-known retailers and manufacturers (Figure 4-2). You can navigate the Quicken Picks Web site like any other site to get the details for deals and take advantage of them to save money.

Participating Financial Institutions

If you're interested in keeping track of your finances with the least amount of data entry, you should be considering Quicken's online features Transaction Download and Online Payment. The beginning of this chapter explained the benefits of these features. Chapters 6 and 11 tell you how to use them. But you can't use them until you've set up an account with a participating financial institution and applied for the online account services you want to use.

When you create a bank, credit card, or investment account, Quicken prompts you to enter the name of your financial institution. Quicken can

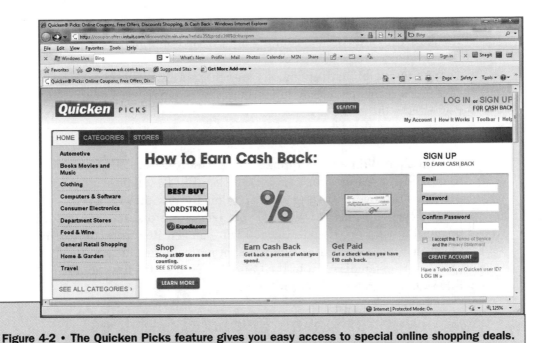

Figure 4-2 • The Quicken Picks feature gives you easy access to special online shopping deals.

determine whether your financial institution is one of the participating financial institutions, as many are. If you've already set up your accounts for online account services, you can skip this section. But you may find it useful if you're shopping around for another financial institution and want one that works with Quicken.

Finding a Participating Institution

Participating financial institutions offer four types of online financial services:

- **Banking Account Access** enables you to download bank account transactions directly into your Quicken data file.
- **Credit/Charge Card Access** enables you to download credit or charge card transactions directly into your Quicken data file.
- **Investment Account Access** enables you to download brokerage and other investment account transactions directly into your Quicken data file.
- **Payments** enables you to send payment instructions from within Quicken. This makes it possible to pay bills and send payments to anyone without writing a check.

If your bank, credit card company, or brokerage firm is not on the list when you are setting up a new account, you have two options:

Change financial institutions.   I know it sounds harsh, but if your bank or credit card company doesn't support online banking services with Quicken and you really want to use this feature, you can find a financial institution that does support it and open an account there.

Use Quicken Bill Pay and Quicken Visa Credit Card.   If you're interested only in the Bill Pay feature, you can use Quicken Bill Pay. This enables you to process payments from your existing bank accounts from within Quicken. There's no need to change banks or wait until your bank signs on as a participating financial institution. If you'd like to earn Quicken Rewards, consider the Quicken Visa Credit Card. You can learn more about Quicken Bill Pay and Quicken Visa Credit Card in the Quicken Services window; choose the More From Quicken tab to display it.

Applying for Online Financial Services

Before you can take advantage of the online feature in Quicken, you must apply for a user name and password from your financial institution. This gets the wheels turning to put you online. It may take a few days to get the necessary access information, so apply as soon as you're sure you want to take advantage of the online financial services features.

Banking

This part of the book explains how to use Quicken Personal Finance Software to keep track of the bank and credit card accounts in the Banking tab. It starts by explaining the basics of manually recording bank and credit card transactions, and then tells you how you can take advantage of online transaction entry and payment processing features such as Transaction Downloads and Online Bill Pay. It provides details about how you can tap into the power of Quicken to automate many entry tasks, thus saving you time. It also explains how to reconcile accounts and how to use Quicken's reporting features to learn more about what you have and how you're doing financially. This part has five chapters:

Chapter 5:   *Recording Bank and Credit Card Transactions*

Chapter 6:   *Using Online Banking Features*

Chapter 7:   *Automating Transactions and Tasks*

Chapter 8:   *Reconciling Your Accounts*

Chapter 9:   *Examining Your Banking Activity*

Part Two

Recording Bank and Credit Card Transactions

Chapter 5

In This Chapter:

- *Creating banking accounts*
- *Entering payments and other transactions*
- *Using splits and tags*
- *Writing and printing checks*
- *Entering credit card transactions*
- *Transferring money*
- *Working with existing transactions*
- *Adding notes and attachments*

At Quicken's core is its ability to manage your bank accounts. This is probably Quicken's most used feature. You enter the transactions, and Quicken Personal Finance Software keeps track of account balances and the source and destination of the money you spend. You can even have Quicken print checks for you.

Using similar transaction entry techniques, Quicken can also help you keep track of credit card accounts. You enter transactions as you make them or at month's end when you receive your statement and pay your bill. Quicken keeps track of balances and offers you an easy way to monitor what you used your credit card to buy. It also enables you to keep an eye on how much your credit cards cost you in terms of finance charges and other fees.

Getting Started

Before you can use Quicken to track bank and credit card transactions, you should prepare by creating the necessary accounts and learning how recording transactions works. In this section, I provide an overview of the banking account types, along with examples of transactions you might make. I also provide detailed step-by-step instructions for creating banking accounts.

Overview of Accounts and Transactions

Most of the transactions you track with Quicken will involve one or more of its bank, credit card, and cash accounts. Here's a closer look at each account type, along with some transaction examples. As you read about these accounts, imagine how they might apply to your financial situation.

Bank Accounts

Quicken offers two types of accounts that you can use to track the money you have in a bank:

- **Checking** accounts include check writing privileges. These accounts usually have a lot of activity, with deposits to increase the account balance and checks that decrease the account balance.
- **Savings** accounts are for your savings. These accounts usually don't have as much activity as checking accounts. You can use a savings account to track the balance in a certificate of deposit (CD), holiday savings club, or similar savings account.

Generally speaking, bank account transactions can be broken down into three broad categories: payments, deposits, and transfers.

Payments   Payments are cash outflows. Here are some examples:

- You write a check to pay your electric bill.
- You withdraw money from your savings account to buy a gift for your mother.
- You use your ATM card to withdraw spending money from a bank account.
- You use your debit card to buy groceries.
- You pay a monthly checking account fee.

Deposits Deposits are cash inflows. Here are some examples:

- You deposit your paycheck into your checking account.
- You sell your old computer and deposit the proceeds into your savings account.
- Your paycheck or Social Security check is deposited into your bank account as a direct deposit.
- You earn interest on your savings account.

Transfers A transfer is a movement of funds from one account to another. Here are some examples:

- You transfer money from an interest-bearing savings account to your checking account when you're ready to pay your bills.
- You transfer money from a money market account to your home equity line of credit account to reduce its balance.

Credit Card Accounts

Credit card accounts track money you owe, not money you own. Some credit cards, such as MasterCard, Visa, American Express, and Discover, can be used in most stores that accept credit cards. Other credit cards, such as Macy's, Dillard's, and Shell, can be used only in certain stores. But they all have one thing in common: if there's a balance, it's usually because you owe the credit card company money.

Credit card account transactions can also be broken down into two categories: charges and payments.

Charges Charges result when you use your credit card to buy something or the credit card company charges a fee for services. Here are some examples:

- You use your Visa card to buy a new computer.
- You use your Discover card to pay for a hotel stay.
- You use your Shell card to fill the gas tank on your boat at the marina.
- A finance charge based on your account balance is added to your Macy's bill at month's end.
- A late fee is added to your MasterCard bill because you didn't pay the previous month's bill on time.
- A fee is added to your American Express bill for annual membership dues.

The opposite of a charge is a *credit*. Think of it as a negative charge; don't confuse it with a payment. Here are two examples:

- You return the sweater you bought with your American Express card to the store you bought it from.
- In reviewing your MasterCard bill, you discover that a merchant charged you in error, and you arrange to have the incorrect charge removed.

Payments Payments are amounts you send to a credit card company to reduce your balance. Here are three examples:

- You pay the minimum amount due on your Visa card.
- You pay $150 toward the balance on your Macy's card.
- You pay the balance on your American Express card.

Cash Accounts

Quicken also offers cash accounts for tracking cash expenditures. For example, you might create an account called My Wallet or Spending Money and use it to keep track of the cash you have on hand. Cash accounts are like bank accounts, but there's no bank. The money is in your wallet, your pocket, or the old coffee can on the windowsill.

Cash accounts have two types of transactions: receive and spend.

Receive When you receive cash, you increase the amount of cash you have on hand. Here are some examples:

- You withdraw cash from the bank for weekly spending money.
- You sell your *National Geographic* magazine collection for cash at a garage sale.
- You get a $20 bill in a birthday card from your grandmother.

Spend When you spend cash, you reduce your cash balance. Here are some examples:

- You buy coffee and a newspaper and pay a bridge toll on your way to work.
- You give your son his allowance.
- You put a $20 bill in the birthday card you send to your granddaughter.

Creating Banking Accounts

Chapter 3 briefly discusses how to use the Account Setup dialog to create new Quicken accounts. Here are the details for creating Banking tab accounts.

In the Setup tab, scroll to Checking and Savings Accounts to display a list of accounts already set up in Quicken. Then click the Add Checking Account button to display the Account Setup dialog as seen in Figure 5-1. You create credit card and cash accounts in their areas as discussed later in this chapter.

In the Banking tab, click Options | Add An Account. You see a dialog asking what type of account you want to set up as seen here. Choose the type of

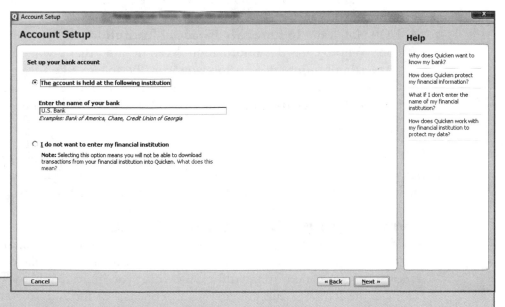

Figure 5-1 • The Account Setup dialog helps you quickly set up your various accounts.

account and click Next. Note that if you have already set up an account and named a financial institution, you are prompted with a screen asking if you would like to use an existing financial institution or a new one.

Entering Financial Institution Information

Quicken's extensive online account access features make it possible to automate data entry and account reconciliations for accounts held in participating financial institutions. To take advantage of these features, if you're creating a bank or credit card account, Quicken usually starts the account creation process by prompting you to enter the name of your financial institution.

You have two options:

- **The Account Is Held At The Following Institution** enables you to specify the bank in which the account is held. Type the name of the bank in the text box. Quicken displays a drop-down list that attempts to match the characters in the text box to those in its internal database of supported financial institutions. If your bank appears on the list, click it to select and enter it. Otherwise, finish typing and click Next. If you entered the name of a financial institution Quicken does not recognize, it displays a dialog that attempts to match what you typed with the name of a financial institution it recognizes. If none of these is your institution, click None Of These Is My Bank—*use name of institution*. If you choose this option, Quicken reminds you that you cannot use online services..
- **I Do Not Want To Enter My Financial Institution** tells Quicken that you don't want to enter this information. Keep in mind that if you don't enter financial institution information, you won't be able to take advantage of Quicken's online banking features for this account. However, you can activate the online banking features later. I discuss online banking in Chapter 6.

If the account is held at a financial institution that supports Quicken's transaction download feature, a dialog like the one in Figure 5-2 appears. Enter the information provided by your financial institution and click Next.

Completing the Account Setup Online

As I discuss in Chapter 6, financial institutions that support transaction download enable you to download bank or credit card account balance and transaction information from within Quicken. If you indicated that you want to complete the account setup online, Quicken opens a connection to your bank and you see a message like the one shown next.

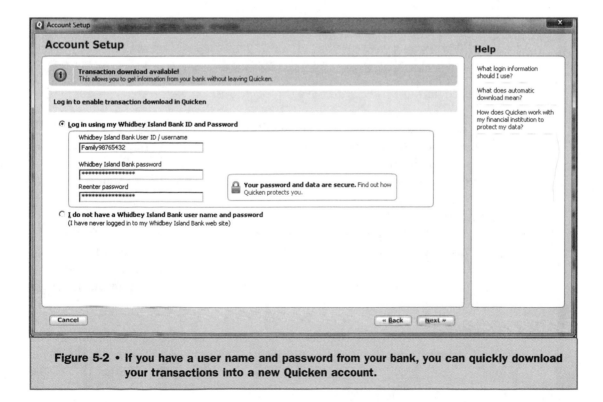

Figure 5-2 • **If you have a user name and password from your bank, you can quickly download your transactions into a new Quicken account.**

Quicken connects to the Internet to exchange some information with your bank or credit card company. A dialog may appear to ask for additional information to prove you are authorized to access the account; provide information as required. When it's finished, it displays a dialog like this one, which lists all the accounts you have with that financial institution:

For each account listed, you have three options:

- To match the account to an existing Quicken account, select the Exists In Quicken option and choose the account name from the drop-down list that appears. This option is only available if you have already set up at least one banking account in Quicken but have not yet set up that account for online account access.
- To create a new Quicken account for the account, select the New In Quicken option and enter a name for the account in the text box beside it.
- To exclude an account from your Quicken data file, remove the check mark in the box to the left of the account. You can go back and add the account for online services later, if you choose. See "Editing Existing Accounts" later in this chapter.

When you're finished setting account options, click Next. Quicken downloads the information into the account you specified as shown in Figure 5-3. Finally, Quicken summarizes the accounts that have been added. Click Done.

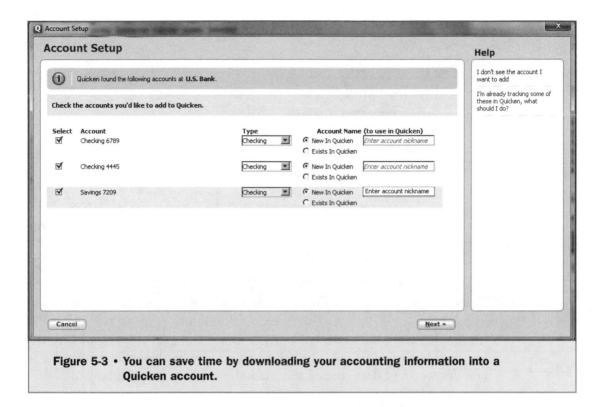

Figure 5-3 • You can save time by downloading your accounting information into a Quicken account.

I explain how to work with downloaded transactions in Chapter 6.

Completing the Account Setup Manually

If the account is not held at a financial institution that supports Quicken's transaction download feature, or if you indicated that you want to set up the account manually, Quicken prompts you to enter a name for the account. Enter a descriptive name in the Account Name/Nickname box and click Next. As shown in the illustration on the next page, Quicken prompts you to enter your account ending statement date and balance.

For checking, savings, and credit card accounts, you have three options:

- Enter the ending statement date and balance from your most recent account statement as shown below. This is the quickest, most accurate way to create an account. The statement date becomes your account's start date, and you will enter only those transactions that were made after that date or that did not clear that statement.

- Enter the ending statement date and balance from an earlier account statement. This is also an accurate way to create the account, but it will require that you play "catch up" to enter more transactions into Quicken. (If you use transaction downloads, however, you may be able to have several months' worth of data entered automatically for you; I explain how in Chapter 6.)

• Enter today's date and **0** in the dialog. This is fast, but it certainly isn't accurate. You'll eventually have to either adjust the beginning balance for the account or use the reconciliation feature to create an adjusting entry after your first reconciliation.

For a cash account, unless you plan to enter transactions you made before you created the account, you'll probably use today's date and the contents of your wallet or pocket as the starting balance information.

If you are creating a credit card account, click the Next button.

Quicken confirms that the account setup is complete. Click the Done button.

Tips for Creating Banking Accounts

Here are a few additional things to keep in mind when creating accounts for the Banking tab:

• Give each account a name that clearly identifies it. For example, if you have two checking accounts, don't name them "Checking 1" and "Checking 2."

Instead, include the bank name (such as "USA Bank Checking") or account purpose (such as "Joint Checking") in the account name. This prevents you from accidentally entering a transaction in the wrong account register.

- If you create a bank or credit card account with a balance date and amount from a bank statement—the recommended way—be careful not to enter transactions that already appear on that statement or in previous statements.

- Entering your credit limit for a credit card account enables Quicken to alert you when you get close to (or exceed) your limit. If a credit card account doesn't have a credit limit—for example, an American Express card—you may want to enter your own personal spending limit. This makes it possible to take advantage of Quicken's alerts feature to prevent overspending in that account.

- Using a cash account to track every penny you spend, from the cup of coffee you buy at work in the morning to the quart of milk you pick up on your way home that evening, isn't for everyone. You may prefer to track only large cash inflows or outflows and record the rest as miscellaneous expenses.

Editing Existing Accounts

After you have added an account, you can easily make changes to it. For example, it can be confusing when an account does not appear available to match when downloading transactions from your financial institution because it has already been enabled for online access. You can prevent this confusion by temporarily deactivating online services for that account before you start your download.

Deactivating Online Services

1. From the Account Bar, right-click on the account you want to edit. From the context menu that opens, click Edit Account to display the Account Details dialog.
2. Choose the Online Services tab. Click the Remove From One Step Update button. A message box appears asking if you want to deactivate the online service. Click Yes. A connection message box briefly appears while the service is deactivated.
3. Depending on the type of connection your financial institution offers, you may see a Remove Connection button. If so, click it.
4. Click OK to complete the deactivation.

Adding Other Account Information

As you work with your accounts, there may be other information you want to include. For example, your credit card limit may be raised, or your interest rate changed on a savings account. To enter the new information:

1. From the Account Bar, right-click the account name you want to edit to open the Account Details dialog.
2. In the General Information tab, the left side of the dialog has different fields, depending on the type of account.
   - Checking and savings accounts let you change the following:
     - Account Name
     - Description
     - Whether or not the account is tax deferred
     - Interest Rate
     - Maximum and minimum balances for which you can be alerted
   - For credit card accounts, you can change the following:
     - Account name
     - Account description
     - Interest rate
     - Credit limit
   - Investing accounts let you change the
     - Account name
     - Description
     - Whether or not the account is tax deferred
     - An option to show the cash in the investment account in a checking account
   - For all account types, the information on the right side of the dialog is the same. You can change the following:
     - The location of the account within Quicken's centers
     - The financial institution—useful if your bank merges with another
     - The account number
     - The name of a contact at the financial institution
     - The phone number of the institution
     - The financial institution's web pages, including the banking activity pages
     - Any other comments you have about the account

Entering Transactions

To make the most of Quicken, you must enter transactions for the accounts you want to track. You can do this manually, as discussed in this chapter, or, if the account is enabled for Online Account Services, you can track your account activity automatically via download, as discussed in Chapter 6. Either way, you'll need to know how to enter transactions for banking accounts.

You can enter transactions in several ways, based on the type of transaction:

- Use *registers* to record virtually any type of transaction, including manual checks, bank account payments and deposits, credit card charges and payments, and cash receipts and spending.
- Use the *Write Checks* window to record checks to be printed by Quicken.
- Enter *transfers* to transfer money from one account to another.

Using Account Registers

Quicken's account registers offer a standard way to enter all kinds of transactions. As the name suggests, these *electronic account registers* are similar to the paper checking account register that comes with your checks.

You can open an account's register as follows:

- In the Banking tab, click Banking Actions | Banking Accounts and choose the name of the account from the drop-down menu as shown here.
- If the Account Bar is displayed, click the name of the account you want to open.

Add Account
Checking
Money Market
Brokerage (Cash)
Checking 6789
My Wallet
Casual Account
Cash Account

The account window appears. If necessary, click the Transactions button to display the account register window (see Figure 5-4). Use it to enter and record transactions.

Overview of the Account Register

Before I begin my discussion of entry techniques, let's take a closer look at the account register window.

Downloaded Transactions At the bottom of the account register are two tabs of information as seen in Figure 5-5. If these tabs are not visible, you can tell Quicken to show them. From the menu bar, click Edit | Preferences | Quicken Preferences | Downloaded Transactions and clear the *Automatically add downloaded transactions to register* check box.

Download Transactions or **Downloaded Transactions** displays a setup form for enabling transaction download or a list of transactions that have already been

Figure 5-4 • Here's the account register window for a checking account.

Figure 5-5 • The bottom half of the account register window displays any downloaded transactions and a list of your Bill and Income Reminders.

downloaded but not yet accepted into the account. I explain how to set up and work with the transaction download and online payment features in Chapter 6.

Bill and Income Reminders Bill and Income Reminders tab (see Figure 5-6) displays a list of upcoming, due, and overdue scheduled transactions. I tell you more about scheduled transactions in Chapter 7.

You can show or hide this information in the bottom half of the register window by clicking the small arrow button on the right end of the bar on which the tabs appear.

The Action Bar

This window's Action Bar, as seen in Figure 5-7, includes a number of subtabs and menus you can use for working with transactions and changing the window's view:

1. Click **View | Account Overview** to display a recap of your current accounts as shown in Figure 5-8.
2. The **Acct** subtab lists each of your accounts. In the example shown in Figure 5-9, the Checking account is open and the Overview button selected.
   - The **Transactions** button displays the account register.

Status	Due	Pay To / Receive From	Amount	Web	Action
Bills					
Due Soon	10/2/2009	Western National Mortgage	-825.00		Enter Edit▼ Skip
Deposits and Other Scheduled Transactions					
Due Soon	9/25/2009	Acme Tool	1,500.00		

Download Transactions | Bill and Income Reminders (2 Due)

Add Reminder ▼ | Manage Reminders | Lowest Balance Forecast before 10/12/2009: 41,754.28

Figure 5-6 • You'll never forget another payment when you use Quicken Reminders.

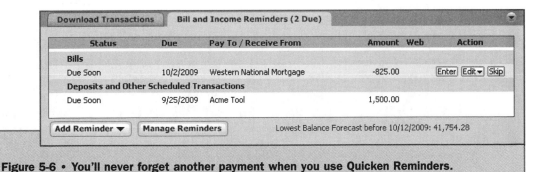

Figure 5-7 • The Action Bar gives you quick access to all your banking activities.

| Accounts ▾ | Update | Home | Bills | **Banking** | Investing | Net Worth | Planning | More | Setup |

View ☐ View ▾

Tools ✏ Calendar
✏ Banking Tools ▾

Actions ▸ Banking Actions ▾

Spending and Savings Accounts ⚙ Options ▾

Account	Min Bal.	Interest %	Ending Balance
Spending			
⚡ Checking	0.00	Set	22,747.74
Money Market	0.00	Set	29,589.67
Brokerage (Cash)	0.00	Set	1,707.01
Checking 6789	0.00	Set	139.12
Single Mutual Fund (Cash)	0.00	Set	0.00
Work Funds	0.00	Set	1,521.00
Ckg - Misc	0.00	Set	354.59
My Wallet			45.00
Casual Account	0.00	Set	50.00
Cash Account			0.00
Checking 2	0.00	Set	0.00
		Subtotal	**54,278.54**
Savings			
Savings	0.00	Set	73,852.08
Vacation Savings	0.00	Set	25,444.81
		Subtotal	**99,296.89**
		Total	**153,575.43**

Credit Card Accounts ⚙ Options ▾

Account	Credit Limit	Available	Interest %	Balance
Credit Card - Seattle	10,000.00	10,000.00	9.0%	0.00
Credit Card - Island	7,500.00	7,500.00	Set	0.00
Total	**17,500.00**	**17,500.00**		**0.00**

⚡ To Do   🖱 Help

Figure 5-8 • The Account Overview gives you all of your account balances in one place.

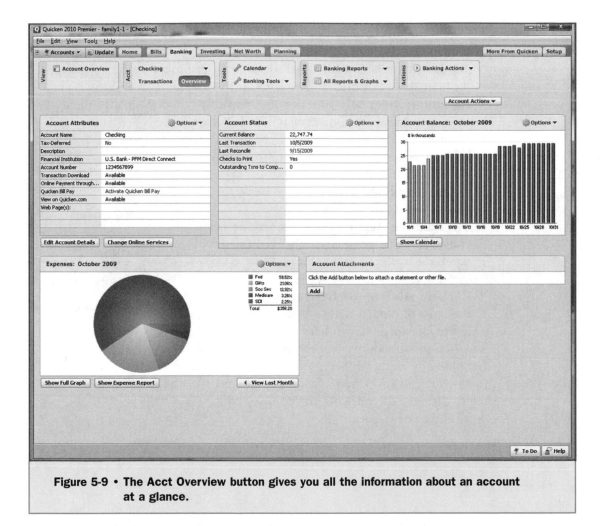

Figure 5-9 • **The Acct Overview button gives you all the information about an account at a glance.**

- The **Overview** button displays graphical information about each account as shown in Figure 5-9.
3. The **Tools** subtab has a Calendar button and a Banking Tools button.
    - **Calendar** opens the calendar which you can use to see exactly what will happen on each day this month, or for months into the future. See Chapter 7 for more information about the Calendar.
    - Click **Banking Tools** to display the menu shown here.

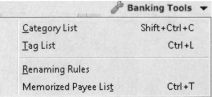

- Click **Category List** (or use your keyboard shortcut keys of SHIFT-CTRL-C) to open the list of categories.
- **Tag List** is available with either a click of your mouse or the keyboard shortcut SHIFT-L. I discuss Tags later in this chapter.
- **Renaming Rules** help you identify items that you download. I discuss more about downloading transactions in Chapter 4.
- **Memorized Payees** are those payees you pay regularly. You can open the list from this menu or use the keyboard shortcut CTRL-T.

4. The **Reports** subtab, offers a link to banking reports as well as all other reports.
   - The **Banking Reports** menu, as seen here, lets you display and print all of Quicken's standard reports that pertain to banking. I discuss banking reports in Chapter 9.
   - Click the **All Reports & Graphs** to see the types of reports that Quicken can create for you as shown here.

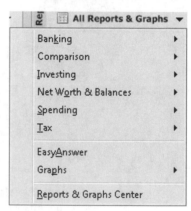

5. The **Actions** subtab displays the Banking Action menu as shown here. From this menu, you can add a new account, open the register for any of your current accounts, and write and print checks.

6. From the account register, the **Show** drop-down list, shown here, lets you filter the register to show just the transactions you choose to see.

7. The next drop-down list allows you to filter the register for specific time periods or customize the time period to display.

8. The **Find** icon displays the Quicken Find dialog, which you can use to search for transactions based on a variety of criteria. I explain how to search for transactions later in this chapter, in the section titled "Searching for Transactions."

9. The **Account Actions** menu, shown on the next page, has several sections. In the Banking tab, the Account Actions menu offers activities that relate to banking.

- **Transactions** has four links:
  - **Setup Online** opens the Setup Account Online dialog.
  - **Edit Account Details** opens the Account Details dialog.
  - **Write Checks** opens the Write Checks dialog as discussed later in this chapter.
  - **Reconcile** opens the reconciliation dialog. I discuss reconciling your accounts in Chapter 8.
  - **Transfer Money** opens the transfer dialog. See "Transferring Money" later in this chapter.
- **Reporting** offers links to banking and register reports.
  - **Register Report** displays all of the transactions in this account's register for a period you specify. I discuss more about report in Chapter 9.
  - **Expense Summary Graph** displays a graph of all of your expenses, by category, for the year to day as seen here.

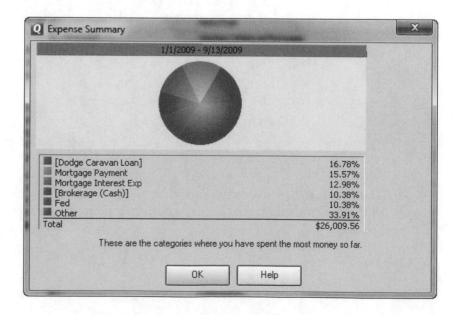

- **More Reports** opens a report menu from which you can choose several reports as shown here.

- **Print Transactions** opens the Print Register dialog from which you can print transactions, including the detail for splits, for a period you designate as seen here.

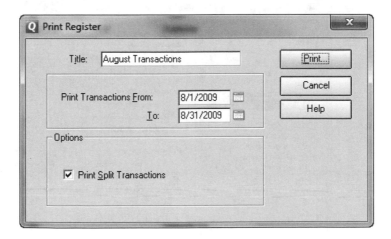

- **Register Views and Preferences** lets you set how this register displays:
  - **Two-Line Display** shows two lines as seen in Figure 5-4. If you clear that check box, you will see the payee, the category, and the amount on just one line.
  - **Sorting Options** allows you to tell Quicken how to organize your transactions in this register.
- **Register Preferences** opens the Quicken Register Preferences dialog as seen here. I discuss Preferences in Appendix B.

Basic Entry Techniques

To enter a transaction, first, open a register by clicking **Transactions** in the Acct subtab on the Action Bar. Begin by clicking in the first empty line at the end of the account register window (refer to Figure 5-4). This activates a new, blank transaction. You can then enter transaction information into each field and press ENTER to complete the transaction.

Although the entry process is pretty straightforward, here are a few things to keep in mind when entering transactions.

Advancing from Field to Field   To move from one text box, or *field*, to another when entering transactions, you can either click in the next field's text box or press the TAB key. Pressing TAB is usually quicker.

Using Icons   Icons appear when certain fields are active:

- When the Date field is active, a calendar icon appears. You can click it to display a calendar, and then click calendar buttons to view and enter a date.

- When one of the two Amount fields is active, a calculator icon appears. You can click it to use a calculator and enter calculated results.
- When the Payee or Category field is active, a Report button appears. You can click this button to display a pop-up report of transactions in that category or for that payee, like the one shown here.

Menu buttons, which look like triangles pointing down to a horizontal line, display drop-down lists of items applicable to the active field. You can enter an item by choosing it from the list's options.

Using the Num Field The Num field is where you enter a transaction number or type. You can enter any number you like or use the drop-down list (shown here) to display a list of standard entries; click an option to enter it for the transaction. You can also press the + or – key on the keyboard to increment or decrement the check number while the Num field is active.

- **Next Check Num** automatically increments the most recently entered check number and enters the resulting number in the Num field.
- **ATM** is for ATM transactions. You may also want to use it for debit or check card transactions.
- **Deposit** is for deposits.
- **Print Check** is for transactions for which you want Quicken to print a check. Quicken automatically enters the check number when the check is printed.
- **Send Online Payments** is for accounts that you have enabled online bill payments
- **Transfer** is for a transfer of funds from one account to another.
- **EFT**, which stands for Electronic Funds Transfer, is for direct deposits and similar transactions.
- **Online** is for a transaction you initiated online.

```
Next Check Num
ATM
Deposit
Print Check
Send Online Payme
Transfer
EFT
Online

    Edit List
```

The Payee Drop-down List and QuickFill When you begin to enter information in the Payee field, a drop-down list of existing payees or payers appears. As shown next, as you type, Quicken narrows down the list to display only those names that match what you have typed. You can enter an existing name from the list by selecting it. Quicken will fill in details from the most recent transaction for that name for you. This is Quicken's QuickFill feature, which you will learn more about in Chapter 7.

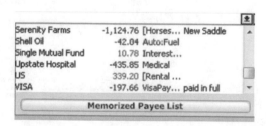

Automatic Categorization After entering a payee for the first time, Quicken may fill in the category for you. This is Quicken's automatic categorization feature, which enters categories based on thousands of payee names programmed into it. You'll find that in most cases, Quicken assigns an appropriate category. But you can change the category if you like and, from that point on, Quicken's QuickFill feature will use the category you assign for future transactions to that payee. Chapter 7 provides more information about QuickFill.

Using the Category Drop-down List The Category drop-down list organizes category and transfer accounts as they are in the Category List window (which I discuss and illustrate in Chapter 3). This drop-down list may appear automatically when you begin to enter a category in the Category field of the transaction area; if it does not, you can click the menu button on the right side of the field to display it. You can narrow down the display of categories by clicking a heading on the left side of the drop-down list. Then click the category name to enter it into the field.

Entering New Categories If you type in a category that does not exist in the Category List, Quicken displays the New Category dialog (shown here), which offers to create a new category with that name. Click Yes to use the Set Up Category dialog to create a new category, or click No to return to the register and enter a different category. If you turn off the Prompt Before Creating New Categories check box, Quicken automatically displays the Set Up Category dialog every time you enter a category that does not exist in the Category List. I explain how to create categories in Chapter 3.

Entering Subcategories When you choose a subcategory from the Category field's drop-down list, Quicken automatically enters the subcategory's parent category name, followed by a colon character (:) and the subcategory name. To type in a subcategory, use the first letter or two of the category, the colon, and then the first letter or two of the subcategory. QuickFill will match the category:subcategory. Here's what it might look like in a register entry:

State Farm	
Insurance:Automobile	to 3/2010

Entering Multiple Categories To enter more than one category for a transaction, click the Split button on the right side of the transaction entry area. I explain how to enter transactions with splits a little later in this chapter, in the section titled "Using Splits."

Using Tags As discussed in Chapter 3, a tag is an optional identifier for specifying what a transaction applies to. Quicken displays a Tag field in the transaction form. To include a tag in a transaction, simply enter the tag in that field. Quicken may display a drop-down list of valid tags for you to choose from. If you type in a tag name that is not on the Tag List, Quicken displays the Set Up Tag window so you can create the tag on the fly. I explain how to create tags in Chapter 3.

Entering Memos You can enter a brief memo (up to 64 characters) about the transaction in the Memo field to the right of the Tag field. This memo can help you remember what a transaction is for.

Using Transaction Buttons As shown in Figure 5-4, four buttons appear on the line above or below the active transaction. You can use these buttons to work with the transaction:

- **Enter** enters the transaction into the account register. If Quicken's sound option is turned on, you should hear a cash register *ch-ching* sound when you click it. (You can turn Quicken sounds on or off in the Quicken Preferences dialog, which I discuss in Appendix B.)
- **Edit** displays a menu of editing options for the transactions. I discuss some of the Edit menu's commands later in this chapter, in the section titled "Changing Transactions."
- **Split** opens the Split Transaction window for the transaction. I explain how to enter a transaction with splits in the next section.

- **Attach** (a paper clip icon) displays a menu that enables you to add a follow-up flag, note, or electronic image attachment to the transaction. I explain how to attach items to transactions later in this chapter, in the section titled "Adding Notes and Attachments."

Using Splits

A *split* is a transaction with more than one category. For example, suppose you pay one utility bill for two categories of utilities—electricity and water. If you want to track each of these two expenses separately, you can use a split to record each category's portion of the payment you make. This enables you to keep good records without writing multiple checks to the same payee.

To record a transaction with a split, click the Split button in the account register or Write Checks window when entering the transaction. The Split Transaction window, which is shown next, appears. Click in the first blank line and select a category. If desired, enter a memo for the category in the Memo field. Then enter the amount for that category in the Amount field. Repeat this process for each category you want to include in the transaction. Here's what the Split Transaction window might look like with two categories entered:

	Category	Memo	Amount
1.	Groceries	Weekly groceries	99 67
2.	Charitable Donations	gave $5 in cash for food bank	5 00
3.			
4.			
5.			
6.			
7.			
8.			
9.			
10.			
11.			
12.			
13.			
14.			
15.			
16.			

Split Total: 104.67
Remainder: 0.00
Transaction Total: 104.67

If you entered a transaction amount before clicking the Split button, you can monitor the Remainder and Transaction Total values in the Split Transaction window to make sure you've accounted for the entire transaction amount. If you entered an incorrect amount, you can click the Adjust button to adjust the transaction amount to match the Split Total.

When you're finished entering transaction categories, click OK or press ENTER. If you left the transaction amount empty before clicking the Split button, a dialog appears, asking if you want to record the transaction as a payment or deposit. Select the appropriate option and click OK.

As shown next, the word *Split* appears in the Category field for the transaction in the account register window:

Two buttons appear beside the Category field when you activate a transaction with a split:

- The green check mark displays the Split Transaction window so you can review and edit the transaction.
- The red *X* clears all lines from the split. Use this option with care—it permanently removes all category information from the transaction.

Tracking Credit Cards with Quicken

Tracking bank account transactions and balances is just one part of using Quicken. It's also a great tool for tracking credit cards. Knowing how much you owe on your credit cards helps you maintain a clear picture of your financial situation.

How you use Quicken to track your credit cards depends on how accurate you want your financial records to be and how much effort you're willing to spend to keep Quicken up-to-date.

Credit Card Tracking Techniques

You can use either of two techniques for paying credit card bills and monitoring credit card balances with Quicken:

- Use your checking account register or the Write Checks window to record amounts paid to each credit card company for your credit card bill. Although this does track the amounts you pay, it doesn't track how much you owe or the individual charges.

- Use a credit card account register to record credit card expenditures and payments. This takes a bit more effort on your part, but it tracks how much you owe and categorizes what you bought.

In my opinion, it's worth the extra effort to track your credit card expenditures and balances in individual credit card accounts. And if you utilize Quicken's Transaction Download feature for your credit card accounts, as I discuss in Chapter 6, it won't take much time or effort to get the job done.

Recording Strategies

You can also use two strategies for recording transactions in credit card accounts. Choosing the strategy that's right for you makes the job easier to handle.

Enter as You Spend   One strategy is to enter transactions as you spend. To do this, you must collect your credit card receipts—which might be something you already do. Don't forget to jot down the totals for any telephone and online shopping you do. Then, every day or every few days, sit down with Quicken and enter the transactions.

While this strategy requires you to stay on top of things, it offers two main benefits:

- Your Quicken credit card registers always indicate what you owe to credit card companies. This prevents unpleasant surprises at month-end or at the checkout counter when you're told you've reached your limit. It also enables you to use the alerts feature to track credit card balances; I tell you about that in Chapter 9.
- At month-end, you don't have to spend a lot of time entering big batches of transactions. All (or at least most) of them should already be entered.

I'll be the first to admit that I've never been able to use this strategy. I just don't like holding on to all those pieces of paper. (Of course, since signing up for Transaction Download, all this information is entered automatically for me. You can learn more about Transaction Download in Chapter 6.)

Enter When You Pay   The other strategy, which you may find better for you, is to enter transactions when you get your monthly statement. With this strategy, when you open your credit card statement, you'll spend some time sitting in front of your computer with Quicken to enter each transaction. If there aren't many, this isn't a big deal. But it could take some time if there are many transactions to enter.

Of course, the main benefit of this strategy is that you don't have to collect credit card receipts and spend time throughout the month entering your transactions. But you still have to enter them! This is the method I use for the one credit card I have that I cannot access online yet.

Entering Credit Card Transactions

Entering credit card transactions isn't very different from entering checking account or savings account transactions. Here are a few examples which are illustrated in Figure 5-10.

Entering Individual Charges Open the account register for the credit card account. Then enter the charge transaction, using the name of the merchant that accepted the charge as the payee name. If you don't want to include a transaction number or receipt number, you can leave the Ref box empty.

Entering Credits Enter the transaction just as if it were a charge, but put the amount of the credit in the Payment box. This subtracts it from your account balance.

Entering Finance Charges In the credit card account register, enter the name of the credit card company as the payee and the amount of the finance charge as a charge. You can use the Interest Exp category for the transaction.

Figure 5-10 • This example shows some typical transactions in a credit card register.

Entering Payments In the account register for your checking account or in the Write Checks window, enter a payment transaction with the credit card company name in the Payee box. Enter the credit card account name in the Category text box; you should find it as a transfer account in the Category drop-down list that appears when you activate the field. The checking account register transaction should look like the one shown next. Figure 5-10 shows what this transaction looks like in the credit card account register.

First Island Bank	340	99
[Credit Card - Island]		

Recording Credit Card Rebates Some credit card companies offer rebates for purchases. How you record a rebate depends on how the rebate is received:

- To record a rebate received as a check, deposit the check as usual and enter the amount of the rebate as a deposit in that account.
- To record a rebate received as a reduction in the credit card account balance, enter the amount of the rebate in the credit card account as a payment. (Just remember that a rebate is not a payment that counts toward your monthly obligation to the credit card company.)

What you use as a category for this transaction is completely up to you. You may want to use the Interest Exp account, thus recording the rebate as a reduction in your interest expense. Or, perhaps, if the rebate applies to a certain purchase only, you'd use the category you originally used for that purchase. For example, I have a credit card that gives me a 5 percent rebate on fuel purchases. I record the rebate using the Fuel category I created to track fuel expenses. If you have a lot of credit cards that offer rebates, you may want to create a Rebate income account and use that as the category for all rebate transactions. These are just suggestions. There is no right or wrong way to do it.

Entering Cash Transactions

Although Quicken enables you to keep track of cash transactions through the use of a cash account, not everyone does this. The reason: most people make many small cash transactions every day. Is it worth tracking every penny you spend? That's something you need to decide.

Personally, I don't track all cash transactions. I track only expenditures that are large or tax-deductible. You may want to do the same. If so, you still need to set up a cash account, but you don't need to record every transaction. That's what I do; Figure 5-11 shows an example.

Cash Receipts Cash receipts may come from using your ATM card, cashing a check, or getting cash from some other source. If the cash comes from one of your other accounts through an ATM or check transaction, when you record that transaction, use your cash account as the transfer in the Category field. That increases your cash balance. Here's what the transaction might look like in your checking account:

Cash		250 00
[My Wallet]		

Important Cash Expenditures In your cash account, record large, tax-deductible, or other important cash expenditures like any other transaction. Be sure to assign the correct category.

Other Cash Expenditures Throughout the week, you may spend 50¢ for a newspaper, $3 for a cup of coffee, and about $12 for lunch at your favorite hamburger joint. Recording transactions like these can be tedious, so don't bother if you don't want to. Instead, at the end of the week, compare your cash on hand to the balance in your cash account register. Then, enter a transaction to record the

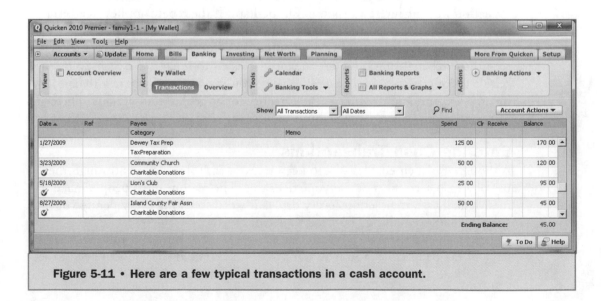

Figure 5-11 • Here are a few typical transactions in a cash account.

difference as an expenditure. You can use the Misc category and enter anything you like in the Payee field.

Writing Checks

Quicken's Write Checks window uses a basic check-like interface to record checks. You enter the same information that you would write on an actual check. You then tell Quicken to print the check based on the information you entered. (I explain how to print checks later in this chapter, in the section titled "Printing Checks.")

To open the Write Checks window, choose Banking | Banking Actions | Write and Print Checks or press CTRL-W. The Write Checks window, which is shown in Figure 5-12, appears. The name of the account from which you are writing this check appears in the drop-down list near the top of the window. If you need to choose another account, click the down arrow. Enter the necessary information for a check and record the transaction.

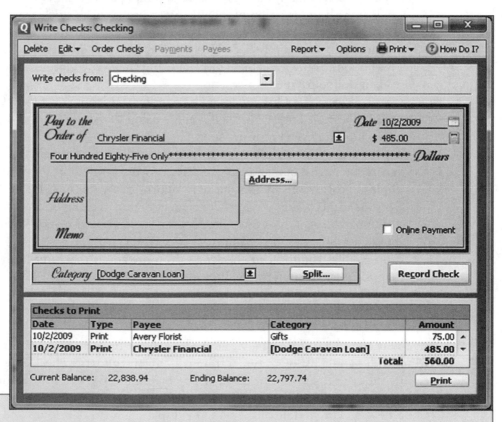

Figure 5-12 • Here's the Write Checks window, with a check already created.

Overview of the Write Checks Window

The Write Checks window is a busy place, with a lot of information and options. Before I explain how to use it to enter transactions, let's take a look at its options.

The Button Bar   The Write Checks window's button bar includes a number of buttons and menus for working with transactions and changing the window's view:

- **Delete** deletes the selected transaction. When you click this button, a dialog appears to confirm that you really do want to delete the transaction.
- **Edit** is a menu full of commands for creating, editing, and working with transactions. I discuss many of these commands later in this chapter, in the section titled "Working with Existing Transactions."
- **Order Checks** displays the Checks & Supplies page of the Quicken Services window, with information on how you can order check stock that is compatible with Quicken.
- **Payments** displays the Bills & Deposits list, which is discussed in Chapter 7. This option is only available if you are using the Write Checks window to send an online payment instruction.
- **Payees** displays the Online Payee List window, which is covered in Chapter 6. This option is only available if you are using the Write Checks window to send an online payment instruction.
- **Report** displays a menu of reports that are available for the selected transaction. Use commands to generate reports from within the Write Checks window. Learn more about Quicken's reporting features in Chapter 9.
- **Options** displays the Quicken Preferences dialog, which you can use to customize the way the Write Checks window looks and works; learn more about customizing Quicken in Appendix B.
- **Print** enables you to print checks. Learn more about that later in this chapter, in the section titled "Printing Checks."
- **How Do I?** displays the Quicken Personal Finances Help window, with a list of topics related to the Write Checks window.

Account List   The Write Checks From drop-down list near the top of the window displays a list of accounts from which you can write checks. Be sure to choose the correct account from the list before entering check information.

Check Form   The middle of the window displays a form that looks and works a lot like a paper check. This is where you enter transaction information.

Checks To Print The Checks To Print area of the window lists all of the checks that have been entered in the Write Checks window that have not yet been printed. When you enter a transaction in the Write Checks window, it is added to this list.

Entering Transactions in the Write Checks Window

The Write Checks window (refer to Figure 5-12) is like a cross between a paper check and Quicken's account register window. You fill in the check form like you would fill in the blanks on a paper check. Quicken's QuickFill feature makes data entry quicker and easier by recalling entry information from similar transactions to the same payee, and its automatic categorization feature can automatically "guess" the category for many new transactions. You must enter a valid Quicken category in the Category field, just as you would when entering a transaction in the account register. Clicking the Record Check button completes the transaction and adds it to the Checks To Print list (see Figure 5-12), as well as the account register.

Consult the section "Using Account Registers," earlier, for details about the information that should be entered into most fields. Here are a few additional things to consider when entering transactions in the Write Checks window:

Addresses on Checks If you enter an address on the check, you can mail the check using a window envelope. The address is automatically added to the Quicken Address Book. You can click the Address button in the Write Checks window to display the Edit Address Book Record dialog, which you can use to modify an address in the Address Book.

Check Memos If you enter a note on the memo line of a check, it may be visible if you mail the check in a window envelope.

Transferring Money

You can also record the transfer of funds from one account to another. You might find this feature especially useful for recording telephone or ATM transfers.

Using the Transfer Dialog

One way to record a transfer is with the Transfer dialog. Open the account register window for one of the accounts involved in the transfer transaction and click Account Actions | Transfer Money. The Record A Transfer Between

Quicken Accounts dialog, which is illustrated next, appears. Choose the source and destination accounts from the drop-down lists, enter a transaction date and amount, and click OK.

Recording a Transfer in the Account Register Window

The Transfer dialog isn't the only way to record a transfer. You can also record a transfer in the account register window of either the source or destination account. When you choose Transfer (TXFR) from the Num drop-down list, the Category drop-down list displays only transfer accounts. Choose the other transfer account from the list and complete the transaction.

The following illustrations show a transfer from one checking account to another. Here's what the source (Checking) account transaction looks like:

9/7/2009	TXFR	Money Market Account	15,000 00
		[Money Market]	

And here's what the corresponding destination (Money Market) account transaction looks like:

9/7/2009	TXFR	Money Market Account	15,000 00
		[Checking]	

Working with Existing Transactions

So far, this chapter has concentrated on entering transactions. What do you do when you need to modify a transaction you already recorded? That's what this section is all about.

Searching for Transactions

The Quicken Find dialog includes several commands to help you locate and work with transactions as shown here.

- **Search** offers a drop-down list that enables you to search for transactions in several ways as seen here.

- **Match If** lets you narrow the criteria for the search.

- **Find** enables you to narrow the search even more closely.

The following sections take a closer look at each of these commands. They also explain how you can use the new Find icon on the Action Bar to find transactions quickly.

Using the Find Command

To use the Find command, begin by opening an account register or Write Checks window for the account that you want to search. Click the Find icon on the register's Action Bar or press CTRL-F. The Quicken Find dialog appears.

Start by choosing an option from the Search drop-down list, which includes all register fields for a transaction. Then choose a Match If option to indicate how the search criteria should be matched. Enter the search criteria in the Find box. If you enter a space in the Find box, Quicken searches for entries for which the Search field is blank; this is a great way to find uncategorized transactions. To search backward (relative to the currently selected transaction), turn on the Search Backwards check box.

After setting up the search, if you click the Find button, Quicken selects the first match found in the window. If you click the Find All button, Quicken displays the Search Results window, which lists all the matches it found. You can double-click a match to view it in the account register window.

Using the Edit Transaction Command

If you select the Edit Transaction(s) button in the Search Results window, as shown here, the Find and Replace dialog appears.

The top part of the dialog looks and works much like the Quicken Find dialog. You can turn on the Show Matches In Split check box at the bottom of the dialog if you want Quicken to find all matches, including those that appear in splits. Once you set up the search and click the Find All button, a list of matches appears in the bottom half of the dialog, as shown next. Click beside each found item you want to change to place a green check mark there. Then set options in the Replace and With boxes. Click Replace to replace all checked items with the replacement option you specified.

Sorting Transactions

You can click a register's column heading or use the Sort options to change how your transactions are displayed. Click Account Actions | Sorting Options in the Action Bar of the register's account in the Banking tab to change the sort order of transactions. For example, sorting by check number groups the transactions by the Num field, making it easy to find a specific check. You can quickly move to a specific date or transaction number by dragging the scroll box on the scroll bar.

Changing Transactions

Quicken enables you to change a transaction at any time—even after it has been cleared. This makes it possible to correct errors in any transaction you have entered.

Making Simple Changes If all you want to do is change one of the fields in the transaction—such as the category, date, or number—simply find the transaction in the appropriate account register, make changes as desired, and click the Enter button to record them.

Using the Edit Menu The Edit menu appears when you click the Edit button in the account register window for the currently selected transaction. It offers other options for working with a selected transaction:

- **Enter** enters the transaction in the register. Choosing this command is the same as clicking the Enter button or pressing ENTER.
- **Restore Transaction** enables you to change a transaction back to the way it was before you started changing it. This option is available only if you have made changes to the selected transaction.
- **Split** opens the Split window for the transaction. Choosing this command is the same as clicking the Split button. You learned how to use the Split feature earlier in this chapter, in the section titled "Using Splits."
- **Notes And Flags** displays the Transaction Notes And Flags dialog (which is shown later in this chapter, in the section titled "Adding Notes, Flags, and Alerts") so you can add transaction notes, flag the transaction in a specific color, or create an alert for follow-up.
- **Attachments** displays the Transaction Attachment dialog (shown later in this chapter, in the section titled "Attaching Checks, Receipts, or Other Images") so you can attach checks, receipts, and other images to the transaction.
- **Tax Line Item Assignments** displays the Tax Line Item Assignments dialog, which you can use to assign a line item to the transaction's category. Learn more about using the Tax Line Assignments feature of Quicken in Chapter 18.
- **Cut Transaction(s)** copies the selected transaction and removes it from the account register.
- **Copy Transaction(s)** copies the selected transaction without removing it from the account register.
- **Paste Transaction(s)** pastes the last-copied transaction into the current account register. This option is available only after a transaction has been cut

or copied. You might want to cut a transaction to paste it into another register if you realize that you entered it in the wrong register.

- **Edit Transaction(s)** displays the Find And Replace dialog (shown earlier in this chapter, in the section titled "Searching for Transactions") so you can use the Replace feature to modify the selected transaction(s).
- **New** enables you to create a new transaction for the account. This does not affect the currently selected transaction.
- **Delete** deletes the selected transaction. This is the same as clicking the Delete button in the button bar. Remember that deleting a transaction removes the transaction from the Quicken data file, thus changing the account balance and category activity.
- **Undo Delete** restores the transaction you just deleted. You must use this command immediately after deleting a transaction to restore the transaction.
- **Insert Transaction** enables you to insert a transaction before the selected transaction in the account register. This does not affect the currently selected transaction.
- **Move Transaction(s)** displays the Move Transactions(s) dialog, which you can use to move a transaction from the current account register to a different account register. Simply choose an account name from the drop-down list and click OK to complete the move.
- **Undo Accept All Transactions** restores accepted transactions to unaccepted status. This command is available only if the last thing you did was accept transactions. Learn more about accepting transactions in Chapter 6.
- **Memorize Payee** tells Quicken to add the selected transaction to its list of memorized payees. Memorized payees are used for the QuickFill feature, which is discussed in Chapter 7.
- **Schedule Bill Or Deposit** enables you to schedule the transaction for a future date or to set up the transaction as a recurring transaction. Learn more about scheduling transactions in Chapter 7.
- **Void Transaction(s)** marks the selected transaction as void. This reverses the effect of the transaction on the account balance and category activity without actually deleting the transaction.
- **Reconcile** enables you to indicate whether the transaction should be marked as Not Reconciled, Cleared, or Reconciled. Learn how to reconcile accounts in Chapter 8.
- **Revert to downloaded payee name** (not shown) enables you to revert to the transaction payee downloaded from your financial institution's server. This option only appears if the transaction has been downloaded and its payee name has changed.

- **Find** displays the Find dialog, which is discussed earlier in this chapter, in the section titled "Searching for Transactions."
- **Find Next** searches for transactions matching the previously entered Find criteria.
- **Go To Matching Transfer** displays the selected transaction in the account register for the other part of a transfer. For example, if the selected transaction involves the checking and savings accounts and you are viewing it in the checking account register, choosing the Go To Transfer command displays the same transaction in the savings account register. This command is available only if the selected transaction includes a transfer.
- **Go To Specific Date** enables you to move to a different date within the register. This does not affect the currently selected transaction.
- **Cancel Payment** (not shown) sends a cancel payment instruction to your bank to stop an online payment. This option is available only for online payments that have not yet been made.
- **Amount Spent On** *category* opens a Category Report for this category.
- **Launch Mini-Report For** displays a small report window of the current payee's or category's transactions. The option that appears depends on the field that is selected when you display the menu.

Selecting More Than One Transaction You may need to work with more than one transaction at a time. To do this, you need to select multiple transactions. Here's how:

- To select several individual transactions in an account register, hold down CTRL and click each transaction you want to include. The transactions change color to indicate they are selected.
- To select a range of transactions, click to select the first transaction in the range. Then hold down SHIFT and click the last transaction in the range. All transactions between the first and the last transaction change color to indicate they have been selected.

Adding Notes and Attachments

Quicken's attachment feature enables you to add notes, flags, reminders, and image files to a transaction or account. This makes it possible to store all kinds of digital information in your Quicken data file, including cancelled checks, receipts, or photographs.

Adding Notes, Flags, and Alerts

You can add a note, color-coded flag, or follow-up alert—or all three—to any Quicken transaction. You do this in the account register window.

First, select the transaction you want to add the item to. Then click the Attach icon (the small paper clip) for the transaction and choose Add Follow-Up Flag or Add Note, or click Notes and Flags or Attachments from the Edit button for the transaction. The Transaction Notes And Flags dialog, shown next, appears.

What Does This Mean to You? Transaction Attachments

If there's such a thing as a "Paperwork Reduction Act," then why do I seem to keep accumulating more and more paper? Bank statements, canceled checks, receipts. It never seems to end. But I know that the moment I throw away an important tax-related document, that's the day I'll get a letter from Uncle Sam, asking to see it.

That's where Quicken's electronic image attachment feature can help. If you have a scanner, you can digitize important papers and attach their image files to the transactions or accounts they relate to. Then, when you need to consult the document, you can quickly and easily find it in Quicken and view it onscreen. You can even print a copy, with the click of a button!

Sure beats dealing with file boxes.

- To add a note, type the text of the note into the Notes box. This adds a note icon to the transaction, beneath the date. Pointing to the icon displays the note in a screen tip box.
- To flag the transaction, turn on the Flag This Transaction check box. Then choose a color from the drop-down list. This adds a flag icon, in the color

you indicated, to the transaction, beneath the date. (The flag icon replaces the note icon if the transaction also has a note.)

- To create a follow-up alert, turn on the Alert For Follow Up On check box and enter a date in the box beside it. (You can add a follow-up alert only if the transaction is already flagged.) This adds an alert to the Alerts Center window, which is discussed in Chapter 9.

Click OK to save your settings.

Attaching Checks, Receipts, or Other Images

Quicken also enables you to attach image files from a file on disk, a scanner, or the clipboard to transactions or accounts. You can use this feature to file digital copies of important documents with the transactions or accounts they relate to.

Attaching Images to Transactions

You attach an image to a transaction in the account register window. Begin by selecting the transaction you want to attach the item to. Then click the Attach button for the transaction and choose an option from the Attach Electronic Image submenu that appears; or choose Attachments from the menu that appears when you click the Edit button for the transaction.

In the Transaction Attachments dialog that appears (see Figure 5-13), use the Attach New or Attach Another drop-down list to choose the type of attachment you want to add: Check, Receipt/Bill, Invoice, Warranty, or Other. Then click one of the Image From buttons:

- **File** displays the Select Attachment File dialog, which you can use to locate, select, and open a file on disk. The file must be in a format readable by Internet Explorer, such as JPG, GIF, TXT, HTML, PDF, and PNG. When you click Open, the file's content appears in the Transaction Attachment dialog.
- **Scanner** may display the Select Source dialog, which you can use to select your scanner. It then displays your scanner's standard scanning interface, which you can use to scan an image. When the scan is complete, the image appears in the Transaction Attachment dialog.
- **Clipboard** pastes the contents of the clipboard into the Transaction Attachments dialog. (To use this option, you should select and copy an image *before* opening the Transaction Attachment dialog.)

Quicken allows you to add as many attachments as you like to a transaction. To add other attachments, just repeat the process to attach another item. When

Figure 5-13 • Use the Transaction Attachments dialog to attach images to a transaction.

you're finished, click Done to close the Transaction Attachments dialog. An Attachment icon appears beneath the transaction date to indicate that items are attached.

Working with Attachments

Once a file has been attached to a transaction, you can view, remove, replace, or print it at any time.

To work with a transaction attachment, click the Attachment icon for the transaction. The Transaction Attachments dialog (refer to Figure 5-13) opens. Click the thumbnail image or icon for the attached item to work with it.

You can use buttons in the Transaction Attachments dialog to work with attachments:

- **Help** (which appears as a question mark) displays the Quicken Personal Finances Help window, with links to topics about attaching digital images to transactions and accounts. Click a link to view the help information.
- **Print** (which appears as a small printer icon) prints the attachment.
- **Export** saves the attachment as a file on your disk.
- **Delete** removes the attachment.
- **Done** closes the dialog.

Printing Checks

Quicken's ability to print checks enables you to create accurate, legible, professional-looking checks without picking up a pen (or a typewriter). In this section, I explain how to print the checks you enter in the Write Checks window, discussed earlier in this chapter.

Getting the Right Checks

Before you can print checks from Quicken, you must obtain compatible check stock. Quicken supports checks in a number of different styles:

- **Standard checks** print just checks. There's no voucher or stub.
- **Voucher checks** pair each check with a similarly sized voucher form. When you print on a voucher check, the transaction category information, including splits and tags, can be printed on the voucher part.
- **Wallet checks** pair each check with a stub. When you print on a wallet check, the transaction information is printed on the stub.

In addition to these styles, you can get the checks in two different formats for your printer:

- **Page-oriented** checks are for laser and inkjet printers.
- **Continuous** checks are for pin-feed printers.

A catalog and order form for checks may have been included with your copy of Quicken. You can use it to order checks. If you have an Internet connection, you can order checks online from within Quicken by choosing More From Quicken | Quicken Services | Other Services | Order Checks & Supplies, or by clicking the Order Checks button in the button bar of the Write Checks window (see Figure 5-12).

Setting Up

Quicken must also be set up to print the kind of checks you purchased. You do this once, and Quicken remembers the settings.

Choose File | Printer Setup | For Printing Checks to display the Check Printer Setup dialog, shown next. Use the drop-down lists and option buttons to specify settings for your printer and check stock. Following are a few things to keep in mind when making settings in this dialog.

Partial Page Printing Options

If you select the Page-Oriented option and either Standard or Wallet checks in the Check Printer Setup dialog, you can also set options for Partial Page Printing Style. This enables you to set up the printer for situations when you're not printing an entire page of checks.

- **Edge** is for inserting the page against one side of the feeder. The left or right edge of the checks enters the feeder first.
- **Centered** is for centering the page in the feeder. The left or right edge of the checks enters the feeder first.
- **Portrait** is also for centering the page in the feeder, but in this case, the top edge of each check enters the feeder first.

If your printer supports multiple feed trays, you can also set the source tray for partial and full pages by choosing options from the Partial Page Source and Full Page Source drop-down lists.

Continuous Printing Options

If you select the Continuous option and either Standard or Wallet checks in the Check Printer Setup dialog, the dialog changes to offer two Continuous options:

- **Bypass The Driver** should be turned on for a continuous printer that skips checks or prints nothing.
- **Use Low Starting Position** should be turned on for a continuous printer that cuts the date or logo off your checks.

Checking the Settings for Page-Oriented Checks

If you're using page-oriented checks, you can check your settings by printing a sample page on plain paper. Here's how:

1. Click the Align button in the Check Printer Setup dialog.
2. In the Align Checks dialog that appears, click the Full Page Of Checks button.
3. In the Fine Alignment dialog, click the Print Sample button.
4. When the sample emerges from your printer, hold it up to the light with a sheet of check stock behind it. The sample should line up with the check.
5. If the sample does not line up properly with the check stock, set Vertical and/or Horizontal adjustment values in the Fine Alignment dialog. Then repeat steps 3 through 5 until the alignment is correct.
6. Click OK in each dialog to accept your settings and close it.

Printing

Once setup is complete, you're ready to print checks.

Open the account register for the account you want to print checks for. Then insert the check stock in your printer and choose File | Print Checks, or click the Print button in the Write Checks window. The Select Checks To Print dialog, which is shown next, appears. Enter the number of the first check that will be printed in the First Check Number box. Then set other options as desired. If you select the Selected Checks option, you can click the Choose button to display a list of checks and check off the ones you want to print. Click Done in that window to return to the Select Checks To Print dialog.

When you click Print First or OK, Quicken sends the print job to your printer. It then displays a dialog asking if the checks printed correctly. You have two options:

- If all checks printed fine, just click OK.
- If a problem occurred while printing the checks, enter the number of the first check that was misprinted, and then click OK. You can then go back to the Select Checks To Print dialog and try again.

Using Online Banking Features

Chapter 6

In This Chapter:

- *Benefits and costs of online banking*
- *Setting up Online Account Services*
- *Downloading and comparing transactions*
- *Setting up payees*
- *Processing online payments and transfers*

Life can be pretty hectic sometimes—too hectic to keep track of your bank accounts, pay bills before they're overdue, and buy stamps to mail your bills. Quicken Personal Finance Software's Online Account Services enable you to do most (if not all) of your banking from the comfort of your own home so banking can be a lot less of a chore. Several features can be used separately or together:

- **Transaction Download** enables you to download bank and credit card account activity, and transfer money online between accounts.
- **Online Payment** enables you to pay bills online, without manually writing or mailing a check. (Quicken Bill Pay offers the features of Online Payment, even if your bank does not support it.)

This chapter explains how these features work and how you can use them to save time while keeping track of your finances.

The instructions in this chapter assume that you have already configured Quicken for an Internet connection. If you have not done so, do it now. Chapter 4 provides the instructions you need to set up and test an Internet connection. This chapter also assumes that you understand the topics and procedures discussed in Chapters 3 and 5. This chapter builds on many of the basic concepts discussed in those chapters.

Online Account Services

Here's a closer look at Quicken's Online Account Services, including what the services are, how they work, and how you can expect to benefit from them.

Transaction Download

Quicken's Transaction Download feature can perform several tasks, depending on your financial institution. Here's the scoop.

How It Works

Generally speaking, financial institutions can support Transaction Download three ways.

Direct Connect   Many financial institutions support direct communication between Quicken and the financial institution's server. This so-called *Direct Connect* method is the most powerful way to use the Transaction Download feature. To download transactions, you simply click a button in Quicken's Online Center window, provide brief instructions and a PIN, and wait while Quicken gets the information you want. At the same time, Quicken can send information such as payment or transfer instructions to your bank for processing. In this two-way communication, Quicken does all the work.

Express Web Connect   If a financial institution does not support Direct Connect but does support the download of transactions from its Web site, it may support a download method called *Express Web Connect*. This one-way communication downloads transactions directly into Quicken without requiring you to manually visit the financial institution's Web site.

 If you're already using Quicken with Web Connect and your financial institution supports Express Web Connect, Quicken will automatically prompt you to convert the download method to Express Web Connect. I highly recommend doing so, as it will simplify and speed up the download of transactions from your financial institution to your Quicken data file.

Web Connect   Many financial institutions that don't support Direct Connect or Express Web Connect enable you to manually download specially formatted *Web Connect* files. To do this, you must log in to your financial institution's Web site using the information your financial institution supplies, navigate to a download page, and indicate what data you want to download. Once the Web Connect file has been downloaded, Quicken reads it and knows exactly which Quicken account it applies to.

Downloaded Transactions

Bank account transaction downloads include all deposits, checks, interest payments, bank fees, transfers, ATM transactions, and debit card transactions. Credit card transaction downloads include all charges, credits (for returns or adjustments), payments, fees, and finance charges. Quicken displays all of the transactions, including those you have not yet entered in your account register, as well as the current balance of the account. A few clicks and keystrokes is all it takes to enter the transactions you missed. This feature makes it virtually impossible to omit entries, while telling you exactly how much money is available in a bank account or how much money you owe on your credit card account—no more surprises in that monthly statement.

Additional Features of Direct Connect

If your financial institution supports Direct Connect, you may also be able to take advantage of the following two features:

Transfer Money Between Accounts   If you have more than one bank account at the same financial institution, you can use Online Account Access to transfer money between accounts. Although many banks offer this feature by phone or on their Web sites, initiating the transaction from within Quicken is quicker and easier and has the added benefit of entering it into your Quicken data file. Just enter a transfer transaction and let Quicken do the rest.

Send E-Mail Messages to Your Financial Institution   Ever call the customer service center at your bank or credit card company to ask a question? If you're lucky, real people are waiting to answer the phone. But if you're like most people, your financial institution uses a call routing system that requires you to listen to voice prompts and press telephone keypad keys to communicate with a machine. Either way, when a real person gets on the line, you have to provide all kinds of information about yourself just to prove that you are who you say you are. *Then* you can ask your question. The e-mail feature that's part of Direct Connect enables you to exchange e-mail messages with your bank or credit card company's customer service department. You normally get a response within one business day.

Online Payment and Quicken Bill Pay

Online Payment enables you to send a check to anyone without physically writing, printing, or mailing a check. You enter and store information about the payee within Quicken. You then create a transaction for the payee that includes the payment date and amount. You can enter the transaction weeks or months in advance if desired—the payee receives payment on the date you specify.

Online Payment is one of the least understood Quicken features. Many folks think it can be used to pay only big companies like the phone company or credit card companies. That just isn't true. You can use Online Payment to pay any bill, contribute to your retirement account, donate money to a charity, or send your brother a birthday gift.

How It Works

Suppose you use Quicken to send online payment instructions to pay your monthly bill at Joe's Hardware Store. You've already set up Joe as a payee by entering the name, address, and phone number of his store, as well as your account number there. Quicken sends your payment instructions to your bank, which stores it in its computer with a bunch of other online payment instructions. When the payment date nears, the bank's computer looks through its big database of payees that it can pay by wire transfer. It sees phone companies and credit card companies and other banks. But because Joe's store is small, it's probably not one of the wire transfer payees. So the bank's computer prepares a check using all the information you provided. It mails the check along with thousands of others due to be paid that day.

Joe's wife, who does the accounting for the store (with Quicken Home & Business, in case you're wondering), gets the check a few days later. She deposits it with the other checks she gets that day. The amount of the check is deducted from your bank account and your account balance at Joe's. If you use Transaction Download, the check appears as a transaction. It also appears on your bank statement. If your bank returns canceled checks to you, you may get the check along with all your others.

When the Money Leaves Your Account   The date the money is actually withdrawn from your account to cover the payment varies depending on your bank. There are four possibilities:

- One to four days before the payment is processed for delivery
- The day the payment is processed for delivery
- The day the payment is delivered
- The day the paper check or electronic funds transfer clears your bank

To find out when funds are withdrawn from your account for online payments, ask your bank.

The Benefits of Online Payment

Online Payment can benefit you in several ways. You can pay your bills as they arrive, without paying them early—the payee doesn't receive payment before the payment date you specify. You don't have to buy stamps, and the bank never forgets to mail the checks.

Quicken Bill Pay

If your bank does not support Online Payment, you can still take advantage of this feature by signing up for Quicken Bill Pay. This service works with your checking account like Online Payment does.

Costs

The cost of Quicken's online account services varies from bank to bank. Check with your bank to determine the exact fees. Here's what you can expect:

- Transaction Download is often free to all customers or to customers who maintain a certain minimum account balance. Otherwise, you could pay up to $10 for this service.
- Online Payment is sometimes free, but more often it costs from $5 to $10 per month for 20 to 25 payments per month. Each additional payment usually costs 40¢ to 60¢. Again, some banks waive this fee if you maintain a certain minimum balance.
- Quicken Bill Pay is $9.95 for up to 20 payments and $2.49 for each set of five payments after that. (These prices are subject to change.)

Security

If you're worried about security, you must have skipped over the security information in Chapter 4. Go back and read that now.

**What Does This Mean to You?
Online Payment Costs**

If you think Online Payment sounds expensive, do the math. Here's an example. I get 20 payments per month for $5. If I had to mail 20 checks, it would cost me $8.80 in postage. So I'd actually save $3.40 per month if I made 20 online payments. Even if I don't make 20 payments a month, I also don't have to stuff envelopes, apply return address labels, or stick on stamps. My bills get paid on time, I earn more interest income, and I haven't bounced a check in more than ten years.

Does it sound like I'm sold on this feature? You bet I am!

It explains how Quicken and financial institution security works to make Online Account Services safe.

Setting Up Online Account Services

To use the Online Account Services supported by Quicken, you must configure the appropriate Quicken accounts. This requires that you enter information about your financial institution and the account with which you want to use these features.

Applying for Online Account Services

Before you can use one of the online account services, you must apply for it—learn how at the end of Chapter 4. Normally, all it takes is a phone call, although some banks and credit card companies allow you to apply online.

To learn more about and apply for Quicken Bill Pay, choose More From Quicken | Quicken Services | Visit Quicken Bill Pay. After reading the information about Quicken Bill Pay that appears in your browser window, click the Start Now. It's Free! button to begin the process.

The application process for these services usually takes a week but may take less. You'll know that you're ready to go online when you get a letter with setup information. The setup information usually consists of the following:

PIN (Personal Identification Number)   You'll have to enter this code into Quicken when you access your account online. This is a security feature, so don't write down your PIN on a sticky note and attach it to your computer monitor. There is a chance that your financial institution may send this information separately for additional security.

Customer ID Number   This is often your Social Security number or taxpayer identification number.

Bank Routing Number   Although your bank might send routing number information, Quicken won't need it. It knows what financial institution you're using based on the information you provide when you create the account. That's why it's so important to choose the correct financial institution when you create an account.

Account Number for Each Online Access–Enabled Account   This tells your financial institution which account you want to work with. In many instances, Quicken may not need this information either.

Setting Up Online Account Services

With customer ID and PIN in hand, you're ready to set up your account (or accounts) for Online Account Services. You can set up the account in a number of ways; rather than cover them all, this section covers the most straightforward method.

Keep in mind that if you set up an account using the online method, as discussed in Chapter 4, and you already have online account access enabled at your bank, your account may already be set up for online access. You can tell if it is by following the instructions in the "Checking Online Account Service Status" section, later in this chapter.

Setting Up for Direct Connect, Express Web Connect, and Quicken Bill Pay

If you have not already activated online services with your bank, click Banking | *<the account you want to set up>* | Account Actions | Set Up Online, as shown here. If the account is already set up for online access, the Account Action menu will show Update Now instead of Set Up Online.

The Account Setup dialog appears. Quicken displays a dialog like the one shown next, which lists of all the financial institutions you are using that have Online Account Services enabled and the User ID for those accounts—even if you have only one. If the account you are setting up is at one of the listed financial institutions, select that institution. Otherwise, click No, The Account Is at a Different Institution Or Has A Different Login. In either case, click Next.

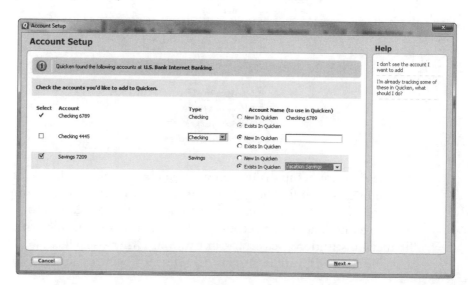

If you selected a login from the list, Quicken has you enter the password for this financial institution and user account. Click Next to continue.

If you click No, Quicken opens the Account Setup dialog so you can select your financial institution. The Account Setup dialog is discussed in Chapter 3.

Quicken connects to the Internet again to fetch more information. You may be asked for additional information by your financial institution. If so, enter that information and click OK.

A list of the accounts held at this financial institution displays as shown here. Choose the account you want to use and click Next.

Quicken displays a dialog telling you that you have successfully set up the account(s). Here's what mine looks like. Click Done.

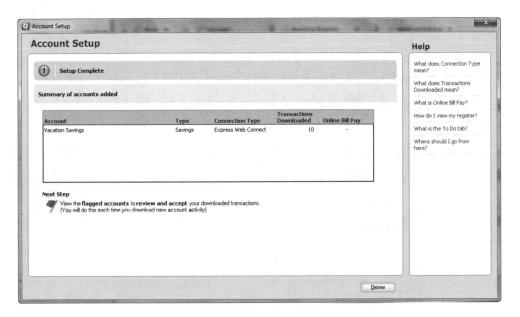

Checking Online Account Service Status

You can confirm that an account has been set up for Online Account Services and determine what kind of connection it uses.

Choose Setup | Checking and Savings Accounts to view your banking accounts. Each account will display the type of connection as shown below:

Account Name	Type	Transaction Download ⑦	Online Bill Pay ⑦	
Brokerage (Cash)	Checking	—	No (Activate Bill Pay)	Edit
Checking	Checking	*Not Available*	No (Activate Bill Pay)	Edit
Checking 6789	Checking	Yes (Express Web Connect)	No (Activate Bill Pay)	Edit
Money Market	Checking	*Not Available*	No (Activate Bill Pay)	Edit
Savings	Savings	*Not Available*	No (Activate Bill Pay)	Edit
Vacation Savings	Savings	Yes (Express Web Connect)	—	Edit
Other	Checking	*Not Available*	No (Activate Bill Pay)	Edit
Single Mutual Fund (Cash)	Checking	—	No (Activate Bill Pay)	Edit

= Checking and Savings Accounts　　Why use this?

Add Checking and Savings accounts to track spending, reconcile statements, download bank activity and more.

[Add Checking Account] [Add Savings Account]

If the "Improve Connection" link appears for an account, you can change the connection method to one that's easier to use. If a link like this appears for one of your accounts, click it and follow the instructions that appear to upgrade your connection.

You can also add online services to an account in the account's Account Action subtab. Open the account's register and click Account Actions | Set Up Online.

You can also right-click the account name on the Account Bar, click Edit Account to open the Account Details dialog. Click the Online Services tab. You can use this dialog to activate or, in this case, remove this account from One Step Updates.

More About Transaction Download

Quicken makes a distinction between two types of downloaded transactions:

- **Online transaction instructions** are those transactions that have been sent to your financial institution but have not yet cleared your account. For example, suppose you used your bank's Web site to pay one of your bills.

This transaction is in your bank's computer server, but it hasn't been completed or cleared. When you download transactions for that account, Quicken downloads the payment instruction so you can record it as an upcoming payment in your account.

- **Cleared transactions** are those transactions that have cleared your account and are included in your current account balance. For example, suppose you made a deposit at the bank. As soon as the bank accepts the deposit, the deposit is said to have "cleared" and is included in your current bank account balance. Cleared transactions can include deposits, checks, online payments, ATM transactions, debit card transactions, bank or interest fees, and interest earnings.

By default, all downloaded transactions are loaded into your register automatically. If you want to review your downloaded transactions before they have been entered into your register automatically, click Edit | Preferences | Quicken Preferences | Downloaded Transactions and clear the Automatically Add Downloaded Transactions to Registers check box.

The Online Center

While you can access online services in the various tabs, you can also use the Online Center to work with Quicken's online features. This window gives you access to all the lists and commands you need to download transactions, create payments, transfer money, and exchange e-mail with your financial institution.

Using the Online Center Window

To open the Online Center window, choose Tools | Online Center. Figure 6-1 shows what the Transactions tab of this window looks like with one of my financial institutions selected.

   A number of button bar buttons and menus enable you to work with the window's contents:

- **Delete** removes the selected item. This button is not available in all tabs of the Online Center window.
- **Payees** (if you have set up online payments) displays the Online Payee List window, which is discussed later in this chapter in the section titled "Entering Online Payee Information."
- **Repeating** (if you have set up online payments) displays the Repeating Online tab of the Scheduled Bills & Deposits list window. Learn more about

Figure 6-1 • The Online Center window gives you access to online features for your accounts.

using this feature later in this chapter, in the section titled "Scheduling Repeating Online Payments."

- **Contact Info** displays the Contact Information dialog for the currently selected financial institution. You can use the information in the dialog to contact the bank or credit card company by phone, Web site, or e-mail.
- **Password Vault** gives you access to Quicken's Password Vault feature, which is discussed in Chapter 7. (This option may appear only if you have online banking features enabled for accounts at more than one financial institution.)
- **Renaming Rules** displays the Renaming Rules For Downloaded Transactions dialog. Learn how to use the renaming feature later, in the section titled "Renaming Downloaded Payees."
- **Print** prints the transactions that appear in the window.
- **Options** displays a menu of commands for working with the current account or window.

Downloading Transactions

One of the main features of Online Account Services is the ability to download transactions from your financial institution into Quicken. You do this with the Update/Send button of the Online Center window (refer to Figure 6-1). Here's how you can take advantage of this feature.

Connecting to the Financial Institution with Direct Connect or Express Web Connect

If your financial institution supports Direct Connect or Express Web Connect, you can download all transactions from within Quicken.

In the Online Center window, choose the name of your bank or credit card company from the Financial Institution drop-down list. If necessary, click the Update/Send button. The One Step Update Settings dialog, which is shown next, appears. Click to toggle the check marks beside the instructions you want to send, enter your password, and click Update Now.

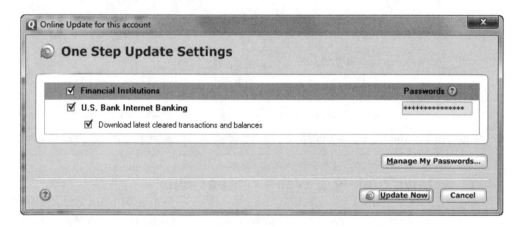

Quicken might display a dialog offering to save your passwords. If you click Yes, follow the instructions in Chapter 7 to set up the Password Vault feature. You may then need to reinitiate the download procedure.

Wait while Quicken connects to your bank. A status dialog appears while it works. When Quicken has finished exchanging information, the status dialog disappears and the One Step Update Summary window (see Figure 6-2) takes its place. Continue following the instructions later in the chapter, in the section titled "Viewing Downloaded Transactions."

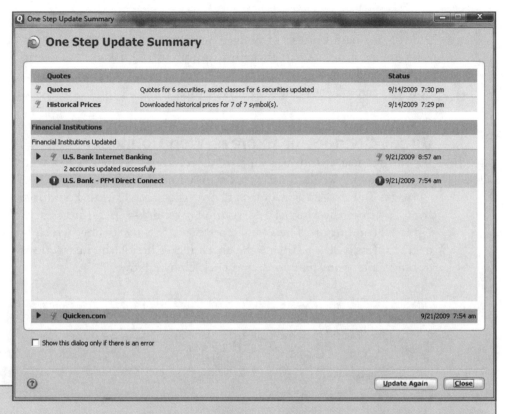

Figure 6-2 • The One Step Update Summary window summarizes the activity of online sessions.

Downloading a Web Connect File

If your financial institution supports Web Connect but not Express Web Connect, you'll have to log in to your financial institution's Web site and manually download the statement information just as you did when you first set up the account for Online Account Services.

In the Online Center window, choose the name of your bank or credit card company from the Financial Institution drop-down list. If necessary, click the Update/Send button. Quicken connects to the Internet and displays your financial institution's login page. Log in, navigate to the page where you can download statements, and download the statement or transactions you want. If necessary, switch back to Quicken. It should automatically import the transactions you downloaded into the correct account. Newly downloaded transactions have a small blue ball icon, as shown in the illustration. Transactions that

⊚	9/4/2009	5049
⊚	9/9/2009	
⊚	9/10/2009	
⊚	9/15/2009	5050

have been matched to scheduled transactions have both a blue ball and a calendar icon.

Click the Close button in the One Step Update Summary window to dismiss it. Then, use the Account Bar or some other method to open an account with downloaded transactions.

If you have chosen to turn off the Automatically Add Downloaded Transactions To Register preference, your downloaded transactions will appear in the Downloaded Transactions tab at the bottom of the register window. From there, you can use the directions in "Comparing Downloaded Transactions to Register Transactions."

Keep in mind that the first time you connect via Direct Connect, the bank normally sends all transactions from the past 60 or more days. (One of my banks sends a full year of transactions, with a maximum of 250 transactions!) After that, only new transactions will be downloaded. For Web Connect downloads, you can often specify the transaction period when you set up the download.

Comparing Downloaded Transactions to Register Transactions

Your job is to compare the downloaded transactions to the transactions already entered in your account register. This enables you to identify transactions that you neglected to enter or that you entered incorrectly. In addition, because Quicken will automatically enter a date, transaction number, and amount—and in the case of some transactions, the payee and category (based on previously memorized transactions)—using this method to enter a transaction can be much faster than entering it manually in the account register window.

The Status column in the bottom half of the account register window (refer to Figure 6-3) identifies three types of transactions:

- **Match** identifies transactions that match those in the register. This will happen if the transaction has already been entered in the Quicken register.
- **New** identifies transactions that do not appear to be in the register.
- **Accepted** identifies matched transactions that you have accepted. When a downloaded transaction has been accepted, a small **c** appears in the Clr column of the account register to indicate that the item has cleared the bank but has not yet been reconciled.

When you select a transaction in the bottom half of the window, the transactions below it shift down to make room for a blank line with an Accept button and an Edit menu. You can use these to work with the selected transaction.

Figure 6-3 • Turn off automatic download to see your downloaded transactions appear on the bottom half of the register window.

Accepting a Matched Transaction If a transaction matches one in the register, you can accept it by selecting it in the list at the bottom of the window and clicking the Accept button.

Entering and Accepting a New Transaction To enter and accept a new transaction, select the transaction in the bottom half of the window. Fill in any missing details, including the payee, category, and memo. Then click Enter in the top half of the window or Accept in the bottom half. Quicken enters and accepts the transaction.

Unmatching a Matched Transaction   If a matched transaction really shouldn't be matched, select it in the bottom half of the window and choose Unmatch from the Edit pop-up menu

- **Unmatch** tells Quicken that it got the match wrong, but this command lets Quicken attempt to match it to another transaction. As a result, it may come up with another match. It's your job to determine whether the new match is correct. If it can't find a match, the status changes to New.
- **Make Transaction New** tells Quicken that the transaction shouldn't match any existing transaction. The status changes to New and Quicken can then treat it as a new transaction.
- **Make All Transactions New** tells Quicken to make all of the downloaded but not yet accepted transactions new so you can manually match them.

Manually Matching a Transaction   If a downloaded transaction identified as New should match one in the register, or if a single transaction corresponds to multiple transactions in your account register, you can manually match them up. In the bottom half of the window, select the transaction that you want to match manually, and click the Edit button, which is shown below, appears. Click Match Manually to open the Manually Match Transactions dialog. Turn on the check box(es) for the transaction(s) you want to include in the match. When you click Accept, Quicken creates an entry for the transaction. If the transaction included multiple register transactions, the entry Quicken creates includes each of the register transactions on a separate split line. You can click the Split button for the transaction to edit it as desired. Learn how to work with splits in Chapter 5.

Deleting a New Transaction   To delete a new transaction, select the transaction in the bottom half of the account register window and click Edit and choose Delete from the Edit pop-up menu, as shown here. A confirmation dialog appears; click Yes to remove the transaction from the list.

| Delete |
| Match Manually |
| Make New |
| Make All New |
| |
| Unmatch |
| Revert to Original Payee |
| Show Renaming Rules |

Accepting All Downloaded Transactions
Accept All accepts all transactions into your account register without reviewing them one by one. Keep in mind that some

transactions may not be properly categorized, and some transactions may be matched to the wrong transaction, making it appear as if the downloaded transaction disappeared. I don't use Accept All without first examining each downloaded transaction to ensure it matched to the register transaction I expect.

Renaming Downloaded Payees

One of the potentially annoying things about entering transactions by accepting downloaded activity information is the way your bank identifies payees. For example, my bank identifies the payee for my cable television company as "CableAmerica{026-144710}" instead of plain old "CableAmerica."

Fortunately, Quicken's renaming rules feature can automatically rename bank-assigned payee names with names you prefer. In fact, the first time you complete a download of bank or credit card transactions, Quicken is likely to rename a bunch of payees all at once. You'll see the Rename Your Payees dialog, which summarizes all of the payee names Quicken wants to rename. When you click Apply Settings, Quicken changes the payee names as listed in the dialog and applies those renaming rules from that point forward.

You can also create and apply your own renaming rules. You do this with the Renaming Rules For Downloaded Transactions dialog, which is shown here:

To open this dialog, click the Renaming Rules button at the bottom of the Downloaded Transactions tab of the register window or choose Tools | Renaming Rules. The top half of the dialog lists all the renaming rules that have already been created. The bottom half of the dialog has options you can select to enable the Renaming feature and let Quicken automatically create renaming rules for you. (I recommend selecting On for both options.)

You can use buttons to the right of the list to add, modify, or remove renaming rules.

New   Clicking the New button displays the Create Renaming Rule dialog. Enter the name you want to see as the payee name in the Change Payee To box. Then choose an option from the first drop-down list to determine which field Quicken should match, choose a match option from the middle drop-down list, and enter match text in the text box. For example, if I wanted to change every downloaded item containing the text *CableAmerica{026-144710}* to *CableAmerica*, I'd set the dialog as shown here. You can click the Add New Item link to add another line of matching criteria; doing so tells Quicken to match *any* criteria you enter. When you click OK in the dialog, the renaming rule is added to the list as shown in the illustration.

Edit   Clicking the Edit button displays the Edit Renaming Rule dialog, which looks and works just like the Create Renaming Rule dialog just shown. This dialog enables you to modify settings for the selected renaming rule.

Delete   Clicking the Delete button removes the selected renaming rule from the list. You'll have to click OK in the confirmation dialog that appears to remove the rule.

Making Online Payments

The Add Transaction Reminder enables you to enter online payment instructions for accounts for which you have enabled the Online Payment feature. Figure 6-4 shows what it looks like.

The rest of this section explains how to set up online payees, enter payment information for one-time and repeating payments, and work with payment instructions.

Figure 6-4 • Use the Add Bill Reminder window to create online payments.

Entering Online Payee Information

To send payments from your account, your bank must know who and where each payee is. To ensure that your account with the payee is properly credited, you must also provide account information. You do this by setting up online payees.

- From the Bills tab, click Add Reminder tab.
- In the How section, select the account from which you will be paying the bill from the drop down list.
- In the Payment Method field, select Online Bill Pay.
- Enter the information into the Payee field in the Add Bill Reminder window. Press TAB to open the Set Up Online Payee dialog, as seen here.

- Enter the name of the Online Payee in the Name field and any description that might be needed in the optional Description field.
- Enter a mailing address, city, state and ZIP code. If you skip over one of these required fields, Quicken will prompt you for the information.
- Enter an Account # and Phone. Again, if you do not enter this information, you are prompted for it.
- Click OK when you have completed entering the information. The Confirm Online Payee Information message appears displaying the information you just entered, as shown here. *Check the information in this box carefully.* If there is an error, your payment might not reach the payee or it might not be properly credited to your account. Remember, your bank will not be sending

a billing stub with the payment—just the payment. When you're satisfied that the information is correct, click Accept. The payee is added to the list. If the information is not correct, click Cancel to return to the Set Up Online Payee dialog.

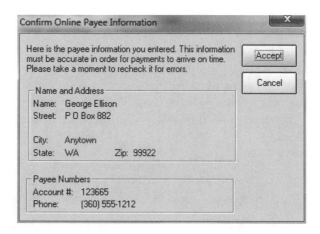

If you choose, you can also work with online payees through the Online Center. Click Tools | Online Center | Payees to open the Online Payee List.

- **New** enables you to create a new online payee.
- **Edit** enables you to modify the information for the selected online payee.
- **Delete** removes the selected online payee. Deleting a payee simply deletes the payee's information from the Online Payee List window. It does not change any transactions for a payee. You cannot delete a payee for which unsent payment instructions exist.
- **Use** switches you back to the Payments tab of the Online Center window and inserts the selected payee into the payment form.
- **Report** displays a report of all payments made to the selected online payee.
- **Print** prints a list of online payees.
- **Financial Institution** offers a drop down list of all the institutions for which you have enabled online bill pay. Choose the institution that has the account from which you will be paying this payee.
- The payees you have added for the displayed institution are listed below, showing the payee name, the lead time for this payee, and the account number as shown in the illustration.

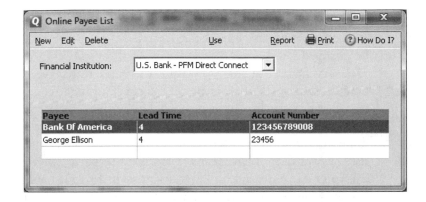

Entering Payment Instructions

To enter additional online payment instructions, click Tools | Online Center | Payments, as seen in Figure 6-5. Fill in the fields in the middle of the window with the payment information:

Figure 6-5 • **The Payments tab in the Online Center can also be used to enter information about online payments.**

- **Processing Date** is the date the bank should begin processing the payment. For some banks, this date is fixed based on the Delivery Date field and can't be changed.
- **Delivery Date** is the date you want the payee to receive payment. This is the date the bank will either write on the check or make the electronic funds transfer. The check may be received before that date, depending on the mail (if the check is mailed). The date you enter, however, must be at least the same number of business days in advance as the lead time for the payee—usually four days. That means if you want to pay a bill on Wednesday, June 29, you must enter and send its instructions to your bank on or before Friday, June 24. To process payment as soon as possible, just enter today's date and Quicken will adjust the date for you. For some banks, the delivery date cannot be changed; instead, specify a Processing Date that allows enough time for the payment to be made on a timely basis.
- **Payee** is the online payee to receive payment. Quicken's QuickFill feature fills in the payee's name as you type it. If desired, you can choose it from the drop-down list of online payees. If you enter a payee that is not in the Online Payee List window, Quicken displays the Set Up Online Payee dialog so you can add the new payee's information. This enables you to create online payees as you enter payment instructions.
- **$** is the amount of the payment.
- **Category** is the category for the transaction. You can enter a category, choose one from the drop-down list, or click the Split button to enter multiple categories.
- **Memo**, which is optional, is for entering a note about the transaction.

When you've finished entering information for the transaction, click Enter. The transaction appears in the list in the bottom half of the window with the words

---

What Does This Mean to You? Payment and Delivery Dates

Don't let the Processing Date and Delivery Date options confuse you. The Delivery Date is the important date. It determines whether your payment will make it to the payee on time. Whenever possible, I give the bank an extra two days. So, for example, if a bill is due on June 29, I'd instruct the bank to pay on June 27. This isn't because I don't have confidence in Quicken or my bank. It's because I have less confidence in the Postal Service.

If the Delivery Date field on your form can't be changed, don't panic. Just enter a Processing Date at least four days (or six, if you're extra cautious like me) before the date you want the payment to arrive. That should give your bank enough time to get the payment to the payee without getting you in trouble.

"Payment request ready to send" in the Status column beside it. You can repeat this process for as many payments as you want to make.

Entering Online Payments in the Account Register

Another way to enter an online payment instruction is to simply enter the transaction in the appropriate account register. Click the Bills tab, then click Manage Reminders and double-click the transaction on the list, or click Enter. The Enter Transaction dialog appears with SEND in the Method/Check Number field, as seen next. Make any changes or additions in the dialog, and Click Enter Transaction to enter it into the register. You may find this method quicker, especially if you've worked with Quicken for a while and are familiar with the account register window.

Scheduling Repeating Online Payments

Some payments are exactly the same every month, such as your rent, a car loan, or your monthly cable television bill. You can set these payments up as repeating online payments.

Here's how it works. You schedule the online payment once, indicating the payee, amount, and frequency. Quicken sends the instructions to your bank. Thirty days before the payment is due, your bank creates a new postdated payment based on your instructions and notifies you that it has created the payment. Quicken automatically enters the payment information in your account register with the appropriate payment date. The payment is delivered on the payment date. This happens regularly, at the interval you specify, until you tell it to stop. Because you don't have to do a thing to continue paying regularly, the more payments you make with this feature, the more time you save.

(Using this feature to pay an amortized loan such as a mortgage works a little differently. Learn about it later in this chapter, in the section titled "Linking a Repeating Online Payment to an Amortized Loan.")

In the Add Transaction Reminder window, click the This Is A Repeating Online Payment check box, as seen next. The Delivery Method will immediately change to Automatic. You can also click Tools | Online Center | Repeating to open the Add Transaction Reminder window.

There are two very important things to remember when using the Add A Transaction Reminder dialog to create a repeating online payment:

- Choose Online Bill Pay from the Payment Method drop-down list. This tells Quicken that the payment will be made online.
- Turn on the This Is A Repeating Online Payment check box. This tells Quicken to send one instruction for multiple repeating payments.

When you click OK to save the payment instruction, it appears in the Repeating Online tab of the Bill And Income Reminder list window as seen in Figure 6-6.

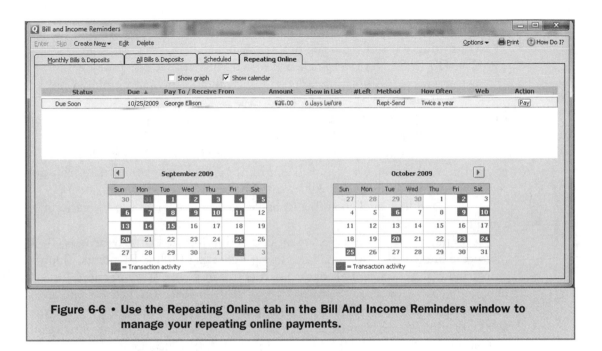

Figure 6-6 • Use the Repeating Online tab in the Bill And Income Reminders window to manage your repeating online payments.

You can use button bar options to work with items listed in the Bill And Income Reminders list window:

- **Enter** records the selected repeating online payment in the register.
- **Skip** skips payment of the selected repeating online payment.
- **Create New** enables you to create a new scheduled transaction or paycheck. Learn more about this menu in Chapter 7.
- **Edit** displays the Edit Repeating Online Payment dialog, shown here, so you can modify the details of the repeating online payment.
- **Delete** removes the repeating online payment from the list, thus canceling future payments. You must click Delete in the confirmation dialog that appears to remove the transaction.

- **Options** offers commands for changing the sort order of payments in the list.
- **Print** prints a list of repeating online payments.
- **How Do I?** displays the Quicken Personal Finances Help window with instructions for completing tasks with the Bill and Income Reminder list.

Linking a Repeating Online Payment to an Amortized Loan

Repeating online payments are perfect for paying off loans. After all, loan payments are the same every month and must be paid by a certain date. You can set up a repeating online payment instruction, send it to your financial institution, and let Quicken and your bank makes the payments automatically every month for you.

Set up the repeating online payment instruction for the loan payment as instructed in the earlier section "Scheduling Repeating Online Payments." Don't worry about all the categories that are part of a loan payment transaction. Just choose the loan account as the category. You don't even have to get the date or amount right. When you link the transaction to the loan, Quicken will make the necessary adjustments. Be sure to click Authorize to save the payment instruction.

Choose Net Worth | Loan Details or press CTRL-H to display the Loans window. If necessary, choose the loan account's name from the Choose Loan menu in the button bar to display the information for the loan for which you want to use the payment instruction.

Click the Edit Payment button to display the Edit Loan Payment dialog. Then click the Payment Method button. In the Select Payment Method dialog, select Repeating Online Payment. Then choose the repeating online payment instruction you created from the Repeating Payment drop-down list. It might look something like this:

Click OK in each dialog to dismiss it. Quicken links the loan payment to the repeating online payment instruction. It makes changes to the payment instruction, if necessary, to match the payment categories and split information. The next time you connect to your financial institution, the instruction will be sent and payments will begin.

Sending Payment Instructions

Once your payment instructions have been completed, you must connect to your bank to send the instructions. In the Online Center window, click the Update/Send button. Quicken displays the Online Update window, which lists all of the payment instructions, including any repeating payment instructions. Enter your password and click the Update Now button.

> ### What Does This Mean to You? Repeating Online Loan Payments
>
> Setting up a loan payment as a repeating online payment has got to be one of the best timesaving features available in Quicken. It does all kinds of neat things for you.
>
> First, it ensures that your loan payment is made regularly, on a timely basis, with no monthly effort on your part. Second, it automatically adjusts the balance of your loan principal account (a debt account) by accurately calculating interest and principal paid for every entry. (You know these amounts change every month, right? Can you imagine doing the entries manually? Egads!) And since the loan account balance is updated with every payment, your net worth is always up-to-date.
>
> Just set it and forget it. That should be this feature's slogan. And if you're in a fog about how to set up a loan in Quicken, don't fret. I explain all in lucky Chapter 13.

Wait while Quicken connects to your bank's server and sends your payment (or payment cancellation) instructions. When it has finished, it displays the Online Update Summary window. Click Done.

In the Payments tab of the Online Center window, the words "Scheduled for delivery on" followed by the payment date appear in the Status column beside the payment instructions that have been sent to your bank.

Canceling a Payment

Occasionally, you may change your mind about making a payment. Perhaps you found out that your spouse already sent a check, or that you set up the payment for the wrong amount. For whatever reason, you can cancel an online payment that you have sent to your bank—as long as there's enough time to cancel it.

Here's how it works. When you send a payment instruction to your bank, it waits in the bank's computer. When the processing date (determined by the number of days in the payee's lead time and the payment date) arrives, the bank makes the payment. Before the processing date, however, the payment instructions can be canceled. If you send a cancel payment instruction to the bank before the processing date, the bank removes the instruction from its computer without sending payment to the payee. Quicken won't let you cancel a payment if the processing date has already passed. If you wait too long, the only way to cancel the payment is to call the bank directly and stop the check.

Keep in mind that canceling a payment instruction isn't the same as stopping a check. If you send the cancel payment instruction in time, the bank should not charge a fee for stopping the payment.

Canceling a Regular Online Payment   In the Online Center window, select the payment that you want to cancel and click the Cancel Payment button. Click Yes in the confirmation dialog that appears. Use the Update/Send button to send the cancel payment instruction.

Stopping a Single Repeating Online Payment   In the Online Center window, select the payment you want to stop and click the Cancel Payment button. Click Yes in the confirmation dialog that appears. Use the Update/Send button to send the cancel payment instruction. Note that the payment may not appear in the Online Center window unless you have reviewed and approved all downloaded payment transactions, as instructed earlier in this chapter.

Stopping All Future Payments for a Repeating Online Payment   In the Repeating tab of the Bill And Income Reminders window, select the payment you want to stop and click Delete. Click Delete in the confirmation dialog that appears. The transaction is removed from the list. Then use the Update/Send button in the Online Center window to send the cancel payment instruction.

Transferring Money Between Accounts

If you have more than one account enabled for Online Bill Pay via Direct Connect at the same financial institution, you can transfer money from one account to the other directly from Quicken.

- From the Account Bar, select the account you from which you want to transfer the funds.
- Click Banking | Account Actions | Transfer Money.
- The Record A Transaction Between Quicken Accounts dialog appears as seen on the top of the next page.

Enter the transfer information—source account, destination account, and amount—in the fields in the middle of the window. When you click Enter, the information is added to the list of transfers at the bottom of the window. The transaction will appear in both check registers with TXFR in the Num field, as seen here.

9/25/2009	TXFR	Transfer Money		125 00	
🖉		[Small Checking]			

Like payment instructions, you must send transfer instructions to your bank in order for the transaction to take place. Click the One Step Update button on the Account Bar to send the information.

Exchanging E-mail with Your Financial Institution

You can use the E-mail tab of the Online Center window to exchange e-mail messages with financial institutions for which you have enabled Online Account Services via Direct Connect. Keep in mind that not all financial institutions support this feature. Also, remember that this communication is between you and your financial institution, not Intuit (makers of Quicken). It is intended primarily for exchanging information about your account, not technical support for using Quicken.

Creating an E-mail Message

In the E-mail tab of the Online Center window, click Create. If a Create dialog like the one shown here appears, use it to set general options for your e-mail message. If your message is about an online payment, choose the account from the Account drop-down list and select the payment from the Payments scrolling list.

When you click OK, a Message window appears. Use it to compose your e-mail message. When you click OK, the message is saved. It appears in the bottom half of the E-mail tab of the Online Center window, ready to be sent to your financial institution.

Exchanging E-mail Messages

Using e-mail is a lot like having a box at the post office. When you write a letter, you have to get it to the post office to send it to the recipient. When you receive a letter, you have to go to the post office and check your box to retrieve it. E-mail works the same way. Connecting is a lot like going to the post office to send and retrieve messages.

In the Online Center window, click the Update/Send button. Quicken displays the Online Update window, which includes any e-mail messages you may have created that need to be sent. Enter your password and click the Update Now button. Then wait while Quicken establishes an Internet connection with your bank and exchanges e-mail.

Reading an E-mail Message

When your bank sends you an e-mail message, it appears in the E-mail tab of the Online Center window. To read the message, select it and click Read. The message appears in a message window. If desired, you can click the Print button to print the message for future reference.

Automating Transactions and Tasks

Chapter 7

In This Chapter:

- *QuickFill and memorized payees*
- *Scheduled transactions*
- *Calendar*
- *Billminder*
- *Paycheck Setup*
- *Address Book*
- *One Step Update and the Password Vault*
- *Scheduling updates*

Quicken Personal Finance Software includes a number of features to automate the entry of transactions. This chapter tells you about QuickFill, Billminder, and the other features you can use to automate transaction entries or remind yourself when a transaction is due. It also explains how you can use Quicken's One Step Update feature to handle all of your online tasks at once. I'm sure you'll agree that these features can make data entry and other Quicken tasks quicker and easier.

Before you read this chapter, make sure you have a good understanding of the data entry techniques covered in Chapter 5. This chapter builds upon many of the basic concepts discussed there.

QuickFill and Memorized Payees

As you enter transactions, Quicken is quietly working in the background, memorizing transaction information for each payee. It creates a database of memorized payees. It then uses the memorized payees for its QuickFill feature.

How It Works

QuickFill works in two ways:

- When you enter the first few characters of a payee name in the Write Checks or account register window, Quicken immediately fills in the rest of the name. When you advance to the next text box or field of the entry form, Quicken fills in the rest of the transaction information based on the last transaction for that payee.
- You can select a memorized payee from the drop-down list in the Payee field of the Write Checks or account register window. Quicken then fills in the rest of the transaction information based on the last transaction for that payee.

QuickFill entries include amounts, categories, and memos. They can also include splits and tags. For example, you might pay the cable or satellite company for television service every month. The bill is usually the same amount each month. The second time you create an entry with the company's name, Quicken fills in the rest of the transaction automatically. You can make adjustments to the amount or other information as desired and save the transaction. It may have taken a minute or so to enter the transaction the first time, but it'll take only seconds to enter it every time after that.

By default, the QuickFill feature is set up to work as discussed here. If it does not, check the QuickFill options to make sure they are set properly. I tell you how in Appendix B.

Working with the Memorized Payee List

If desired, you can view a list of memorized payees, as shown in Figure 7-1. Just choose Tools | Memorized Payee List or press CTRL-T.

Button Bar Buttons

You can use buttons on the button bar to add, modify, or delete memorized payees or work with the Memorized Payee List:

- **Go To Find And Replace** displays the Find And Replace dialog, which you can use to replace payee names. Learn how to use the Find And Replace dialog in Chapter 5.

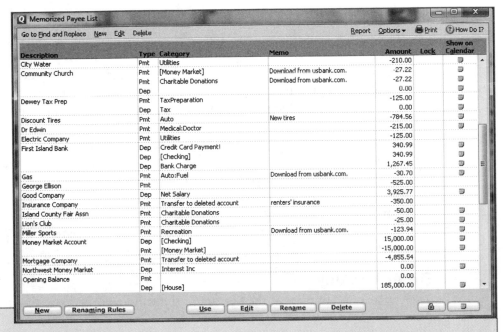

Figure 7-1 • **Each line in the Memorized Payee List represents the last transaction recorded for a payee.**

- **New** displays the Create Memorized Payee dialog, shown next, which you can use to create brand-new transactions without actually entering them into any register of your Quicken data file. Just fill in the fields to enter transaction information and click OK. The new transaction appears in the Memorized Payee List window.

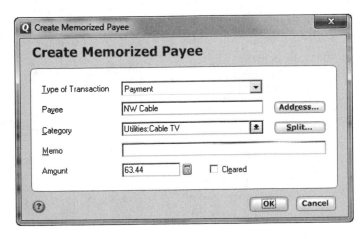

- **Edit** displays the Edit Memorized Payee dialog for the currently selected transaction. This dialog looks and works like the Create Memorized Payee dialog.
- **Delete** displays a dialog asking you to confirm that you really do want to delete the selected memorized payee. If you delete the transaction, it is removed from the Memorized Payee List only—not from any register in the Quicken data file.
- **Report** displays a Payee Report for the currently selected payee transaction.
- **Options** offers commands for changing the sort order and other view options for the Memorized Payee List.
- **Print** prints a list of memorized payees.
- **How Do I?** displays the Quicken Personal Finances Help window with additional information for completing tasks with the Memorized Payee List window.

Other Options

You can also use buttons at the bottom of the window to work with a selected payee:

- **New** displays the Create Memorized Payee dialog, discussed and shown earlier.
- **Use** enters the selected transaction into the active account register or Write Checks window and fills in the transaction's information for you. You must click the Enter button to accept the entry.
- **Edit** displays the Edit Memorized Payee dialog for the currently selected transaction. This dialog looks and works like the Create Memorized Payee dialog.
- **Rename** displays the Merge And Rename Payees dialog, shown here, which you can use to enter a new name for the selected payee. (To rename multiple payees at once, hold down CTRL and click each payee in the list to select them all before clicking the Rename button.) Enter a new name in the dialog and click OK to change the payee name. If the Create Renaming Rules For Future Downloaded Transactions check box is turned on, Quicken displays the Edit Renaming Rule dialog, so you can modify the

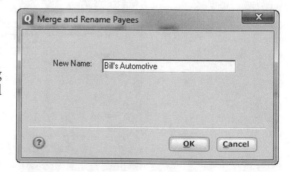

renaming rule Quicken suggests. Learn how to create renaming rules in Chapter 6.

- **Delete** enables you to delete the selected memorized payee. This does not remove any transactions from Quicken registers.
- **Lock** (a padlock icon) toggles the locked setting for the selected transaction. When locked, the payee's transaction will not be rememorized if you make any changes to it when you use it.
- **Calendar** (a calendar page icon) toggles the calendar setting for the selected transaction. When enabled, the payee's transaction will appear on the Calendar (refer to Figure 7-6).

> You may want to build a Memorized Payee list from all of your existing cash flow accounts. To do so:
>
> 1. From the menu bar, click Tools.
> 2. Hold down CTRL-SHIFT and click Memorized Payee List
> 3. Your new Memorized Payee List displays.

Bills and Income Reminders

One of my favorite Quicken features is the ability to tell Quicken about the bills, deposits, and other transactions that need to be made in the future—especially the ones that happen on a regular basis. This feature, when fully utilized, doesn't just prevent you from forgetting to pay bills; it can completely automate the transaction entry process.

This part of the chapter tells you more about bill and income reminders, including how to set up and use them.

Overview of Scheduled Transactions

Generally speaking, you can use two types of scheduled transactions:

- **One-time transactions** are future transactions that you expect to record only once. For example, suppose you are arranging to purchase some furniture. You have already paid a deposit for the furniture and you know that the balance will be due at month-end, when the furniture is delivered. You can schedule that month-end payment in advance.
- **Recurring transactions** are transactions that occur periodically, on a regular basis. Many of your monthly bills are good examples: rent or mortgage payments, car payments, utility bills—unfortunately, there are too many to list!

Reminders aren't only for payments. You could create a reminder for incoming funds, too, such as an expected bonus or a monthly child-support check you receive. You can even schedule your paycheck—but I recommend using Quicken's Paycheck Setup feature, which is discussed later in this chapter, to do that.

Making the Most of Bill and Income Reminders

Quicken's Reminders feature is one of the best timesaving features Quicken offers. By taking full advantage of this feature, you can minimize the time you spend entering transactions into Quicken. That's a good thing, right? After all, you have better things to do with your time than punch numbers into a computer.

Here are a few suggestions from a seasoned Quicken user (yours truly) about how you can make the most of the feature. See how many you can use—and how much time they can save you.

Set up all recurring transactions as scheduled transactions. *Recurring payments* are things like monthly and quarterly bills for rent, mortgage, insurance, utilities, and other regular bills. *Recurring deposits* are things like your paycheck, commissions, and other regular income. Set them all up, even if the amounts vary from one payment or deposit to the next. Not only does having these transactions set up in advance make them quick and easy to enter, but it enables you to take advantage of Quicken's budgeting and forecasting features, which is covered in Chapter 17.

Use Paycheck Setup to track gross pay and deductions. Paycheck Setup may take a bit of time to set up, but it can save you a lot of time and effort while keeping close track of your gross pay and all deductions. This enables you to utilize Quicken's tax planning and reporting features, which is discussed in Chapter 19, without spending a lot of time to enter data. Be sure to set up all paychecks for the people included in your Quicken data file—normally you and, if you're married, your spouse.

Let Quicken automatically enter transactions whenever possible. If Quicken automatically enters transactions for you, entering recurring transactions is a real no-brainer. Quicken does all the entry work; all you do is make the payment or deposit. The only unfortunate thing about this option is that it works best with transactions that have the same amount each time they are made. Still, I'm sure you'll find enough transactions to take advantage of this.

Use the Online Payment or check printing feature. Scheduled transactions seem to work best when coupled with either Quicken's Online Payment feature, which is covered in Chapter 6, or its check printing feature, which is covered in Chapter 5. (Of the two, I prefer online payments, for reasons I expound in Chapter 6.) Once the transaction is entered, Quicken can either automatically send payment instructions when you connect to your financial institution or automatically print checks for payments when you print all checks. So not only is Quicken entering the transaction details for you, but it's making the payments, too! (Ah, if only it could go out, get a job, and earn the money you spend so you don't have to.)

Record transactions several days in advance. You don't have to wait until you make a payment or deposit to record the associated transaction. You can enter transactions in advance so your account register reflects both the current and future balances. Just be sure to enter the transaction due dates rather than entry dates when entering them into Quicken. I especially like doing this for payments, because Quicken can clearly show me that even if I have a nice fat balance today, transactions due over the next few days may leave considerably less to work with. I use this, in effect, as a very short-term forecasting tool. (Quicken's Cash Flow Forecast feature, which is covered in Chapter 17, does a better job of predicting the future.)

Set up reminders based on how often you use Quicken. When you schedule a transaction and indicate that Quicken should prompt you to enter it, you can specify the number of days in advance that you should be reminded. Set this value based on how often you use Quicken. For example, if you use Quicken only once a week, set this value to 10. If you use Quicken every other day, set it to 4. This way, you're sure to be reminded in time to enter a scheduled transaction and make the payment or deposit associated with it.

Remember that creating a reminder is not the same as recording a transaction. You must record a transaction to have it appear in the appropriate register, print a check for it, or send an online payment instruction for it. Creating the reminder is only part of the job—the big part. You still have to make sure each transaction is entered in a timely manner. That's why I recommend using automatic entry and reminders whenever possible—so you don't forget to finish the transaction entry job.

Creating a Reminder

You create a scheduled transaction in Quicken with the Add Transaction Reminder dialog, which is shown in Figure 7-3. To open this dialog, choose Bills | Manage Reminders or press CTRL-J to display the All Bills & Deposits tab of the Bill and Income Reminders window. Then choose Scheduled Bill or Deposit from the Create New menu on the button bar.

I should mention here that there are a number of different versions of this dialog, depending on how you access it. For example, if you click the Add Bill button in the Bill Reminders area of the Setup tab's View subtab (shown next), the Add Bill Reminder dialog appears. Similarly, if you click the Add Other Income button in the Income and Transfer Reminders area (also shown next), the Add Income Reminder dialog appears. These dialogs and others like it all enable you to perform pretty much the same task: schedule a transaction. The Add Transaction Reminder dialog, however, makes it possible to schedule most kinds of transactions—simply select one of the Type options at the top of the dialog (refer to Figure 7-3)—while the other dialogs are for specific types of transactions.

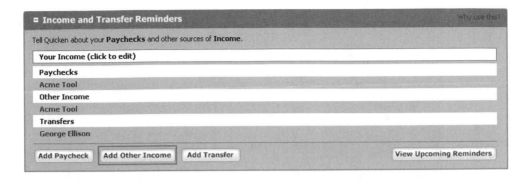

No matter which dialog you open, you can use it to enter information about the transaction, including the account, payee, category or transfer account, memo, and scheduling information. You can click the Split button to enter more than one category for the transaction. When you're finished setting up the transaction, click OK to save it.

The Add Transaction Reminder dialog has quite a few options, some of which don't appear elsewhere in Quicken. Here's a closer look at each of them.

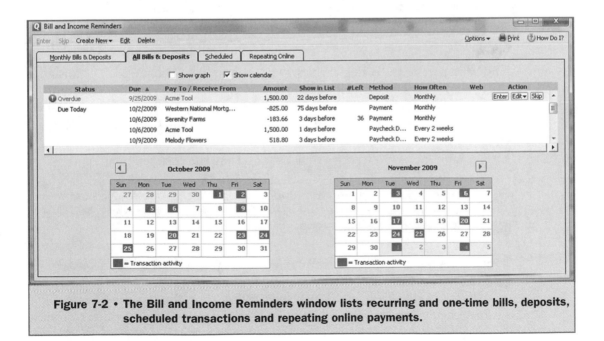

Figure 7-2 • The Bill and Income Reminders window lists recurring and one-time bills, deposits, scheduled transactions and repeating online payments.

Figure 7-3 • Use one of the three radio buttons along the top of the Add Transaction Reminder dialog to add transactions for bills, deposits, and other items.

Who

The Who part of the dialog enables you to specify who you are paying (for bill or payment), or who has paid you (for income, deposit, or transfer). You can enter text in the field or choose a QuickFill transaction from the drop-down list. Clicking the Address button enables you to enter an address for the person or entity in the field.

The Amount area offers two options for setting the transaction amount:

Fixed Amount The Fixed Amount option displays a text box you can use to enter a dollar amount that the transaction will always use. You can change the amount when the transaction is entered, if necessary.

Variable Amount The Variable Amount option enables you to estimate the amount. When you select this option, an estimate may appear beside a Change link. To set or change the estimate, click the link. This displays the Change Estimate dialog (shown next), which you can use to set variable amount options:

- **Do Not Estimate** tells Quicken not to display an estimated amount. This is the default option.
- **Estimated Amount** enables you to enter an estimated amount. This is useful for expenses that are always approximately the same, such as a cable television bill which may vary slightly from month to month.
- **Estimate From Last *N* Payments** enables you to specify how many previous transactions Quicken

should average to calculate an amount. This is a rolling average; Quicken's calculation will change every time the payment is made. If you select this option, be sure to enter the number of transactions Quicken should include for average calculation purposes. This is useful for bills that may vary from month to month on a trend, such as electricity or natural gas. Note that until you have entered the payment *N* times, the estimate may not be what you expect.

- **Estimate From One Year Ago** tells Quicken to estimate based on your payment to the same payee last year around the same time. This is useful for seasonal expenditures.
- **Use Full Credit Card Balance** tells Quicken to use the credit card account's balance when calculating a payment. This is especially useful for credit card accounts that must be paid in full when due, such as American Express. This option is available only if the transaction is to make a credit card payment.

When

The When area enables you to set transaction scheduling options. How you set these options determines when you will be reminded about the transaction. They can also make it possible for the transaction to be entered automatically.

Next Due Date   The next due date is the transaction date or the first date for a repeating transaction.

Reminder   The Reminder area enables you to set how far in advance you should be reminded about the transaction or whether Quicken should just enter it automatically. Click the Change link beside the reminder description to display a dialog like the one shown next. Set options as desired and click OK.

- **Remind Me *N* Days In Advance** enables you to set the number of days Quicken should remind you in advance. The default setting is 3.
- **Automatically Enter The Transaction In Register *N* Days Before The Due Date** lets you enter the number of days in advance that Quicken should automatically enter the transaction in the appropriate register.
- **Use Only Business Days For Reminder Days** excludes weekends and holidays from the calculation of the number of days in advance to remind you about or enter the transaction.

How Often?   Use the How Often? Options to set up a recurring transaction. First, choose an option from the drop-down list. Your options are Only Once, Weekly, Every Two Weeks, Twice A Month, Every Four Weeks, Monthly, Every Two Months, Quarterly, Twice A Year, Yearly, Estimated Tax (which follows the IRS estimated tax payment schedule), Variable Weeks, and Variable Months. Then set options in the area beneath the list; the options change based on the frequency you select.

End On   For a recurring transaction, you can click the Change link beside the end date to display the End Reminders dialog (shown next) to specify when the recurring transaction should end:

- **No End Date**, which is the default option, keeps the transaction scheduled until you delete it or set another option in this dialog.
- **End On** enables you to set a specific date for the last transaction.
- **End After *N* Reminders** enables you to specify the number of transactions before they automatically end.

How

The How area of the dialog enables you to set options that control how the payment, deposit, or transfer will be made. The options that appear vary depending on the type of transaction you are setting up a reminder for.

Pay From Account/Add To Account/From Account This is the account you will pay from (for a bill or payment), add funds to (for income or a deposit), or transfer money from (for a transfer). All accounts except hidden accounts, will appear in the drop-down list.

Payment Method For bills or payments, you can choose a payment method. The method you choose determines how the transaction will appear in your account register when it is entered, and it may trigger other Quicken features. You can choose from three options on the Payment Method drop-down list:

- **Manual Payment** records the transaction as a payment, which decreases the balance in a banking account. The Num field in the account register for the transaction remains blank; you can always fill it in later if desired. Use this option for handwritten checks or cash payments.
- **Online Bill Pay** records the transaction as an online payment, which decreases the balance in a banking account. The Num field in the account register is set to SEND, which signals Quicken to send the transaction with other payment instructions. If you choose this option, you can turn on the This Is A Repeating Online Payment check box to set up the payment as a repeating online payment. Learn more about repeating online payments in Chapter 6.
- **Print Check With Quicken** records the transaction as a payment using a check to be printed. This decreases the balance in a banking account. The Num field in the account register is set to PRINT, which signals Quicken to include the transaction with other checks to be printed. Use this option for scheduling transactions using Quicken's check printing feature, which Chapter 5 discussed in greater detail.

Delivery Method Quicken now enables you to specify a delivery method for bills, payments, income, deposits, or transfers. Use the Delivery Method drop-down list to choose from options such as Automatic, Bank Web Site, In Person, Mail, Other, or Payee Web site. Although this does not affect how Quicken records the transaction, it helps you keep track of how a transaction was completed.

Web Site This option enables you to enter the URL for the payee or payor's Web site. You can click the Go button beside the Web address to open the payee's site in your default Web browser.

Track Spending

The Track Spending area of the dialog enables you to set the category or account, tag, and memo for the transaction.

Category/Account For a bill, payment, income, or deposit, you can use the Category field to set the category or transfer account for the transaction. For a transfer transaction, this field becomes the Account field, which you can use to set the account that funds are being transferred into.

Tag If you have selected to display the Tag field, you can use the Tag drop-down list to assign a tag to the transaction. Using the tag feature of Quicken is completely optional.

Memo To provide just a little bit more detail about the transaction, you can enter a short note in the Memo field. This is also optional.

Viewing Reminders

Quicken displays reminders in four places: the Bills tab, the Manage Reminders window, the Bill and Income Reminder lists that appear in various places throughout Quicken, and the Bill Reminders areas in the Setup tab's View | Quicken Setup subtab. Here's a quick look at each.

The Bills Tab

Quicken's new interface includes a Bills tab, which you can use to view upcoming bills and other scheduled transactions in a number of different ways. Each view is a different look at your bills, with two options that appear in the Action Bar.

- Manage Reminders displays the Bill and Income Reminders window (refer to Figure 7-2).
- Add Reminder enables you to add a bill, income, paycheck, or transfer reminder as discussed earlier in this chapter.

The Bills tab has two subtabs:

Upcoming Timeline The Timeline subtab (Figure 7-4) shows each upcoming scheduled transaction with a note-like interface. Click one of the transaction buttons and its details appear in the middle of the window. Use the horizontal scroll bar at the bottom of the window to display upcoming transactions. You can use a transaction's buttons to Enter, Skip, or Edit the transaction. Clicking a Show History button displays a payment history for that payee.

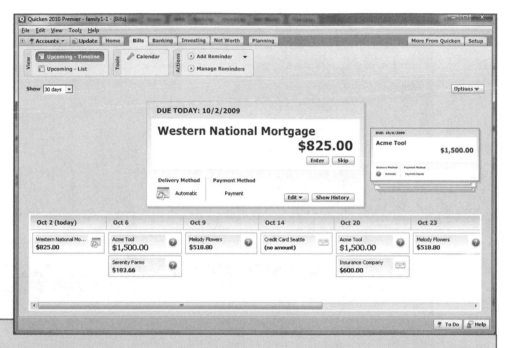

Figure 7-4 • Upcoming Timeline subtab of the Bills tab displays icons and details for upcoming scheduled transactions.

Upcoming List   This subtab (Figure 7-5) shows upcoming transactions in a list view. You can select a transaction and click a button in the Action column to work with it. The Show drop-down list enables you to select a time period of upcoming transactions to show.

Calendar   The Tools:Calendar subtab (Figure 7-6) shows all transactions in a calendar view that includes transactions and their amounts, as well as ending total banking account balance. You can use the arrows by the current month area to scroll through months. Learn more about how the Calendar works later in this chapter.

The Bills and Income Reminders Window

In the Bills tab, click Actions | Manage Reminders to open the Bill and Income Reminders window (refer to Figure 7-2) which displays current and future transactions. The Bill and Income Reminders window has four tabs that organize the transactions as discussed in "Window Tabs" below.

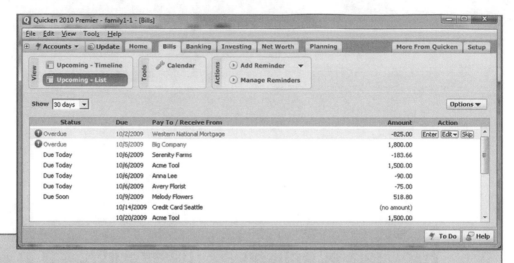

Figure 7-5 • The Upcoming – List subtab of the Bills tab lists upcoming transactions.

Figure 7-6 • The Bills tab's Tools:Calendar subtab shows bills on a calendar.

Transaction Button Bar Options You can use button bar options to create, edit, delete, or enter scheduled transactions:

- **Enter** opens the Enter Transaction dialog as shown here. Enter the appropriate information and click Enter Transaction.

- The **Edit** button to the right of a transaction displays a menu that allows you to modify the just the current transaction or this and all future transactions. If you choose to modify all future transactions, the Edit Bill Reminder dialog opens. The Edit Bill Reminder dialog is covered next.
- **Skip** enables you to skip the payment (or next payment) of that transaction.

Bill and Income Reminder Button Bar Options

- **Create New** enables you to create a new scheduled transaction or paycheck. Learn how to add a scheduled transaction earlier in this chapter and how to add a paycheck later in this chapter.
- **Edit** opens the Edit Bill Reminder dialog in which you can modify each area of the reminder as shown in Figure 7-7
- **Delete** removes the scheduled transaction. It does not remove any transactions that have already been entered in a register.
- **Options** offers commands for changing the way the Bill and Income Reminders window is sorted.
- **Print** prints a list of scheduled transactions.
- **How Do I?** displays the Quicken Personal Finances Help window with instructions for completing tasks with the Bill and Income Reminders window.

Window Tabs

- **All Bills & Deposits** (refer to Figure 7-2) displays all types of scheduled transactions.

Figure 7-7 • The Edit Bill Reminder dialog helps you change every part of your reminder.

Figure 7-8 • The All Bills & Deposits tab of the Bill and Income Reminders window shows you both overdue and current bills.

- **Monthly Bills & Deposits** (see Figure 7-8) displays all transactions for the month. You can click the arrows beside the name of the month to view transactions for other months.
- **Scheduled** (see Figure 7-8) displays the deposits and payments that have been scheduled for this month.
- **Repeating Online** (see Figure 7-8) lists repeating payments you have scheduled to be paid online.

Display Check Boxes Two check boxes enable you to display additional information in the window, as shown in Figures 7-2 and 7-8.

- **Show Graph** displays a column chart showing cash flow for a selected account for the month.
- **Show Calendar** displays one or two calendars that indicate dates on which transactions will be made.

Bill and Income Reminders Lists

Bill and Income Reminders lists appear in a number of places throughout Quicken. For example:

- The Home tab can display a complete list of Bill and Income Reminders. You can click a button beside each transaction to enter, edit, or skip it. You can also display a small graph and calendar to indicate total account balance and transaction dates. Learn how to customize the Home tab in Appendix B.
- Each account register window can include a Bill and Income Reminders list, like the one shown next. The list includes only the transactions scheduled for that account. You can click a button beside each transaction to enter, edit, or skip it. If this list does not appear in the bottom of a register window, click the Bill and Income Reminders tab to display it. If you don't see the tab, click Edit | Preferences | Quicken Preferences | Download Transactions, and clear the Automatically Add Downloaded Transactions To Registers check box.

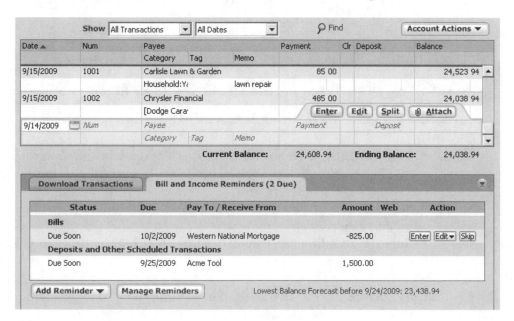

Buttons and Menu Commands The Bill and Income Reminders lists often include several buttons at the bottom of the list and may include an Options menu at the top of the list. You can use these buttons and menu commands to get more information about transactions, display the Bill and Income Reminders List window, add scheduled transactions, or set up a paycheck. The options that appear vary depending on where the list appears within Quicken.

Schedule These? The Schedule These? list in a Bill and Income Reminders list, when present, displays transactions that Quicken "thinks" you might want to schedule for the future. It builds this list based on categories used in the transactions or transactions you have entered more than once. Here are a few things you can do to work with this list:

- To schedule a transaction in the list, click the Yes button beside it. Quicken displays the Edit Bill Reminder dialog so you can turn the transaction into a scheduled transaction.
- To remove a transaction from the list, click the No button beside it.

Calendar

Quicken's Calendar keeps track of all your transactions—past and future—by date. Quicken's calendar appears on the Bills and Banking tabs' Action Bars in the Tools subtab (refer to Figure 7-6). You may also open the calendar from Tools | Calendar, or by pressing CTRL-K.

Calendar Button Bar Options You can use button bar options to work with the window's contents:

- **Go To Date** enables you to go to a specific calendar date. Click the calendar icon and use the tiny calendar that appears to locate and select the date you want. Or enter the date in the edit box and click the Go button.
- **Arrow** buttons on either side of the month name enable you to move from one month to another.
- **Add Note** enables you to enter a note for the selected date. The note you enter appears on the calendar (refer to the September 17 box in Figure 7-6). To view a note, click it.
- **Options** offers commands for viewing and working with the contents of the Calendar window.
- **Print** prints the Calendar.
- **Help** displays the Quicken Personal Finances Help window with information about using the Calendar.

The Transactions Window When you double-click a calendar date (or single-click a selected date), the Transactions window, which lists all the transactions for that date, appears:
    You can use buttons in the window to work with transactions:

- **Add** enables you to enter a new transaction or create a new scheduled transaction. The dialog that appears when you click this button offers all the options of the Add Scheduled Transaction dialog shown earlier.

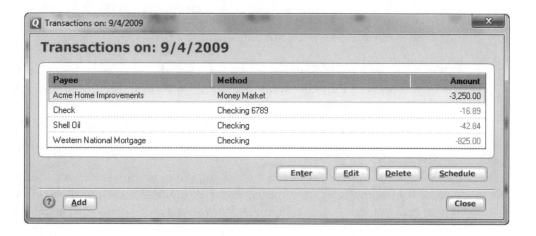

- **Enter** takes you to the currently selected transaction in the appropriate account register, if the transaction has already been entered, and enters the transaction in the register if it has not already been entered into the register.
- **Edit** enables you to modify the currently selected transaction.
- **Delete** removes the selected transaction. This option is only available for transactions that have already been entered.
- **Skip** lets you skip the transaction for this date. This option is only available for transactions that have not been entered.
- **Schedule** enables you to create a new scheduled transaction based on the selected transaction. This option is only available if the currently selected transaction is not a scheduled transaction.
- **Close** closes the window.

Account Balances   The dollar amounts that appear in the bottom of each calendar date box show the total account balances for the accounts displayed in the window, taking all payments into consideration. (You can specify which accounts to include by choosing Select Calendar Accounts from the Options menu in the button bar.) This feature works, in effect, like a simplified forecasting tool. Learn how to use Quicken's more powerful Cash Flow Forecast feature in Chapter 17.

Working with Reminders

Scheduling a transaction was the hard part. (Not very hard, though, was it?) Entering, editing, and skipping a scheduled transaction is easy. Here's one way—in my opinion, the quickest and easiest—to work with reminders.

Click the Bills tab and then click the Upcoming – Timeline button to display that subtab (refer to Figure 7-4). Click the button for the transaction you want to work with in the scrolling horizontal list at the bottom of the window. Then use buttons for the transaction in the main part of the window to work with the transaction:

Enter The Enter button displays the Enter Transaction dialog, which is shown next. Use this dialog to finalize settings for a transaction. When you click Enter Transaction, the transaction is entered into the account register.

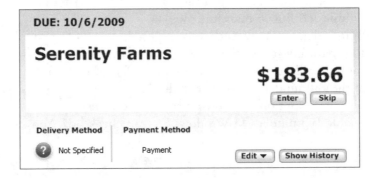

Skip The Skip button skips the transaction. When you click this button, a confirmation dialog appears, asking if you want to skip the transaction that is due and telling you when the next transaction will be due. Click Yes to skip it. The transaction moves down in the list and its due date changes to the next due date.

Edit The Edit button displays the Edit Transaction Reminder dialog, which looks and works very much like the Add Transaction Reminder dialog, shown earlier in Figure 7-3. Use this dialog to modify settings for the transaction's future entries. If the transaction is an instance of a recurring transaction, the Edit button appears as a menu with two options:

- **Only This Instance** displays the Edit Reminder dialog that enables you to change the date and amount of the transaction.
- **This And All Future Reminders** displays the Edit Transaction Reminder dialog, as discussed earlier.

Billminder

Quicken's Billminder feature makes it possible for you to monitor upcoming bills and scheduled transactions without starting Quicken. Let's take a quick look at it.

Quicken Billminder

The Quicken Billminder application, as seen in Figure 7-9, displays a window that summarizes upcoming transactions, as shown next. It also includes a convenient button to run Quicken, should you decide to take action on a listed item.

To open Billminder, you can choose Start | All Programs | Quicken 2010 | Billminder. But to make the most of Billminder, you may want to configure it so it automatically starts each time you start your computer. To do this, click the Options button in the Billminder button bar to display Billminder options as shown next. Turn on the Enable Billminder On Windows Startup check box. You can set other

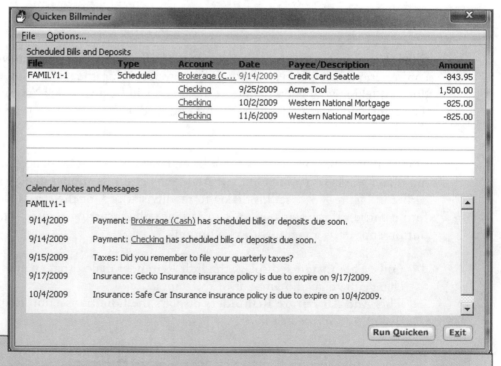

Figure 7-9 • The Billminder can help you remember scheduled bills and deposits.

configuration options as desired to determine when Billminder should appear. Then click OK.

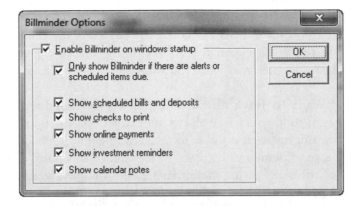

Using Paycheck Setup

Quicken's Paycheck Setup feature offers yet another way to automate transactions. You use it to enter information about your regular payroll check and its deductions. Then, when payday comes along, Quicken automatically enters the payroll deposit information based on the Paycheck Setup transaction.

Although you can use Paycheck Setup to record payroll checks with varying amounts and deductions—such as a check with varying hourly wages or overtime pay—it can be a real timesaver if your paycheck is the same (or almost the same) every payday. If your paycheck does vary, be sure to include all possible deductions, even if their values are often zero. Then it'll be easy to just plug in different values when you need to.

Getting Started

Start by choosing Setup | Income and Transfer Reminders | Add Paycheck. The Paycheck Setup dialog appears. You can also open the Planning tab, click View | Tax Center | Taxable Income YTD | Add Paycheck or Edit Paycheck Note that from the Planning tab, if you have already set up a paycheck, following these instructions displays the Manage Paychecks dialog, which is discussed later in the section titled "Managing Paychecks."

Click New from the Manage Paychecks dialog to display the Paycheck Setup dialog and create a new paycheck. If you entered net payroll information for a paycheck when you created your Quicken data file, you can use this dialog to access and modify the paycheck you created to add detailed payroll information.

The first screen of the Paycheck Setup dialog provides general information about Paycheck Setup and how it works. Click Next to begin.

The first thing Quicken wants to know is whether the paycheck is yours or your spouse's (if applicable) and what the company name is. It uses this information to properly categorize the payroll deductions in each paycheck and to give the paycheck a name. After entering this information, click Next.

Next, Quicken asks what you want to track. You have two options:

- **I Want To Track All Earnings, Taxes, And Deductions** tells Quicken you want to keep track of all payroll deductions when recording a paycheck. This option makes it possible to take advantage of Quicken's tax planning features, which is discussed in Part Six of this book. If you select this option, continue following the instructions in the next section, "Tracking All Earnings and Deductions," after clicking Next.
- **I Want To Track Net Deposits Only** tells Quicken that you just want to track the net take-home pay, not the gross pay and deductions. This option makes setting up a paycheck a bit quicker, but it doesn't tap into Quicken's full power for automatically recording detailed information. If you select this option, continue following the instructions in the section titled "Tracking Net Deposits Only" after clicking Next.

Tracking All Earnings and Deductions

When you indicate that you want to track all earnings and deductions, Quicken displays the Set Up Paycheck dialog (see Figure 7-10). Use this dialog to enter detailed information about the paycheck. It's a good idea to have a recent pay stub on hand when entering information because you'll want it to be as accurate as possible.

Setting Options

Start with the following information:

Account Use the Account drop-down list to choose the account to which the net pay will be deposited. If the check will be deposited to more than one account—for example, if part of the paycheck is deposited to a company credit union savings account—make sure you add the other account and indicate how much is deposited to each account in the Deposit Accounts area near the bottom of the dialog (refer to Figure 7-10).

Start On Enter the date of the next paycheck (or the current paycheck, if you plan to enter this one after setting it up) in the Start On field.

Frequency Use the Frequency drop-down list to indicate how often you receive the paycheck. Then set options, if necessary, to specify dates. The options that appear vary depending on the Frequency you select.

Entry Options Select one of the two entry options in the Scheduling area and set the number of days in advance to enter the transaction. The entry options on the drop-down list are:

- **Remind Me** includes the paycheck in Bill and Income Reminders lists as a reminder to enter the transaction. You may want to use this option if the paycheck's amounts vary each payday or if you have the nasty habit of not depositing your paycheck on the day you get it.
- **Automatically Enter** automatically enters the paycheck in the appropriate account register when it's due. This is the best option to select if the paycheck is the same each payday, especially if you have direct deposit and you know the funds will be deposited on time.

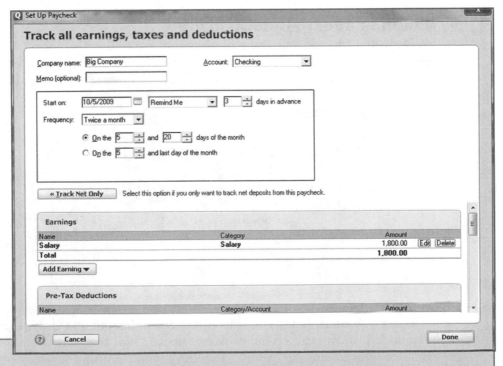

Figure 7-10 • You can use the Set Up Paycheck dialog to enter all details for your paycheck.

Entering Amounts

You can enter an amount by clicking the default amount (0.00) and typing in a replacement value. Or, if you prefer, you can click the Edit button beside an item to display an Edit dialog, which you can use to enter information.

To add another type of item to the dialog, use the Add pop-up menu in the appropriate section. (You can see some examples of the pop-up menus in the next illustration.) For example, to add a pretax deduction, display the Add Pre-Tax Deduction pop-up menu and choose an option. Then enter the details for that item in the dialog that appears. This may seem like a lot of work, but once the paycheck is set up properly, Quicken will take over and do all the hard work for you.

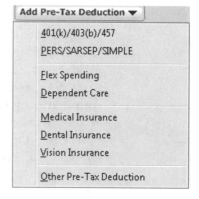

Scroll through the entire pay stub and enter all deductions into the dialog. When you're finished, the Net Pay amount at the bottom of the dialog should match your take-home pay amount.

Entering Year-to-Date Amounts

When you click Done, Quicken displays a dialog asking if you want to enter year-to-date information as shown next. If year-to-date totals appear on the pay stub you used to set up the paycheck, I highly recommend entering this information so all the earnings and deduction information for the current year is included in your Quicken data file.

Select I Want To Enter The Year-To-Date Information and click OK. The Paycheck Year-To-Date Amounts dialog appears. Edit the values in the Year To Date column by clicking each one to select it and entering a replacement value. When you're finished, click Enter.

Tracking Net Deposits Only

When you indicate that you want to track just the net payroll deposits, Quicken displays a Set Up Paycheck dialog. Use this dialog to enter information about the amount you expect to deposit. If you're not sure what the amount will be—like my royalty checks, which vary from one quarter to the next—you can leave the Amount field set to 0.00; if you do so, don't tell Quicken to enter the paycheck without prompting you, or it will enter 0 each payday!

Be sure to set the correct options throughout the dialog, especially in the Scheduling area. These options are discussed earlier in this chapter, in the section titled "Setting Other Options." When you're finished, click Done.

Managing Paychecks

Once you have at least one paycheck set up, you can use the Manage Paychecks dialog to modify it, delete it, or add another. Choose Planning | View:Tax Center | Taxable Income YTD | Edit Paycheck button. The Manage Paychecks dialog, which is shown next, appears. It lists all paychecks that have been set up in Quicken. You can use the buttons on the bottom of the dialog to work with paychecks.

New The New button displays the Paycheck Setup dialog, discussed earlier in this chapter, so you can set up a paycheck.

Edit The Edit button displays the Edit Future Paychecks dialog for the currently selected paycheck. This dialog looks and works much like the Set Up Paycheck dialogs shown earlier. Use it to modify the paycheck setup for all future paychecks. Making changes in this dialog does not modify recorded paycheck transactions.

Delete   The Delete button deletes the selected paycheck. This does not delete any paycheck transactions already recorded—just the scheduled paycheck transaction. You'll have to click Yes in a confirmation dialog to remove the paycheck from Quicken.

Entering Paycheck Transactions

Entering a paycheck transaction is just as easy as entering a scheduled transaction. Display a Bill and Income Reminders list in which the paycheck appears, then click the Enter button beside the paycheck. The Edit Current Paycheck And Enter Into Register dialog appears. It displays all of the information you entered when you set up the paycheck. Modify values and options as necessary and click Enter. The paycheck's information is recorded.

Address Book

Quicken's Address Book feature automatically stores the address information you enter when using the Write Checks window. You can also use this feature to modify or delete existing information or add new records. Keeping track of addresses with the Address Book makes it easy to insert addresses when writing checks and to look up contact information when you need to follow up on transactions.

Displaying the Address Book Window

Choose Tools | Address Book to display the Address Book window (see Figure 7-11). It lists all the records in the Address Book.

You can use button bar buttons and menus to work with Address Book window contents:

- **New** enables you to create a new Address Book record.
- **Edit** enables you to edit the selected record.
- **Delete** removes the Address Book record. It does not affect transactions in which the record was used.
- **Modify** offers several commands for modifying the selected record or selecting multiple records.
- **Sort** enables you to change the order of records in the window.

Figure 7-11 • Use the Address Book to keep track of the organizations and individuals you do business with.

- **Print** offers commands for printing Address Book record information.
- **How Do I?** displays the Quicken Personal Finances Help window with instructions for working with the Address Book.

Adding or Modifying Address Book Records

To add a new Address Book record, click New on the button bar of the Address Book window. The Edit Address Book Record dialog, which is shown next, appears.

You can also use the Edit Address Book Record dialog to edit an existing record. Simply select the record in the Address Book window and click the Edit button in the button bar.

The Edit Address Book Record dialog has five tabs for record information. Click a tab to display its options, and then enter the information you want to store. Here's what you can enter in each of the five tabs:

- **Payee** is for the information that would normally appear in a Write Check window, as well as some additional contact information.
- **Contact** is for the name, title, phone numbers, and Web site of a specific person.
- **Secondary** is for a secondary mailing address and e-mail address.
- **Personal** is for personal information, such as spouse and children's names, birthday and anniversary, and still more phone numbers.
- **Miscellaneous** is for additional information, such as user-defined fields and notes.

Printing Entry Information

You can print the information in the list in three formats: list, labels, and envelopes.

Start by selecting a record and the Group drop-down list at the top of the Address Book window to display the records that you want to print. Click Print to open a drop-down list of printing options.

If you want to change the format of a specific record, choose that record and click Format to open the Format Print Check Address dialog as seen here. Set the options and click OK.

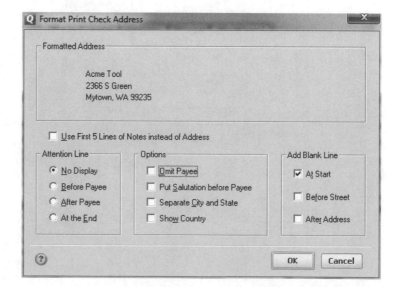

List Choosing List displays a Print dialog just like the one that appears when printing Quicken reports. Use it to enter printing options, and then click OK to print the list. Consult Chapter 9 for more information about printing lists and reports.

Labels Choosing Labels displays the Print Labels dialog. It includes a list of commonly used Avery label products; be sure to select the right one before you click the Print button to print. To print a sheet of return address labels, choose an address from the drop-down list in the Return Address area and select the Return Address (Whole Sheet) option in the Print Selection area.

Envelopes Choosing Envelopes displays the Print Envelope dialog. Use it to print #10 envelopes for Address Book records. Just set options in the dialog, put envelope stock into your printer, and click the Print button.

One Step Update and the Password Vault

As discussed in Chapters 6 and 10, the Bank Account Update, Portfolio Export, and WebEntry features use One Step Update to update information on the Web and download transactions entered on the Web. But that's not all One Step Update can do. This feature makes it possible to handle many of your connection chores at once. When used in conjunction with the Password Vault feature, you can click a few buttons, enter a single password, and take a break while Quicken updates portfolio and account information for you. You can even schedule updates to occur automatically when Quicken isn't running.

Using One Step Update

The idea behind One Step Update is to use one command to handle multiple online activities. This eliminates the need to use update commands in a variety of locations throughout Quicken. One command does it all.

Setting Up the Update

Choose Tools | One Step Update or click the Update button in the Account Bar. If a dialog appears, asking if you want to set up the Password Vault, click No for now; I explain how to use this feature later in this chapter, in the section titled "The Password Vault." The One Step Update dialog, which is shown in Figure 7-12, appears. It lists all of the items that can be updated. Check marks appear for each item that will be updated when you connect. You can click the check boxes to toggle the check marks there.

Figure 7-12 • Use the One Step Update dialog to set up and start a One Step Update online session.

The dialog is split into three areas:

Download Quotes, Asset Classes, Headlines and Alerts This area offers one option to download security quotes, asset classes, financial headlines, and security-related alerts. You can select which quotes should be downloaded by clicking the Select Quotes link. Learn more about downloading quotes in Chapter 11.

Financial Institutions The Financial Institutions area lists all the financial institutions for which online account services have been enabled. Your list will differ from the one shown here—unless you have the same financial institutions I have! You can enter your password in a box to the right of each institution name when you're ready to update your data. Note that this part of the dialog scrolls; be sure to scroll down if necessary to set options for financial institutions at the bottom of the list.

Quicken.com   The Quicken.com area lists activities for uploading or exporting your Quicken data with Quicken.com. You can customize these options by clicking the Select Quicken.com Data To Update link. The options include several tabs:

- The **Quotes** dialog helps you to tell Quicken what to download for selected stock symbols. Part 3 discusses investing. You have several buttons from which to choose:

- New Security opens a dialog in which you can enter either a ticker symbol or stock name. Quicken downloads the latest quote for this security. Note here that all quotes are delayed at least 20 minutes.
- Edit Security opens the Edit Security Detail dialog in which you can modify the details of your security as seen on the top of the next page.
- The Lookup Symbol button connects you to the Quicken.com where you can find the ticker symbol for a security by typing in the name.
- The Mark All and Clear All buttons select or unselect the securities on the Quotes list.

- **Portfolio** tab opens a dialog in which you can tell Quicken how to update your investment information. Part 3 discusses investing.
    - You may check or clear the check box to Track My Watch List in Quicken.com
    - Click Send My Shares to track the value of your current holdings
    - Click Send Only My Symbols if you want general information about your stock holdings
- The **Connection** tab gives you several options when updating with Quicken.
    - Quicken Usage Study sends product usage only, no personal information, to Quicken to be used for program improvements.
    - One Step Update can be chosen to run One Step Update when Quicken Starts
    - Quicken.com Login helps you manage your Quicken.com password and member information.

Updating Information

Make sure check marks appear beside the items you want to update in the One Step Update dialog. If necessary, enter passwords in the text boxes beside financial institutions for which you want to update data. Then click Update Now. If Quicken offers to save your passwords, click No for now. Learn how to use the Password Vault feature later in this chapter. Quicken establishes a connection to the Internet and begins transferring data.

When the update is complete, the One Step Update Summary dialog appears. As shown in Figure 7-13, it summarizes the activity for the update. Click the disclosure triangles to the left of financial institution names to reveal a list of accounts and activity. You can click the name of an account in the window to go to that account's register, or click the Close button at the bottom of the window to dismiss it.

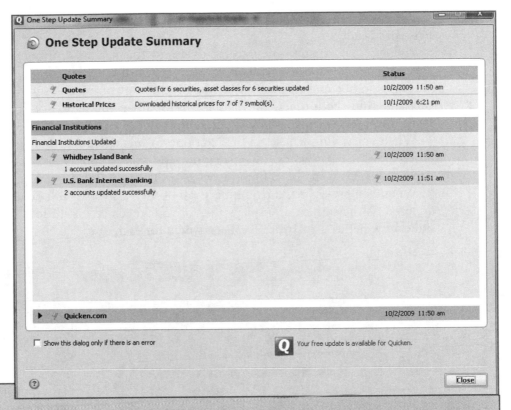

Figure 7-13 • **The One Step Update Settings dialog displays all your chosen activity for the One Step Update process.**

The Password Vault

You might find it a nuisance to have to type in each password when you use the One Step Update feature—especially if you connect to more than one or two financial institutions. This is when the Password Vault can help.

Quicken's Password Vault feature enables you to store all your financial institution passwords in one central location. The passwords are then protected with a single password. When you use One Step Update, you enter just one password to access all financial institutions. You must have Online Account Access or Online Payment set up with at least one institution to use the Password Vault feature.

Setting Up the Password Vault

Choose Tools | Online Center | Password Vault or Tools | Password Vault | Setup New Password Vault. The Password Vault Setup dialog appears. It provides some introductory information. Click Next to display the first window of the Password Vault Setup

Follow the instructions in each tab to choose financial institutions and enter corresponding passwords. You'll enter each password twice because the characters you type do not appear onscreen; this is a secure way of making sure you enter the same thing both times. You can do this for any combination of financial institutions for which you have set up online access.

When you've finished, select the No option when asked whether you want to enter additional passwords. The dialog prompts you to enter a password to protect the Password Vault. Enter it twice in the boxes and click Next.

When you click Next, the Summary tab of the Password Vault Setup window appears. As shown next, it displays a list of your financial institutions and indicates whether a password has been stored for each one.

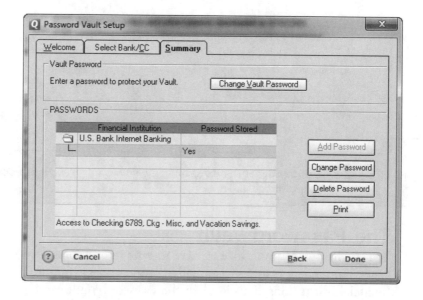

You can use buttons in this dialog to change or delete a selected password, print all passwords, or change the Vault password. When you've finished working with the window's contents, click Done. Quicken creates the Password Vault.

Using the Password Vault

Using the Password Vault is easy. Simply choose Tools | One Step Update or click the Update button in the Account Bar. You will no longer be prompted for any passwords. Simply continue using One Step Update in the usual way with one difference: you don't have to enter passwords for any of the financial institutions for which a password has been entered in the Password Vault.

You can also use the Password Vault in conjunction with the Update/Send button in the Online Center window, which is discussed in Chapters 6 and 11. Clicking that button automatically displays the Vault Password dialog. Enter your password and click OK; Quicken performs the update.

Editing the Password Vault

Once you've created a Password Vault, you can modify it to change passwords or add passwords for other financial institutions. Choose Tools| Password Vault | Add or Edit Passwords. In the Edit Password Vault dialog that appears, click the Change Vault Password button to change the password to your Password Vault. Click Change Password to change the passwords for any account. Click Delete Password to delete an account's password. When you've finished, click Done.

Deleting the Password Vault

You can delete the Password Vault if you decide you no longer want to use it. Choose Tools | Password Vault | Delete Vault and All Saved Passwords. Then click Yes in the confirmation dialog that appears. Quicken deletes the Password Vault. From then on, you'll have to enter passwords for each financial institution when you use One Step Update.

Scheduling Updates

You can schedule updates to occur when you're not using Quicken. Then, when you start Quicken, your data file is already updated with information from your financial institutions, and, if you've disabled automatic transaction download, ready to review and accept into your account registers. Your Quicken.com information can also be automatically updated based on information in your Quicken data file.

Setting Up the Schedule

To set up a schedule, begin by choosing Tools | Schedule Updates. The Schedule Updates dialog, which is shown on the top of the next page, appears. Set options in each area of the dialog and click OK.

Here's a look at each of the options:

Items To Schedule The Items To Schedule area lists all of the items in the One Step Update dialog discussed earlier in this chapter. Click to toggle check marks beside each item you want to include in the schedule.

Schedule The Schedule area determines when the updates will occur. Turn on check boxes for each day of the week you want the updates to occur, and then

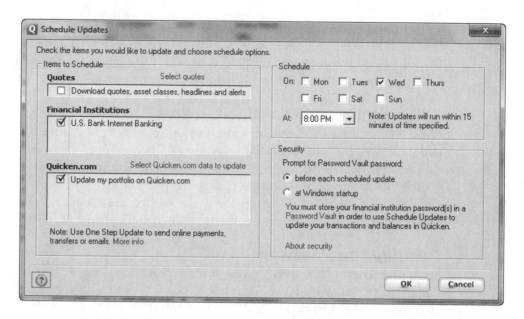

choose a time from the At drop-down list. Since your computer must be running for the updates to take place, set options for when you know your computer will be turned on. Updates will not occur, however, if Quicken is running; this ensures that the automated feature does not interrupt your work with Quicken.

Security Security options enable you to indicate when your computer should prompt you for the Password Vault password. (The Password Vault feature must be set up and used in conjunction with scheduled updates.) You have two options:

- **Before Each Scheduled Update** displays the Password Vault Password dialog just before each update. You may want to select this option if the update is scheduled for a time when you expect to be at work on your computer. This is a more secure option, since it requires you to be present just before the update takes place. If you're not around, however, the update will not take place as scheduled.
- **At Windows Startup** displays the Password Vault Password dialog when you start Windows. This option can make scheduled updates more convenient, since you don't have to be around when they occur.

Using the Schedule

Using the schedule is easy. First you must exit Quicken, since a scheduled update will not occur when Quicken is running. Eventually, the Vault Password dialog will appear. When it appears depends on the schedule and security options you set. Enter your password in the dialog and click Update. Quicken does the rest.

Changing the Schedule

To change the schedule, choose Tools | Schedule Updates to display the Schedule Updates dialog. Make changes in the dialog as desired to modify settings. To cancel scheduled updates, turn off the check boxes beside each day of the week. When you're finished making changes, click OK.

Reconciling Your Accounts

Chapter 8

In This Chapter:

- *Starting a reconciliation*
- *Comparing transactions*
- *Making adjustments*
- *Reconciling credit card accounts*
- *Printing a reconciliation report*
- *Identifying reconciled items*

One of the least pleasant tasks of manually maintaining a bank account is balancing or reconciling it monthly. If you're good about it, you faithfully open your bank statement each month and use the form your bank provides to balance the account. There's a lot of adding when it comes to totaling the outstanding checks and deposits, and the longer you wait to do the job, the more adding you'll need to do. And for some reason, it hardly ever comes out right the first time you try. Maybe you've even failed so many times that you've given up. I knew someone who'd open a new checking account once a year just so she could start fresh after 12 months of not being able to balance her account. That's *not* something I recommend.

In this chapter, I explain why you should reconcile your bank statements and how you can do it—quickly and easily—with Quicken Personal Finance Software.

Reconciling Bank Accounts

Reconciling an account refers to the process of comparing transactions in your account register to transactions on the account statement sent to you by your bank. Transactions that match are simply checked off. Transactions that appear only in one place—your account register or the bank's account statement—need to be accounted for.

In this section, I cover the basics of reconciling a bank account with Quicken: comparing transactions, making adjustments, and finishing up.

Getting Started

To reconcile a bank account, you must have the statement for the account. Bank statements usually come monthly, so you won't have to wait long.

With statement in hand, open the account register for the account you want to reconcile. Click the Account Action button on the Action Bar and choose Reconcile. What happens next depends on whether the account is enabled for online access.

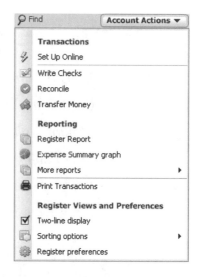

Accounts Without Online Account Access

If the account is not enabled for online access, the Statement Summary dialog, which is shown next, appears. It gathers basic statement information prior to reconciling the account. Enter information from your bank statement in the appropriate boxes. (Enter service charge and interest earned information only if you have not already entered it in the account register.) Then click OK to continue.

What Does This Mean to You? Reconciling Accounts

Stop right there! Read this!

I know you were about to skip this chapter. But don't do it. Here's why.

Reconciling your checking account is important. It helps you locate differences between what you think you have in the account and what the bank says you have. It can help you track down bank errors (which do happen once in a while) or personal errors (which, unfortunately, seem to happen more frequently). Completely balancing your checking account and making adjustments as necessary can prevent you from accidentally bouncing checks when you think you have more money than you really do. That can save you the cost of bank fees and a lot of embarrassment.

If you keep track of all bank account activity with Quicken, reconciling your bank accounts is easy. You don't need to use the form on the back of the bank statement. You don't even need a calculator. Just use Quicken's reconciliation feature to enter beginning and ending balances, check off cleared transactions, and enter the transactions you missed. You'll find you're successful a lot more often with Quicken helping you out.

You can use Quicken's reconciliation feature to balance any Quicken cash flow account—including credit card accounts. Although this chapter concentrates on checking accounts, I provide additional information for reconciling credit card accounts, too.

So stifle that yawn and keep reading!

Accounts with Online Account Access

If the account is enabled for online account access, Quicken may begin by displaying a dialog that reminds you to download recent transactions or compare downloaded transactions to transactions in your register. If so, be sure to do this; it's the only way you can be sure that all transactions recorded by the bank are included in your account register.

Quicken displays the Reconcile Online Account dialog:

As you can see, this dialog offers two options for reconciling the account:

- **Paper Statement** enables you to reconcile the information in your Quicken account register to your bank statement. It is a traditional account reconciliation, and it works just like the account reconciliation you perform for an account without online account access. If you select this option, you must enter the bank statement ending date and ending balance in the appropriate boxes.
- **Online Balance** enables you to reconcile the account to the balance that was last downloaded for the account. If you select this option, you don't have to enter anything in the boxes. Turning on the Auto Reconcile After Compare To Register check box tells Quicken to reconcile the account to your financial institution's online balance automatically each time you download and accept transactions. With this Auto Reconcile feature enabled, you never have to reconcile the account again.

After setting options in this dialog, click OK to continue.

Comparing Transactions

The next step in reconciling the account is to compare transactions that have cleared on the statement with transactions in your account register. For this, Quicken displays the Statement Summary window (shown in Figure 8-1), which displays all payments, checks, and deposits.

You can use button bar buttons within this window to work with its contents:

- **New** switches you to the account register window for the account you are reconciling so you can enter a new transaction.
- **Edit** switches you to the selected transaction in its account register window so you can modify it.
- **Delete** removes the selected transaction from the account register.
- **Back To Statement Summary** displays the Statement Summary dialog shown earlier or the Reconcile Paper Statement dialog (which is similar to the top half of the Reconcile Online Account dialog shown earlier) so you can check or change entries there.
- **View** offers options to change the sort order of the window's contents.
- **How Do I?** displays the Quicken Personal Finances Help window with instructions for reconciling accounts.

Figure 8-1 • Use the Statement Summary window to compare your register transactions to your bank statement transactions.

Reconciling to a Bank Statement

Your job is to check off the items in the window that also appear on your bank statement. While you're checking off items, be sure to check off the same items with a pen or pencil on your bank statement.

If the account is enabled for online account access and you have been downloading and comparing transactions regularly to accept them into your account register, many of the transactions in the Reconcile Bank Statement window may already be checked off. This speeds up the reconciliation process.

While you're checking off transactions in Quicken and on your bank statement, look for differences between them. Here are some of the differences you might encounter:

- An item that appears on the bank statement but not in your account register is an item that you did not enter. You may have omitted the transaction for a number of reasons. Perhaps it was a bank adjustment that you were not informed about. Or maybe you simply forgot to enter a check. To enter an omitted transaction, click New on the button bar to switch to the register window. Enter the transaction in the register, click Enter, and click the Return To Reconcile button to continue the reconciliation. Then click to place a check mark in the Clr column beside the item to mark it cleared.

- An item that appears on both your account register and bank statement but has a different amount or date could be due to an error—yours or the bank's. If the error is yours, you can edit the transaction by double-clicking it in the Reconcile Bank Statement window. This displays the account register window with the transaction selected. Edit the transaction and click the Enter button. Then click the Return To Reconcile button to continue the reconciliation.
- Items that appear in your account register but not on the bank statement are items that have not yet cleared the bank. These are usually transactions prepared just before the bank's closing date, but they can be older. Do not check them off. Chances are, you'll check them off the next time you complete a reconciliation. If, during a bank reconciliation, you discover any uncleared items that are older than two or three months, you should investigate why they have not cleared the bank. You may discover that a check (or worse yet, a deposit) was lost in transit.

Reconciling to an Online Balance

If you've recently downloaded and accepted transactions for the account, reconciling to an online balance shouldn't take much effort. Items you've already reviewed and accepted will be checked off. Some more recent transactions may not be checked off because they haven't cleared your bank yet. Your job is to look for older transactions that appear in your Quicken account register that aren't checked off. These could represent stale payments that may have been lost in transit to the payee or errors (or duplications) you made when manually entering information into your Quicken account register. Follow up on all transactions more than 60 days old to see why they haven't been included with your downloaded transactions.

Finishing Up

When you reconcile a bank account with Quicken, your goal is to make the difference between the Cleared Balance and the Statement Ending Balance zero. You can monitor this progress at the bottom of the Statement Summary window, as shown in Figure 8-1.

When the Difference Is Zero

If you correctly checked off all bank statement items and the difference is zero, you've successfully reconciled the account. Congratulations. Click the Finished button.

If You Can't Get the Difference to Zero

Sometimes, try as you might, you just can't get the difference to zero. Here are a few last things to check before you give up:

- Make sure all the amounts you checked off in your account register are the same as the amounts on the bank statement. Keep in mind that if you made a transposition error—for example, 19 instead of 91—the difference will be evenly divisible by 9.
- Make sure you included any bank charges or earned interest.
- Make sure the beginning and ending balances you entered are the same as those on the bank statement.

If you checked and rechecked all these things and still can't get the difference to zero, click Finished. Quicken displays a dialog like the one shown here that indicates the amount of the difference and offers to make an adjustment to your account register for the amount. Click Adjust to accept the adjustment. The amount of the adjustment will be recorded without a category.

But next month, don't give up!

First-Time Reconciliations

A while back, I was contacted by a reader who was having difficulties understanding how to reconcile an account for the first time. He seemed to think he needed to come up with some kind of "plug figure" to get the reconciliation to work. He hadn't even *tried* performing the reconciliation, too worried about what *might* happen. Oddly enough, he was an accountant. I suspect that he was over-thinking the situation, but I understand what he was concerned about and decided to address it in the book.

Suppose you have a checking account that you've been using for several years. Recently, you purchased and installed Quicken. You followed my instructions to set up your checking account as a Quicken account, using the ending balance on your most recent bank statement—say it was dated 7/11/09—as the beginning balance in the account. After setting up the account, you entered all transactions dated after 7/11/09 into the account register.

August rolls along and you receive your 8/12/09 bank statement. Following the instructions in this chapter, you reconcile the account for the first time. But you discover that the 8/12/09 bank statement includes checks you wrote *before* 8/11/09 that were outstanding (had not cleared the bank) as of the 7/11/09 bank statement. If you don't consider these transactions in your reconciliation, there is a difference between the cleared balance and the statement ending balance. What do you do about these transactions?

This is what was confusing my accountant friend. He thought he needed to make some kind of adjusting entry in Quicken *before* starting the reconciliation. Instead, consider the following two options:

- If you want to record the transactions in your Quicken data file—perhaps to make charges to categories more complete—record them. You can do this during the reconciliation by clicking the New button on the Statement Summary window's button bar (refer to Figure 8-1). I explain how earlier in this chapter. Once the transactions have been entered, be sure to check them off in the Statement Summary window. The difference should go away.
- If you don't want to record the transactions—perhaps you don't care about the categories that would be affected—let Quicken make an adjusting entry for you at the end of the reconciliation. That's the "plug figure" my accountant friend was looking for. He didn't realize that Quicken would take care of it for him.

Once that first reconciliation is complete, you should have no further problems—unless, of course, the 9/12/09 bank statement includes one or more very old checks from before 7/11/09. Then the same situation results, with the same options and resolution.

The moral of this story: Trust Quicken. Even if you can't figure out the accounting procedures behind your finances, Quicken can.

Other Reconciliation Tasks and Features

Quicken offers a number of other reconciliation features that you might find useful. Here's a quick look at them.

Reconciling Credit Card Accounts

You can reconcile a credit card account the same way you reconcile a bank account. If you try to enter all credit card transactions as you make them throughout the month, it's a good idea to use the reconciliation feature to compare your entries to the credit card statement, just to make sure you didn't miss any. If you simply enter all credit card transactions when you get your statement, reconciling to the statement really isn't necessary.

When you begin the reconciliation process, Quicken displays either the Statement Summary dialog or the Reconcile Online Account dialog, depending on whether the credit card account has online account access features enabled. The dialogs are similar to the ones that appear when you reconcile a bank account.

Enter information in the appropriate text boxes and click OK to move on to the Statement Summary window, which looks and works almost exactly like the Statement Summary window that was shown in Figure 8-1.

If you can't successfully get the credit card reconciliation to work, Quicken offers to make adjustments. The following illustration shows the Adjusting Register To Agree With Statement dialog for a hopelessly messed-up account that needs adjustments to opening balance, payments, and charges. Choose a category for each adjustment and click Adjust to make the adjusting entries.

At the conclusion of a credit card reconciliation, Quicken may display the Make Credit Card Payment dialog (shown here), offering to prepare a credit card payment for you. This is particularly handy if you like to pay your credit card bill after reconciling your statement to your entries. Select an account and payment method and click Yes. Quicken prepares the transaction for you.

Printing a Reconciliation Report

At the end of a reconciliation, Quicken displays a dialog that offers to create a reconciliation report. If you click Yes, the Reconciliation Report Setup dialog, shown here, appears. Set report options in the dialog and click the printer icon to print the report.

I don't usually create reconciliation reports. I have enough paper filed away! But if your reconciliation required an adjusting entry, it might be a good idea to document it by printing a reconciliation report. You can then file the report with your bank statement and canceled checks.

Identifying Reconciled Items

As shown in the next illustration, Quicken uses the Clr column in an account register to identify items that either have cleared the bank or have been reconciled:

- **c** indicates that the item has cleared the bank. You'll see a **c** in the Clr column beside items that you have checked off during a reconciliation if you have not completed the reconciliation. You'll also see a **c** beside items downloaded and accepted using Quicken's online account access feature, which I discuss in Chapter 6.
- **R** indicates that the item has been reconciled.

To make it even more obvious that a transaction either has cleared your financial institution or has been reconciled, reconciled transactions appear in gray print rather than black. You can see this in Figure 8-2.

You can toggle the gray color of reconciled transactions to black via Quicken preference Register | Register Appearance | Gray Reconciled Transactions. The "Standard" view for new users is Gray Reconciled Transactions by default.

To prevent errors in your account registers, do not edit transactions that have been reconciled.

Figure 8-2 • Outstanding transactions in your check register are in black, while items that have cleared your bank are in grey.

Examining Your Banking Activity

In This Chapter:

- *Banking overview*
- *Using alerts*
- *Types of reports and graphs*
- *Creating reports and graphs*
- *Customizing and saving reports and graphs*
- *Printing reports and graphs*

At this point, you'll probably agree that entering financial information into Quicken Personal Finance Software is a great way to organize it. But sometimes organizing information isn't enough. Sometimes you need to see concise summaries of the information you entered, in the form of balances, activity reports, and graphs.

Quicken provides the kind of information you're looking for, in the form of snapshots, reports, and graphs. This chapter concludes the discussion of Quicken's banking area by telling you about the snapshots of information it offers and how you can take advantage of its alerts. It also explains how you can create, modify, and save standard and custom reports and graphs for all Quicken tabs.

A Closer Look at the Banking Tab

The previous chapters in this part of the book have explored many aspects of Quicken's banking area, including accounts, transaction entry, Online Account Services, automation features, and reconciliations. But the banking area also offers a place for examining the results of your work with banking accounts and features.

In this part of the chapter you will go on a guided tour of the banking area's reporting and graphing features so you can learn about the information you can find there.

The Cash Flow View

The Cash Flow view (see Figure 9-1), which is available from Planning tab | View subtab | Cash Flow button, provides a summary of your projected cash flow for a month. You can click the arrows on either side of the month name to view this information for previous or future months.

The Cash Flow view features a number of snapshots:

+ In – Out = What's Left The top of the Cash Flow view summarizes incoming funds, outgoing funds, and what's left to save or spend. You can click links in this area to view pop-up reports with details for the summarized values, like the image on the next page:

Figure 9-1 • The Cash Flow view shows projected cash flow information for a month.

Other Expenses	close ✕
Expenses	
Category	Amount
Uncategorized	228.46
Groceries	104.67
Charity	100.00
Household:Yard Service	85.00
Publications	58.44
Auto:Fuel	42.84
Total	**$619.41**

Banking Reminders The Banking Reminders tab at the bottom of the Cash Flow view lists banking reminders. You can use the Show drop-down list to specify which transactions should appear and how they should be formatted. Enter, Edit, and Skip buttons for items that have not yet been recorded appear so you can enter them into Quicken, edit them, or skip them for the month. You can use the buttons at the bottom of the snapshot to add bills and deposits and show the Bill And Income Reminders window. Using Quicken's reminder features is explained in Chapter 7.

Account Balance Graph The Account Balance Graph tab at the bottom of the Cash Flow view's window (shown next) summarizes the balance of cash flow accounts for the period being viewed. You can use the Show drop-down list to specify which accounts should appear in the graph.

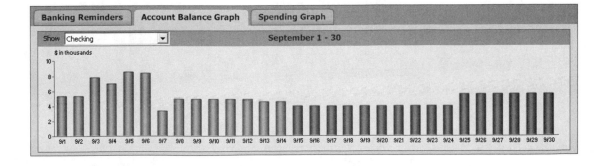

Spending Graph   The Spending Graph tab at the bottom of the Cash Flow view's window (shown next) displays two spending graphs for the month: Spending by Category and Spending by Payee. You can click buttons at the bottom of each graph to display a full graph, customize the graph, or access the Spending Planner feature of Quicken. I explain how to work with report and graph windows and customize graphs later in this chapter and tell you about the Spending Planner next.

Spending Planner

Quicken's Spending Planner, which is shown in Figure 9-2, is like a live budget where you can easily see income and spending based on payee and category. You can use this feature to help you take control of your spending and to save money.

Expected Income   Quicken automatically calculates your expected monthly income based on scheduled paychecks and other income. You can change this amount by clicking the Edit button near the top of the view and entering a new value in the Set Expected Income dialog that appears (shown here).

| Home | Bills | Banking | Investing | Net Worth | Planning | | More From Quicken | Setup |

View	Spending Planner	Lifetime Planner	Tools	Tax Tools ▾	Other Tools ▾	Reports	Spending Reports ▾
	Cash Flow	Tax Center		Financial Calculators ▾			All Reports & Graphs ▾

◄ September 2009 ►

September 2009   Total Monthly Allocation ⑦ $4,750 [Edit]

| $1,494 | $615 | $2,641 |

■ Scheduled Bills   ■ Categorized   ☐ Left Over
                             Spending

Type	Allocation	Actuals	Left Over	Rollover Reserve ⑦
⊟ Credit Card Debt ⑦	$0	—	—	—
General	0 [Apply]	—	—	—
⊟ Savings ⑦	$0	—	—	$0
General	0	—	—	0
[Create New Savings Target]				
⊟ Scheduled Bills ⑦	$1,494	—	$485	$0
Chysler Financial, Inc.	485	Due: 10/24/2009	485	0
Serenity Farms	184	184	0	0
Western National Mortgage	825	825	0	0
[Manage My Bills]				
⊟ Categorized Spending ⑦	$3,256		$2,641	-$5
Auto	130		130	0
Clothing	100		100	0
Dining	100		100	0
Entertainment	100		100	0
Groceries	100	100	0	-5
[Choose Categories to Watch]				
Totals	**$4,750**			

[Show Spending Report]

Figure 9-2 • Quicken's Spending Planner helps you take control of your spending.

Credit Card Debt and Savings You can indicate how much you plan to allocate to your credit card debt and savings by entering values in the Allocation box beside each item. (You may have to click the + sign beside a type heading to display an item as shown in Figure 9-2.) If you want to save for a specific purpose, you can click the Create New Savings Target button and use the Create New Savings Target dialog (shown on the next page) to enter a name and amount to save.

Scheduled Bills Quicken lists your scheduled bills and other transactions in the Scheduled Bills area so you know what expenses to expect for the month. You can adjust the allocation for a payee by entering a different value in the Allocation column box beside it. You can display the Bill And Income Reminders window, which I discuss in detail in Chapter 7, by clicking the Manage My Bills button at the bottom of the Scheduled Bills list.

Categorized Spending Quicken also displays expenses by category, showing allocated and actual amounts graphically. This makes it easy to see if you've already spent more for a category than you've allocated for it. You can change a category's allocation by entering a new value in the Allocation box beside it. To change the list of categories that appears in the view, click the Choose Categories To Watch button and use the Choose Categories dialog that appears (shown next) to check off the categories you want to monitor.

Rollover Reserve The far right column of the Spending Planner worksheet shows the Rollover Reserve. This is the difference between an allocated amount and the actual amount. Rollover reserves can accumulate from one month to the next.

For example, suppose you allocated $150 per month for Entertainment. This month, however, you only spent $100. The remaining $50 goes into a rollover reserve so you can spend it in the future without exceeding your allocation for that category. Of course, if you spent more than $150 this month for Entertainment, the rollover is a negative value, meaning you must spend less next month.

You can move a rollover reserve from one payee or category to another. Click the button in the Rollover Reserve column at the far right end of the worksheet for a payee or category. Then use the Edit Rollover Reserve dialog (shown next) to indicate how you want the rollover moved. When you click OK, Quicken adjusts the rollover reserve as you specified.

The Summary View

In versions of Quicken prior to 2010 there was a Summary view in the Banking tab that displayed a number of snapshots with useful information about your banking accounts. If you liked this view, as I did, you can easily create it. Open the Home tab and in the View subtab, click the down arrow next to the highlighted view, and select Add A Custom View. In the Custom View dialog, type **Summary View** for the View Name. If Alerts is not in the Chosen Items list, click in the Available Items list and click Add. Similarly, if they are not in the Chosen Items list, add the following from the Available Items list: Spending And Savings Accounts, Credit Card Accounts, and Bill And Income Reminders, in that order. When you click OK, you'll see a Summary View, close to what was in previous Quicken versions, as shown in Figure 9-3.

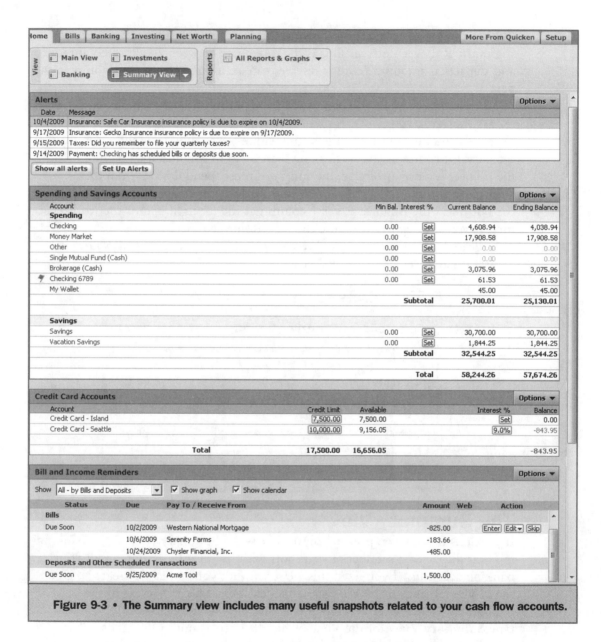

Figure 9-3 • The Summary view includes many useful snapshots related to your cash flow accounts.

In your new Summary View, all snapshots include an Options menu and possibly buttons that you can use to work with the snapshot. For example, the Alerts snapshot at the top of the view has buttons and Options menu commands for showing, setting up, and deleting alerts. I discuss many of these options throughout this part of the book; you can explore the others on your own.

Here's a brief summary of each snapshot in the Summary View.

Alerts The Alerts snapshot lists alerts you have set up. You can click blue links to go to the account or other items the alert applies to. I tell you how to set up and use banking related Alerts later in this chapter, in the section titled "Banking Alerts."

Spending And Savings Accounts The Spending And Savings Accounts snapshot lists all of your checking, savings, and cash accounts, along with their current and ending balances. You can click links to view the account register, set up balance alerts, and set interest rates.

Credit Card Accounts The Credit Card Accounts snapshot lists all of your credit card accounts along with their current and ending balances. You can click links to view the account register, set the credit limit, and specify the interest rate.

Bill And Income Reminders The Bill And Income Reminders snapshot lists all of your bills, deposits, and other scheduled transactions. It may also display a list of transactions that Quicken thinks you may want to schedule. Buttons beside each item enable you to enter, edit, or skip a scheduled transaction, or to schedule or ignore a suggested transaction. I tell you more about working with scheduled transactions in Chapter 7.

The Analysis & Reports View

Once again a favorite view in versions of Quicken prior to 2010, Analysis & Reports, can be easily created in 2010. Open the Home tab and in the View subtab click the down arrow next to the highlighted view and select Add A Custom View. In the Custom View dialog, type **Analysis & Reports View** for the View Name. Remove all items in the Chosen Items list and add the following from the Available Items list: Expenses, Income vs. Expenses, and Budget, in that order. When you click OK, you'll see an Analysis & Reports View, close to what was in previous Quicken versions, as shown in Figure 9-4.

The Analysis & Reports View includes snapshots that summarize and help you analyze entries into your banking accounts. Most of these snapshots give you a glimpse of Quicken's extensive and highly customizable reporting features, which I discuss later in this chapter, in the section titled "Working with Reports and Graphs."

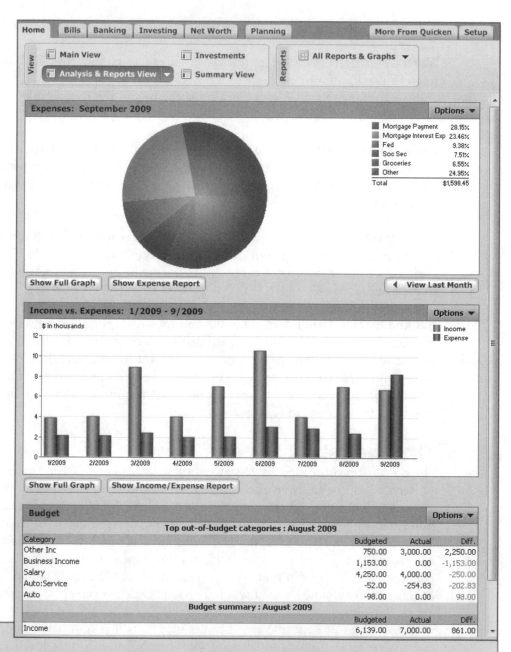

Figure 9-4 • The Analysis & Reports view includes snapshots that help you understand your finances.

Here's a quick look at the snapshots in the Analysis & Reports view.

Expenses The Expenses snapshot displays a pie chart of your expenses for the current or previous month.

Income vs. Expenses The Income vs. Expenses snapshot displays a column chart of your year-to-date income and expenses.

Budget The Budget snapshot displays information from your budget, including the top five out-of-budget categories, and a summary of your budgeted and actual income and expenses. To use this snapshot, you must set up a budget using Quicken's budgeting feature, as discussed in Chapter 17. Otherwise, the image in this area will be instructions on how to do that.

Alerts

The Alerts snapshot in the Summary view (refer to Figure 9-3) lists alerts that have been established. Having them at the top of the window helps make sure that you don't miss them.

In this section, I tell you about the kinds of alerts Quicken offers for banking and explain how to set them up.

Banking Alerts Overview

Quicken offers seven different alerts that you can set up for cash flow accounts. To enable them, open the Tools menu, choose Alert Center, click the Setup tab, and then open the Banking category. Here's an explanation of each of them:

- **Account Min. Balances** enables you to set minimum balances for your checking and savings accounts. You can set a minimum amount and a reminder amount for each account, as shown in Figure 9-5. Quicken can alert you when the account balance falls below the reminder amount you specify.
- **Account Max. Balances** enables you to set maximum balances for your checking and savings accounts. Quicken alerts you when the account balance climbs above the amount you specify.
- **Credit Card Limits** enables you to set limits for your credit card accounts. You can set a limit amount and a reminder amount. Quicken alerts you if the balance exceeds the reminder amount.
- **Check Reorder Notice** tells Quicken to alert you when you reach a certain check number. You can set this option for checking and savings accounts.

This feature can be used whether you use checks provided by your bank or another printer, or checks you purchase exclusively for use with Quicken.

- **Monthly Expenses** enables you to specify maximum monthly spending amounts for any Quicken expense category. If you exceed the limit you specified, Quicken alerts you.
- **Savings Goals** tells Quicken to alert you when you fall behind on a savings goal. This option works directly with Quicken's Savings Goals feature, which I cover in Chapter 17.
- **Online Services Available** tells Quicken to alert you when one of your financial institutions supports Online Account Services. Quicken can learn about new financial partners when you connect to the Internet to utilize other features. I tell you more about Online Account Services in Chapter 6.

In addition, Quicken offers three other General category Reminder Alerts that fall in the banking area.

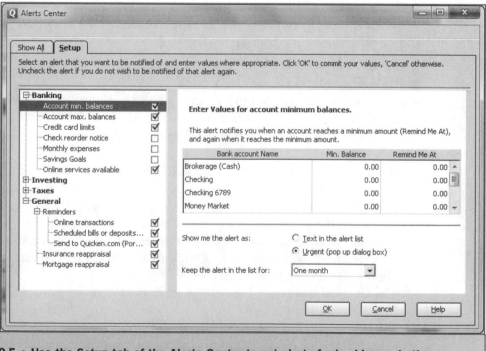

Figure 9-5 • Use the Setup tab of the Alerts Center to set alerts for banking and other accounts.

- **Online Transactions** tells Quicken to remind you to download transactions from your financial institution if you haven't done so for 30 days or more.
- **Scheduled Bills Or Deposits Due Soon** tells Quicken to remind you in advance of any scheduled transactions that are due.
- **Send To Quicken.com** tells Quicken to remind you to export your portfolio to Quicken.com when holdings change.

Setting Up Alerts

You set up alerts with the Setup tab of the Alerts Center window, as shown in Figure 9-5. You can then click the name of one of the alerts to view and set it. Figure 9-6 shows the Monthly Expenses alert.

Setting Basic Options

To set an alert, begin by selecting the name of the alert on the left side of the window. If necessary, click the check box to place a check mark within it. Then click the value you want to change on the right side of the window and enter a new value. Not all alerts have values you can change; for example, the Online Services Available alert is a simple on or off setting made with the check mark.

Figure 9-6 • Use Alerts to notify you when you have exceeded your budget.

What Does This Mean to You? Cash Flow Alerts

If you're juggling multiple bank and credit card accounts, Quicken's Banking alerts can really help you keep your sanity. After all, who can keep track of all those balances and keep them where they should be?

For example, suppose you have a checking account and a money market account. The checking account may be free, but only if the balance is at least $1,000. The money market account earns interest, but you're allowed to make only a limited number of monthly expenditures, so it can't replace the checking account. This kind of situation is perfect for Quicken's Alerts feature. Set it up so Quicken tells you when your checking account balance is getting too low—so you can transfer money in from your money market account and avoid paying fees—or too high—so you can transfer money out to your money market account and earn interest on it.

The Alerts feature can also prevent embarrassment at a checkout counter by warning you when a credit card balance is getting dangerously close to its limit. Likewise, it can remind you to pay your credit card bill, so even if your balance is relatively low, you won't forget to make that monthly payment on time.

If you're trying to keep spending under control, Quicken can be a good friend. You can use its Alerts feature to set up maximum spending amounts for specific categories. Find yourself dining out too often? Set the maximum Dining category expenditure for the month. Just can't resist another pair of shoes in the mall? Set the maximum Clothing category expenditure. Then, when you enter the expenditure that puts you over the maximum for the month, Quicken firmly informs you that it's time to stop.

It's like having an impartial financial manager looking over your shoulder.

Setting Other Options

You can set two additional options in the bottom half of the window.

Show Me The Alert As Choose from two options for showing the alert:

- **Text In The Alert List** displays the alert as an item in an Alerts snapshot only, which you can see in the Alerts Center Show All tab and when you add Alerts to another view.
- **Urgent (Pop Up Dialog Box)** displays the alert in a dialog when you start Quicken. You must dismiss this in-your-face alert by clicking the OK button in the dialog before continuing to work with Quicken.

Keep The Alert In The List For You can set the amount of time the alert should remain in the Cash Flow Alerts snapshot. The default setting is One Month, but you can use the drop-down list to choose from One Day, One Week, One Month, One Quarter, or One Year.

Finishing Up

When you're completely finished setting alerts, click OK to close the Alerts Center window. The alerts will work quietly in the background, watching your finances. When it's time to go to work, they appear as you specified.

Working with Alerts

Once you've set up alerts, you can view, modify, or delete them as desired. Here's how.

Viewing Alerts

As shown in Figure 9-3, you can add Alerts so they will appear in a snapshot in any custom view.

You can also view alerts in the Show All tab of the Alerts Center window (see Figure 9-7). Click the Show All Alerts button in any Alerts snapshot or open the Tools menu and choose Alert Center | Show All tab to display them.

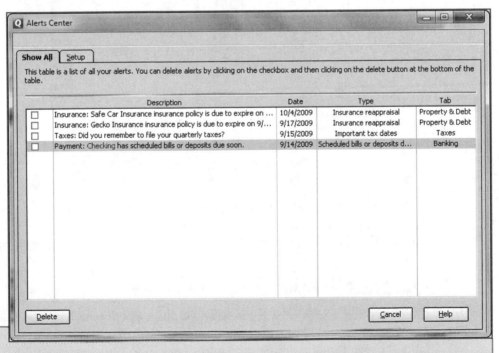

Figure 9-7 • The Show All tab of the Alerts Center window enables you to view and delete specific alerts.

Modifying Alerts

You can change the way an alert works at any time. Open the Tools menu and choose Alert Center | Setup tab (refer to Figure 9-5). Then follow the instructions in the earlier section titled "Setting Up Alerts" to change alert settings.

Deleting Alerts

To delete an alert, display the Show All tab of the Alerts Center (refer to Figure 9-7). Turn on the check box beside each alert you want to delete and click the Delete button. A confirmation dialog appears, as shown next. Click OK to delete the alert.

To prevent a deleted alert from getting reestablished and appearing again in the future, use the Setup tab of the Alerts Center window (refer to Figure 9-5) to turn off the check box for the alert in the list on the left side of the window.

Quicken Reporting Overview

Quicken offers a variety of reports and graphs, each of which can be customized to meet your needs. I like to think of reports and graphs as the "fruits of my labor." I spend time entering data into Quicken so Quicken can crunch the numbers for me. I use the reports and graphs it creates to analyze my spending habits, find ways to save money, and submit information to financial institutions when I apply for loans or credit cards.

In this section, I tell you about the types of reports and graphs Quicken offers. Then I explain how you can use a variety of techniques to quickly create reports and graphs based on the information in your Quicken data file. Although I'll concentrate on reports and graphs for the banking area, the techniques in this part of the chapter apply to the reports and graphs you create for any Quicken data, regardless of where it appears.

Types of Reports and Graphs

Within Quicken are essentially two kinds of reports and graphs: standard and saved. Here's an overview of each one.

Standard

Quicken includes a number of standard reports and graphs that are organized by topic: Banking, Spending, Comparison, Investing, Tax, Net Worth & Balances, Business, and EasyAnswer. For example, the Banking topic includes Banking Summary, Cash Flow, Cash Flow By Tag, Missing Checks, Reconciliation, and Transaction reports. These reports and graphs clearly show banking-related information. EasyAnswer reports and graphs answer

---

What Does This Mean to You? Reporting

Okay, so you're not a corporation with stockholders and SEC reporting requirements. And maybe you're not even involved in any kind of business where reports could help you maximize profits. But that doesn't mean you won't find Quicken's reporting features useful.

I found Quicken extremely useful a few years ago when I applied for a mortgage for a rental property I wanted to buy. I'd been faithfully entering my transactions into Quicken for years and had a complete record of everything I owned and owed. Rather than manually filling out the lengthy forms required by the lender, I created Quicken reports that provided the same information. I also whipped up reports that summarized my current net worth, detailed my investment portfolio, and totaled my year-to-date income and expenses. I sent all these reports to the bank with copies of my recent tax returns. I got a positive answer within a few days. And I didn't even need to take out a calculator!

A friend of mine has a tax preparer do his returns every year. (I guess he hasn't learned about the benefits of TurboTax yet.) In the old days, before he started using Quicken, he'd spend hours with his tax guy, answering questions and shuffling through piles of paper and handwritten notes. Now he uses Quicken to create reports of his income and expenses, including detailed reports for things like charity contributions and medical expenditures. He spends less than an hour with his tax guy and, because they both save time, his tax preparation bill is half what it used to be.

As you can see, reports aren't just for businesses. They're for people like you and me, too.

specific, predefined questions, such as, "Where did I spend my money during the period…?" and "How much did I spend on…?" You select a question and then provide optional information, such as a date range, payee, or account. Quicken gathers the information and generates the report or graph.

Saved You can create custom reports and graphs by customizing the standard reports and graphs. This multiplies your reporting capabilities, enabling you to create reports or graphs that show exactly what you need to show. When you save your custom reports and graphs, they can be re-created quickly, with just a few mouse clicks, to display current information.

Creating Reports and Graphs

With Quicken, creating a report or graph is as simple as clicking a few buttons. You can use several techniques: choosing a report or graph from the Reports menu, setting options in the Reports & Graphs center window, using the Report button or menu on button bars, and choosing commands from contextual menus. In this section, I explain how to use all of these techniques.

Reports & Graphs Center

The Reports & Graphs center window (see Figure 9-8) offers one way to create reports and graphs. Open the Home tab or any of the other tabs except the Bills tab, in the Reports subtab choose All Reports & Graphs | Reports & Graphs Center to display it. Click one of the topics on the left side of the window to display a list of the available reports and graphs. The icon that appears to the left of the report name indicates whether you can create a report, a graph, or both.

To create a report or graph, click its name on the left side of the window and then set the Date Range option in the settings area that appears beneath it. You can click the Customize button to further customize the report or graph, as I explain later, in the section titled "Customizing Reports and Graphs." Then click Show Report or Show Graph to display the report or graph. Figures 9-9 and 9-10 show examples of reports.

The All Reports & Graphs Menu

The All Reports & Graphs menu, which is shown on the next page, can be opened from the Reports subtab of any tab except Bills. It includes a number of submenus, each of which corresponds to a report topic. To create a report or graph from the All Reports & Graphs menu, click a topic submenu, and then click a report name. Quicken creates the report with default date settings. Figure 9-10 shows an example of a report created directly from the Reports menu.

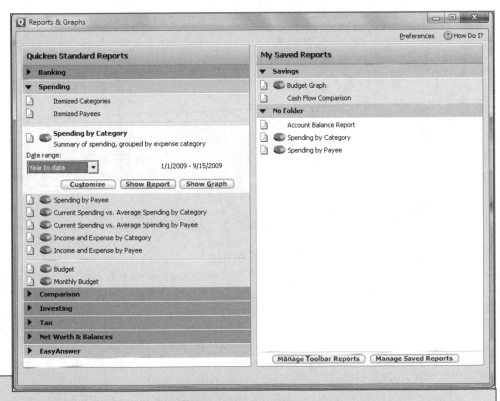

Figure 9-8 • You can use the Reports & Graphs center window to create reports or graphs.

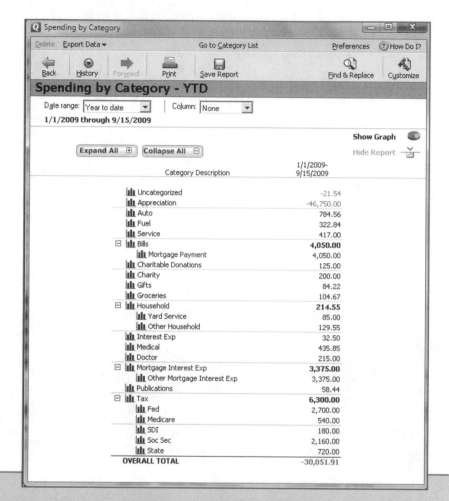

Figure 9-9 • A Spending By Category report lists expenses by category.

Reports from Other Menus

You can also create a report by using the menus in some windows. This normally creates a report based on information selected within the window.

For example, you could create a Register report for a specific account by choosing Register Report from the Account Actions menu at the top of the register for that account.

A Report button also appears in an account register window when you activate the Payee or Category field. Clicking this button displays a pop-up *mini report* of recent activity for the payee or category, as illustrated on page 224 and discussed briefly in Chapter 5. Clicking the Show Report button in the mini

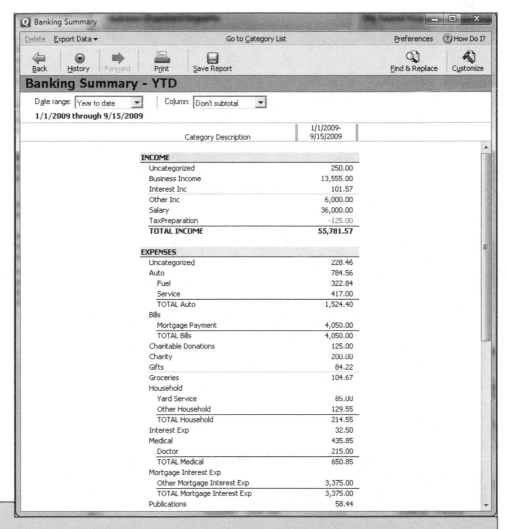

Figure 9-10 • A Banking Summary report summarizes income and expenses.

report opens a report window with the information, although the Show Report button does not display in the mini report if you clicked on a Category field with a split. See this illustration at the top of the next page.

Contextual Menus

The contextual menu that appears when you right-click (click the right mouse button) while pointing to an item sometimes includes a command that will create a report for the item. For example, right-clicking the name of a payee in

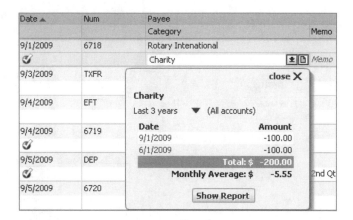

the account register window displays a menu that includes the Payments Made To command. Choosing this command creates a Payee report that lists all payments made to that payee.

Working with Reports and Graphs

Although Quicken's standard reports and graphs can often provide just the information you need onscreen, you may want to do more with them. In this section, I explain how you can customize reports and graphs, save the reports and graphs you create so they're easy to re-create, and print reports and graphs so you have hard copies when you need them.

Working with a Report Window

When you create a report or graph, it appears in a report window. Figures 9-9 and 9-10 show examples. This window has a number of features and options you can use to work with reports.

Button Bar Buttons

The report window includes a number of button bar buttons that work with report contents:

- **Delete** deletes the report from the report list. This button is gray if the report has not been added to the report list. I tell you more about the report list in the section titled "Saving Reports and Graphs," later in this chapter.
- **Export Data** is a menu that includes commands for exporting the report's contents in three ways: export Report To Excel Compatible Format, Copy Report To Clipboard, and Export To PDF Format.

- **Go To Category List** displays the Category List window.
- **Preferences** displays the Quicken Preferences dialog for Reports And Graphs so you can set preferences for all reports and graphs you create. Reports And Graphs preferences are described in Appendix B.
- **How Do I?** displays the Quicken Personal Finances Help window with information about creating reports and graphs.

Toolbar Buttons

The report window also includes a number of toolbar buttons:

- **Back**, which is available only if you are viewing a subreport (see Figure 9-9), returns to the parent report. I explain how to create subreports later in this chapter.
- **History** displays a list of the parent report and all subreports you have created. Choose the name of a report to display it. If you choose the Show Report List command, a Report History navigation bar appears, listing all reports related to the window (see Figure 9-11). You can click the Hide Report List button to hide the list.

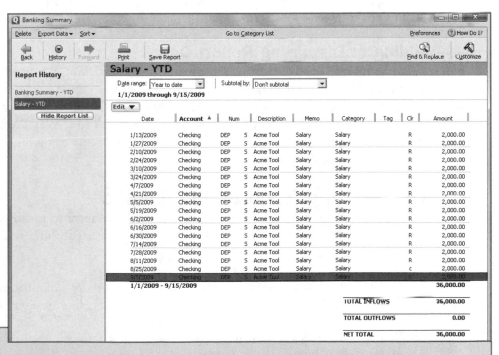

Figure 9-11 • **A subreport with the Report History list displayed.**

- **Forward**, which is available only if you have clicked the Back button, displays the previously viewed report in the window.
- **Print** sends the report or graph to the printer.
- **Save Report** saves the report. I tell you more about saving reports in the section titled "Saving Reports and Graphs," later in this chapter.
- **Find & Replace** displays the Find And Replace dialog, which you can use to modify transactions that make up the report. The Find And Replace feature of Quicken is discussed in Chapter 5.
- **Customize** displays the Customize dialog, which you can use to customize the currently displayed report. I explain how to use the Customize dialog later in this chapter, in the section titled "Customizing Reports and Graphs."

Hide/Display Graph/Report

If a report includes a graph, either the graph or a Show Graph button will appear at the top of the report window. Clicking the Show Graph button will display the graph. The button will then turn into a Hide Graph button; clicking it hides the graph. Similarly, the report window may include a Hide Report or Show Report button, depending on whether the report is displayed or hidden.

You can display a large graph instead of a report, as shown in Figure 9-12, by clicking the Show Graph button and then clicking the Hide Report button.

Hiding or Displaying Report Detail

You can show or hide the details for some reports by clicking a + or – button beside a report line. For example, clicking the – button beside Bills in Figure 9-9 collapses the subcategories beneath Bills to show just the main category totals. The button then turns into a + button, which you click to display the hidden detail. The Expand All or Collapse All buttons do the same thing, but for all categories and subcategories.

Customizing Reports and Graphs

You can customize just about any report or graph you create so it shows only the information you want to display. When you can customize it, however, depends on how you create it:

- When you create a report or graph using the Reports & Graphs center window (refer to Figure 9-8), you can customize it before or after you create it.
- When you create a report using other commands, you can customize it only after you create it.

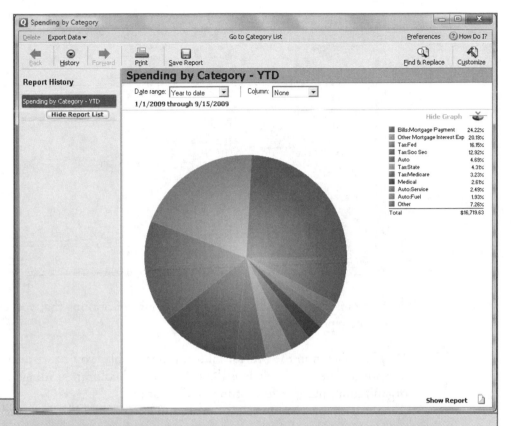

Figure 9-12 • The Spending By Category graph, with the corresponding report hidden.

Customization options vary from one type of report or graph to another. It's impossible to cover all variables in this chapter. I will, however, tell you about the most common options so you know what to expect. I'm sure you'll agree that Quicken's reporting feature is very flexible when you go beyond the basics.

Using the Customize Dialog

To customize a report or graph, click the Customize button in the options area for the report or graph in the Reports & Graphs center window (refer to Figure 9-8) or the Customize button at the top of the report window (refer to Figures 9-9 through 9-12). The Customize dialog, which is shown on the next page, appears. The dialog's full name includes the name of the report or graph.

The Customize dialog includes up to seven tabs of options that you can set to customize the report:

- **Display** (shown in the previous illustration) enables you to set display options for the report, such as the title, row and column headings, organization, number formatting, and columns.
- **Accounts** enables you to select the accounts that should be included in the report. Quicken will include transactions or balances in only the accounts you specify in the report.
- **Categories** enables you to select the categories to include in the report. If desired, you can use this tab to include only transactions for which the payee, category, or memo contains certain text.
- **Payees** makes it possible to select the payees to include in the report. If desired, you can use this tab to include only transactions for which the category, payee, or memo contains certain text.
- **Tags** enables you to select the tags to include in the report. If desired, you can use this tab to include only transactions for which the payee, tag, or memo contains certain text. This tab, which appears only if you have at least one tag defined, makes it possible to generate reports by tag. I tell you about tags in Chapter 3.
- **Category Groups** enables you to select the category groups to include in the report. I tell you about category groups in Chapters 3 and 17.
- **Advanced** enables you to set additional criteria for transactions to be included in the report, such as amount, status, and transaction type.

No matter which tab is selected, you also have access to the Date Range area, which you can use to specify a date or range of dates for the report.

Once you have set options as desired, click the Show Report, Show Graph, or OK (for both) button. (The button that appears varies depending on whether you can create a report, a graph, or both from within the dialog and how you opened the dialog.) If you are creating the report or graph from the Reports & Graphs center window (refer to Figure 9-8), Quicken creates the report or graph to your specifications. If you are customizing an existing report or graph, Quicken creates a subreport of the original report or graph and displays it in the same report window.

If the custom report or graph isn't exactly what you want, that's okay. Just click the Customize button in the report or graph window and change settings in the Customize dialog to fine-tune the report or graph. When you click OK, Quicken creates a new subreport. You can repeat this process until the report or graph is exactly the way you want it.

Using the Customize Bar

The Customize bar near the top of a report window (see Figures 9-9 through 9-12) offers another way to customize a report or graph. Use it to change date ranges, modify subtotal settings, or set columns for the report. Quicken immediately creates a subreport based on your revised settings and displays it in the same report window. For example, Figure 9-13 shows breaking out Spending By Category, shown as a single year-to-date amount in Figure 9-9, into monthly amounts by opening the column drop-down menu and choosing Month.

Using QuickZoom

The QuickZoom feature enables you to create a report or graph on the fly. Simply double-click a report line item, graph bar, or legend item. Quicken generates a new subreport for the item you double-clicked and displays it in the same report window.

Working with Subreports

Quicken creates a subreport each time you customize an existing report or graph, or create a QuickZoom report and save it. As you can imagine, it's easy to accumulate quite a few of these subreports when experimenting with Quicken's reporting features.

To view a specific subreport, choose its name from the History menu in the report window's toolbar. The view changes to switch to the report.

You can also choose Show Report List from the History menu in the toolbar to display the Report History list, shown in Figure 9-11. Click the name of the report you want to view to display it.

Figure 9-13 • Many reports can be broken out by month or other time period with the column menu.

You can click the Back or Forward button at the top of the navigation bar to move among subreports you have already viewed.

To delete a subreport, display the subreport and then click the Delete button in the button bar.

Saving Reports and Graphs

You'll often create a predefined report and customize it to create a report you want to be able to see again and again. Rather than creating and customizing the report from scratch each time you want to see it, you can save the report's settings. Then, when you want to view the report again, just select it from a list and it appears. You can do the same for graphs.

Saving a Report or Graph

To save a report or graph, start by creating, customizing, and displaying it. When it looks just the way you want, click the Save Report button in the report window's toolbar. The Save Report dialog, which is shown next, appears.

Enter a name and description for the report or graph in the appropriate boxes. To save the report or graph in a specific folder, choose the folder name from the Save In drop-down list. You can create a new folder by clicking the Create Folder button, entering a name for the folder in the dialog that appears, and clicking OK. To save all versions of the report that you create, turn on the Save Report History check box. When you're finished setting options, click OK to save the report.

Viewing a Saved Report or Graph

When you save a report or graph, it appears in a number of places throughout Quicken, organized by folder if you have saved them into specific folders.

The Reports & Graphs Center Window   Saved reports and graphs appear in the My Saved Reports area of the Reports & Graphs center window (refer to Figure 9-8). Click the name of the report or graph and click Show Report or Show Graph to display it.

The My Saved Reports & Graphs Submenu   Saved reports and graphs also appear on the My Saved Reports & Graphs submenu under the All Reports & Graphs menu. (This submenu appears only if at least one report has been saved.) Choose a report name to display it.

The Quicken Toolbar   If you used the Manage Toolbar Reports dialog to add saved reports to the toolbar, as discussed in the section titled "Managing Toolbar Reports" later in this chapter, they appear as toolbar buttons. Click the button to display the report. If you display a saved report folder on the toolbar (also selected in Manage Toolbar Reports dialog), it appears as a pop-up menu button that lists the reports within it.

Managing Saved Reports

Quicken offers two tools for managing saved reports: the Manage Saved Reports and Manage Toolbar Reports dialogs. You can open both of these dialogs by clicking the appropriate button within the Reports & Graphs center window (refer to Figure 9-8).

Managing Saved Reports   The Manage Saved Reports dialog, shown next, enables you to organize saved reports by folder, edit report settings, or delete reports. Select the item you want to work with in the report list and click a button.

- **Create Folder** displays the Create New Report Folder. Enter a name for the folder in the Name box and click OK. The folder appears in the list.
- **Move To Folder** displays the Move To Report Folder dialog. Choose a different folder from the Name drop-down list and click OK. The item moves to that folder.
- **Rename Folder** displays the Rename Report Folder dialog. Enter a new name for the folder in the Name box and click OK. The folder's name changes.
- **Edit** displays the Edit Saved Report dialog, which enables you to enter a new name and description for the report. Click OK to save your changes.
- **Delete** removes the selected item. When you click this button, a confirmation dialog appears. You must click OK to permanently delete the item.

Managing Toolbar Reports The Manage Toolbar Reports dialog, shown next, enables you to specify which saved reports and folders should appear on the toolbar. Turn on the check box beside each folder or report you want to appear. Then click OK to save your settings.

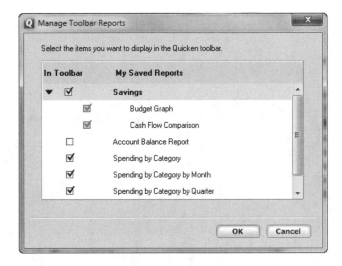

Printing Reports and Graphs

You can print reports and graphs. This enables you to create hard copies for your paper files or for use when applying for loans or completing your tax returns.

To print a report, subreport, or graph, begin by displaying it in the report window. Then click the Print button in the window's toolbar. The Print dialog appears (see Figure 9-14). Set options as desired and click Print.

Here's a look at the available options.

Print To Print To options determine the destination of the printed report or graph. You have two choices:

- **Printer** prints to the printer you choose from the drop-down list, which includes all printers, faxes, and related devices set up in Windows. This is the option you'll probably select most often. Clicking the Properties button displays the Properties dialog for the currently selected printer.
- **Export To** makes it possible to export the report information in one of three formats you choose from the drop-down list: Text File, Tab-Delimited (Excel-Compatible) Disk File, or PRN (123-Compatible) Disk File. This option is only available if you are printing a report without a graph.

Figure 9-14 • Use the Print dialog to preview your report and send it to your printer.

Print Range The print range determines which pages will print. You can use this if the printout is expected to be more than one page. The default setting is All, which prints all pages of the report. To print a range of pages, select Pages, and then enter the page numbers for the page range you want to print.

Copies The Copies box determines how many copies of the report will print. If you enter a value greater than 1, you can turn on the Collate check box to collate the copies as they are printed.

Page Scaling Page Scaling options enable you to resize a report or graph to a specific percentage or to fit on a certain number of pages. These options are only available for certain printers.

Print What You can toggle two check boxes to determine whether Quicken should print a graph or report or both. The options that are available depend on what's in the report window.

Orientation Orientation determines how the printed report will be viewed. The options are Portrait or Landscape. These are standard options offered by all programs. The icon beside each orientation option illustrates it.

Ink Color Select one of three options to determine the ink color and quality of the printout: Color (available only if a color printer is selected from the Printer drop-down list), Grayscale, or Draft.

Fonts Use the two Change Font buttons to change the header and body typefaces of the report or graph. Clicking the button displays the Font dialog, which you can use to set standard font options, such as font, size, and style.

Preview The Preview area shows a thumbnail preview of the document. You can click the buttons in the Viewing Page area to scroll through all pages of the report. To change the margins for the document, click the Adjust Margins button. The Preview area changes, as shown next, to offer boxes for entering margin values. To view a full-size preview, click the thumbnail in this area or click the Preview button at the bottom of the dialog.

Investing

This part of the book explains how you can use Quicken Personal Finance Software to track your investments. It begins by explaining the basics of tracking investments in Quicken and then goes on to explain how you can use Quicken's online investment tracking features to download investment information from your brokerage firm and exchange information with Quicken.com. Along the way, it provides a wealth of information you can use to invest wisely and maximize your investment returns. Finally, it explains how you can use Quicken's Investing tab and reporting features to keep an eye on your portfolio and investment returns. This part has three chapters:

Part Three

Entering Your Investment Transactions

Chapter 10

In This Chapter:

- *Setting up investment accounts*
- *Recording investment transactions*
- *Adding and editing securities*
- *Using the Security Detail View window*

Investments offer individuals a way to make their money grow. Although more risky than deposits made to an FDIC-insured bank, stocks, bonds, mutual funds, and other types of investments have the potential to earn more. That's why many people build investment portfolios as a way to save for future goals or retirement.

In this chapter, you will be introduced to investments and portfolio management and then you will learn how to use Quicken Personal Finance Software to keep track of the money you invest.

Quicken Investment Basics

An *investment* is a security or asset that you expect to increase in value and/or generate income. There are many types of investments—Table 10-1 lists some of them. This chapter concentrates on the investments you can track with the features in Quicken's Investing tab.

Type of Investment	Type of Account
CD	Savings account or standard brokerage account
Money market fund	Savings account or standard brokerage account
Stocks in your possession	Standard brokerage account
Brokerage account with one or more securities, with or without an associated cash, checking, or interest-earning account	Standard brokerage account
Employee stock options	Standard brokerage account
Employee Stock Purchase Plan (ESPP)	Standard brokerage account
Dividend Reinvestment Program (DRIP)	Standard brokerage account
Bonds, including U.S. Savings Bonds	Standard brokerage account
Treasury bills	Standard brokerage account
Single mutual fund with no cash balance	Single mutual fund account
Variable or fixed annuities	Standard brokerage account
401(k) or 403(b) plan	401(k) or 403(b) account
529 Educational Savings Plan	529 plan account or Educational IRA (529) account
Traditional IRA, Roth IRA, Education IRA, or Sep IRA	IRA account
Keogh Plan, SEP-IRA, or SIMPLE-IRA	Keogh plan or SEP-IRA account
Real estate	Asset account
Real estate investment trusts (REITs) or partnerships	Standard brokerage account

Table 10-1 • Quicken Accounts for Various Investment Types

Before you learn how to use Quicken to track your investments, here's a review of Quicken's investment accounts and a more detailed explanation of why investment tracking is so important.

Your Quicken Portfolio

The term *portfolio* refers to the total of all of your investments. For example, if you have shares of one company's stock, shares in two mutual funds, and a 401(k) plan account, these are the items that make up your portfolio.

Types of Investment Accounts

Your Quicken portfolio can include four types of investment accounts. You can have as many investment accounts as you need to properly represent the investments that make up your portfolio.

Standard Brokerage A standard brokerage account is for tracking a wide variety of investments handled through a brokerage firm, including stocks, bonds, mutual funds, and annuities. Like the account at your brokerage firm, it can track income, capital gains, performance, market values, shares, and cash balances for multiple securities.

IRA or Keogh Plan An IRA or a Keogh account is for tracking a variety of retirement accounts, including standard IRA, Roth IRA, Coverdell Education Savings Account (formerly known as Education IRA), SEP-IRA, SIMPLE-IRA, and Keogh plans.

401(k) or 403(b) A 401(k) or 403(b) account is for tracking 401(k), 403(b), or 457 plans, in which you make regularly scheduled, pretax contributions toward investments for your retirement. This type of account can track performance, market value, and distribution among investment choices. If you (and your spouse) have more than one plan, you should set up a separate account for each.

529 Plan A 529 plan account is for tracking 529 educational savings plans. These plans enable multiple family members to make pretax contributions to invest money for a family member's college education. This type of account enables you to track cash, money market, and securities activity and balances.

Choosing the Right Type of Account

Sometimes, it's not clear which kind of account is best for a specific type of investment. Table 10-1 offers some guidance.

Keep in mind that you can also track many types of investments in asset accounts. But Quicken's investment accounts enable you to better track and report on the income, capital gains, and performance of your investments.

This chapter concentrates on investment accounts tracked in standard brokerage, IRA or Keogh, 401(k) or 403(b), and 529 plan accounts.

The Importance of Portfolio Management

At this point, you may be wondering why you should bother including investment information in your Quicken data file. After all, you may already get quarterly (or even monthly) statements from your broker or investment firm.

What you may not realize, however, is how you can benefit from keeping a close eye on your investments. Take a look at what portfolio management with Quicken can do for you.

Centralizing Your Investment Records

Unless you have only one brokerage account for all your investments, you probably get multiple statements for the stocks, bonds, mutual funds, and other investments in your portfolio. No single statement can provide a complete picture of your portfolio's worth—however, Quicken can. By entering the transactions and values on each statement within Quicken, you can see the details of your entire portfolio in one place.

Knowing the Value of Your Portfolio on Any Day

Brokerage statements can tell you the value of your investments on the statement's ending date, but not what they're worth today—or what they were worth on July 1, 2004. Quicken, however, can tell you what your portfolio is worth on any day for which you have entered—or, better yet, downloaded—security prices, and it can estimate values for dates without exact pricing information. If you like to keep your portfolio's value up-to-date with the latest security prices, you can retrieve prices online. Chapter 11 shows you how to take advantage of this feature.

Keeping Track of Performance History

Manually compiling a complete pricing and performance history for an investment is no small task, especially for periods spanning multiple statements. If you consistently enter investment information in your Quicken data file, however, preparing performance charts and reports is as easy as choosing a menu command or clicking a button.

Calculating Capital Gains Quickly and Easily

Calculating the gain on the sale of an investment isn't always easy. Considerations include not only the purchase and selling prices, but also commissions, fees, stock splits, and purchase lots. Quicken can take all the work out of calculating capital gains, even if you're just considering the sale and want to know what its impact will be. This is extremely helpful at tax time, as Chapter 18 explains.

Creating Investing Accounts

Before you can begin tracking your investments with Quicken, you must set up the investment accounts you'll need. Basic information about setting up accounts is contained in Chapter 3. This chapter provides the specifics for creating investing accounts. As you'll see on the following pages, when you create an investment account, Quicken not only prompts you for basic account information, but also gathers information about your security holdings. When you're finished creating an account, it's all ready to use for entering transactions and creating reports.

Begin by selecting the Investing tab, and then click the Add Investing Accounts link, shown here.

Note that you can also open the Investing tab by choosing Accounts | Investing from the Accounts Bar. You will not see the screen as shown here if you have previously set up any investing accounts. If you have previously setup an investing account, create another investing account by clicking Investing | Investing Actions | Investing Accounts | Add Account.

Choosing the Type of Investing Account

The Account Setup dialog, which you get by following the instructions above, shown in Figure 10-1 will be displayed.

The first thing you need to do is indicate the type of account you want to create. Select the appropriate option; you can refer to Table 10-1 if you need help deciding. The option you select will determine certain settings for the account. For example, if you choose an IRA or Keogh plan, Quicken will set tax-deferred options that would not be set if you selected a Standard Brokerage account. Then click Next.

Figure 10-1 • The Account Setup dialog is where you select the type of investment account you want to establish.

Entering Financial Institution Information

Quicken's extensive online account access features make it possible to automate data entry for accounts held in participating financial institutions, including many brokerage firms. (Chapter 4 contains more about how you can find a participating financial institution.) To take advantage of these features, Quicken starts the account creation process for Standard Brokerage, IRA or Keogh Plan, or 401(k) or 403(b) accounts by prompting you to enter the name of your brokerage firm. As shown next, you have two options:

- **The Account Is Held At The Following Institution** enables you to specify the brokerage firm or other financial institution in which the account is held. Simply type to start entering an institution name in the box. As you type, Quicken displays a drop-down list that attempts to match the characters to those in its internal database of supported financial institutions. If your financial institution appears on the list, click it to select and enter it. Otherwise, finish typing and click Next. If you entered the name of a financial institution Quicken does not recognize, it displays a dialog that enables you to select one with a similar name or keep the one you entered.

- **I Do Not Want To Enter My Financial Institution** enables you to complete the account setup process without entering an institution name. Select this option if the account you are creating is not held at a financial institution—for example, an account to track the value of securities in a safe deposit box.

Entering Other Basic Information

Quicken may display dialogs that prompt you for additional information about the account. The dialogs that appear and the order in which they appear vary, depending on the financial institution you indicated. Although this makes it difficult to explain the process in a linear manner, I can give you a good idea of what you can expect to see.

Completing an Account Setup with Download Options

If your account is with an institution that is able to download transactions, you will see this screen on the top of the next page:

If you already have an ID and password, enter them into the Account Setup dialog. If not, click I Do Not Have A User Name And Password, and click Next. Quicken will take a few minutes to look for your accounts.

When your accounts are found, you will then be able to choose which accounts you want to add to Quicken. Select the check box of the account you want, type a name for the account that identifies it for you, and click Next.

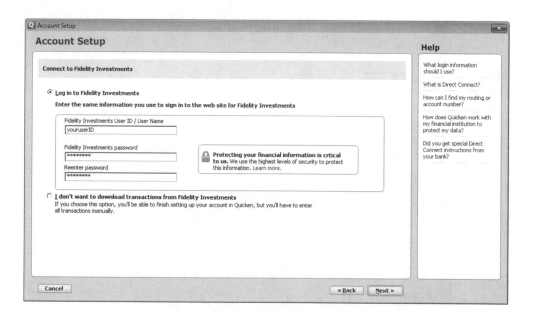

Your account will be downloaded for you. But first you will have to enter the ticker symbols for the stocks you own. Refer to the "Securities Held" for instructions on how to complete the setup in this case.

Completing the Account Setup Manually

If you don't have a customer ID and PIN for your brokerage account or are not interested in setting up the account for online features, you can enter your security information manually. You can always enable online features later, as explained in Chapter 11. If you select the option I Do Not Want To Enter My Financial Institution, click Next to continue. What Quicken does next depends on the type of investment account you are creating. The following illustrations show some of the dialogs Quicken may display and information it may prompt you for. Click the Next or Done button in each dialog to move through the account creation process. You will initially be asked for a name or nickname by which the account will be identified, as shown here:

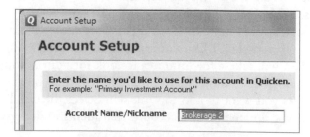

Account Name and Other Basic Information Depending on your account, you'll be asked for other information. Quicken displays dialogs that prompt you to enter certain types of accounts and other basic information, including the following, as shown here:

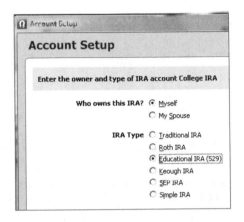

For IRAs

- Who owns the IRA
- What type of an IRA is it

For 401(k) or 403(b) Accounts You will need to enter variations of this basic information for several types of accounts, most notably 401s:

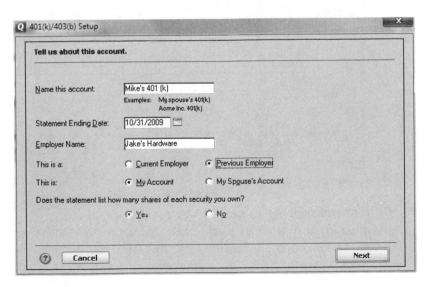

- Statement ending date
- Employer name
- Who owns the account
- Whether you have loans (and how many) against the account
- What securities you have in the account
- Whether you want to set up your paycheck information

For 401(k) or 403(b) accounts, Quicken displays a dialog that asks whether you want to track loans against the account. If you have any loans against the account, be sure to indicate how many you have. Quicken will then display one or more dialogs prompting you for information about your loan(s).

Securities Held A dialog like the one shown next prompts you to enter security ticker symbols and names. Enter one security per line, using the TAB key to move from one box to the next. If you don't know the ticker symbol for a security, you can click the Ticker Symbol Lookup button to look it up online. If you need to enter more than 10 securities in the dialog, click the Add More button to add more lines. Don't enter bonds in this dialog; you can add them later.

Current Holdings Quicken displays a dialog that offers to go online to download security names, recent prices, fundamentals, and asset classes. If your Internet connection is not automatically connected, such as with DSL, select Connect Now and click Next. Quicken connects briefly to check the ticker symbols you entered and then displays a dialog like the one shown next. Enter the total number of shares for each security. If the type of security—Stock, Mutual Fund, or Other—is incorrect, select the correct option. When you click Next, Quicken displays a dialog that confirms your entries. Click Done.

Paycheck Setup When you create a 401(k) or 403(b) account, Quicken displays a dialog that asks whether you want to set up your paycheck. Quicken's Paycheck Setup feature is great for automatically entering 401(k) contributions and loan payments. Chapter 7 contains more about this feature.

Working with Placeholder Entries

Quicken automatically creates special transactions, called *placeholder entries*, in investment accounts when you enter—either manually or via online account access—current holding information for securities as part of the account setup process. These transactions make it possible to get up and running quickly with Quicken's investment tracking features, but they lack the information Quicken needs to create accurate investment reports.

Here's how it works. When you create an investment account, you tell Quicken what securities are in the account and how many shares of each security you currently own. But Quicken doesn't know when you bought those shares or what you paid for them. Without this historical cost information, Quicken can't calculate your return on investment or your capital gains (or losses) when you sell the security.

Although you can work with a Quicken investment account as soon as it's created, to get the most out of Quicken's investment tracking features, you should replace the placeholder entries it creates with investment cost information. This section explains how.

Viewing Placeholder Entries for an Account

You can find an account's placeholder entries with the rest of the transactions for that account. Click the Investing tab, then choose the name of the account you want to work with from the pop-up menu at the top of the window. With that account displayed, click the Transactions button. Figure 10-2 shows an example of an investment account that includes three placeholder entries—the third is selected.

If placeholder entries are not visible, you may need to set the preference for viewing hidden investment transactions. Select Edit | Preferences | Quicken

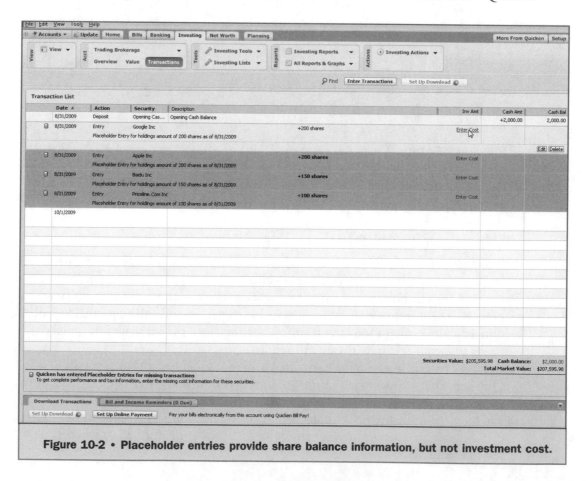

Figure 10-2 • Placeholder entries provide share balance information, but not investment cost.

Preferences. Select Investment Transactions in the Select Preferences Type pane, then select the Show Hidden Transaction check box. Click OK to save the preference.

Entering Cost Information for Placeholder Entries

To enter security cost information, begin by selecting the placeholder entry you want to work with. Click the Enter Cost link to display the Enter Missing Transactions dialog shown here.

Q Enter Missing Transactions   X

Enter Missing Transactions for Apple Inc

This security is missing all or part of its transaction history. When you downloaded or manually entered transactions, the total number of shares in those transactions did not equal the total number of shares you own. Quicken has added a Placeholder Entry to account for missing transactions.

To get complete performance reporting and tax calculations, enter the missing transactions now.

Apple Inc Transactions as of 10/5/2009

Date	Transaction	Description
	Enter Missing Transactions to complete cost basis	

Holdings as of 10/5/2009	Shares	Cost
Total shares you own:	500	×
Shares from transactions (above)	0	0.00
Shares in Placeholder Entry	**500**	**Unknown**

[Enter Missing Transaction...]   [Estimate Average Cost...]

[Help]   [Finish Later]

Transactions entered in the investment account before the date of the placeholder entry will not affect the cash balance of the investment account. Be sure to enter transactions dated before the placeholder entry using the placeholder entry's Enter Cost link.

Two buttons at the bottom of the dialog offer methods for entering historical cost information for a security: Enter Missing Transaction and Estimate Average Cost.

Enter Missing Transactions This option enables you to enter the individual transactions that make up the total number of shares you hold. In most cases, these transactions would include purchases, stock dividends, and stock splits.

This option gives you the most accurate records, but if you have many transactions, entering them all could be time-consuming. When you click this button, Quicken displays the Shares Bought dialog, which enables you to enter transaction details for a security acquisition. You will find how to enter transactions, such as purchases and stock dividends, later in this chapter, in the section titled "Recording Investment Transactions."

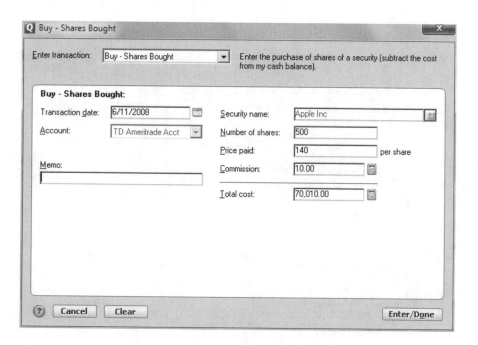

Estimate Average Cost This option enables you to enter an average estimated cost for all of the shares you hold. Although this method is less accurate than entering individual transactions, it's a lot quicker and may be sufficient if you don't need detailed records of stock costs. You can always go back later and use the Enter Missing Transaction button to record more accurate acquisition details. When you click this button, a dialog like the one shown next appears. Enter either the total cost of the shares in the Cost box or the average price per share in the Price/Share box. Quicken makes any necessary calculations. Click OK to save the entry.

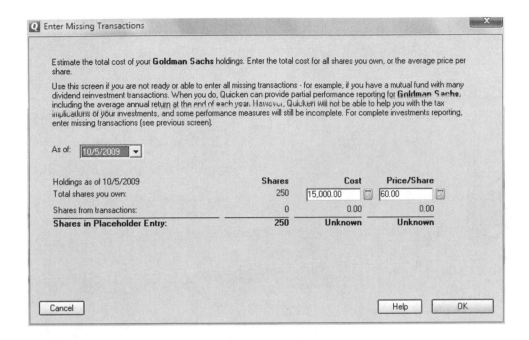

Viewing Investment Accounts

To view an account's information, click the Investing tab and then choose the name of the account you want to view from the pop-up menu near the top of the window. Then click one of the three buttons at the top of the account window: Overview, Value, or Transactions. This part of the chapter takes a quick look at each of these views.

Overview

An investment account's Overview screen (see Figure 10-3) displays a number of snapshots full of information about the account.

Holdings The Holdings area lists each of the securities held in the account, along with information about each one. You can use various buttons and menus in the Holdings area to work with this information.

- **Options** offers commands to change the view preferences, include sold security lots in the display, get quotes online, or display a complete portfolio. These options are discussed more throughout this chapter and in Chapter 11.

Figure 10-3 • Here's an example of the Overview screen for an account with holdings in three different securities.

- **Show** enables you to display a variety of information about the securities, including Value (the default selection), Recent Performance, Historic Performance, or Tax Implications.
- **As Of** enables you to see the account's status on a certain date. Change the date in this box, and Quicken recalculates the information as of that date.
- **Download Historical Prices** displays the Get Historical Prices dialog, which you can use to get price history for securities you own or watch. Learn more about downloading stock prices in Chapter 11.

Account Attributes The Account Attributes area displays basic information about the account. Menus and buttons in this area enable you to modify this information.

- **Options** offers commands to create a new account, view or edit comments, set tax attributes, set or browse Web pages for the account, and store transaction fees.
- **Edit Account Details** displays the General Information tab of the Account Details dialog, which you can use to enter or edit basic information about the account, including its name, tax-deferred status, account number, and contact information.
- **Change Online Services** displays the Online Services tab of the Account Details dialog, which you can use to enable, disable, or change online services for the account. Learn more about online services in Chapter 11.

Account Status The Account Status area provides information about the status of the account, including the account's value and transactions and download dates. The Options menu in this area offers commands to reconcile the account or view all accounts in the Account List window.

Investing Activity The Investing Activity area summarizes the activity in the account by quarter and provides capital gain (or loss) information. Menus and buttons in this area enable you to view various investment reports, or your entire portfolio, and to scroll through each year's recorded data. Chapter 12 discusses investing reports and Portfolio view.

Account Attachments The Account Attachments area enables you to attach statements or other files to the account. This makes these documents easy to find when you need them. Learn how to attach files in Chapter 5.

Value View

An investment account's Value subtab (see Figure 10-4) displays three graphical representations of the account's performance. Each snapshot includes an Options menu and one or more buttons to view other graphs or reports.

Account Value Vs. Cost Basis The Account Value Vs. Cost Basis graph uses bars to represent the account's value and a line to represent the cost of the securities. Ideally, the line should be below the tops of the bars, indicating that the securities cost less than they're worth.

Asset Allocation The Asset Allocation chart displays the distribution of your investment among various types of investments, such as large-cap stocks, small-cap stocks, international stocks, bonds, and cash.

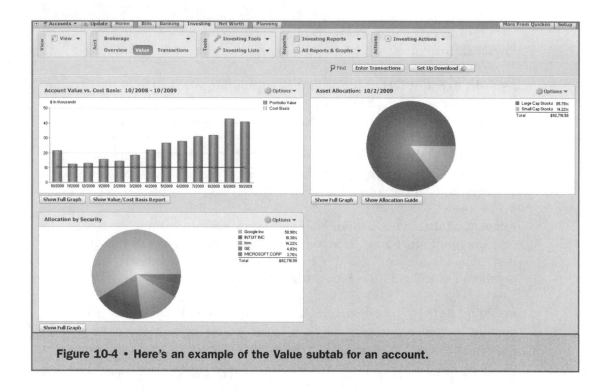

Figure 10-4 • Here's an example of the Value subtab for an account.

Allocation By Security The Allocation By Security chart displays the distribution of your investment among the securities in the account.

Transactions View

An investment account's Transactions List (see Figures 10-2 and 10-5) displays the transactions that have been entered for the account, along with the current cash balance. You can click a transaction to display Edit and Delete buttons for it; Edit enables you to modify the transaction, and Delete enables you to delete it. You can also use buttons at the top of the window to enter transactions and, if the account is set up for online account access, to download transactions from your financial institution. Chapter 11 tells more about online access.

Recording Investment Transactions

The most important part of properly tracking investments is recording all investment transactions. This includes purchases, sales, dividends, and other activity affecting your portfolio's value.

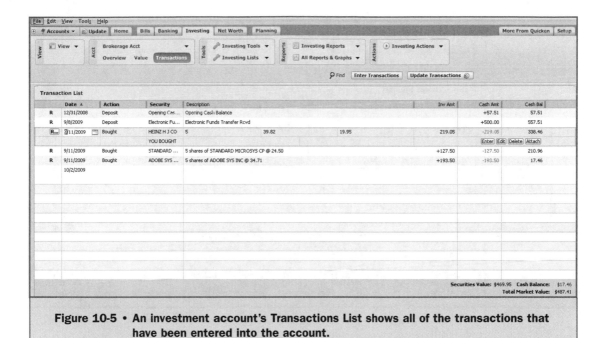

Figure 10-5 • An investment account's Transactions List shows all of the transactions that have been entered into the account.

Before you enter a transaction, you must have all of its details. In most cases, you can find the information you need on a monthly statement, confirmation form, or receipt you receive from your broker or investment firm. The information varies, depending on the transaction, but it generally should include the security name, transaction date, number of shares, price per share, and any commissions or fees.

This section provides some information and advice for entering the most common transactions into investment accounts.

Using the Investment Transaction Dialog

You enter transactions into an investment account with the investment transaction dialog. This dialog, which is named for the type of transaction you are entering, is a fill-in form with all of the fields you need to enter transaction details.

To open the investment transaction dialog, click the Enter Transactions button in the Transactions view for the account in which you want to enter the transaction (refer to Figures 10-2 and 10-5). It looks like the dialog shown on the next page when you first open it:

Investment Actions

To use the investment transaction dialog, you must begin by choosing a transaction type (or *action*) from the Enter Transaction drop-down list. There are dozens of action types organized into two categories: Investment Transactions and Cash Transactions.

Investment Transactions Investment transactions directly affect your security or investment account balances.

- **Buy – Shares Bought** (shown earlier) enables you to add shares to an investment account. The cost of the shares (plus any commissions) is deducted from the account's cash balance (or another account's cash balance).
- **Sell – Shares Sold** enables you to remove shares from an investment account. The proceeds from the sale (net of any commissions) are added to the account's cash balance (or another account's cash balance).
- **Div – Stock Dividend (Non-Cash)** enables you to add shares of a security paid as a dividend.
- **Reinvest – Income Reinvested** enables you to account for investment income (such as dividends) that is reinvested in the security. This is common with dividend reinvestment plans and mutual funds.

- **Inc – Income (Div, Int, Etc.)** enables you to record income from interest, dividends, and capital gain distributions.
- **Add – Shares Added** enables you to add shares to an investment account without an exchange of cash. You might use this option to add shares received as a gift.
- **Remove – Shares Removed** enables you to remove shares from an investment account without an exchange of cash. You might use this option to remove shares you have given to someone else as a gift.
- **Adjust Share Balance** enables you to create a placeholder entry transaction to make your share balance agree with your brokerage statement. You can enter cost information later, as discussed earlier in this chapter, in the section titled "Working with Placeholder Entries."
- **Stock Split** enables you to record additional shares received as a result of a stock split.
- **Return Of Capital** enables you to record the return of part of your investment capital.
- **Miscellaneous Expense** enables you to record investment expenses other than commissions.
- **Margin Interest Expense** enables you to record the amount of interest paid as a result of purchasing securities on margin.
- **Bonds Bought** enables you to record the purchase of bonds.
- **Grant Employee Stock Option** enables you to record the receipt of an employee stock option.
- **Exercise Employee Stock Option** enables you to use an employee stock option to buy stock.
- **Reprice Employee Stock Option** enables you to change pricing information for stock options.
- **Bought ESPP Shares** enables you to buy shares in an employee stock purchase program.
- **Sold ESPP Shares** enables you to sell shares purchased through an employee stock purchase program.
- **Short Sale** enables you to record a short sale of a security.
- **Cover Short Sale** enables you to record the purchase of stock to cover a short sale.
- **Corporate Name Change** enables you to record the change of the name of a company for which you own stock. This preserves the old name information; simply editing the security name in the Edit Security dialog does not.
- **Corporate Securities Spin-Off** enables you to record securities obtained through a spin-off of a smaller company from one of the companies in which you own securities.

- **Corporate Acquisition (Stock For Stock)** enables you to record securities obtained in exchange for other securities you own, normally as a result of a corporate acquisition.
- **Cash Transferred Into Account** enables you to record the transfer of cash into the investment account.
- **Cash Transferred Out Of Account** enables you to record the transfer of cash out of the investment account.
- **Shares Transferred Between Accounts** enables you to move shares from one Quicken investment account to another.
- **Reminder Transaction** enables you to enter an investment reminder that will appear each time you start Quicken. You may find this option useful if you want to conduct a transaction at a future date and are worried that you may forget to do it. If the Reminder Transaction has a future date, the reminder will not appear in the Alerts list until that future date.

Cash Transactions Cash transactions affect the cash balance in an investment account. These actions make it possible to track an investment account's cash balance without using a linked cash account.

- **Write Check** enables you to record a check written from an investment account.
- **Deposit** enables you to record a cash deposit to an investment account.
- **Withdraw** enables you to record the withdrawal of cash from an investment account.
- **Online Payment** enables you to record an online payment from the investment account's cash balance. To use this feature, the account must be enabled for Online Payment or Quicken Bill Pay. Chapter 6 discusses Online Payment.
- **Other Cash Transaction** enables you to record any type of transaction that affects the investment account's cash balance.

Completing the Transaction

Investment transaction dialogs and forms are generally self-explanatory and easy to use. Simply fill out the fields in the form, and click one of the Enter buttons.

- **Enter/New** enters the current transaction and redisplays the investment transaction dialog so you can enter another transaction.
- **Enter/Done** enters the current transaction and dismisses the investment transaction dialog.

Entering Common Transactions

Although page count limitations make it impossible to review every kind of investment transaction in this book, here's a look at a few common transactions. They should give you a solid understanding of how the investment transaction dialogs work so you can enter your transactions.

Buying Shares

A security purchase normally involves the exchange of cash for security shares. In some cases, you may already own shares of the security or have it listed on your Watch List. In other cases, the security may not already exist in your Quicken data file, so you'll need to set up the security when you make the purchase.

Start by choosing Buy – Shares Bought in the investment transaction dialog to display the Buy – Shares Bought dialog, shown earlier. Enter information about the shares you have purchased.

- **Transaction Date** is the date of the transaction.
- **Account** is the name of the account in which the transaction should be recorded. You cannot change the option chosen from this drop-down list if you are entering a transaction from within the account's Transaction View window; if it's wrong, click Cancel, open the correct account register, and start over.
- **Security Name** is the name of the security. If you enter the name of a security that doesn't already exist in Quicken, the Add Security To Quicken dialog, which is discussed later in the section titled "Adding a New Security," appears so you can add the security to Quicken.
- **Number Of Shares** is the number of shares purchased.
- **Price Paid** is the per-share price.
- **Commission** is the amount of commissions you paid to your brokerage or investment firm.
- **Total Cost** is calculated by Quicken. Enter the Total Cost and Number of Shares and let Quicken calculate the Price Paid. The Total Cost and Number of Shares is what gets reported on IRS Schedule D when you sell the shares. However, if you're recording the purchase of a fractional number of shares and this amount is off by a penny or two, use the Commission field to adjust the Total Cost. The net effect of tiny adjustments like this is negligible.
- **Use Cash For This Transaction** enables you to specify an account from which the Total Cost should be deducted. By default, this option is set to use cash from the same investment account.

When you're finished entering information about the transaction, click one of the Enter buttons. The transaction appears in the Transactions tab for the account.

If you want to add security shares to an account without an exchange of cash, use the Add – Shares Added action. Its form asks for most of the same information but does not affect any cash balances.

Selling

A security sale also involves the exchange of cash for security shares. Normally, you dispose of shares you already own, but in some instances, you may sell shares you don't own. This is called *selling short*, and it is a risky investment technique sometimes used by experienced investors. (To record short sale transactions, use the Short Sale or Cover Short Sale action.)

To sell shares, choose Sell – Shares Sold in the investment transaction dialog to display the Sell – Shares Sold dialog, which is shown next. Enter information about the shares you have sold.

- **Transaction Date** is the date of the transaction.
- **Account** is the name of the account in which the transaction should be recorded. You cannot change the option chosen from this drop-down list if you are entering a transaction from within the account's Transaction View

window; if it's wrong, click Cancel, open the correct account register, and start over.

- **Security Name** is the name of the security. You can choose an option from the drop-down list.
- **Sell All Shares In This Account** tells Quicken to automatically enter the total number of shares you own in the Number Of Shares box.
- **Number Of Shares** is the number of shares sold.
- **Price Received** is the per-share price.
- **Commission** is the amount of commissions you paid to your brokerage or investment firm.
- **Specify Lots** enables you to specify which shares you are selling when you have multiple purchase lots. You can use this option for additional control over capital gains. For example, if you want to take advantage of long-term capital gains tax breaks, you could sell shares that have been in your possession for more than 12 months. If you want to record a loss, you could sell shares that cost more than the selling price. Obviously, your options will vary, depending on the lots, their acquisition prices, and your selling price. If you select this option, click the Specify Lots button to display a dialog like the one shown next. (This dialog may include an Enter Missing Transactions button if placeholder entries exist for the security.) Use the dialog to enter shares in each lot you are selling, or select one of the Auto Select options and click OK. If you don't use the Specify Lots button to select lots, Quicken automatically sells the oldest shares (First In, First Out, or FIFO, method).

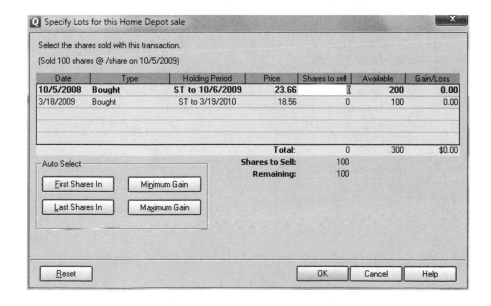

Consult your tax professional if you want to select lots other than FIFO to determine what the IRS limitations might be.

- **Total Sale** is calculated by Quicken dividing the total sale amount by the number of shares. Total Sale can also be determined by multiplying the per-share price by the number of shares and deducting the commission. This is the proceeds from the sale. The technique Quicken uses is determined by the data you enter.
- **Record Proceeds?** enables you to specify an account to which the net proceeds should be added.

When you click one of the Enter buttons, Quicken records the transaction.

Dividend Payments and Other Income

Many investments pay dividends, interest, or other income in cash. (That's why they're so attractive to an investor!) Recording this activity in the appropriate account register enables Quicken to calculate performance accurately while keeping account balances up-to-date.

Keep in mind that many mutual funds are set up to reinvest income, rather than pay it in cash. Do not use the steps in this section to record a reinvestment of income. Instead, use the Reinvest Income action to enter transaction information.

To record dividend or interest income, choose Inc – Income (Div, Int, Etc.) from the drop-down list in the investment transaction dialog to display the Inc – Income dialog, shown next. Enter information about a cash payment on an investment.

- **Transaction Date** is the date of the transaction.
- **Account** is the name of the account in which the transaction should be recorded. You cannot change the option chosen from this drop-down list if you are entering a transaction from within the account's Transaction View window; if it's wrong, click Cancel, open the correct account register, and start over.
- **Transfer Account** enables you to specify an account into which the income is deposited. Leave this blank if the cash is deposited directly into the investment account.
- **Memo** enables you to enter a brief note about the transaction.
- **Security Name** is the name of the security. You can choose an option from the drop-down list. If the transaction isn't related to a specific security—for example, interest paid on a cash balance in a brokerage account—you can leave this field blank.
- **Dividend**, **Interest**, **Short-Term Cap Gain Dist**, **Mid-Term Cap Gain Dist**, **Long-Term Cap Gain Dist**, and **Miscellaneous** are fields for entering various types of income. In most cases, you'll use only one or two of these boxes.
- **Total Proceeds** is the total of all income amounts, calculated by Quicken.
- **Category For Miscellaneous** is the category you want to use to record miscellaneous income. This field is available only if you enter a value in the Miscellaneous field.

When you click one of the Enter buttons to record the transaction, it appears in the Transactions tab for the account.

Other Transactions

Other transactions are just as easy to enter as purchases, sales, and income. Simply choose the appropriate option from the drop-down list in the investment transaction dialog and enter the transaction information in the form that appears. If you have the transaction confirmation or brokerage statement in front of you when you enter the transaction, you have all the information you need to record it.

If you need additional guidance while entering a transaction, click the Help button (question mark icon) in the Enter Transaction dialog to learn more about the options that must be entered.

Entering Transactions in the Transaction List

Quicken also enables you to enter investment transactions directly into the Transaction List window. This feature makes entering transactions quicker for experienced Quicken users.

To begin, scroll down to the blank line at the bottom of the Transaction List. Click the line to activate it, and enter the transaction date in the Date column. Then choose an action from the pop-up menu in the Action column and press TAB. The two lines for the transactions fill in with italicized reminders of the information you should enter into each field, as shown next. Fill in the fields with transaction details and click Enter.

Transaction List						
Date ▲	Action	Security	Description	Inv Amt	Cash Amt	Cash Bal
10/5/2005	Deposit	Opening Cas...	Opening Cash Balance		+12,050.00	12,050.00
6/11/2008	Bought	Apple Inc	500 shares of Apple Inc @ 140	+70,010.00	N/A	12,050.00
10/5/2008	Bought	Home Depot	200 shares of Home Depot @ 23.66	+4,742.00	N/A	12,050.00
3/18/2009	Bought	Home Depot	100 shares of Home Depot @ 18.56	+1,866.00	N/A	12,050.00
10/5/2009	Entry	Goldman Sachs	+250 shares	+15,000.00		
	Placeholder Entry for holdings amount of 250 shares as of 10/5/2009					
10/5/2009	Bought					

[Enter] [Edit] [Delete] [Attach]

Editing Transactions

Quicken offers two ways to edit transactions: with the investment transaction dialog and in the Transaction List.

Editing Transactions with the Investment Transaction Dialog

In the Transactions subtab for the account (refer to Figure 10-5), select the transaction you want to edit, and click the Edit button beneath it. Edit the transaction in the dialog that appears, and click Enter/Done to save your changes.

A few transaction types cannot be edited: Exercise Employee Stock Option and Sold ESPP Shares. These transactions must be deleted and re-entered if a change is needed.

Editing Transactions in the Transaction List

In the Transactions view for the account (refer to Figure 10-5), select the transaction you want to edit. Click in the field you want to modify, and make the desired change. When you're finished, click Enter.

Keep in mind that to use this technique successfully, you must have a complete understanding of the components of the investment transaction you're trying to change. If you're not sure how to edit the transaction directly as discussed here, I highly recommend that you use the investment transaction dialog to make changes to transactions.

Adjusting Balances

Occasionally, you may need to adjust the cash balance or number of shares in an investment account or update the balance in a 401(k) account. Here's how.

Updating an Account's Cash Balance

You can adjust the balance in an investment account with a cash balance. In the Account Bar, click the name of the account you want to adjust. Then choose Investing | Investing Actions | Investing Activities | Update Cash Balance. The Update Cash Balance dialog, which is shown here, appears. (Note that this dialog will not display downloaded cash balance information if the account is not enabled for online access.) Enter the date and the correct balance in the text boxes, and click Done. Quicken creates an adjusting entry.

Updating an Account's Share Balance

You can adjust the number of shares in an investment account. In the Account Bar, click the name of the account you want to adjust. Then choose Investing | Investing Actions | Investing Activities | Update Share Balance to display the Adjust Share Balance dialog, shown here. (This is the same as choosing the Adjust Share Balance action in the investment transaction dialog.) Enter the adjustment date, security, and correct number of shares in the dialog. When you click Enter/Done, Quicken creates a placeholder entry that adjusts the share balance. Learn more about placeholder entries in the section titled "Working with Placeholder Entries," earlier in this chapter.

Updating 401(k) or 403(b) Balances

401(k) or 403(b) account balances change every time you make a contribution through your paycheck. To adjust the balance, click the name of the 401(k) or 403(b) account in the Account Bar to open it. If necessary, click its Overview button. Click the Update 401(k) Holdings button on the button bar. Then follow the prompts in the Update 401(k)/403(b) Account dialog that appears to update the information. Click Next to display the next page. When you're finished, click Done to record the adjustment.

Remember, if you set up your paycheck as discussed in Chapter 7, Quicken will automatically record contributions to your 401(k) or 403(b) account every payday.

Working with Securities

This chapter talks a lot about securities. But exactly what are they?

In Quicken, a security is a single investment that has a share price. Examples of securities include stock shares for a specific company, bonds for a specific company, and mutual funds offered by investment firms. Normally, when you own a security, you own a certain number of shares. To calculate the total value of the security, you'd multiply the number of shares you own by the most recent per-share price.

This part of the chapter explains how you can use the Security List, Add Security To Quicken, Edit Security Details, Security Type List, Investing Goal List, and Security Detail View windows to view, add, and work with securities.

Security List

The Security List window (see Figure 10-6) simply lists the securities in Quicken's data file. You can use this window to add, edit, delete, or hide securities, including

Figure 10-6 • Use the Security List window to view, add, edit, or remove securities that you own or watch.

watch *list securities*—securities you don't own but want to monitor. To open this window, choose Investing | Investing Lists | Security List or press CTRL-Y.

Using the Button Bar

Button bar buttons enable you to work with the list's items.

- **New** enables you to create a new security.
- **Edit** enables you to modify the currently selected security.
- **Delete** removes the currently selected security from your Quicken data file. You cannot delete a security that has been used in a transaction.
- **Choose Market Indexes** enables you to add common market indexes, such as the Dow Jones Industrial Average and the S&P 500 Index, to the Security List. This lets you download quotes for these indexes when you download security prices, as discussed in Chapter 11.
- **Hide (x)** removes the currently selected security from all lists without actually deleting it. To view a hidden security, choose View Hidden Securities from the Options menu on the button bar. To unhide a security, view and select it, and then click the Hide button on the button bar.
- **Report** displays a Security Report for the selected security.
- **Options** displays a menu that enables you to toggle the view of hidden securities.
- **Print** prints a list of securities.
- **How Do I?** displays the Quicken Personal Finances Help window with additional information about using the Security List window.

Adding a New Security

To add a new security to your Quicken data file—either as a holding or a Watch List item—click the New button in the button bar of the Security List window (refer to Figure 10-6). The Add Security To Quicken dialog appears, displaying screens that prompt you for information about a security.

As shown next, Quicken starts by prompting you for the security's ticker symbol and name. Although the ticker symbol is required if you want to use Quicken's online features to download security values (as discussed in Chapter 11), entering the correct ticker symbol when you have an Internet connection can automate much of the security setup process. If you don't know the ticker symbol and have an Internet connection, you can click the Look Up button to connect to the Internet and look up the symbol.

The first screen also offers a check box labeled Include This Security On My Watch List. Selecting this check box tells Quicken to track the security, even if you don't own any shares.

When you click Next, Quicken connects to the Internet to obtain information about the security based on its ticker symbol. If it finds the ticker symbol, it displays the information it has downloaded in the Add Security To Quicken dialog. Click Done to add the security to the Security List.

If Quicken can't find information about the security on the Internet, it displays a dialog like the one shown here, enabling you to correct the ticker symbol or add the security manually. If you made an error when entering the ticker symbol, you can enter the correct symbol in the Ticker Symbol

text box and click Next to try looking it up on the Internet again.

If you select the Add Manually option, select a security type—Bond, CD, Emp. Stock Option, ESPP, Market Index, Mutual Fund, Other, Stock, or U.S. Savings Bond—and click Next. Another dialog appears, prompting you for additional information about the security, such as its asset class (for a stock), asset class mixture (for a mutual fund), and bond type and maturity and call dates (for a bond). Enter whatever information you have for the security and click Done to add the security to the Security List.

Editing a Security

You can edit a security to correct or clarify information you previously entered for it. Select the security's name in the Security List window (refer to Figure 10-6), and click the Edit button on the button bar. The Edit Security Details dialog appears; the illustrations on the top of the next page show what it looks like for a stock (left) and for a mutual fund (right). Enter or edit information in the dialog, and click OK to save your changes.

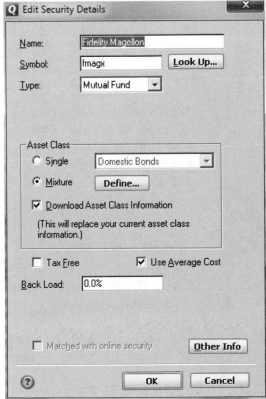

Security Type List

The Security Type List, which is shown here, displays a list of security types. To display this list, choose Investing | Investing Lists | Security Type List.

You can use button bar buttons to modify the list.

- **New** enables you to create a new security type. Clicking this button displays the Set Up Security Type dialog, which you can use to enter a name for the security type.
- **Edit** enables you to change the name of the currently selected security type.
- **Delete** enables you to remove the currently selected security type from the list.

Be cautious about editing or deleting security types. You can cause yourself some serious headaches by doing so.

- **Print** prints the Security Type List.
- **How Do I?** displays the Quicken Personal Finances Help window with instructions for working with the Security Type List.

Adding or removing security types does not affect the drop-down list in the Add Security To Quicken dialog, which lists standard security types.

Investing Goal List

As illustrated here, the Investing Goal List window displays a list of all investment goals. You may find investment goals useful for organizing your investments based on what you expect them to do for you. You can assign a goal to a security by clicking the Other Info button in the Edit Security Details dialog for the security.

To show the Investing Goal List window, choose Investing | Investing Lists | Investing Goal List. You can use button bar buttons to modify the list if desired.

- **New** enables you to create a new investment goal. Clicking this button displays the Set Up Investing Goal dialog, which you can use to enter a name for the goal.
- **Edit** enables you to change the name of the currently selected investment goal.
- **Delete** enables you to remove the currently selected investment goal from the list.
- **Print** prints the Investing Goal List.
- **How Do I?** displays the Quicken Personal Finances Help window with instructions for working with the Investing Goal List.

Security Detail View

The Security Detail View window (see Figure 10-7) provides a wealth of information about a specific security, including value and performance information, transactions, and price or market value history. You can use this window to edit transactions, update prices, edit a security, or open the Portfolio or account register windows.

To open the Security Detail View window, choose Investing | Investing Tools | Security Detail View, click the name or ticker symbol for a security in an account's Overview screen (refer to Figure 10-3), or double-click the name of a security in the Security List window (refer to Figure 10-6). To switch from one security to another, use the drop-down list in the upper-left corner of the Security Detail View window.

Figure 10-7 • The Security Detail View window displays all kinds of information about a security you own or watch.

Button Bar Buttons

The button bar buttons in the Security Detail View window enable you to edit and update security information.

- **Edit Security Details** displays the Edit Security Details dialog, which is discussed earlier in this chapter, in the section titled "Editing a Security."
- **Update** is a menu full of options for using an Internet connection to update current and historical price information for securities you own or watch. These options can be a real timesaver, as discussed in Chapter 11.
- **Online Research** is a menu full of options for using an Internet connection to research a security. These options are discussed in Chapters 11 and 12.
- **Report** displays a Security Report, which summarizes all activity for the security.
- **How Do I?** displays the Quicken Personal Finances Help window with additional information about using the Security Detail View window and its options.

Snapshots

The Security Detail View window is organized into snapshots of information about the currently selected security.

- **Security Details** displays general information about the security. You can click the Edit Security Details button to edit the information in this snapshot.
- **Holdings** provides information about your holdings of the security.
- **Quote** provides information from the most recently downloaded quote. (Learn how to download quotes in Chapter 11.)
- **Transaction History** lists all transactions involving that security.
- **Price History** or **Market Value Chart** displays either the price history or the market value for the security as a chart, respectively. You can specify which chart to display by choosing an option from the pop-up menu in the upper-left corner of the chart. Clicking the More Charting button displays the Multiple Security Charting window, which is discussed in Chapter 11.

Using Transaction Download and Research Tools

In This Chapter:

- *Accessing an overview of your accounts*
- *Setting up Transaction Download*
- *Downloading transactions*
- *Comparing downloaded transactions to register transactions*
- *Reviewing account balance details*
- *Comparing downloaded holdings to recorded holdings*
- *Downloading stock quotes*
- *Exporting your portfolio to Quicken.com*
- *Using online research tools*

Quicken offers three separate features for tracking investments online:

- **Downloading Transactions** enables you to download transactions and balances for your investment accounts. This helps automate the entry of investment transactions and keeps your Quicken records in sync with your brokerage firm's records.
- **Quotes, News, And Alerts Download** enables you to obtain current and historical quotes, asset allocation information, and news headlines about individual stocks, mutual funds,

and other investments. This automates the tracking of market values and provides valuable information you can use to make better investment decisions. This feature can also alert you to important information about securities you own or watch.

- **Quicken.com Update** enables you to put a copy of your investment portfolio on the Quicken.com Web site, where you can track its value from any computer connected to the Internet—without Quicken.

This chapter tells you about each of these features and explains how they can help you save time and stay informed about your investments. It also tells you about some of the features on Quicken.com that can help you research investments.

The instructions in this chapter assume that you have already configured your computer for an Internet connection. If you have not done so, do it now. Chapter 4 provides the information you need to set up and test an Internet connection for Quicken. This chapter also assumes that you understand the topics and procedures discussed in Chapters 3 and 7, and it builds on many of the basic concepts discussed in those chapters.

Transaction Download

You can download transactions, balance details, and holdings information directly from the financial institutions with which you maintain investment accounts. Each transaction can then be entered into your Quicken investment account with the click of a mouse button. You can also review downloaded account balance details and compare downloaded holdings information to the information recorded in your portfolio.

Using the Overview Window

The Overview window, as you learned in Chapter 10, allows you to view most information about an account. It is the starting point when it comes to dealing with your investments. To see this view, click Investing | Overview. In the Acct area of the Action Bar, click the account name down arrow to choose the specific account you want to view. Figure 11-1 shows this view for a simple Fidelity account entitled "Brokerage Acct." From Overview, you can access Holdings, Account Attributes, Account Status, and Investing Activity. You can initiate either a manual or automatic download of transactions.

Many brokerage and investment firms support the downloading of transactions. Assuming you have entered your investment account, as described in Chapter 10, you can learn whether your brokerage firm supports this feature

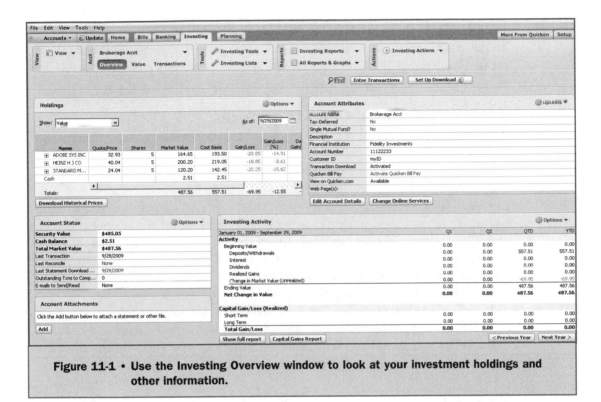

Figure 11-1 • Use the Investing Overview window to look at your investment holdings and other information.

by checking the Account Attributes area. As shown here, the word *Available* appears beside Transaction Download in the Account Attributes area if your brokerage firm supports this feature. If you have already initiated downloading for an account, as is true in Figure 11-1, you will see *Activated* instead.

Setting Up Transaction Downloads

To download transactions for an account, you must first configure the account for it. This requires that you enter additional information for the account(s) you want to track, including the account number, your user ID, and a password.

Applying for Transaction Downloads

Before you can download transactions, you may need to apply for it. Learn how at the end of Chapter 4. Normally, all it takes is a phone call, although many brokerage and investment firms allow you to apply online through the company Web site.

Not all brokerage firms have an application process. Some brokers simply provide Quicken access information on their Web sites. To access your account with Quicken, you simply configure Quicken with the same user ID and password you use to access your account via the Web. There's no need to wait for an application to be processed and additional information to be sent. Check your brokerage firm's Web site to see if these instructions apply to you.

If you do need to apply for Quicken access to your account, it may take up to a week for the application to be processed. You'll know that you're ready to go online when you get a letter with setup information. The setup information may consist of the following:

Customer ID   This may be your Social Security number or some other ID the brokerage firm provides.

Account Number   This is the account number for your account at the brokerage firm.

Password or PIN   You'll have to enter your password or PIN into Quicken when you download transactions. If your brokerage firm sends this information, they may send it separately for additional security.

Setting Up the Account and Downloading Transactions

Setting up Transaction Download is similar to setting up online account services for a bank account or credit card account. When the information is correctly set up, the process happens quickly.

When you have selected an account to look at, look for a Set Up Download button in either the Overview or Transactions subtab for the account. When you click the Set Up Download button, Quicken immediately connects to your financial institution through the Internet and gets information about the financial institution you have selected. When it has retrieved the information, the login screen appears (shown next), where you can enter your user ID and password in the appropriate boxes. Then click Next.

If you do not have a password and ID from the financial institution, you cannot download transactions. In that case, click I Do Not Have A User ID And Password, and click Next. Your update session will be canceled. You will need to establish an ID and password with your financial institution before you can download transactions into Quicken.

Quicken connects to the Internet to download transactions and balances for your account. When it's finished, you will see your transactions in the lower panel of the window, as seen in Figure 11-2. You can see on the Downloaded Transactions tab how many transactions have been downloaded. You can also see the date of the latest download to the right of the update buttons.

Downloaded Transactions After Setting Up

After you have set up Quicken to automatically download transactions, you will see a different set of dialogs. When you click Update Transactions, you will see the Online Update For This Account dialog. It allows you to update the account in one step. Enter your password and click Update Now. You will see a Save Passwords dialog that allows you to click Yes to save your password in Quicken, or you can click No. If you click Yes, you will bypass the need to load the password each time you update your files. If, for security purposes, you'd rather

Figure 11-2 • You can download transactions from a financial institution and then choose to accept them all or individually before they are added to your Quicken account.

reenter the password each time, just click Don't Ask Me This Again, and click No. You'll see a One Step Update Summary dialog that shows a summary of what has been done, as shown on the top of the next page. Click Close. After you have accepted your transactions, as explained next, click Done, if needed, to close the Downloaded Transactions tab.

The Set Up Download button changes to an Update Transactions button once the account is set up for online access. The Update Transaction button is displayed when there are downloaded transactions to accept. If there are no transactions to accept, the button is labeled Set Up Download. The button behaves the same for both labels.

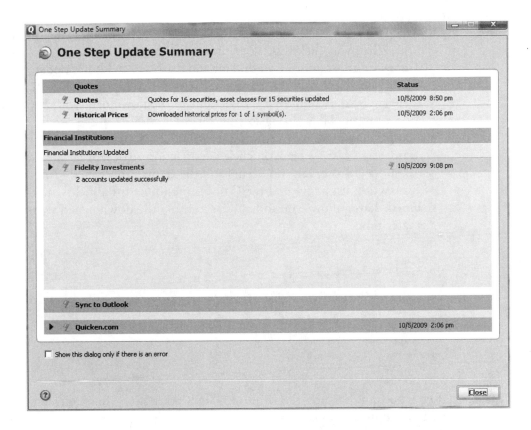

Reviewing and Accepting Transactions

You'll have an opportunity to review each of the downloaded transactions before deciding to accept them into your "official" Transaction List. Consult Chapter 6 for details. In most cases, you'll simply select a new or matched transaction and click the Accept button to accept it. Because Quicken will automatically enter most transaction information, using this method to enter an investment transaction can be much faster than entering it manually. If Quicken needs additional information about the transaction, it displays a dialog prompting you for the information it doesn't have.

Remember that downloaded transactions that have not been accepted may not be entered in your Investment Transaction List. Thus, your register and portfolio balances may be misstated until you accept all downloaded transactions.

Once the data from your financial institution has been successfully downloaded into Quicken, you need to accept the transactions. You have these options.

- **Accept All** allows you to accept all of the transactions into the Transaction List. When you click this, all of the transactions are transferred to the Transaction List and the Cash Amt and Cash Bal fields are updated. The Downloaded Transactions pane will disappear. When you click Accept All, if there are Sold or Removed transactions in the download, you may need to follow prompts in a dialog so you can enter additional required information.
- **Accept** allows you to accept any transactions you have selected into the Transaction List. When you click a transaction to accept it and then click Accept, a "register" sound occurs and the transaction is placed in the Transaction list above and the Cash Amt and Cash Bal fields are updated.
- **Finish Later** allows you to handle accepting the downloaded transactions at a later time.

	Date ▲	Action	Security	Description	Inv Amt	Cash Amt	Cash Bal
	9/7/2009	Withdraw	Opening Cas...	Opening Cash Balance			0.00
c	9/8/2009	Deposit	Electronic Fu...	Electronic Funds Transfer Rcvd		+500.00	500.00
c	9/11/2009	Bought	HEINZ H J CO	5 shares of HEINZ H J CO @ 39.82	+219.05	-219.05	280.95
c	9/11/2009	Bought	STANDARD ...	5 shares of STANDARD MICROSYS CP @ 24.50	+142.45	-142.45	138.50
c	9/11/2009	Bought	ADOBE SYS ...	5 shares of ADOBE SYS INC @ 34.71	+193.50	-193.50	-55.00
c	9/30/2009	Deposit	Interest Ear...	Interest Earned		+0.01	-54.99
	10/1/2009	XIn				+57.51	2.52
▼	10/5/2009	Action					

Transaction List

Enter | Edit | Delete | Attach

If your account balance as downloaded does not match your Quicken balance, an extra adjusting transaction will be added, as shown above for a missing Beginning Balance.

Renaming Transactions

Renaming rules are not very helpful in investment accounts. The rules only affect payee names, and only cash transactions have payees. However, you may want to rename some transactions in order to make them consistent with your naming conventions, or to avoid cluttering your Transaction List with a variety of names that don't give you the information needed. In this case, you can create rules telling Quicken how to change the names of downloaded transactions. You can "rename" securities in downloaded transactions by matching the downloaded security to a security in your Security List. Once the Matched With Online Security link is established, the security will be renamed to the name from the Security List. For example, TD Ameritrade downloads GE as GENERAL ELECTRIC CO COM, but you may prefer your Security List to use "General Electric," so transactions for GE are renamed to General Electric.

To rename transactions, click the Renaming Rules button in the Downloaded Transactions tab or follow the menu path Tools | Renaming Rules. The

Renaming Rules For Downloaded Transactions dialog is displayed. It shows the list of existing rules—by default, "Do Not Rename" is initially the only rule.

To create a new rule, click New. The Create Renaming Rule is displayed, as shown here.

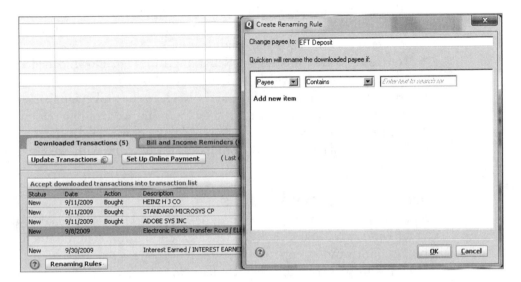

1. In the Change Payee To text box, type the name you want to have.
2. In the next text box, click the down arrow to choose between "Payee" and "Memo."
3. Next click the down arrow to choose between "Is Equal To," "Starts With," or "Contains."
4. In the last text box, type the text you want to change.

Upon creating the rule, click OK and then click Done to make the renaming action happen.

Using the Online Center Window

You can also use the Online Center to download account information and compare it to data in your Quicken file. From the menu bar, choose Tools | Online Center. If necessary, choose the name of your brokerage firm from the Financial Institution drop-down list near the top of the window

The button bar offers a number of options you can use for working with the Online Center window:

- **Delete** deletes a selected item.

- **Contact Info** displays the Contact Information dialog for the currently selected financial institution. You can use the information in the dialog to contact the bank or credit card company by phone, Web site, or e-mail.
- **Password Vault** gives you access to Quicken's Password Vault feature, which I discuss in Chapter 7. (This option only appears if you have enabled online account services for accounts at more than one financial institution and have not yet set up the Password Vault feature.)
- **Renaming Rules** displays the Renaming Rules For Downloaded Transactions dialog, which is discussed in this chapter.
- **Trade** connects to the Internet and displays your brokerage firm's home page in an Internet window. You can then log in to make online trades.
- **Print** prints the transactions listed in the window.
- **Options** displays a menu of commands for working with the current window.

Downloading Transactions

To download transactions, make sure the brokerage firm is selected in the Online Center window and then click the Update/Send button. The Online Update For This Account window appears.

Enter your password and click Update Now. Wait while Quicken connects to your financial institution. A Quicken One Step Update Status window appears during the connection.

When Quicken is finished exchanging information, a One Step Update Summary window appears to summarize the activity that took place while you waited. Click Close. If you display the Online Center window again, you'll see the transactions you downloaded in the bottom half of the window's Transactions subtab.

Reviewing Transactions

To compare downloaded transactions to register transactions, click the Compare To List button in the Online Center window. Refer to the section earlier in the chapter, "Reviewing and Accepting Transactions" to read about the displayed window.

Adjusting the Cash Balance

If the cash balance in your Quicken account doesn't match the cash balance at your brokerage firm, you can adjust the cash balance with the Update Cash Balance dialog, like the one shown next. Click Investing | Investing Actions | Investing Activities | Update Cash Balance. Enter the correct cash balance and the date, and click Done. Quicken adjusts the account accordingly.

Reconciling Your Account

To keep your electronic investing accounts reconciled to your statement, you can perform a periodic reconciliation. If your account does not match your statement, you can adjust it with the Reconcile This Account dialog. Choose Investing | Overview and on the Account Status pane, click Options | Reconcile This Account. The Statement Summary dialog will appear. Enter the starting and ending cash balance amounts and the statement ending date, and click OK.

A list of the transactions is displayed, as shown in Figure 11-3. On the left are those transactions that decrease the cash balance, and on the right are those that increase it. As you click each transaction, the difference in the lower-right area of the dialog reflects the increase or decrease. Your account is successfully reconciled when the difference is equal to zero. If you want to start by marking all of the transactions, click Mark All. This is particularly helpful when you have a lot of

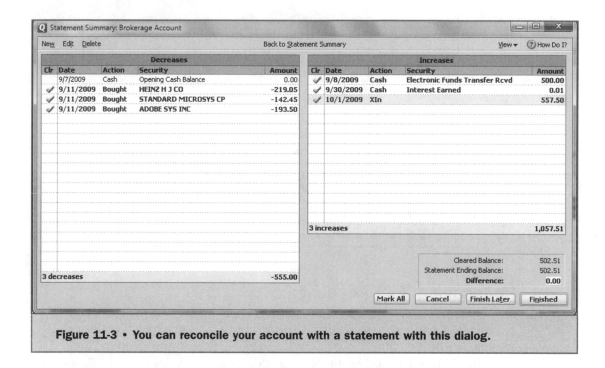

Figure 11-3 • You can reconcile your account with a statement with this dialog.

transactions. When you have marked all and are finished, click Finished. If you want to return to this at a later time, click Finish Later.

When you have reconciled your account, a message will be displayed offering you the opportunity to create a reconciliation report. Click Yes or No.

Adjusting Holdings

If the holdings amounts in Quicken don't match what you've downloaded, the Enter Transactions dialog, which is shown on the top of the next page, can be used to adjust your holdings. Click Investing | Overview for the account you want to adjust, and then click Enter Transactions. On the Enter Transaction drop-down menu, select the type of transaction you want. Buy – Shares Bought and Sell – Shares Sold are the most typical. Fill in the information needed, and when you are finished, click Enter/Done.

Reviewing Balances

When you download transactions from your financial institution, you also receive detailed account balance information. To review this information, click Investing | Overview for the account you want to review, and look at the Account Status pane. Here's what it might look like:

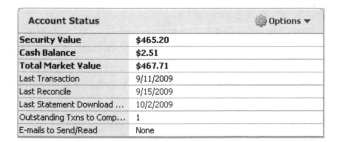

Account Status	⚙ Options ▼
Security Value	**$465.20**
Cash Balance	**$2.51**
Total Market Value	**$467.71**
Last Transaction	9/11/2009
Last Reconcile	9/15/2009
Last Statement Download ...	10/2/2009
Outstanding Txns to Comp...	1
E-mails to Send/Read	None

Reviewing Holdings

Your financial institution also sends you information about your individual holdings. You can review this information in the Overview window and compare it to the information in your portfolio.

To review holdings, click Investing | Overview for the account you want to review, and look at the Holdings pane. Here's the Holdings pane for the same account shown in the previous illustration:

If you want to adjust your holdings, refer to the section to "Adjust Holdings," earlier in this chapter.

Downloading Quotes, Headlines, and Alerts

Quicken enables you to download up-to-date stock quotes, news headlines, and alerts for the securities in your portfolio and on your Watch List. You set up this feature once and then update the information as often as desired. You can even download historical price information so you can review price trends for a security that only recently caught your eye.

Because the quote and headline download feature is built into Quicken, it doesn't rely on your brokerage firm for information. That means you can download quotes, headlines, and alerts even if your brokerage firm doesn't offer the downloading of transactions. All you need is an Internet connection.

Setting Up the Download

Before you can get quotes online, you must set up the feature. Choose Edit | Preferences | Customize Online Updates. If necessary, click the Quotes tab in the Customize Online Updates dialog that appears, as shown next. Click to place a green check mark to the left of each security or index you want to download quotes, headlines, and alerts for. Then click OK. To add securities to the list, click New Security. If you don't know the symbol for it, click Look Up Symbol. Click OK when you're finished.

Setting Up a Watch List

To set up a group of securities you don't own but want to track, create a Watch List. Click Investing | View | Account Overview. Under the Watch List area, click Select Securities To Watch. A Security List dialog will be displayed, as shown here. The menu contains commands for you to manage the list: click New to add new securities, Edit to change a name or symbol, Delete to remove a security from the list, or Choose Market Indexes to add them to the list. Place a check mark on each security or index that you want to track on the Watch List. When you are done, click the Close icon in the upper-right corner of the window.

Security	Symbol	Type	Asset Class	Watch
ADOBE SYS INC	ADBE	Stock	Large Cap Stocks	☑
Apple Inc	aapl	Stock	Large Cap Stocks	☑
Dow Jones Industrials	DJI	Market Index	Unclassified	☑
Fidelity Magellon	fmagx	Mutual Fund	Asset Mixture	☑
GE	ge	Stock	Large Cap Stocks	☑
Goldman Sachs	GS	Stock	Large Cap Stocks	☐
Google Inc	goog	Stock	Large Cap Stocks	☑
HEINZ H J CO	HNZ	Stock	Large Cap Stocks	☑
Home Depot	HD	Stock	Large Cap Stocks	☐
Htm	htm	Stock	Small Cap Stocks	☑
INTUIT INC	INTU	Stock	Large Cap Stocks	☑
MICROSOFT CORP	MSFT	Stock	Large Cap Stocks	☑
NASDAQ Composite	COMPX	Market Index	Unclassified	☑
Russell 2000	IUX	Market Index	Unclassified	☐
S&P 500 Index	INX	Market Index	Unclassified	☐
STANDARD MICROSYS CP	SMSC	Stock	Small Cap Stocks	☐

If you have any securities already on your Watch List, you won't see the Select Securities To Watch link. Instead, use CTRL-Y or click the Options menu to open the Security List, and select the Watch check box for the desired securities.

Updating Information

You can update quotes and information any time you like. Choose Investing | Account Overview. You will see a summary of your Investment and Retirement Accounts and your Watch List, as seen in Figure 11-4.

To update either your Investment and Retirement Accounts or the Watch List, click one of the two Options menus and click Download Latest Quotes. Quicken connects to the Internet and begins downloading information. While it works, a Quicken Online Update Status dialog shows you what's going on. When the dialog disappears, the information is updated.

Viewing Downloaded Quotes and Headlines

You can view quotes and news headlines for a security in two places:

- **Security Detail View** window, shown in Figure 11-5, displays quote information for individual securities. To open this window, choose Investing | Account Overview. Click a stock in the Watch List, or click Investing Tools | Security Detail View. The Security Detail View dialog will appear.
- **Portfolio** window (see Figure 11-6), which I discuss in greater detail in Chapter 12, displays quotes and news headlines for all securities you own or watch. To display this window, choose Investing | Portfolio, or press CTRL-U.

View				Acct		Tools		Reports		Actions	
▣ Account Overview	▣ Asset Allocation	▣ Online Portfolio		Brokerage Acct ▼		✐ Investing Tools ▼		▣ Investing Reports ▼		▶ Investing Actions ▼	
▣ Performance	▣ Portfolio					✐ Investing Lists ▼		▣ All Reports & Graphs ▼			

Investment and Retirement Accounts					⚙ Options ▼
Account	Cost Basis	Gain/Loss	Gain/Loss (%)	Day Gain/Loss	Day Gain/Loss (%)
Investment					
Brokerage Acct	557.51	-69.95	-12.55	-10.10	-2.03
IRA acct	0.00	0.00	0.00	0.00	0.00
Subtotal	557.51	-69.95	-12.55	-10.10	-2.03
Retirement					
TD Ameritrade	5,000.00*	146,634.00*	2,932.68*	-244.95	-0.16
Total	5,557.51*	146,564.05*	2,637.23*	-255.05	-0.17

*Placeholder Entries for missing data are used in these calculations. Show me.

Watch List				⚙ Options ▼
Name	Day Change	Day Change (%)	Quote/Price	
ADOBE SYS INC	▼	- 1.78	-5.13	32.93
Apple Inc	📷 ▼	- 0.7719	-0.41	185.38
Dow Jones Industrials			n.a.	
Goldman Sachs Group Inc	📷 ▲	+ 1.08	+0.59	183.58
HEINZ H J CO	▲	+ 0.22	+0.55	40.04
Home Depot Inc	📷 ▼	- 0.43	-1.58	26.83
NASDAQ Composite			n.a.	
STANDARD MICROSYS CP	▼	- 0.46	-1.86	24.04

Online quotes delayed at least 20 minutes. Updated 9/29/2009 at 5:38 pm local time.

Figure 11-4 • **The Account Overview view displays important information about your accounts and Watch List items.**

Figure 11-5 • The Security Detail View window shows information about a security.

Viewing Stock Quotes

The Security Detail View window (see Figure 11-5) offers the most detailed quote information. You can find detailed information in the left side of the window. If you have been faithfully downloading quotes for your securities (or you have downloaded historical quotes, as discussed in the section titled "Downloading Historical Quote Information" later in this chapter), a chart of the price history appears in the body of the window. You can use the drop-down list in the top-left corner of the window to switch from one security to another.

In the Portfolio window, downloaded quotes appear beside the security name or ticker symbol. Stock quotes are delayed 20 minutes or more during the trading day. Quotes for mutual funds are updated once a day by around 6:00 P.M. eastern time. Prior to that, you'll see the previous day's prices with *est* beside the price (short for *estimate*), indicating that the price has not been updated

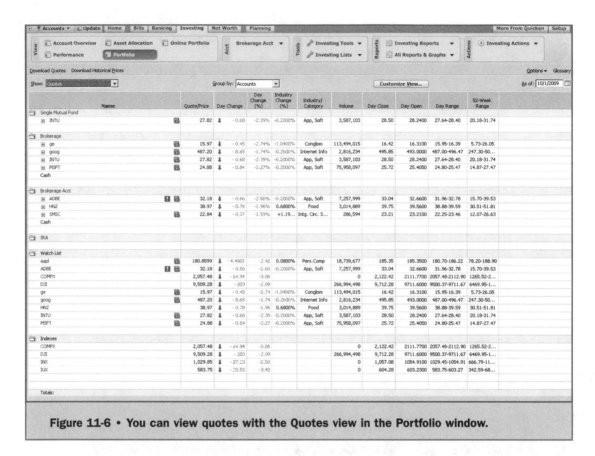

Figure 11-6 • You can view quotes with the Quotes view in the Portfolio window.

since the previous trading day. Choose Quotes from the Show drop-down list near the top of the window to see more quote details, as shown in Figure 11-6.

You can also view stock quotes by selecting the security in the Security Detail View window (double-click the stock name) and choosing Edit Price History from the Update menu on the button bar. This displays the Price History window, which displays all of the recorded stock quotes for the security, as shown here. You

Price History for: INTUIT INC

Date	Price	High	Low	Volume
10/5/2009	28.25	28.27	27.60	3,106,464
10/2/2009	27.77	28.07	27.56	2,315,306
10/1/2009	27.82	28.40	27.64	3,585,877
9/30/2009	28.50	28.58	27.92	4,185,574
9/29/2009	28.25	28.48	28.06	2,754,791
9/28/2009	28.23	28.50	27.75	3,163,810
9/25/2009	27.65	27.82	27.55	3,082,559
9/24/2009	27.64	27.98	27.46	4,445,067
9/23/2009	27.80	28.26	27.62	4,663,520
9/22/2009	27.87	28	27.27	5,306,591
9/21/2009	27.47	27.84	27.35	3,443,255
9/18/2009	27.77	27.93	27.40	3,730,019
9/17/2009	27.64	27.95	27.55	3,450,797
9/16/2009	27.89	27.97	27.39	4,910,771

can use buttons in this window's button bar to add, modify, or remove price information, as discussed in Chapter 12.

Viewing Security News

Quicken may display up to three icons in the Name column of the Portfolio view window, one example is shown in the illustration. Each icon displays pertinent information when you hover the cursor over it. If an information box includes an underlined link, clicking the link opens a Web page with more information using Quicken's built-in Web browser.

- The exclamation point icon displays alert information about the security, such as major price fluctuations and information about earnings announcements.
- The newspaper icon displays news headlines related to the security. Click the title to download the whole article.
- The H (shown) or L icon indicates that the security has reached a 52-week price high or low.

Watch List											
aapl	Google Inc (goog)						172.16	0.0000	-	78.20-174.47
	GeoEye Celebrates GeoEye-1 Satellite's First Year in Space									
ADBE	PR Newswire						34.65	0.0000	-	15.70-45.26
	Google Dominates Internet Landscape in India and Brazil									
COMPX	PR Newswire						2,080.90	0.0000	-	1265.52-2...
	National Federation of the Blind Endorses Google Books Settlement Before Congress									
DJI	PR Newswire						9,605.41	9598.0800	9535.96-9631.11	6469.95-1...
goog	↓more...						472.14	0.0000	-	247.30-47...
HNZ	39.90	↑	+ 0.07	+0.18	0.0600%	Food	1,805	39.83	0.0000	-	30.51-52.95
INTU	27.86	↑	+ 0.02	+0.07	0.4000%	App, Soft	2,845	27.84	0.0000	-	20.18-32.00
MSFT	25	↑	+ 0.14	+0.56	0.4000%	App, Soft	42,810	24.86	0.0000	-	14.87-27.66

Downloading Historical Quote Information

Quicken enables you to download up to five years of historical quotes for any security you own or watch. Choose Investing | Investing Actions | Historic Prices. Quicken displays the Get Historical Prices dialog, shown here.

Choose a time period from the drop-down list at the top of the dialog. Your choices are Month, Year, Two Years, and Five Years. Make sure check marks appear beside all securities for which you want to get historical quotes. (Click Mark All to get prices for all on the list.)

Then click the Update Now button. Quicken connects to the Internet and retrieves the information you requested. When it's done, it displays the One Step Update Summary window. Click Close to dismiss the window. You can review the quotes that were downloaded in the Security Detail view window (refer to Figure 11-5).

Downloading Asset Class Information

For each security you own or watch, you can include asset class information. This enables you to create accurate asset allocation reports and graphs. Chapter 10 explains how to enter asset class information manually; Chapter 12 explains how you can use this information to diversify your portfolio to meet your investment goals.

The trouble is that most mutual funds consist of many investments in a variety of asset classes. Manually looking up and entering this information is time-consuming and tedious. Fortunately, Quicken can download this information from the Internet and enter it for you.

Choose Investing | Investing Actions | Asset Class Changes. Quicken displays the Download Security Asset Classes dialog, which looks and works very much like the Get Historical Prices dialog shown in the previous illustration. Make sure check marks appear beside all securities for which you want to download asset class information, and then click the Update Now button. Quicken connects to the Internet and retrieves the information you requested. When it's done, it displays the One Step Update Summary window. Click Close to dismiss the window. The asset classes are automatically entered for each security.

Use Quicken.com for Updates

Using Quicken.com enables you to track your portfolio's value on the Web. Although you can do this without Quicken by manually customizing and updating the default portfolio Web page at Quicken.com, it's a lot easier to have Quicken automatically send updated portfolio information to Quicken.com for you.

To use the Quicken.com update feature, you must register Quicken. (Quicken will remind you if you haven't completed this step.) During the registration process, you will enter a Member ID and Password that you need to remember.

The registration process sets up a private Quicken.com account for you to store your portfolio data.

Exporting Your Portfolio

In Quicken, choose Investing | Investing Actions | Update Portfolio on Quicken.com. The Portfolio tab of the Customize Online Updates dialog appears, as shown next. If this dialog does not appear, you can display it by choosing Edit | Preferences | Customize Online Updates and then clicking the Portfolio tab in the dialog.

Click to place green check marks beside each account that you want to track on the Web. If you also want to track Watch List items on the Web, turn on the Track My Watch List On Quicken.com check box. Finally, select one of the upload options:

- **Send My Shares** exports the ticker symbols and the number of shares of each security you own for your portfolio. This enables you to track both prices and portfolio values.
- **Send Only My Symbols** exports just the ticker symbols for your portfolio. This enables you to track prices but not portfolio values.

When you're finished, click OK. You'll see the updated information in the Investing | Portfolio window.

Updating the Password Vault

You may want to use Quicken's Password Vault to store the different passwords that you have for your various financial institutions. Your passwords are protected with encryption. Click Tools | Password Vault | Set Up New Password Vault. The Password Vault Setup dialog will appear. Click Next. The Select Bank/CC tab will display, as shown here. The financial institutions for which you currently have established Internet connections are listed. Click the financial institution you want, and click Next.

You'll next see the Enter The Password dialog. Enter the password you use to access your financial institution account, and then reenter it to confirm it is accurate. Click Next. Now you'll be asked to enter and reenter a password for the Password Vault itself. Click Next. The Summary tab is now displayed, showing your account and its user ID. At this point you can change or delete your password. Click Done to finish.

Checking Your Portfolio on the Web

Once your portfolio has been updated, you can view it at any time from any computer with Web access. (Figure 11-7 shows an example.) Use a Web browser to navigate to www.quicken.com/. When prompted, log in. If the contents of your portfolio does not appear on the page, scroll down on the Quicken Home page and under My Account, click Online Portfolio. To see its performance, click the Performance heading beneath the Portfolio Analysis tab, and scroll

Figure 11-7 • Once your portfolio has been exported, you can view it on the Web from any computer—provided that you have logged in to your private Quicken.com account.

down to see the whole page. Do some creative management by clicking the Manage Web Portfolio & Watchlists heading.

Using Online Research Tools

Quicken offers access to a number of research tools on Quicken.com. You can use these tools to find and learn about securities before you invest.

This part of the chapter tells you a little about Quicken's online research tools so you can explore them on your own. I think you'll find them valuable resources for making wise investment decisions.

When you click Investing | Investing Tools | Online Research | Investment Research, you will be directed to the Quotes & Research tab of the Quicken Investing pages of Quicken.com. In it you have access to several research tools.

You can switch from one to another by clicking the appropriate navigation tag: Snapshot, One-Click Scorecard, Evaluator, and Headlines.

Quote Lookup

The Quote Lookup feature enables you to look up stock ticker symbols. These symbols are required to use Quicken's Online Research features for getting quotes and obtaining information about securities on the Web.

Choose Investing | Investing Tools | Online Research | Quote Lookup. Quicken displays the Symbol Lookup dialog in a Quicken browser window. Type all or part of the security name in the text box, and click Search. Quicken organizes the results by security type: Stocks, Mutual Funds, ETFs, and Indices. Click the tab of the security type you want, and examine the securities it found that matched the criteria you entered. You can note the ticker symbol and use it to get quotes or enter new securities.

Multiple Security Charting

Quicken displays a chart of a security's prices in the Security Detail View window. This is a great way to see trends in a single security's values. But what if you want to see multiple charts? Or to see a popular index? That's where Multiple Security Charting comes in.

To begin, choose Investing | Investing Tools | Online Research | Multiple Security Charting. The Multiple Security Charting window, which is shown next, appears. Use it to set options and select securities for the charts you want to create. To select more than one security, hold down CTRL while clicking each security name. When you click the Go Online To Chart button, Quicken connects you to the Internet and displays a Yahoo! Finance page with the charts you requested.

One-Click Scorecard

One-Click Scorecard instantly prepares reports that help you evaluate a security before you invest, using a variety of well-known analysis techniques and strategies.

To get started, choose Investing | Investing Tools | Online Research | One-Click Scorecard. Quicken connects to the Internet and first asks for your Member ID and password. It then displays the Quotes & Research tab of the Quicken Investing pages on Quicken.com. In the Quote text box, type the ticker symbol for the security you want to evaluate, and click Go. After a moment, Quicken displays a snapshot of the requested security. If you wish, click One-Click Scorecard to return to that view.

If you find yourself in another part of the site, return to the One-Click Scorecard by clicking the Quotes & Research tab and clicking One-Click Scorecard on the toolbar. The report that appears automatically displays the results based on the recommended investing strategy for that type of investment. For example, the recommended strategy for a stock with strong growth and value characteristics is Robert Hagstrom's *The Warren Buffet Way*. Read through the report to learn more about the analysis.

Security Evaluator

The Security Evaluator instantly prepares a detailed, six-report analysis of stocks that includes historical trends and industry comparisons. This information can help you determine whether a security's performance may meet your investing goals.

To get started, choose Investing | Investing Tools | Online Research | Evaluator. Quicken connects to the Internet and displays the Quotes & Research tab of Quicken Investing pages on Quicken.com. Enter the ticker symbol for the security you want to evaluate and click Go. After a moment, Quicken displays a snapshot of the security. Click Evaluator on the toolbar to see a detailed analysis page full of information for the security.

Mutual Fund Finder

Quicken's Mutual Fund Finder enables you to search for mutual funds based on criteria you provide. To get started, choose Investing | Investing Tools | Online

Research | Mutual Fund Finder. Quicken connects to the Internet and displays the Screener Settings page of the Mutual Fund Screener on Yahoo! Finance. Click a link for one of the Preset Screens or enter search criteria and click the Find Funds button at the bottom of the page. The results appear in an Internet window. You can click a link in the More Info column of the list to learn more about a listed fund.

Evaluating Your Position

In This Chapter:

- *Using the Investing tab*
- *Setting Investment alerts*
- *Using Investment analysis and reports*
- *Understanding the Portfolio window*
- *Using the Asset Allocation Guide*
- *Using the Portfolio Rebalancer*
- *Using the Portfolio Analyzer*
- *Previewing your Buy/Sell Decisions*
- *Estimating Capital Gains*

A s you enter transactions into Quicken—whether manually or automatically via the transaction download—Quicken builds a portrait of your investment portfolio and performance. If you're serious about investing, you can use this information to evaluate your investing position and fine-tune your portfolio to diversify and maximize returns.

Quicken's Investing tab offers a wide range of tools—including reports, graphs, alerts, analysis tools, and reference materials—that you can use to evaluate and strengthen your investment positions. This chapter takes a closer look at the features that can make you a better investor.

Using the Investing Tab

The Investing tab should be your first stop for evaluating your investment position. Each of its five views includes snapshots with calculated information and links to more information on Quicken and Quicken.com features. Because the Investing tab always displays the most recent information it has, its windows are most useful immediately after downloading quotes, news, and research information, as discussed in Chapter 11.

To open the Investing tab window, click the Investing tab near the top of Quicken's main window. One of the Investing tab's views appears. Click the button for the view you want to see.

This part of the chapter takes you on a guided tour of Quicken's Investing tab so you know exactly how you can use it to monitor your investments.

Exploring the Account Overview

The Account Overview (you may have to expand the View submenu), which is shown in Figure 12-1, offers snapshots with general information about your investment accounts and investments, as of the last time they were updated. Watch List securities are shown with the latest updated prices.

Setting Investment Alerts

Investment alerts are downloaded automatically with quotes and news headlines, as discussed in Chapter 11. They appear in the Portfolio view in the Investing tab window. You can hover your cursor over an alert icon to view why the alert has been issued. You can then click a link to view additional information either in your Quicken data file or on the Web.

Investment and Retirement Accounts					Options ▾
Account	Cost Basis	Gain/Loss	Gain/Loss (%)	Day Gain/Loss	Day Gain/Loss (%)
Investment					
Single Mutual Fund	3,750.00	10,135.00	270.27	0.00	0.00
Brokerage	10,309.46	24,313.88	235.84	0.00	0.00
Brokerage Acct	557.51	-99.55	-17.86	0.00	0.00
IRA	0.00	0.00	0.00	0.00	0.00
Subtotal	**14,616.97**	**34,349.33**	**235.00**	**0.00**	**0.00**
Total	**14,616.97**	**34,349.33**	**235.00**	**0.00**	**0.00**

Watch List				Options ▾
Name	Day Change	Day Change (%)		Quote/Price
ADOBE SYS INC			e.st.	32.35
Apple Inc			e.st.	184.90
Dow Jones Industrials			e.st.	9,487.67
GE			e.st.	15.36
Google Inc			e.st.	484.58
HEINZ H J CO			e.st.	38.85
INTUIT INC			e.st.	27.77
MICROSOFT CORP			e.st.	24.96
NASDAQ Composite			e.st.	2,048.11

Figure 12-1 • The Account Overview displays information about your investment accounts as of the most recent update.

There are ten investment alerts:

- **Price And Volume** consists of three alerts. Price alerts notify you when a security's price rises above or falls below values you specify. Volume alerts notify you when the sales volume of a security exceeds a value you specify. You must set options for these alerts on Quicken.com.
- **Download Quotes Reminder** reminds you to download quotes from Quicken.com.
- **Maturity Date Reminder** reminds you when a CD or bond reaches its maturity date.
- **Stocks Ratings And Analysis** notifies you when ratings and analysis information becomes available for stocks you track.
- **Mutual Funds Ratings And Analysis** notifies you when ratings and analysis information becomes available for mutual funds you track.
- **Tax Implications On Sale** notifies you of your tax implications when you sell a security.
- **Cap. Gains For The Year** notifies you if you exceed your capital gains limit for the year.
- **Tax Efficient Investments** provides you with information about investments that are more tax-efficient than those you already have.
- **Mutual Fund Distributions** provides you with information about mutual fund distributions.
- **Securities Holding Period** provides you with information about holding periods for securities you own.

The alerts I find most useful are Price And Volume, Maturity Date Reminder, Stocks Ratings And Analysis, and Cap. Gains For The Year. These alerts give me timely information that I need to know without subjecting me to information overload.

Setting Up Alerts   To set up investment alerts, click Investing | Account Overview, and then on the right of the Investment And Retirement Accounts pane, click Options | Setup/Edit Investing Alerts. Quicken displays the Setup tab of the Alerts Center window, shown next, which Chapter 9 discusses in greater detail. On the left side of the window, click the name of an alert you want to set, and then set options for the alert in the right side of the window. (You must set some alerts, such as the Price And Volume alert, on Quicken.com.) You can disable an alert by removing the check mark beside its name. When you are finished making changes, click OK to save them.

Deleting Alerts   To remove an alert from the Portfolio view, select Tools | Alerts Center, and click the Show All tab. Then uncheck any alerts you want to deselect, and click Delete.

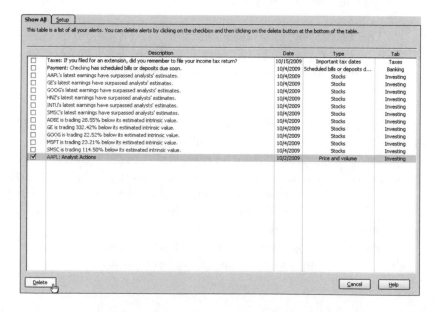

Reviewing Investment & Retirement Accounts

The Investment & Retirement Accounts snapshot lists all of your investment accounts, including those for retirement, along with their current market values. (Market value is determined by the most recently downloaded or entered security values.) You can click the name of an account to view its transactions or overview. The Options menu contains several commands for working with accounts, including downloading updates.

Using Watch Lists

The Watch List snapshot lists all of the securities on your Watch List, along with the most recently entered or downloaded quotes. Click a security's name or symbol to open the Security Detail View window for it. Icons beside a ticker symbol indicate alert and news headlines for a security when you point to them. The Options menu on the Watch List snapshot's button bar offers commands for working with securities and your Watch List.

Studying Your Performance

The Performance view of the Investing tab (see Figure 12-2) displays graphs and tables of information about your investment performance. You can customize many of the snapshots that appear in the Performance view using commands on the snapshot's Options menu. You can further customize the Performance view window by selecting one of the Show Accounts options at the top of the window: All, Investment, Retirement, or Multiple Accounts.

Growth Of $10,000

The Growth Of $10,000 chart illustrates how an investment of $10,000 in your portfolio has grown over the past year. You can turn on check boxes beside popular investment indexes to compare your investment performance to one or more indexes, as shown in Figure 12-2.

Average Annual Return

The Average Annual Return displays the one-year, three-year, and five-year return on each of your investment accounts. If the account has one or more securities in the one-, three-, or five-year period, there will be an Average Annual Return reported for the account. If the account did not exist or no lots of the account's securities existed during the one-, three-, or five-year period, the Average Annual Return will show as N/A.

Figure 12-2 • The Performance view of the Investing tab shows you, at a glance, how your investments are doing.

Portfolio Value vs. Cost Basis

The Portfolio Value vs. Cost Basis graph uses a line graph and a bar graph to illustrate your portfolio's cost basis—what you've invested—and its market value. Ideally, you want the tops of the bars to appear above the line, indicating that your account is worth more than you spent to buy the securities.

Investing Activity

Investing Activity provides quarter-to-date (QTD) and year-to-date (YTD) summaries of your investment values and transactions as well as capital gains information.

Exploring Asset Allocation

The Asset Allocation view of the Investing tab (see Figure 12-3) displays a number of customizable graphs of your investment data, along with a few snapshots with links to other features. Each of the graphs that appears in the

Asset Allocation view can be customized using commands on the graph's Options menu. Buttons beneath each chart enable you to go to a full-sized graph in a report window or view a related report. You can further customize the Asset Allocation view window by selecting one of the Show Accounts options: All, Investment, Retirement, or Multiple Accounts.

Reviewing Your Asset Allocation

Asset Allocation, which is covered in detail later in this chapter, refers to the way your investment dollars are distributed among different types of investments. It's a measure of how well your portfolio is diversified.

The Asset Allocation graph displays two pie charts: Actual Allocation and Target Allocation. Actual Allocation indicates your portfolio's current diversification. Figure 12-3 shows that a heavy majority of the stocks in this account are invested in large-cap stocks. Target Allocation is the allocation you set up with Quicken's Rebalance Portfolio, which is discussed later in this chapter, in the section titled "Using the Rebalance Portfolio." If you have not yet used the Rebalance Portfolio, the Target Allocation pie won't have any slices.

Figure 12-3 • The Asset Allocation view of the Investing tab displays analytical graphs of your investments.

Mutual Fund Ratings from Morningstar

Quicken displays up-to-date ratings from Morningstar, an investment research organization that rates mutual funds based on a variety of criteria. Ratings for mutual funds you track in Quicken are automatically downloaded with asset class and related information. The more stars, the higher the rating.

Allocation By Account

The Allocation By Account chart indicates how your portfolio's market value is distributed among your Quicken investing accounts.

Allocation By Security

The Allocation By Security chart indicates how your portfolio's market value is distributed among different securities. This is a measure of diversification. The more pie slices and the more even the slices, the better your portfolio is diversified among securities. Figure 12-3 shows that too much of the investment in stocks is in a single stock.

Understanding Your Portfolio View

The Portfolio view of the Investing tab (see Figure 12-4) displays all of your investments in one place. Information can be viewed in a wide variety of ways to show you exactly what you need to see to understand the performance, value, or components of your portfolio.

You can open the Portfolio window by clicking the Portfolio view in the Investing tab, by choosing Investing | Portfolio (you may have to expand the View submenu), or by pressing CTRL-U.

Using Portfolio View Options

You can quickly customize the Portfolio window's view by using the Show, Group By, and As Of options right beneath the button bar. There are many view combinations—far too many to illustrate in this book. Here's a brief overview so you can explore these options on your own.

Using Show Options   The Show drop-down list enables you to specify the view that should be used to display the information. Each of the nine predefined views can be customized with the Customize Current View dialog, shown later in this section. You can also customize nine "custom" views to make your own views of the data.

Using Group By Options   The Group By options enable you to select the order in which securities appear. The drop-down list offers seven options: Accounts, Industry, Security, Security Type, Investing Goal, Asset Class, and

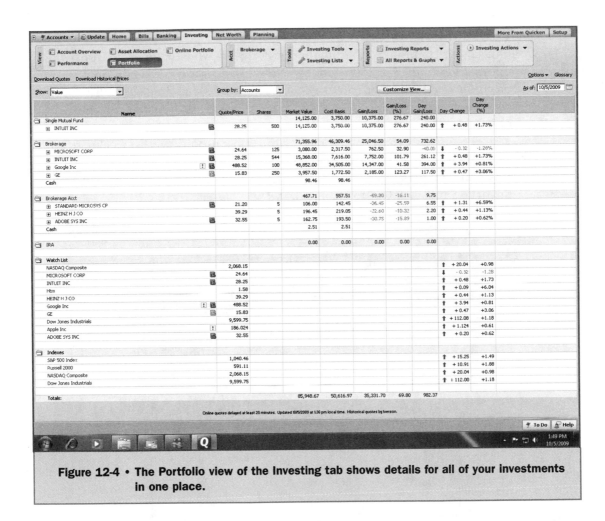

Figure 12-4 • **The Portfolio view of the Investing tab shows details for all of your investments in one place.**

Sector. These options correspond to information entered as part of a security's definition, either manually when you add the security to Quicken or automatically when you download asset class information. Learn how to add securities to Quicken in Chapter 10 and how to download security information in Chapter 11.

Using Portfolio Date   You can use the As Of box to set the date for which you want to view the portfolio. For example, suppose you want to see what your portfolio looked like a month ago, before a particularly volatile market period. Enter that date in the text box. Or you can click the calendar button beside the text box to display a calendar of dates, and then click the date you want to display. The view changes to show your portfolio as of the date you specified.

Customizing a View

Quicken offers an incredible amount of flexibility when it comes to displaying information in the Portfolio window. Not only does it come with nine preconfigured views that you can choose from the Show drop-down list, but it also enables you to create nine additional custom views. You can customize any of these views.

To customize a view, begin by using the Show drop-down list to choose the view you want to customize. Then click the Customize View button. The Customize Current View dialog appears, as shown next. Set options as desired in the dialog and click OK to change the view.

Changing the View Name   To change the name of the view, enter a new name in the Name box.

Selecting Columns to Show   To display a column of information, select it in the Available Columns list and click the Add button beside it. To hide a column of information, select it in the Displayed Columns list and click the Remove button. You can change the order in which columns appear by selecting a column name in the Displayed Columns list and using the Move Up or Move Down buttons to change its order in the list.

Displaying Symbols Rather Than Names   To display a security's ticker symbol rather than its name, turn on the Show Symbols In Name Column check box.

Selecting Accounts to Include   To specify which accounts should appear, toggle the green check marks to the left of the account name in the Accounts To Include list. Only those accounts that are checked will appear. You can change the order in which accounts appear by selecting an account name in the Accounts To Include list and clicking the Move Up or Move Down buttons. To include hidden accounts in the Accounts To Include list, turn on the Show (Hidden Accounts) check box.

Selecting Securities to Include   To specify which securities should appear, toggle the green check marks to the left of the security name in the Securities To Include list. Only those securities that are checked will appear. To include hidden securities in the Securities To Include list, turn on the Show (Hidden Securities) check box.

Setting Portfolio View Options

Quicken also enables you to specify the period for return calculations and the tax rate used in the Portfolio window. Setting these options enables you to fine-tune the way Quicken makes Portfolio window calculations.

Choose Preferences from the Options menu on the Portfolio window's button bar (refer to Figure 12-4). Use the Portfolio View Options dialog that appears (shown here) to set options and click OK. Your options are as follows:

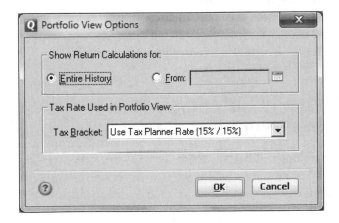

Show Return Calculations For The Show Return Calculations For area offers two options for determining the period for which Quicken calculates the return on investment:

- **Entire History** includes all transactions in the calculations.
- **From** enables you to enter a starting date for calculations. All transactions between that starting date and the current date are included in the calculations.

Tax Rate Used In Portfolio View Use the Tax Bracket drop-down list to choose tax rates that should be used in tax calculations for capital gains. If you are utilizing Quicken's Tax Planner, which is covered in Chapter 19, choose Use Tax Planner Rate. Otherwise, choose the rates that are appropriate for your financial situation.

Tracking Security Values

As the individual views within the Investing tab illustrate, Quicken can automatically do all the math to tell you what your investments are worth—*if* you take the time to enter the per-share prices of each of your securities.

When you record transactions, Quicken automatically records the security price. It uses the most recently entered price as an estimate to calculate the current value of the investment. You may see this in the Portfolio—gray *est.* characters indicate that the price is an estimate. The *est.* characters appear if the current date is on a weekend or holiday, or if you haven't entered or downloaded the current day's prices. Of course, the Portfolio window and all of Quicken's investing reports and charts are a lot more valuable with up-to-date security price information and a history of prices.

You can enter price information in two ways: manually (the hard way) and automatically (the easy way). Learn how to enter security prices manually in this chapter; to learn how to enter prices automatically via Internet download, consult Chapter 11.

Manually Entering Security Prices

Manually entering security prices isn't difficult—it's just time-consuming. And the more securities you track, the more time-consuming it is. But without an Internet connection, this may be the only way you can enter prices into Quicken.

If you track more than one or two securities and want to update price information more often than once a week, skip the rest of this section. You don't want to enter security prices manually. Trust me. It's an extremely tedious task.

Quicken's ability to download stock prices directly from the Internet—even five-year price histories—can save you tons of time and prevent data entry errors. And best of all, it's free. All you need is an Internet connection. Learn about setting up an Internet connection in Chapter 4 and about downloading quotes in Chapter 11.

To enter a security's price manually, start by displaying the Security Detail View window: From the Investing | Portfolio window, click the name of the security for which you want to enter price information. Then choose Edit Price History from the Update button on the button bar. The Price History window for the security appears, as shown next, showing all the price information stored within the Quicken data file for the security.

An alternative way that you may find simpler to enter prices is to press CTRL-U, select the date you want to enter prices for from the As Of date drop-down list, and type the prices into the Quote/Price Share column. Press Enter to record each price.

Date	Price	High	Low	Volume
10/2/2009	27.77	28.07	27.56	2,315,306
10/1/2009	27.82	28.40	27.64	3,585,877
9/30/2009	28.50	28.58	27.92	4,185,574
9/29/2009	28.25	28.48	28.06	2,754,791
9/28/2009	28.23	28.50	27.75	3,163,810
9/25/2009	27.65	27.82	27.55	3,082,559
9/24/2009	27.64	27.98	27.46	4,445,067
9/23/2009	27.80	28.26	27.62	4,663,520
9/22/2009	27.87	28	27.27	5,306,591
9/21/2009	27.47	27.84	27.35	3,443,255
9/18/2009	27.77	27.93	27.40	3,730,019
9/17/2009	27.64	27.95	27.55	3,450,797
9/16/2009	27.89	27.97	27.39	4,910,771
9/15/2009	27.78	27.81	27.20	2,596,389

Price History for: INTUIT INC — New Edit Delete — Print — How Do I?

You can use buttons on the window's button bar to add, edit, delete, and print the price history:

- **New** displays the New Price dialog (shown on the top of the next page). Use it to enter the date and closing price for the security. If you're really interested in stock trading technicals, you can even enter the daily high, low, and volume.
- **Edit** displays the Edit Price dialog for the currently selected price. This dialog looks and works just like the New Price dialog.

- **Delete** removes the selected price. When you click this button, a confirmation dialog appears. You must click OK to delete the price.
- **Print** prints the price list.
- **How Do I?** displays the Quicken Personal Finances Help window, which contains a list of topics about working with the Edit Price History window.

Viewing Market Values and Performance

Once you've entered price information for your securities, you can view their market value and performance information in the Portfolio window (see Figure 12-4) and Security Detail View window. Use options within the windows to modify the information that is displayed. This chapter explained how earlier; additional information is in Chapter 10.

Using Investment Analysis Tools

In addition to the Quicken.com-based investment research tools discussed in Chapter 11, Quicken offers a number of built-in tools that can help you learn more about investing and analyze your investment portfolio.

This part of the chapter introduces these analysis tools so you can explore them more fully on your own.

Understanding Asset Allocation

Many investment gurus say that an investor's goals should determine his or her asset allocation. If you're not sure what your asset allocation should be, Quicken can help. It includes a wealth of information about asset allocation, including sample portfolios with their corresponding allocations. You can use this feature to learn what your target asset allocation should be to meet your investing goals. Then you can monitor your asset allocation and, if necessary, rebalance your portfolio to keep it in line with what it should be.

Using the Asset Allocation Guide

The Asset Allocation Guide explains what asset allocation is, why it's important, and how Quicken can help monitor it in your portfolio. Choose Investing Tools | Asset Allocation Guide. The Asset Allocation Guide window appears (see Figure 12-5).

To take full advantage of this feature, read the information on the right side of the window. You can click links within the text or in the left column to learn more about specific topics. If you're new to asset allocation, you may find the See Model Portfolios link especially useful. It shows suggested asset allocations based on risk and returns for a number of portfolios.

Monitoring Your Asset Allocation

To monitor the asset allocation of your portfolio, you must enter asset class information for each of your investments. You can do this in two ways:

- **Manually enter asset class information.** Although this isn't difficult for stocks, it can be time-consuming for investments that have an asset class mixture, such as mutual funds.

Figure 12-5 • The Asset Allocation Guide explains what asset allocation is and how it can help you meet your investment goals.

- **Download asset class information.** If you have a connection to the Internet, this is the best way to enter this information. With a few clicks, Quicken does all of the work in seconds. The information is complete and accurate. Learn how to download asset class information in Chapter 11.

Viewing Your Asset Allocation

A pie chart of your asset allocation appears in the Asset Allocation Guide window (see Figure 12-5) of the Investing tab (see Figure 12-3). To get more information about a piece of the pie, point to it. A yellow box appears, displaying the asset class, total market value, and percent of portfolio value.

Setting Your Target Asset Allocation

If you know what you want your asset allocation to be, you can set up a target asset allocation. Quicken can then display your target in the pie chart beside the current asset allocation chart on the Investing tab's Asset Allocation window so you can monitor how close you are to your target.

Display the Asset Allocation view of the Investing tab window (refer to Figure 12-3). Then choose Change Target Allocations from the Options menu in the button bar of the Asset Allocation area. The Set Target Asset Allocation dialog appears. Here's what it looks like with a sample allocation already entered:

Enter the desired percentages for each class of asset. When the total of all percentages equals 100, click OK to save your settings. The Target chart in the

Asset Allocation area of the Investing tab window reflects your settings (compare to the unset original in Figure 12-3).

Using the Portfolio Rebalancer

If your current asset allocation deviates from your target asset allocation, you may want to rebalance your portfolio. This means buying and selling investments to bring you closer to your target asset allocation.

Keep in mind that brokerage fees and capital gains impacts often are related to buying and selling securities. For this reason, you should carefully evaluate your investment situation to determine how you can minimize costs and capital gains while rebalancing your portfolio. If small adjustments are necessary to bring you to your target asset allocation, you may not find it worth the cost to make the changes. Use this information as a guideline only!

Quicken can tell you exactly how you must change your current asset allocation to meet your target asset allocation. In the Asset Allocation view and panel of the Investing window, click Options | Rebalance Portfolio. The Portfolio Rebalancer window, shown in Figure 12-6, appears. It provides instructions and shows you how much you must adjust each asset class to meet your targeted goals.

Here's an example. Figure 12-6 indicates that I need $25,361 more invested in Small Caps and $46,577 less invested in large-cap stock. If I wanted to meet my target asset allocation, I could sell $20,000 worth of my large-cap stock investments and reinvest the funds in Small Caps. This would change my asset allocation, bringing it closer to target, without changing the total value of my portfolio.

Understanding Your Portfolio Analyzer

Quicken's Portfolio Analyzer enables you to look at your portfolio in a number of ways. To display it, click Investing | Investing Tools | Portfolio Analyzer. You'll find these options on the left sidebar:

- **Performance** shows your portfolio's average annual rate of return, compared to market indexes like the Dow Jones Industrial Average and the S&P 500 index. It also shows your five best and worst performers, so you can see how individual securities are doing.
- **Holdings** lists your investment accounts and then shows a pie chart of your top ten holdings. Because most experts recommend that no single security take up more than 10 percent of your portfolio, you may find the percentage distribution helpful when considering diversification.
- **Asset Allocation** displays your current actual and target asset allocation so you can see how close you are to your target. How to set up a target allocation was explained earlier in this chapter.

Figure 12-6 • **The Portfolio Rebalancer window tells you what adjustments you need to make to bring your asset allocation closer to target.**

- **Risk Profile** shows how "risky" your portfolio is when compared to the risk associated with specific classes of investments.
- **Tax Implications** summarizes your realized and unrealized YTD capital gains or losses. Capital gains and losses are broken down into two categories: short term and long term.

What's great about the Portfolio Analyzer is that it provides tables and charts to show information about your portfolio, and then it explains everything in plain English so you know what the tables and charts mean. Using this feature regularly can really help you learn about the world of investing and how your portfolio measures up. To give it a try, choose Investing | Investing Tools | Portfolio Analyzer.

Previewing Your Buy/Sell Decisions

Quicken Premier includes a feature called Buy/Sell Preview, which offers a quick and easy way to see the impact of a securities purchase or sale on your finances—including your taxes.

Choose Investing | Investing Tools | Buy/Sell Preview. In the top half of the Buy/Sell Preview window that appears, enter information about the proposed purchase or sale. Quicken automatically enters the most recent price information for a security you own or watch, but you can override that amount if necessary. When you're finished setting options, click Calculate. Quicken displays its results in the bottom half of the window. Here are two examples—one for a purchase and the other for a sale:

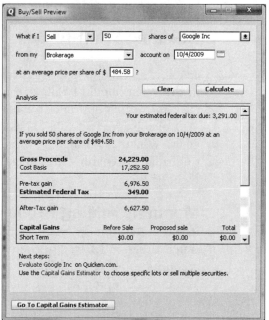

The Buy/Sell Preview feature works with Quicken's Tax Planner, which is discussed in Chapter 19, to calculate the net effect of a sale on your expected tax bill or refund. You can better understand the implications of selling a security on your tax status.

Estimating Capital Gains

Quicken's Capital Gains Estimator enables you to estimate capital gains or losses and their related tax implications *before* you sell a security. The information it provides can help you make an informed decision about which security to sell.

Getting Started

Choose Investing | Investing Tools | Capital Gains Estimator. The Capital Gains Estimator's welcome window appears.

Start by reading the information in the right side of the window. It explains what the Capital Gains Estimator does and offers links for learning more about specific terms and topics. Then click each of the links in the left side of the window, in turn, to step through the process of setting up the Capital Gains Estimator for your situation. You'll be prompted to name and choose a scenario, select taxable investment accounts to include, set your tax rate, and enter capital loss carryover information. When you enter complete and accurate information, Quicken can provide a more accurate indication of tax impacts.

Deciding What to Sell

Quicken Premier users can tap into a feature in the Capital Gains Estimator that enables Quicken to help you decide which securities to sell. Follow instructions in the What Should I Sell? screen to tell Quicken your goals for the sale, and click the Search button at the bottom of the window.

A dialog appears while Quicken makes complex calculations to meet your goals. When it's finished, you can click the View Results button in the dialog to display a scenario with Quicken's recommendation and the results (see Figure 12-7).

Manually Adding Proposed Sales

If you prefer, you can manually indicate proposed sales in the Scenario window (refer to Figure 12-7). The Step 1 area shows all the securities you hold in the accounts you selected during the setup process.

You can add a proposed sale in two ways:

- Double-click the name of the security you want to sell. Then enter the number of shares and sales price in the Add To Scenario dialog that appears (shown here) and click OK. If you have multiple purchase lots for the security, this automatically sells the oldest lots first.

Figure 12-7 · Quicken displays its recommendations as a scenario.

- If necessary, click the plus sign (+) to the left of the security that you want to sell to display the purchase lots. Then click the lot you want to sell. This enables you to specify exactly which lots are to be sold in the Proposed Sales area.

No matter which method you use, the sale is added to the Step 2 area of the window, which lists all of the proposed sales (see Figure 12-7).

To adjust the number of shares to be sold, click in the Shares To Sell field for the proposed sale (in the Step 2 area) and enter a new value. The value you enter must be less than or equal to the number of shares purchased in that lot.

You can set up proposed sales for up to three scenarios—just click the Scenario link on the left side of the window to see and set that scenario's options. You can mix and match any sales you like to reach your goal.

Reading the Results

When all information has been entered, you can see the true power of the Capital Gains Estimator. It tells you about the proceeds from the sales, as well as the gain or loss. If you scroll down in the What If Scenarios screen (refer to Figure 12-7), you'll find more information about the proposed sale and its tax implications in the Step 3 area, including the gross profit and net proceeds from proposed sales. You can click links to view the results of additional calculations, such as the tax situation before and after executing the proposed sales and gain or loss on the proposed sales. Do the same for each scenario to see how they compare—then make your selling decision.

Net Worth

This part of the book explains how you can use Quicken Personal Finance Software's Net Worth features to keep track of your property and loans. It starts with coverage of assets, such as a car and home, and the loans that you may have used to finance them. Then it moves on to tell you how you can use the Net Worth tab and other Quicken features to monitor expenses related to your assets and debt. This part of the book has two chapters:

Chapter 13:   Monitoring Assets and Loans

Chapter 14:   Keeping Tabs on Your Net Worth

Part Four

Monitoring Assets and Loans

In This Chapter:

- *Assets and debts defined*
- *Loan basics*
- *Setting up asset and loan accounts*
- *Tracking a loan*
- *Adjusting asset values*

Assets and debts (or liabilities) make up your net worth. Bank and investment accounts, which I cover in Chapters 5 and 10, are examples of assets. Credit card accounts, which I cover in Chapter 5, are examples of debts. But you may want to use Quicken Personal Finance Software to track other assets and debts, including a home, car, recreational vehicle, and related loans. By including these items in your Quicken data file, you can quickly and accurately calculate your net worth and financial fitness.

This chapter explains how to set up asset and debt accounts to track your possessions and any outstanding loans you used to purchase them.

The Basics

Before you begin, it's a good idea to have a clear understanding of what assets, debts, and loans are, and how they work together in your Quicken data file.

Assets and Debts

An asset is something you own. Common examples might be your house, car, camper, computer, television set, and patio furniture. Most assets have value—you can sell them for cash or trade them for another asset.

Although you can use Quicken to track every single asset you own in its own asset account, doing so would be cumbersome. Instead, you'll normally account for high-value assets in individual accounts and lower-value assets in a group asset account. For example, you may create separate asset accounts for your home and your car, but group personal possessions, such as your computer, television, and stamp collection, in a single group asset account. This makes it easy to track all your assets, so you have accurate records for insurance and other purposes.

A *debt* is something you owe—often to buy one of your assets! For example, if you buy a house, chances are you'll use a mortgage to finance it. The mortgage, which is a loan that is secured by your home, is a debt. You can use Quicken to track all of your debts, so you know exactly how much you owe at any given time.

Loans

A *loan* is a promise to pay money. Loans are commonly used to buy assets, although some folks often turn to debt consolidation loans to pay off other debts—this is discussed further in Chapter 17.

Here's how it works. The lender gives the borrower money in exchange for the borrower's promise to pay it back. (The promise is usually in writing, with lots of signatures and initials.) The borrower normally pays back the loan to the lender with periodic payments that include interest on the loan balance or *principal.* The amount of the loan is reduced after each payment. The borrower incurs interest expense while the lender earns interest income.

While most people think of a loan as something you owe (a debt), a loan can also be something you own (an asset). For example, say you borrow money from your brother to buy a car. In your Quicken data file, the loan is related to a debt—money that you owe your brother. In your brother's Quicken data file, the loan is related to an asset—money that is due to him from you.

Types of Loans

There are several types of loans, some of which are designed for specific purposes. Here's a quick summary of some of what's available, along with their pros and cons.

This list is not exhaustive. Financial institutions are always coming up with new loan products, and it's impossible to keep up with them here. If you're interested in a loan product that isn't mentioned in this chapter, consult the financial institution that is offering it to learn more about how it works and what it can do for you.

Mortgage

A *mortgage* is a long-term loan secured by real estate. Most mortgages require a down payment on the property of 10 percent or higher. Monthly payments are based on the term of the loan and the interest rate applied to the principal. The interest you pay on a mortgage for a first or second home is tax-deductible. If you fail to make mortgage payments, your house could be sold to pay back the mortgage.

A *balloon mortgage* is a special type of short-term mortgage. Rather than make monthly payments over the full typical mortgage term, at the end of the fifth, seventh, or tenth year, you pay the balance of the mortgage in one big "balloon" payment. Some balloon mortgages offer the option of refinancing when the balloon payment is due.

Home Equity Loans or Lines of Credit

A *home equity loan* or *second mortgage* is a line of credit secured by the equity in your home—the difference between the home's market value and the amount of outstanding debt. Your equity rises when you make mortgage payments or property values increase. It declines when you borrow against your equity or property values decrease. A home equity loan lets you borrow against this equity.

A home equity loan has two benefits: Interest rates are usually lower than other credit, and interest may be tax-deductible. For these reasons, many people use home equity loans to pay off credit card debt; renovate their homes; or buy cars, boats, or other recreational vehicles. But, as with a mortgage, if you fail to make your home equity payments, your house could be sold to satisfy the debt.

Reverse Equity Loans

A *reverse equity loan* provides people who own their homes in full with a regular monthly income. Instead of you paying the lender, the lender pays you. This type of loan is attractive to retirees who live on a fixed income. The loan is paid back when the home is sold—often after the death of the homeowner.

Car Loans

A *car loan* is a loan secured by a vehicle, such as a car, truck, or motor home. Normally, you make a down payment and use the loan to pay the balance of the car's purchase price. Monthly payments are based on the term of the loan and the interest rate applied to the principal. Interest on car loans is not tax-deductible.

Personal Loans

A *personal loan* is an unsecured loan—a loan that requires no collateral. Monthly payments are based on the term of the loan and the interest rate applied to the principal. You can use a personal loan for just about anything. Some people use them to pay off multiple smaller debts so they have only one monthly payment. Interest on personal loans is not tax-deductible.

Loan Considerations

When applying for a loan, a number of variables have a direct impact on what the loan costs you now and in the future. Ask about all of these things *before* applying for any loan.

Interest Rate

The *interest rate* is the annual percentage applied to the loan principal. Several factors affect the interest rate you may be offered:

- **Your credit record** affects the interest rate offered, because a borrower with a good credit record can usually get a better rate than one with a bad credit record. Of course, if your credit record is really bad, you might not be able to borrow money at any rate.
- **The type of loan** affects the interest rate offered because, generally speaking, personal loans have the highest interest rates, whereas mortgages have the lowest. From highest to lowest between these two types are a used car loan, a new car loan, and a home equity reserve or line of credit.
- **The loan term** affects the interest rate offered, because the length of a loan can vary the interest within a specific loan type. For example, for car loans, the longer the term, the lower the rate.
- **The amount of the down payment** affects the interest rate offered, because the more money you put down on the purchase, the lower the rate may be.
- **Your location** affects the interest rate offered, because rates vary from one area of the country to another.
- **The lender** affects the interest rate offered, because rates also vary from one lender to another. Certain types of lenders have lower rates than others.

Two kinds of interest rates can apply to a loan:

- **Fixed rate** applies the same rate to the principal throughout the loan term.
- **Variable rate** applies a different rate to the loan throughout the loan term. For example, the loan may start with one rate and, each year, switch to a different rate. The rate is usually established by adding a certain number of percentage points to a national index, such as Treasury bill rates. A cap limits the amount the rate can change. Mortgages with this type of rate are referred to as *adjustable rate mortgages*, or *ARMs*.

Although ARMs usually offer a lower initial interest rate than fixed-rate mortgages, you should consider the overall economic conditions before deciding on one. For example, when we purchased our first home in the mid-1980s when interest rates were high, we selected an ARM. When interest rates dropped, so did the rate on our mortgage. If we'd selected a fixed-rate mortgage when we bought that home, we would have had to refinance to get the same savings. Rates were much lower when we bought our current home in the late 1990s, so we selected a fixed rate to protect us from possible rate increases in the future. A few years ago, when rates were down again, we refinanced to lock in at an even lower rate and reduce our monthly payments and interest expenses.

You can use Quicken's Refinance Calculator to determine whether it's worthwhile to refinance your home. Using Quicken's calculators is discussed in Chapter 16.

Term

A loan's *term* is the period of time between the loan date and the date payment is due in full. Loan terms vary depending on the type of loan:

- Mortgage loan and home equity reserve loan terms are typically 10, 15, 20, or 30 years.
- Balloon mortgage loan terms are typically 5, 7, or 10 years.
- Car loan terms are typically 3, 4, or 5 years.

Down Payment

A *down payment* is an up-front payment toward the purchase of a home or car. Most mortgages require at least 10 percent down; 20 percent down is preferred.

Keep in mind that if you make only a 10 percent down payment on a home, you may be required to pay for the cost of private mortgage insurance (PMI).

This protects the lender from loss if you fail to pay your mortgage, but it increases your monthly mortgage payments.

Application Fees

Most lenders require you to pay an application fee to process your loan application. This usually includes the cost of obtaining a property appraisal and credit report. These fees are usually not refundable—even if you are turned down.

Mortgage Closing Costs

In addition to the application fee and down payment, many other costs are involved in securing a mortgage and purchasing a home. These are known as *closing costs*. The Real Estate Settlement Procedures Act of 1974 requires that your lender provide a good faith estimate of closing costs. This document summarizes all of the costs of closing on a home based on the mortgage the lender is offering.

Here's a brief list of the types of costs you may encounter. Because they vary from lender to lender, they could be a deciding factor when shopping for a mortgage. Note that most of these fees are not negotiable.

- **Origination fee** covers the administrative costs of processing a loan.
- **Discount or "points"** is a fee based on a percentage rate applied to the loan amount. For example, 1 point on a $250,000 mortgage is $2,500.
- **Appraisal fee** covers the cost of a market-value appraisal of the property by a licensed, certified appraiser.
- **Credit report fee** covers the cost of obtaining a credit history of the prospective borrower(s) to determine creditworthiness.
- **Underwriting fee** covers the cost of underwriting the loan. This is the process of determining loan risks and establishing terms and conditions.
- **Document preparation fee** covers the cost of preparing legal and other documents required to process the loan.
- **Title insurance fee** covers the cost of title insurance, which protects the lender and buyer against loss due to disputes over ownership and possession of the property.
- **Recording fee** covers the cost of entering the sale of a property into public records.
- **Prepaid items** are taxes, insurance, and assessments paid in advance of their due dates. These expenses are not paid to the lender but are due at the closing date.

Tips for Minimizing Loan Expenses

Borrowing money costs money. It's as simple as that. But you can do some things to minimize the cost of a loan.

Shop for the lowest rate. This may seem like a no-brainer, but a surprising number of people simply go to a local bank and accept whatever terms they are offered. You don't have to use a local bank to borrow money for a home, car, or other major purchase. Check the financial pages of your local newspaper or the Quicken Loans page on Quicken.com. And if you're shopping for a car, keep an eye out for low-interest financing deals. Sometimes, you can save a lot of money in interest by buying when the time is right. For example, suppose you have a choice of two five-year car loans for $20,000—one at 7 percent and the other at 7.75 percent. Over the course of five years, you'll pay $1,003 less if you go with the lower rate. That can buy a lot of gas—even at today's fuel prices.

Minimize the loan term. The shorter the loan term, the less interest you'll pay over the life of the loan. The savings can be quite substantial. For example, suppose you have a choice of two loan terms for a $200,000, 6.5 percent mortgage: 15 years or 30 years. If you choose the 15-year mortgage, you'll pay $113,599 in interest, but if you choose the 30-year mortgage, you'll pay a whopping $255,089 in interest—nearly $142,000 more! Neither option is appealing, but the shorter-term mortgage is certainly easier to swallow. The drawback? The monthly payment for the 15 year mortgage is $1,742, while the payment for the 30-year mortgage is just $1,264. Obviously, your monthly spending budget will weigh heavily into the decision.

Maximize the down payment. The less you borrow, the less you'll pay in interest—and the less your monthly payments will be. Take the loan term example just shown. Suppose your budget won't allow you to go with the shorter-term loan—you just can't make those monthly payments. But if you cashed in an IRA worth $30,000 and put that toward the down payment (talk to your tax advisor; you may be able to do this without penalty for the purchase of a first home), you could knock $261 per month off the 15-year loan's monthly payment, which might be enough to fit it into your budget—and save another $17,040 in interest!

Make extra loan payments. If you can't go for a shorter-term loan, consider making extra payments toward the loan's principal. Take another look at the 30-year mortgage example just shown. If you pay an additional $100 per month (increasing your monthly payment to $1,364), you can save more than $55,950 in interest and pay off the loan almost six years early! Or perhaps you get a generous holiday bonus each year. If you put $1,000 of that bonus toward the mortgage each January as an extra payment, you can save $46,760 in interest and pay off the loan more than four years early!

Clean up your credit before applying for a loan.   Loan terms vary based on credit history. To get the best deal, your credit should be as clean as possible. If you think there might be problems in your credit report, get a copy—you can learn how by choosing the Services tab and clicking Free Credit Report in the lower-left corner. Then do what you need to get things cleaned up, but be wary of services that promise to do this for you. Some may not help you.

When evaluating the dollar impact of different loan deals, use Quicken's Loan Calculator. It'll make complex loan payment calculations for you. Chapter 16 explains how to use Quicken's financial calculators, including the Loan Calculator and Refinance Calculator.

Setting Up Accounts

To track an asset or debt with Quicken, you must set up an appropriate account. All transactions related to the asset or debt will be recorded in the account's register.

In this section, you'll read about the types of accounts you can use to track your assets and debts, and how to set up each type of account.

Choosing the Right Account

Quicken offers four Net Worth account types for tracking assets and debts:

- **House**   A house account is used for recording the value of a house, condominium, or other real estate. When you create a house account, Quicken asks whether there is a mortgage on the property. If so, you can have Quicken create a related debt account for you or associate the house account with an existing debt account. This makes it possible to set up both your house asset account and mortgage debt account at the same time.
- **Vehicle**   A vehicle account is similar to a house account, but it's designed for vehicles, including cars, trucks, and recreational vehicles. Quicken asks if there is a loan on the vehicle; if so, it can create a related debt account or link to an existing debt account.
- **Other Asset**   An asset account is for recording the value of other assets, such as personal property. For example, a Quicken data file might include

asset accounts for horses and related equipment, art and antiques, or personal possessions.

- **Debt**   A debt account is for recording money you owe to others. As mentioned earlier, when you create a house or vehicle account, Quicken can automatically create a corresponding debt account for you. You can create a debt account to record other debts that are not related to the purchase of a specific asset. Debt accounts were known as *liability* accounts in previous versions of Quicken.

Creating Asset and Debt Accounts

You create asset and debt accounts with the Account Setup dialog, which walks you through the process of creating the account. Quicken offers a number of ways to open this dialog for an asset or debt account. The most straightforward way to open it for any type of account is to click the Setup tab, scroll down to Property And Debt, and then click what you want to add: an asset, a loan, or a debt. Figure 13-1 shows what the dialog looks like with the Asset account types displayed.

A loan is actually a debt account that has special Quicken features attached to it. Use this option to set up a debt associated with a compounding interest loan, like a mortgage or standard car loan, which is explained later in this chapter.

Figure 13-1 • **The asset Account Setup dialog enables you to set up various asset and debt accounts.**

Chapter 3 explains how to use the Quicken Account Setup dialog to create new Quicken accounts This section provides information about the kinds of data you'll have to enter to create asset and debt accounts.

Account Type

If you select Add Asset, the Account Setup dialog displays a list of asset types: House, Vehicle, or Other Asset. You can see this in Figure 13-1.

Account Name

Give the account a name that clearly identifies the asset or debt. For example, if you have two cars and plan to track them in separate asset accounts, consider naming the account with the make and model of the car. *Jeep Wrangler* and *Chevy Pickup* do a better job identifying the cars than *Car 1* and *Car 2*. When creating a debt account, you may want to include the word *mortgage, loan,* or *payable* in the account name, so you don't confuse it with a related asset.

Starting Point Information

For a vehicle account, Quicken asks for the make, model, and year of the car. Quicken stores this information in the Account Details dialog for the asset. (You can view and edit this information after the account has been created by opening the Net Worth tab | View Account Overview, right-clicking the account, and clicking Edit This Account. Alternatively, open the Setup tab, scroll down to Property And Debt, and click Edit Account opposite the account you want to change.)

Tell Quicken about the vehicle you'd like to track.
Don't worry if you don't have all the details- you can make changes to your account later.

Vehicle Make/Manufacturer	Dodge
Vehicle Model	Caravan
Vehicle Year	2008
When did you acquire this vehicle?	9/24/2008
Purchase Price	24,567.00
Estimate of its Current Value	20,000.00

It's okay to enter approximate values. You will be able to change them later.

For house and vehicle accounts, Quicken prompts you to enter information about the asset's purchase, including the acquisition date and purchase price. You can find this information on your original purchase receipts. Quicken also asks for an estimate of the current value. For a house, this number will (hopefully) be higher than the purchase price; for a car, this number will probably be lower. This is the amount that will appear as the asset account balance. For other assets and debts, Quicken prompts you for a statement date and balance. If you don't know how much to enter now, you can leave it set to zero and enter a value when you know what to enter. I explain how to adjust asset values later in this chapter.

Optional Tax Information

For other asset and debt accounts, you can click a Tax button to enter tax schedule information for transfers in and out of the account. This is completely optional and, in most cases, unnecessary. Chapter 18 explains how to set up Quicken accounts and categories to simplify tax preparation.

Related Mortgage or Loan

When creating a house or vehicle account, Quicken asks whether there is a related mortgage or loan. You have four options, as shown next:

- **Yes. I'd Like To Track This Mortgage/Loan In Quicken. Set Up A New Account For This.** This option tells Quicken that there is a related loan and that Quicken should create a debt account.
- **Yes. I'm Already Tracking The Mortgage/Loan In Quicken.** This option enables you to select an existing debt account to link to the asset.
- **Yes. I Do Not Want To Track the Mortgage/Loan In Quicken.** This option tells Quicken that there is a loan but you don't want to include it in your Quicken data file.
- **No.** This option tells Quicken that there is no loan, so no debt account is necessary. (Lucky you!)

As you've probably guessed or noticed, the use of the word *mortgage* or *loan* in this dialog depends on whether you're creating a house or vehicle asset account. To select any of the Yes options, you must select the first Yes option and then choose one of the options beneath it. Otherwise, choose the No option.

Loan Information

If you indicated that Quicken should track a loan for a house or vehicle, it automatically displays the Loan Setup dialog, which you can use to enter information about the loan. If you set up a debt account, Quicken asks if you want to set up an amortized loan to be associated with the debt. I explain how to set up a loan later in this chapter, in the section "Setting Up a Loan."

The Account Register

When you're finished setting up an asset or debt account (and related loans and loan payments, if applicable), Quicken automatically displays the account's register. Figure 13-2, shown later in the chapter in the section "Recording Other Asset Transactions," shows what a house account might look like. The first transaction, dated 1/1/2000, shows the opening balance, which is the amount paid for the house. The third transaction, dated 7/11/2006, shows an adjustment automatically made by Quicken to increase the account's balance based on my estimate of its worth on the day I created the account.

All transactions that affect an asset or debt account's balance appear in the account register. I tell you more about using account registers for asset and debt accounts later in this chapter, in the section "Recording Other Asset Transactions."

Tracking a Loan

Quicken makes it easy to track the principal, interest, and payments for a loan. Once you set up a loan and corresponding debt or asset accounts you can make payments with Quicken using QuickFill (see Chapter 7), Scheduled Transactions (see Chapter 7), or Online Payments (see Chapter 6). The Loan feature keeps track of all the details, so you don't have to.

Before I explain how to use the Loan feature, let me take a moment to make something clear. A loan is not the same as an asset or debt account. A loan, in Quicken, is information that Quicken uses to calculate the amount of interest and principal due for each payment of an amortized loan, such as a mortgage or car loan. A loan must be associated with an asset account (if you are a lender) or a debt account (if you are a borrower), as well as an income or expense category to record interest income or expense. Loan transactions are recorded in the associated asset or debt account—not in Quicken's loan records. It's possible to delete a loan without losing any transaction data, as explained later in this section. But you can't delete an asset or debt account that has a loan associated with it unless the loan is deleted first.

Setting Up a Loan

You can set up a loan in three ways:

- Create a house, vehicle, or debt account with a related mortgage or loan, as discussed earlier in this chapter. Quicken automatically prompts you for loan information.
- Click the Add A New Loan option in the Options menu of the Loan Summary area of the Net Worth window.
- In the Net Worth tab, open Net Worth Actions in the Actions subtab, and click Add New Loan.

Quicken displays the Loan Setup dialog with EasyStep screens that walk you through the loan creation process. It doesn't matter what the loan is for; the information you need to enter is basically the same. Here's what you can expect.

Type of Loan The Loan Setup dialog starts by prompting you for a loan type. You have two options:

- **Borrow Money** is for loans for which you're borrowing money from a lender, such as a car loan, mortgage, or personal loan. Quicken uses a debt account to record the loan.
- **Lend Money** is for loans for which you're the lender. Quicken uses an asset account to record the money owed from the borrower.

Loan Account The Loan Setup dialog prompts you to enter the account for the loan. Again, you have two options:

- **New Account** enables you to set up a brand-new account for the loan. Be sure to enter a name for the account.
- **Existing Account** enables you to select one of your existing debt accounts for the loan. If you're creating this loan as part of an asset creation process, the account will have already been created, named, and selected for you. Otherwise, this option is available only if you have already created a debt account that isn't already linked to a loan.

Loan Details

No matter how you create the loan, you'll be prompted for information about the loan creation, amount, and payments. It's important to be accurate; get the dates and numbers directly from a loan statement or agreement if possible.

Quicken can calculate some of the values—such as the loan balance and monthly payments—for you. It does this automatically based on your answers to questions in the Loan Setup dialog. Keep in mind, however, that Quicken's calculated amounts may not exactly match those calculated by your bank or finance company.

When you've finished entering loan information in the Loan Setup dialog, a series of Summary tab windows display entered and calculated values. Here's what the Loan Setup dialog's last two Summary screens look like for a $20,000, five-year car loan started on September 24, 2008:

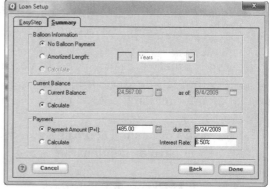

Setting Up Payments

When you set up a loan, Quicken automatically prompts you to set up payment information by displaying the Edit Loan Payment dialog, which is shown on the next page.

Enter information in this dialog to set up the payment. If the total payment should include additional amounts for property taxes, insurance, or other escrow items, click the Edit button. This displays the Split Transaction window, which you can use to enter categories, tags, memos, and amounts to be added to the payment.

In the Transaction area of the dialog, you can specify the type and method for the transaction. For type, three options appear on the drop-down list:

- **Payment** is a transaction recorded in your account register only. You must manually write and mail a check for payment. This is covered in Chapter 5.
- **Print Check** is a transaction recorded in the Write Checks dialog and account register. You can use the Print Check command to print the check, and then you can mail it for payment. This is also covered in Chapter 5.
- **Online Pmt** creates a payment instruction to be processed by your financial institution for use with online payment. This is covered in Chapter 6. This option appears only if at least one of your bank accounts is enabled for Quicken's Online Payment feature.

To indicate the method of payment, click the Payment Method button. The Select Payment Method dialog, shown here, appears. This dialog offers three Payment Type options:

- **Scheduled Bill** is a transaction scheduled for the future. If you select this option, you must also choose options and enter values to specify how Quicken should enter the transaction, which account should be used to pay, and how many days in advance it should be entered and paid. All this is covered in Chapter 7.
- **Memorized Payee** is a transaction memorized for use with QuickFill or Quicken's Calendar. This is also covered in Chapter 7.
- **Repeating Online Payment** is a recurring online payment instruction processed by your financial institution. If you select this option, you must also select a repeating online payment transaction from a drop-down list. If you have not already created a transaction to link to this loan payment, select one of the other options and return to this dialog after you have created the required transaction. Consult Chapter 6 for complete instructions.

Creating an Associated Asset Account

At the conclusion of the payment setup process, Quicken may display a dialog asking if you want to create an asset to go with the loan. This enables you to set up an asset account for the full purchase price of the item you used the loan to buy. Click Yes to create a new account; click No if you have already created one. I discussed creating an asset account earlier in this chapter, in the section titled "Creating Asset and Debt Accounts."

Reviewing Loan Information

The View Loans dialog displays information about your loans, as shown next. You can open this window by opening the Net Worth tab, selecting the loan account, and clicking Loan Details or by pressing CTRL-H.

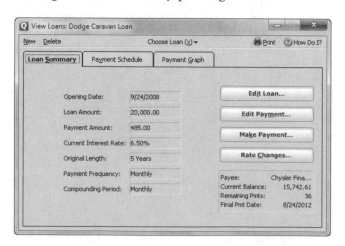

Button Bar Options

The View Loans window's button bar offers options for working with loans:

- **New** enables you to create a new loan. This option was explained earlier in this chapter.
- **Delete** removes the currently displayed loan. If you click this button, a dialog appears, warning that you are about to delete the loan. When you click OK, Quicken removes the loan information, but keeps the debt account and all of its transactions.
- **Choose Loan** displays a menu of your current loans. Use it to choose the loan you want to display in the window.
- **Print** prints a loan payment schedule for the currently displayed loan. The printout includes all of the information in the Payment Schedule tab of the View Loans window, which is shown and discussed momentarily.
- **How Do I?** provides instructions for working with the View Loans window.

Window Tabs

The *tabs* along the top of the window's information area enable you to view various pieces of information about a loan.

Loan Summary   *Loan Summary*, shown earlier, summarizes the loan information.

Payment Schedule   *Payment Schedule*, shown next, displays a schedule of past and future payments. You can turn on the Show Running Totals check box to display cumulative totals, rather than individual payment information.

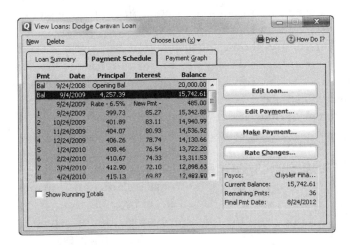

Payment Graph

Payment Graph, shown next, displays a graph of the loan payments. Where the two lines meet indicates the point at which you start paying more toward the loan principal than for interest. You can click a position on a graph line with a magnifying glass tool to display its value.

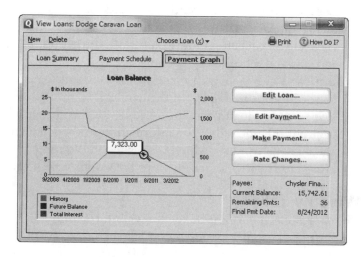

Modifying Loan Information

Once you've created a loan, you can modify it as necessary to record corrections, changes in the interest rate, or changes in payment methods. You can do all these things with buttons in the View Loans window.

Changing Loan Information

If you discover a discrepancy between the loan information in the View Loans window and information on statements or loan agreement papers, you can change the loan information in Quicken.

If necessary, choose the loan account's name from the Choose Loan menu in the button bar to display the information for the loan you want to modify. Then, click the Edit Loan button. A pair of Edit Loan windows enables you to change just about any information for the loan. Modify values and select different options as desired. Click Done in the last window to save your changes. Quicken automatically makes any necessary entries to update the account.

Changing Payment Information

Occasionally, you may want to make changes to a loan's payment information. For example, suppose the real estate taxes on your property are reduced (you can always hope!) and the resulting escrow amount, which is included in the payment, changes. Or suppose you decide to switch payment method from a Scheduled Transaction to a repeating Online Payment.

If necessary, choose the loan account's name from the Choose Loan menu in the button bar to display the information for the loan payment you want to modify. Then click the Edit Payment button. The Edit Loan Payment dialog, shown earlier, appears. Make changes as desired and click OK. Quicken updates the payment information with your changes.

Changing the Interest Rate

If you have an adjustable rate mortgage, you'll periodically have to adjust the rate for the loan within Quicken to match the rate charged by the lender.

If necessary, choose the loan account's name from the Choose Loan menu in the button bar to display the information for the loan whose rate you want to change. Then click the Rate Changes button. The Loan Rate Changes window appears. It lists all the loan rates throughout the history of the loan.

Date	Rate	Principal and Interest
8/27/1994	7.25%	525.00
8/27/1999	7.750%	550.00
8/27/2004	7.0%	500.00
9/27/2009	6.50%	475.00

To insert a rate change, click New in the window's button bar. The Insert An Interest Rate Change dialog appears, as shown here.

Enter the effective date and new rate in the appropriate text boxes. Quicken automatically calculates the new loan payment. When you click OK, the rate appears in the Loan Rate Changes window. Click the Close button to dismiss the window. Quicken recalculates the loan payment schedule for you.

Making a Loan Payment

Although it's usually more convenient to set up a loan payment as a Scheduled Transaction or repeating Online Payment instruction, as discussed earlier, you can also use the View Loans window to make a loan payment. This method is especially useful for making extra loan payments—payments in addition to your normal periodic payments.

If necessary, choose the loan account's name from the Choose Loan menu in the button bar to display the information for the loan for which you want to make a payment. Then click the Make Payment button. A Loan Payment dialog appears, asking whether you are making a regularly scheduled payment or an extra payment. Click the appropriate button.

Making a Regular Loan Payment

If you click the Regular button, the Make Regular Payment dialog, which is shown next, appears. Set options to specify the bank account from which the payment should be made, the type of transaction, the payee information, the date, and a memo for the transaction. If the Type Of Transaction drop-down list is set to Payment, you can enter a check number in the Number box or use one of the options on the Number drop-down list to set a number option. The Category and Amount are already set using values calculated by Quicken—you shouldn't have to change them. Click OK to enter the transaction.

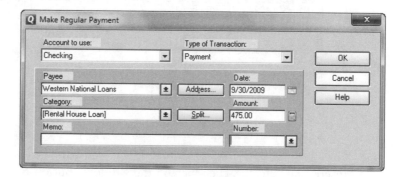

Making an Extra Loan Payment

If you click the Extra button, the Make Extra Payment dialog appears. As you can see in the following illustration, it's almost identical to the Make Regular Payment dialog, with two differences: The loan account is automatically set as the transfer account in the Category field, and the Amount field is left blank. Set options in the dialog to specify payment information, including the amount. Then click OK to enter the transaction.

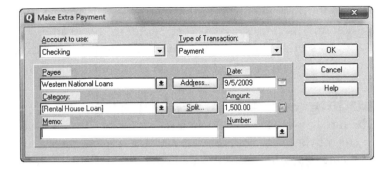

Recording Other Asset Transactions

Part of tracking assets is keeping track of their current values and modifying account balances when necessary. Like bank or investment accounts, which are discussed in Chapters 5 and 10, activity for an asset account appears in its account register.

One way to open an asset's account register is to click the Net Worth tab, choose the name of the asset account from the drop-down menu in the Acct subtab, and, if necessary, click the Transactions subtab. Figure 13-2 shows the account register for a house asset account.

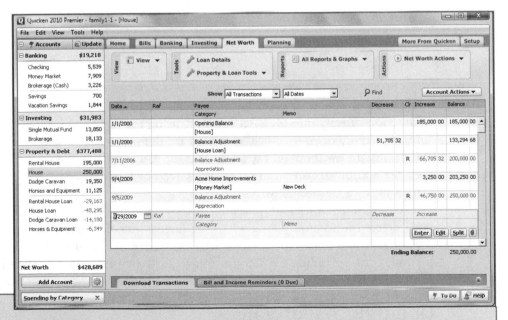

Figure 13-2 • The account register for a newly created asset account shows what you paid for the asset, as well as the estimated market value as of the account creation date.

Use the Tools subtab and the View Loan dialog to work with an asset account register and its entries, as described earlier in this chapter.

In this section, I explain how you can record changes in asset values due to acquisitions and disposals, improvements, market values, and depreciation.

Adding and Disposing of Assets

The most obvious change in an asset's value occurs when you add or remove all or part of the asset. For example, I have a single asset account in which I record the value of my horses and related equipment. When I buy a new saddle, it increases the value of the account. Similarly, when I sell one of my horses, it decreases the value of the account.

In many instances, when you add or dispose of an asset, money is exchanged. In that case, recording the transaction is easy: Simply use the appropriate bank account register to record the purchase or sale, and use the asset account as a transfer account in the Category field. Here's what the purchase of a new saddle might look like in my checking account:

9/5/2009	6721	Serenity Farms		1,124 76		2,113 53
		[Horses and Equipment]	New Saddle			

And here's the same transaction in my Horses and Equipment asset account:

9/5/2009		Serenity Farms			1,124 76	11,124 76
		[Checking]	New Saddle			

If the asset was acquired without an exchange of cash, you can enter the transaction directly into the asset account, using the Gift Received category (or a similar category of your choice) to categorize the income. Similarly, if the asset was disposed of without an exchange of cash, you can enter the transaction into the asset account register using the Gifts Given or Charity (or other appropriate category) to categorize the write-off.

If you have completely disposed of the asset and no longer need the account, don't delete the account! Doing so will remove all income and expense category transactions and uncategorize all transfer transactions related to the account. Instead, consider hiding the account to get it off account lists. I explain how in Chapter 3.

Updating Asset Values

A variety of situations can change the value of a single asset. The type of situation will determine how the value is adjusted. Here are three common examples.

Recording Improvements

Certain home-related expenditures can be considered improvements that increase the value of your home. It's important that you keep track of improvements because they raise the property's tax basis, thus reducing the amount of capital gains you may have to record (and pay tax on) when you sell the house. Your tax advisor can help you determine which expenditures can be capitalized as home improvements.

Since most home improvements involve an expenditure, use the appropriate cash flow account register to record the transaction. Be sure to enter the appropriate asset account (House, Condo, Land, and so on) as a transfer account in the Category field. Here's what a home improvement transaction might look like in my checking account:

9/4/2009	EFT	Acme Home Improvements		3,250 00			12,450 00
		[House]	New Deck				

And here's the same transaction in my House asset account:

9/4/2009		Acme Home Improvements			3,250 00	203,250 00
		[Money Market]	New Deck			

Adjusting for Market Value

Real estate, vehicles, and other large-ticket item assets are also affected by market values. Generally speaking, real estate values go up, vehicle values go down, and other item values can vary either way depending on what they are.

To adjust for market value, click Account Actions | Update Balance at the top of the account register for the asset you want to adjust. The Update Account Balance dialog, which is shown here, appears. Use this dialog to enter the date and market value for the asset. Then select a category or transfer account to record the gain or loss of value.

When you click OK, the entry is added to the account register as a reconciled transaction:

9/5/2009		Balance Adjustment			R	46,750 00	250,000 00
		Appreciation					

If you don't want the adjustment to affect any category or account other than the asset, choose the same asset account as a transfer account. When you click OK, a dialog will warn you that you are trying to record a transfer into the same account. Click OK again. You can see an example of an adjustment like this in Figure 13-2.

Recording Depreciation

Depreciation is a calculated reduction in the value of an asset. Depreciation expense can be calculated using a variety of acceptable methods, including straight line, sum of the year's digits, and declining balance. Normally, it reduces the asset's value regularly, with monthly, quarterly, or annual adjustments.

Depreciation is commonly applied to property used for business purposes, since depreciation expense on those assets may be tax-deductible. If you think depreciation on an asset you own may be tax-deductible, use Quicken to track the depreciation expense. Otherwise, depreciation probably isn't worth the extra effort it requires to track.

To record depreciation, create an entry in the asset account that reduces the value by the amount of the depreciation. Use a Depreciation Expense category to record the expense. The transaction might look something like this:

| 9/1/2009 | Auto:Depreciation | Depreciation Expense | 650 00 | 19,350 00 |

Keep in mind that you can set up monthly, quarterly, or annual depreciation transactions as scheduled transactions. This automates the process of recording them when they are due. I tell you about scheduled transactions in Chapter 7.

Keeping Tabs on Your Net Worth

In This Chapter:

- *The Net Worth tab*
- *Property and debt alerts*
- *Asset and debt account details*
- *Reports and graphs*

When you create asset and debt accounts and enter related transactions into Quicken, as discussed in the previous two chapters, Quicken summarizes your entries and calculates balances. It displays this information in a number of places: the account panel, the Net Worth tabs, account registers and overviews, and reports and graphs. You can consult Quicken's calculated balances and totals at any time to learn about your equity and the expenses associated with your debt and automobile.

This chapter explains how to use Quicken's reporting features to keep tabs on your net worth. As you'll learn in these pages, a wealth of information about your net worth is just a mouse click away.

The Net Worth Tabs

Asset and debt accounts are part of Quicken's Net Worth tab. You can open the Net Worth tab by clicking its tab near the top of Quicken's main window. The Net Worth tab has five subtabs of information about your net worth: View, Acct, Tools, Reports, and Actions. The View subtab has two options: Net Worth (refer to Figure 14-1), which displays graphs representing your net worth in a variety of ways, as well as a year-by-year look at your net worth, and Account Overview (refer to Figure 14-2), which

Chapter 14

Figure 14-1 • The Net Worth view displays graphs and a table representing various components of your net worth.

displays tables of numerical information about your net worth accounts. Together, these charts and tables paint a picture of your overall financial situation.

If the Net Worth tab is not visible, open the View menu and click Tabs To Show | Net Worth.

This part of the chapter takes a closer look at the snapshots in the Net Worth tabs, so you know what you can find there and how you can customize it for your own use.

Figure 14-2 • The Account Overview summarizes Net Worth account information.

Net Worth

The Net Worth snapshot (at the top of Figure 14-1) uses a stacked column graph to indicate your net worth for the past 13 months. The green bar represents your assets, the blue bar represents your debt, and the dark line represents the net of these two amounts. If you're looking for a trend, ideally, the green bars should get taller while the blue bars get shorter. The net effect would be a rise in the dark line. If the dark line is below the baseline, you're in some serious financial trouble because your debts exceed your assets.

Keep in mind that this graph represents all of your accounts in Quicken—including your banking and investment accounts. It's a true view of your net worth trend for the past year.

The Options menu and buttons within the window enable you to view a full-screen version of the graph, a Net Worth report, or the Account List window.

Net Worth By Year

The Net Worth By Year snapshot uses a stacked column graph to show the value of your net worth for each year that Quicken has data, up to a maximum of three full years and year-to-date for the current year. If there's only partial data for a year, the graph isn't reliable for that period. Trend graphs like these are a good reason for using Quicken consistently—only with complete data can you get a complete and accurate picture!

Net Worth Allocation

The Net Worth Allocation chart (refer to Figure 14-1) graphically represents the allocation of your worth between cash or banking accounts, investments, and property and debt accounts. The amount labeled "Total" is really your net worth.

Net Worth By Year Summary

The Net Worth By Year Summary (refer to Figure 14-1) summarizes the ending balances in each of your accounts for the previous three years and the current year to date. This is basically the same data shown in the Net Worth By Year graph, but it's displayed in tabular form with account-level detail. Again, having information like this readily available is a good reason to use Quicken consistently to manage your finances.

Property and Debt Alerts

You can set up alerts in several areas for property and debts, and have Quicken remind you when some action is due.

Setting Up Property and Debt Alerts

To set up an alert, begin by opening the Tools menu and clicking Alert Center (View And Setup). Click the Setup tab, and click the name of the alert you want to set on the left side of the window to display its options on the right. Figure 14-3 shows what the Insurance Reappraisal alert settings might look like with two alerts already set.

Two alerts apply to Net Worth:

Figure 14-3 • Use the Setup tab of the Alerts Center window to set up alerts, such as the Insurance Reappraisal alert shown here.

- **Insurance Reappraisal** (see Figure 14-3) notifies you before an insurance policy expires so you can either reevaluate coverage or shop for a new policy.
- **Mortgage Reappraisal** notifies you before a mortgage changes from variable to fixed (or fixed to variable) so you can consider refinancing. Even if your mortgage doesn't convert, you can use this alert to remind you periodically to check for better mortgage deals.

Both alerts work pretty much the same way. For each alert, enter a name and date in the right side of the window. Select one of the options at the bottom of the window to indicate how you want the alert to appear: as text in the alert list (see Figure 14-4) or as a pop-up dialog that appears when you start Quicken, shown next. Finally, use the drop-down list to specify the length of time the alert should remain in the list and click OK.

Repeat this process for each alert you want to set. When you're finished, click OK.

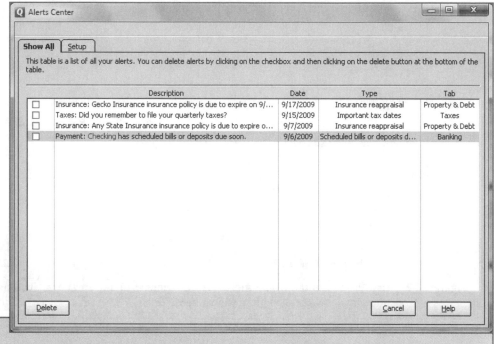

Figure 14-4 • In the Alert Center, you can see currently active alerts and deactivate them.

Working with Property and Debt Alerts

Once you have established property and debt alerts, you can manage them in several ways.

- In the Alert Center's Show All tab (open from the Tools menu and shown in Figure 14-4), you can select the check box opposite an alert and click the Delete button to remove an alert.
- In the Alert Center's Setup tab, you can uncheck an alert category to prevent all the alerts in that category from being displayed in any way.
- If you choose to display the alert as a pop-up dialog when Quicken starts, you can click Don't Show This Type Of Alert As A Popup to stop the pop-up display.

Account Balances

The Property And Debt Accounts area (refer to Figure 14-2) lists all of your property (asset), debt (liability), and credit accounts, and displays each account's current and ending balances. You can click the name of an account to view its account register, which is discussed later in this chapter, in the section titled "Account Details."

One of the nice things about the Property And Debt Accounts area is that it separates assets from debts and provides subtotals for each. The total at the bottom is the net of the two. If this is a negative number, your finances need attention.

The Options pop-up menu at the top of the Property And Debt Accounts area offers several options for working with accounts:

- **Add An Account** option displays the Account Setup dialog, which you can use to create an asset or debt account. I explain how to create accounts in Chapter 3 and provide details specific to asset and debt accounts in Chapter 13.
- **Get Transactions Online** option displays the One Step Update dialog if you have credit cards or other debt with download capability, which you can use to download transactions from your financial institution. One Step Update is explained in Chapter 7, and how to download cash flow account transactions is explained in Chapter 6.
- **View Account List** option displays the Account List window, which you can use to view and manage accounts. The Account List is covered in detail in Chapter 3.

Loan Summary

The Loan Summary (refer to Figure 14-2) lists all of your amortized loans—the ones you set up in the View Loans dialog, as instructed in Chapter 13. It includes several columns of information for each loan:

- **Account** is the name of the account. You can click the account name to view its register, which is discussed later in this chapter.
- **Int. Rate** is the current interest rate.
- **Payments Left** is the number of payments left on the loan. This does not take into consideration any extra payments you may have made that will reduce the loan term.
- **Principal Paid** is the total of the payments made toward the loan balance.
- **Interest Paid** is the total of the interest paid for the loan.
- **Balance** is the ending balance for the account.

The Principal Paid, Interest Paid, and Balance columns contain information calculated by Quicken based on transactions entered in your Quicken data file. It's important to note that the Interest Paid column totals only the amount of interest entered in Quicken. If you set up an existing loan for which payments (including interest) had already been made, Quicken does not include principal or interest already paid on the loan in the totals.

The Options pop-up menu at the top of the Loan Accounts Summary area offers two loan-related options:

- **Add A New Loan** option displays the Loan Setup dialog, so you can create a new loan. This dialog was explained in Chapter 13.
- **Make A Payment** option displays the Loan Summary tab of the View Loans window. To make a payment on a loan, choose the loan name from the Choose Loan pop-up menu, and then click the Make Payment button. The View Loans window and making payments was explained in Chapter 13.

Debt Goals

If you have used Quicken's Debt Reduction Planner, which is discussed in detail in Chapter 17, you may also see the Debt Goals snapshot at the bottom of the Account Overview subtab (refer to Figure 14-2). This snapshot lists the debts you set up in the Debt Reduction Planner, along with the current month's payment and target balance. The Options menu enables you to quickly open and view the Debt Reduction Planner to make changes or review settings in the planner.

Account Details

To learn more about the transactions and balances for a specific account, you can view account details in the Transactions and Overview windows. Select the name of an account from the Acct subtab at the top of the Net Worth tab to open the account you want to view. Then select either Transactions or Overview to open the related window (refer to Figures 14-5 and 14-6).

The Acct subtab of the Net Worth tab may disappear if you make the Quicken window too narrow.

Register

An account's Register window (see Figure 14-5) lists all transactions entered into that account, as well as the ending balance. As I explain in Chapter 13, you can enter transactions directly into the register. Other transactions—such as principal payments for a mortgage or other loan—are automatically calculated and entered by Quicken.

Figure 14-5 • Here's an example of the Register window for a car loan.

Overview

An account's Overview window (see Figure 14-6) is split into five different areas of information about the account: Account Attributes, Account Status, Account Balance (or Equity, for assets with associated loans), Auto Expenses (for vehicles) and Account Attachments.

Account Attributes

The Account Attributes area provides basic information about the account, including its name and description, and whether it can be viewed on Quicken.com.

The Options menu at the top of the area offers several related commands:

- **Create A New Account** displays the Quicken Account Setup dialog, which enables you to create any kind of Quicken account. I explain how to create accounts in Chapter 3.
- **View/Edit Comments** displays the Account Comments dialog, which you can use to enter comments about the account.
- **Set Tax Attributes** displays the Tax Schedule Information dialog, which you can use to choose tax return schedules and lines to associate with transfers in to and out of the account. I explain how this feature works in Chapter 18.
- **Set Web Pages** displays the Set Web Pages dialog. You can use this dialog to enter the Web addresses (or URLs) for up to three Web pages related to

Figure 14-6 • Here's the Overview tab for the vehicle account linked to the car loan.

the account; the addresses you enter appear as clickable links in the Account Attributes area. For example, you can include a link to your mortgage company's home page or login page in the Account Attributes area of your mortgage account, so you can quickly jump to that page when working with Quicken.

• **Browse Web Pages** displays a submenu that lists the Web pages you entered in the Set Web Pages dialog. Choose an option to launch Quicken's built-in browser and view that page on the Internet.

Clicking the Edit Account Details button at the bottom of the Account Attributes area displays the Account Details window, which you can use to enter general information about the account. The fields that appear in this dialog vary depending on the type of account that is displayed. The illustration here shows what it looks like for the account shown in Figures 14-6.

Account Status

The Account Status area provides information about the status of the account, including balance, amount owed or linked account, and equity information. You can click the current balance amount or amount owed/linked account in the Account Status area to view the details behind the amount or to update the current balance of an asset.

The Options pop-up menu offers three related commands:

- **Update My Account Balance** displays the Update Account Balance dialog, which you can use to change the balance of the account. I explain how to modify an account's balance with this dialog in Chapter 13.
- **Manage My Loans** is only available with loan accounts and displays the View Loans dialog, which you can use to add, modify, or delete loans. This dialog is also explained in Chapter 13.
- **View All My Accounts** displays the Account List window, which I cover in Chapter 3.

Account Balance or Equity

The Account Balance or Equity area (refer to Figure 14-6) displays a graphical representation of the balance of the account. (This area is labeled Equity for any asset with an associated loan; it is labeled Account Balance for any other asset or any debt.) You can point to a column to see its exact value.

What's interesting (and extremely useful) about this graph is that if the account is linked to another account, both accounts are displayed on the graph, and your equity—the difference between what an asset is worth and what you still owe on its loan—is charted as a line. Figure 14-6 shows a good example. Although the Overview window is for an asset (a car), it shows the value of the related debt (a car loan). See how the Equity line and Value Of Asset column go down in October 2008? That's because the car's market value was updated that month, thus decreasing both.

The Options pop-up menu offers a number of related commands:

- **Customize This Graph** displays the Customize dialog, which you can use to change the date range and categories included in the graph.
- **Go To A Full Screen View Of This Graph** displays the Account Balance/Equity graph in its own report window, with a Show Report button for its corresponding report. I tell you about creating reports and graphs next in this chapter and in Chapter 9.
- **Report My Net Worth** displays an Account Balance report, with a Show Graph button to display its corresponding graph, discussed in this chapter and in Chapter 9.
- **View All My Accounts** displays the Account List window, which I cover in Chapter 3.
- **Help Reduce My Debt** displays the Debt Reduction dialog, discussed in Chapter 17.
- **Forecast My Future Account Balances** starts Quicken's forecasting feature, which I discuss in detail in Chapter 17.

Auto Expenses

The Auto Expenses area (refer to Figure 14-6), offers a customizable summary of expenses related to your automobile. There are four columns of information.

- **Category** is the full name of the expense category (including subcategory, if applicable).
- **YTD Expenses** is the total year-to-date amount for that category.
- **MTD Expenses** is the total month-to-date amount for that category.
- **Monthly Avg** is the monthly average expenditure for that category.

You can customize the Auto Expenses report by choosing Customize This Report from its Options pop-up menu. The Customize Auto Expenses Component dialog appears. It has three tabs: Accounts (shown next), Categories, and Tags. Click a tab, and then toggle check marks next to account, category, or tag names to include or exclude them from the report. By default, the report includes all accounts and just the Auto category (with its subcategories). But you can make the report include anything you like. When you're finished making changes, click OK to save them. The Auto Expenses area refreshes to reflect your changes.

Clicking the Show Auto Expense Report button at the bottom of the Auto Expenses area displays a report window containing the Auto Expenses report, shown next. Chapter 9 explains how to work with and customize reports.

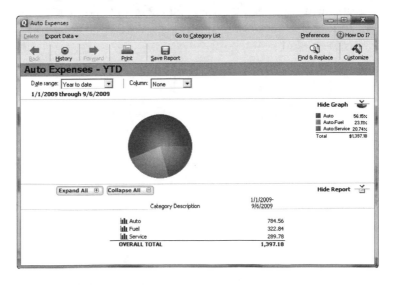

Account Attachments

The Account Attachments area lists all file attachments to the account. I explain how to attach files to an account in Chapter 5.

Reports and Graphs

The information you enter in Net Worth accounts appears on two reports and their corresponding graphs: Account Balances and Net Worth. These reports provide the same information, with slight differences in the order and wording of the presentation.

Creating Reports

To create a report, open All Reports & Graphs in the Reports subtab, select Net Worth & Balances, and click either Account Balances or Net Worth. Quicken makes its calculations and displays the report (see Figure 14-7) in a report window.

Working with the Report Window

The report window works the same for the Account Balances and Net Worth reports as it does for any other Quicken report. Chapter 9 explains how to use buttons and other options in the report window to customize reports, create subreports, and save reports.

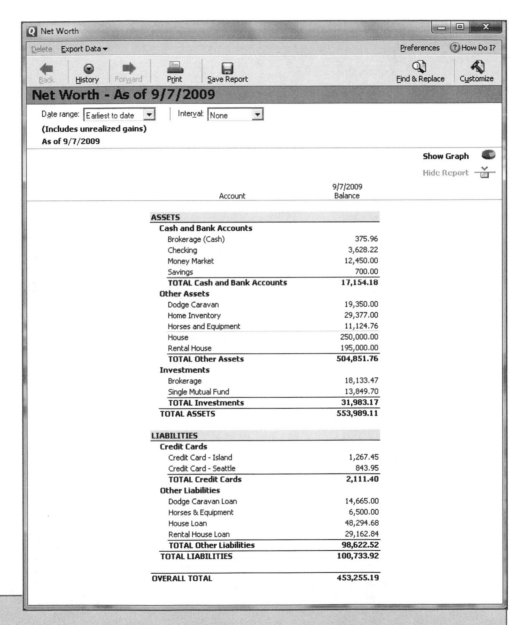

Figure 14-7 • A Net Worth report summarizes the balances in all of your accounts.

Planning

This part of the book tells you about Quicken Personal Finance Software's planning features, which you can use to plan for your retirement, major purchases, and other life events. It covers Quicken's built-in financial calculators, as well as features that can help you save money and make your dreams come true. Its three chapters are:

Part Five

Planning for the Future

In This Chapter:

- *Quicken planning overview*
- *Life event planners*
- *Playing "what if"*

To most people, the future is an unknown, a mystery. After all, who can say what will happen tomorrow, next year, or ten years from now? But if you think about your future, you can usually come up with a few events that you can plan for: your marriage, the purchase of a new home, the birth of your children (and their education years later), and your retirement. (These are just examples—everyone's life runs a different course.) These events, as well as many unforeseen events, all have one thing in common: They affect your finances. This chapter tells you about planning for future events and how tools within Quicken Personal Finance Software can help.

Planning for Retirement

Throughout your life, you work and earn money to pay your bills, buy the things you and your family need or want, and help your kids get started with their own lives. But there comes a day when it's time to retire. Those regular paychecks stop coming, and you find yourself relying on the money you put away for retirement.

Retirement planning is one of the most important financial planning jobs facing individuals and couples. This section tells you about the importance of planning, and offer some planning steps and a word of advice based on personal experience.

The Importance of Planning

Retired people live on fixed incomes. That's not a problem—*if* the income is fixed high enough to support a comfortable lifestyle. You can help ensure that there's enough money to finance your retirement years by planning and saving now.

Poor retirement planning can lead to catastrophic results—imagine running out of money when you turn 75. Or having to make a lifestyle change when you're 65 to accommodate a much lower income.

Planning is even more important these days as longevity increases. People are living longer than ever. Your retirement dollars may need to support you for 20 years or more, at a time when the cost of living will likely be much higher than it is today.

With proper planning, it's possible to finance your retirement years without putting a strain on your working years. By closely monitoring the status of your retirement funds, periodically adjusting your plan, and acting accordingly, your retirement years can be the golden years they're supposed to be.

Planning Steps

Retirement planning is much more than deciding to put $2,000 in an IRA every year. It requires careful consideration of what you have, what you'll need, and how you can make those two numbers the same.

Assess What You Have

Take a good look at your current financial situation. What tax-deferred retirement savings do you already have? A pension? An IRA? Something else? What regular savings do you have? What taxable investments do you have? The numbers you come up with will form the basis of your final retirement funds— like a seed you'll grow.

Be sure to consider property that can be liquidated to contribute to retirement savings. For example, if you currently live in a large home to accommodate your family, you may eventually want to live in a smaller home. The proceeds from the sale of your current home may exceed the cost of your retirement home. Also consider any income-generating property that may continue to generate income in your retirement years or that can be liquidated to contribute to retirement savings.

Determine What You'll Need

What you'll need depends on many things. One simple calculation suggests you'll need 80 percent of your current gross income to maintain your current lifestyle in your retirement years. You may find a calculation like this handy if retirement is still many years in the future and you don't really know what things will cost.

Time is an important factor in calculating the total amount you should have saved by retirement day. Ask yourself two questions:

- **How long do you have to save?** Take your current age and subtract it from the age at which you plan to retire. That's the number of years you have left to save.
- **How long will you be in retirement?** Take the age at which you plan to retire and subtract it from the current life expectancy for someone of your age and gender. That's the number of years you have to save for.

Doing this math tells me that I have only 18 years left to save for a 28-year retirement. I'm glad I've been saving!

Develop an Action Plan

Once you know how much you need, it's time to think seriously about how you can save it. This requires putting money away in one or more savings or investment accounts. I tell you about your options a little later in this chapter.

Stick to the Plan!

The most important part of any plan is sticking to it. For example, if you plan to save $5,000 a year, don't think you can just save $2,000 this year and make up the $3,000 next year. There are two reasons: First, you can't "make up" the interest lost on the $3,000 you didn't save this year, and second, you're kidding yourself if you think you'll manage to put away $8,000 next year.

If you consider deviating from your plan, just think about the alternative: making ends meet with a burger-flipping job in the local fast food joint when you're 68 years old.

Don't Wait! Act Now!

I remember when I first began thinking about retirement. I was 30 or 31 and had been self-employed for about three years. I didn't have a pension or 401(k) plan with my former employer. I didn't have much saved. I had only $2,000 in an IRA. Up until that point, I never worried about retirement—but one day something just clicked, and retirement became something to think about.

I've done a lot of retirement planning and saving since then. While I admit that I don't have a perfect plan (yet), I've certainly come a long way in 12 years. But when I consider how much more I could have saved if I'd begun five years earlier, I could kick myself for waiting.

See for yourself. Table 15-1 shows how $2,500, $5,000, and $7,500 per-year contributions to a tax-deferred retirement account earning 5 percent a year can grow. (These calculations do not take into consideration tax benefits or inflation.)

Start Age	Years of Saving	Savings at Age 62		
		$2,500/year	$5,000/year	$7,500/year
60	2	$5,125	$10,250	$15,375
50	12	$39,793	$79,586	$119,378
40	22	$96,263	$192,526	$288,789
30	32	$188,247	$376,494	$564,741
20	42	$338,079	$676,159	$1,014,238

Table 15-1 • Regular Savings Can Make Your Money Grow

Getting Started with the Quicken Planner

The Planning tab (refer to Figure 15-1) offers access to all of Quicken's built-in planning features, including the Quicken Planner's main plan assumptions and individual financial planners. Once you have set up your plan, the Planning tab provides an up-to-date view of how well your plan is working.

Here's how it works. You start by entering plan assumptions, which include information about you, your current finances, and your tax rate. Quicken makes calculations based on what you entered to display plan results. As you continue working with Quicken, entering transactions that affect your finances, Quicken updates the result of the plan. It also takes into consideration your entries in any of Quicken's other planners, such as the College Planner or Special Purchase Planner.

I won't lie to you: Setting up Quicken Planner assumptions can be time-consuming. But I think that the benefit of using this feature far outweighs the cost (in time) of setting it up. This is especially true if you're settled down and raising a family—Quicken can help you plan for the major events of your life so you're prepared for them. If you don't have the time to set up the Quicken Planner now, make time in the future.

In this section, I explain how to set assumptions for the Quicken Planner and how to view the results of your plan in the Planning tab.

Setting Plan Assumptions

The easiest way to see what plan assumptions need to be made is to view the Plan Assumptions area of the Lifetime Planner. Click Planning | Lifetime Planner. When you first start out, the Plan Assumptions area may look like the illustration here:

Plan Assumptions   ⚙ Options ▾

Click on the links below to set or change your plan assumptions.

About You	Maria & Mike
	2 dependents.
Income	Combined yearly salaries: $145,000
Tax Rate	Effective tax rate: 18%
	After-retirement tax rate: 18% starting in 2026
Inflation	Inflation rate: 3.0%
Savings & Investments	Current savings: $50,277
	Current investments: $84,868
Homes and Assets	Total assets: $508,360
Loans and Debt	You have 4 loan accounts in your plan.
Expenses	Current yearly living expenses: $72,120.

To set details for an assumption category, click its link. This displays a dialog you can use to enter information. Here's a look at each category.

About You

Clicking the About You link displays the About You dialog, which is shown next. Its fields are pretty self-explanatory, so I won't go into much detail. (After all, you should be able to figure out how to enter your name and date of birth!) When you're finished entering information in the dialog, click Done to save it.

Here are some less obvious things to consider when entering data into the About You dialog.

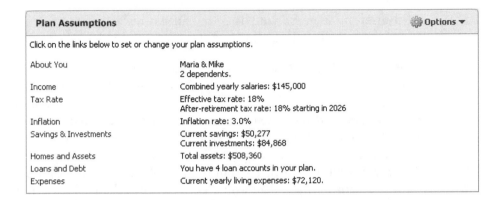

Include Spouse   If you turn on the Include Spouse check box, you can enter information into the Spouse column of the dialog. If you don't have a spouse or don't want to include him or her in your plan, leave that check box turned off.

Life Expectancy   You can either enter what you think might be your life expectancy or click the Calculate button to display the Calculate Life Expectancy dialog. Set options in the dialog, and Quicken tells you how long you may live. Of course, this is an estimate based on current research into life expectancy; you may or may not live to reach the age Quicken suggests.

Children and Dependents   To enter information about children or other dependents, click the New button at the bottom of the dialog. This displays the Add Child/Dependent dialog, in which you can enter the name and date of birth for a dependent. When you click OK, the person's name and age are added to the list. Repeat this process for each child or dependent you need to add. Once a child or dependent has been added, you can select his or her name and click the Edit button to change information about him or her (although I can't see why a name or birth date would change), click the Delete button to remove him or her permanently from the plan, or turn on the Exclude From Plan check box so Quicken doesn't use him or her in its calculations.

Income

Clicking the Income link displays the Income dialog, which is organized into three separate tabs of information. This is where you enter salary, retirement benefits, and other income information for you and your spouse.

Salary   The Salary tab, which is shown here, enables you to record information about current and future salary and self-employment income.

To add an income item, click the New button to display the Add Salary dialog. Then set options to enter information about the income item. As you can see in the following illustration, the Add Salary dialog is extremely flexible, enabling you to enter start and end dates for a salary—which is useful for income from seasonal employment. If you don't need to enter specific dates, choose Already Started from the When Does This Salary Start drop-down list and one of the retirement options from the When Does This Salary End drop-down list. When you click OK, the item is added to the list.

For each item you add, Quicken automatically includes adjustments that specify when the item begins and ends. But you can add other adjustments if you know about changes that will occur in the future. Select the item in the top half of the dialog, and then click the New button at the bottom of the dialog.

Enter information in the Add Salary Adjustment dialog that appears and click OK. The information is added to the bottom half of the Salary tab of the Income dialog.

On the Salary tab, you can select any of the salary or adjustment items and click the Edit or Delete button to change or remove it. You can also select an item and turn on the Exclude From Plan check box to exclude its information from the Quicken Planner.

Retirement Benefits   The Retirement Benefits tab, which is shown here, enables you to enter information about Social Security or pension benefits you are currently receiving or to estimate future benefits.

To estimate future Social Security benefits, enter the age at which you expect to begin collecting benefits and click the Estimate button. The Estimate Social Security Benefits dialog appears. You have two options:

- **Use Rough Estimate** enables you to select a salary range option to estimate benefits.

- **Use Mail-In Estimate From SS Administration** enables you to enter the amount provided by the Social Security Administration on your annual Social Security statement.

   When you click OK, the amount is automatically entered in the Retirement Benefits tab.

   To add a pension, click the New button at the bottom of the Retirement Benefits tab of the Income dialog. This displays the Add Pension dialog, which is shown here. Enter information about the pension and click OK to add it to the Retirement Benefits tab. In that tab, you can select the pension and click Edit or Delete to change or remove it, or select it and turn on the Exclude From Plan check box to exclude it from the Quicken Planner's calculations.

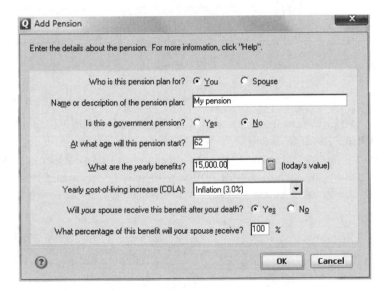

Other Income   The Other Income tab, shown here, enables you to enter income from other sources, such as gifts, child support, and inheritances. Don't use this tab to enter income from investments or rental properties; the Quicken Planner provides other places to enter this information.

To enter an income item, click the New button. Enter information in the Add Other Income dialog, which is shown next. An interesting option in this dialog is the ability to specify how the money will be used: either saved and invested or used to pay expenses. The option you select determines how this income is used in the plan. If you're not sure what to select, leave it set to the default option.

When you click OK, the item is added to the Other Income tab's list. You can edit, delete, or exclude the item from the plan as desired.

Click Done to close the Quicken Planner: Income dialog.

Tax Rate

Clicking the Tax Rate link in the Plan Assumptions area displays the Average Tax Rate dialog shown here. You have two options:

- **Demographic Average**, shown next, enables you to estimate your tax rate based on where you live and what your income is.
- **Tax Returns** enables you to estimate your tax rate based on the total income, total federal taxes, and total state taxes from your most recent tax returns.

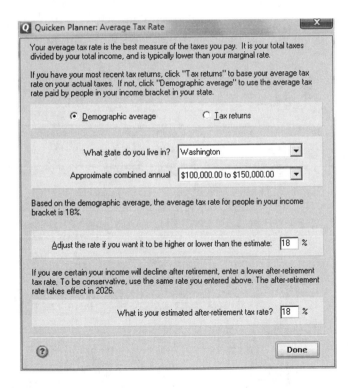

No matter how you estimate the tax rate, you can adjust it by entering a preferred value. You can also enter an estimate of your post-retirement tax rate, which may be lower. Click Done to close the Quicken Planner: Average Tax Rate dialog.

Inflation

Clicking the Inflation link displays the Estimated Inflation dialog, which includes a field you can use to enter the inflation rate you want to use for your plan. Quicken suggests an inflation rate of 3 percent, which is the average inflation rate since 1927, but you can enter any rate you think is correct in the text box. Click Done to save your estimate.

Savings & Investments

Clicking the Savings & Investments link displays the Savings And Investments dialog, which is organized into three tabs. Use this dialog to enter information about current bank and investment accounts, as well as contributions you or your spouse makes regularly to accounts and the return you expect to earn on your investments.

Savings   The Savings tab, which is shown next, lists all of the bank accounts you have set up in Quicken, along with their current balances.

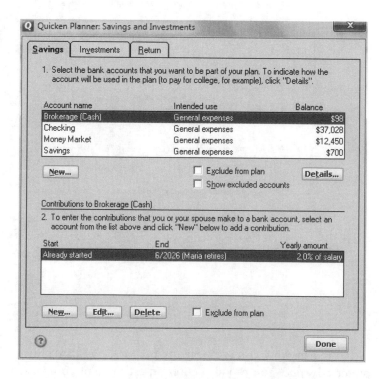

If you have omitted any accounts from Quicken, now is a good time to add them if you want them to be part of your plan. Click the New button to display the Add New Account dialog; Learn how to use this dialog to create new accounts in Chapter 3.

Quicken automatically assumes that each bank account will be used for General expenses. You can change this assumption by selecting an account and clicking the Details button. Choose a new purpose from the drop-down list in the Account Details dialog that appears and click OK. You'll find that until you use Quicken's other planners, General expenses is the only offered option. But if you use another planner—for example, the College Planner—an option for that planner's expense appears in the drop-down list.

If you or your spouse makes regular contributions to one of your bank accounts, you can enter information about that contribution in the dialog. In the top half of the dialog, select the account that receives the contribution. Then click the New button at the bottom of the dialog. Use the Add Contribution dialog that appears to indicate how much you contribute. The dialog will walk you through the process of entering information based on whether the contribution is a percentage of a salary or a base amount that increases each year.

Investments   The Investments tab, which is shown next, lists all of the investment accounts you have set up in Quicken, along with their current market values. Remember, since market value is determined by security prices, the market value is only as up-to-date as the most recently entered or downloaded security prices.

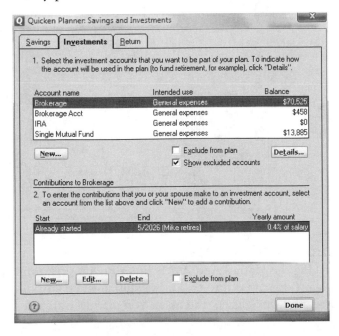

This tab works just like the Savings tab. You can click the New button in the top half of the dialog to add another investment account or click the New button in the bottom half of the dialog to enter regular contribution information for any selected investment account. You can also specify the intended use for any account by selecting the account name and clicking the Details button.

Return   The Return tab, shown next, enables you to specify your expected rates of return for preretirement and postretirement investments. If you turn on the check box near the top of the dialog, additional text boxes appear, enabling you to enter different rates of return for taxable and tax-deferred investments. At the bottom of the dialog, you can enter the percentage of the taxable return that is subject to taxes. This is normally 100 percent, but for your situation, the percentage may be different. Click Done to close the Quicken Planner: Savings and Investments dialog.

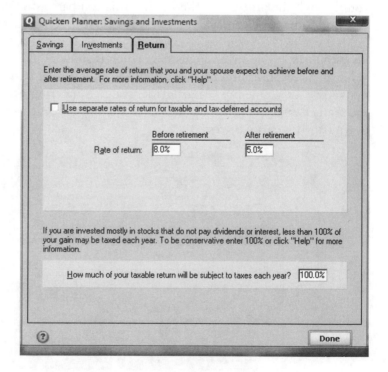

Homes and Assets

Clicking the Homes And Assets link displays the Homes And Assets dialog, which is organized into two tabs. This is where you can enter information about currently owned assets and assets you plan to purchase in the future.

Asset Accounts   The Asset Accounts tab, which is shown next, lists all of the asset accounts you have created in Quicken, including accounts for your home, vehicle, home inventory, and other assets. If you have additional assets that have not yet been entered in Quicken and you want to include them in your plan, click the New button and use the Add New Account dialog that appears to create the new account; I explain how in Chapter 3.

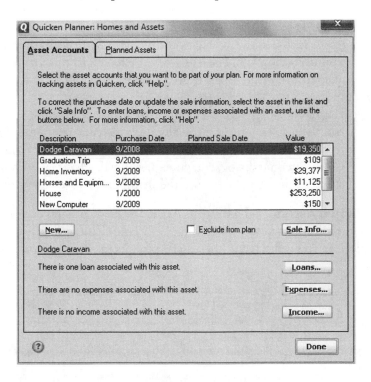

If you plan to sell an asset, you can enter selling information for it. Select the asset in the top half of the dialog, and then click the Sale Info button. A series of dialogs prompts you for information about the asset's purchase and sale date and price, as well as other information that affects how much money you can expect to receive and pay taxes on. This information is then added to your plan.

Three buttons at the bottom of the dialog enable you to associate loans, expenses, and income with a selected asset. This is especially important when working with assets you plan to sell, since the sale of the asset should also end associated debt, expenses, and income.

- **Loans** enables you to link existing loans to the asset or add new loans, including home equity loans. It also enables you to enter information about planned loans—for example, if you plan to use a home equity loan to build an addition on your house sometime next year. You can also enter information about planned payoffs—perhaps you're expecting a big trust fund check (lucky you!) and plan to use it to pay off your house.

- **Expenses** enables you to enter property tax information as well as other expenses related to the asset. For a home, this might include association fees, homeowner's insurance, and estimated maintenance and utility costs. For a car, this might include registration, fuel, service, and insurance. For each expense you add, Quicken prompts you for information about the expense, including how you expect to pay for it—with money in a specific bank account or with a loan. It even enables you to set up a monthly savings target to pay for the item.
- **Income** enables you to enter information about income you expect to earn from the asset. This is especially useful if you own rental property. The dialog that appears when you add an income item is almost the same as the Add Other Income dialog, shown earlier in this chapter. It even allows you to specify how you plan to use the income: for investment or to pay expenses.

Planned Assets   The Planned Assets tab (shown here) enables you to enter information about any assets you plan to purchase in the future. For example, suppose you indicated in the Asset Accounts tab that you plan to sell your home or car on a specific date. If you plan to replace it with another home or car, this is where you'd enter information about the replacement. Quicken uses dialogs that walk you through the process of entering details about the future purchase. Once you've entered planned asset information, you can select the asset in the list and add loans, expenses, and income for it, as well as choose the accounts you plan to use to pay for it. Click Done to close the Quicken Planner: Homes and Assets dialog.

Loans and Debt

Clicking the Loans And Debt link in the Plan Assumptions area displays the Loans And Debt dialog, which is organized into three tabs. This is where you enter information about current and planned loans, as well as information from your debt reduction plan.

Loan Accounts   The Loan Accounts tab, which is shown next, displays information about current loans. This information comes from loans you have set up within Quicken. To add another loan that isn't already recorded in Quicken, click the New button to display the Loan Setup dialog, which is covered in Chapter 13. If you plan to pay off a loan before its last payment date, you can click the Payoff button to enter future payoff information.

Planned Loans   The Planned Loans tab enables you to enter information about loans you plan to make in the future. This does not include any loans you may have already planned in the Homes And Assets dialog discussed earlier. Instead, this is for loans that are not associated with any particular asset, such as a personal loan you plan to pay for flying lessons or a really special vacation.

Debt   The Debt tab includes information from the Debt Reduction Planner, which I cover in detail in Chapter 17. If you have credit card and other debt, it's a good idea to complete the Debt Reduction Planner as part of your overall planning strategy. Click Done to close the Quicken Planner: Loans and Debt dialog.

Expenses

Clicking the Expenses link displays the Expenses dialog, which is organized into four tabs. This is where you enter information about your living expenses, as well as any adjustments to expenses and the expenses for college or other special events.

Living Expenses   The Living Expenses tab, which is shown here, enables you to enter your estimated living expenses using one of two techniques:

- **Rough Estimate** enables you to enter an estimate of your annual living expenses. Using this technique is quicker, but it may not be as accurate as using the Category Detail option.

- **Category Detail** enables you to have Quicken calculate an estimate of your annual living expenses based on transactions already entered in your Quicken data file. This technique is more accurate than Rough Estimate, especially if you have been using Quicken for a while and have a good history of transactions. If you select this method, you can click the Details button that appears in the middle of the dialog to display the Living Expenses Category Detail dialog. Toggle check marks in the list of categories to include or exclude specific categories and enter monthly amounts as desired. When you click OK, Quicken annualizes the amounts and enters them in the Living Expenses tab.

One thing to keep in mind here: Don't include expenses that you may have already included for an asset. For example, if you included car insurance expenses in the Homes And Assets dialog as an expense associated with an automobile, don't include them again here. Doing so would duplicate the expense and overstate your annual expenses.

At the bottom of the dialog, you can enter a percentage of surplus cash—cash left over after paying living expenses—that you want to put into savings.

One really annoying behavior is that each time you use the dialog with the Category detail, the categories you have unchecked are all checked. This inflates your expenses. You must make a note of the categories you wish to exclude and uncheck those categories each time you use the Details dialog.

Adjustments   The Adjustments tab enables you to enter any adjustments to your expenses that are related to planned changes in your life. For example, perhaps you plan to hire a nanny to take care of your child while you go back to work. You can add this planned expense as an adjustment for a predefined period of time. When you click the New button in the Adjustments tab, the Add Living Expense Adjustment dialog appears. The illustration on the next page shows how it might look if I sent my dependent, Alex (okay, so she's just a parrot), to ballet school for a few years.

College Expenses The College Expenses tab enables you to plan for the education of your children—or yourself! Clicking the New button in this tab displays the Add College Expense dialog, shown next, which walks you through the process of entering expected college expenses for a plan member. You'll have to do a little homework to come up with realistic estimates of college costs, including tuition, room, board, books, and supplies. Remember, if you underestimate expenses, your plan won't be accurate. The dialog also prompts you for information about expected financial aid, student loans, and student contributions to cover all sources of financing. If you have a college fund—such as an educational IRA—already set up for the college expense, you can associate it with the expense to indicate how it will be paid for.

Special Expenses   The Special Expenses tab, which is shown here, includes any expenses you may have already added in the Homes And Assets dialog and enables you to enter other one-time or annual expenses you expect to incur. Use this for items like a vacation, wedding, or large purchase. When you click the New button, Quicken prompts you for information about the expense, including the amount and how you expect to finance it. Click Done to close the Quicken Planner: Expenses dialog.

Reviewing and Changing Assumptions
You can review and modify your plan assumptions at any time. Quicken offers a number of ways to do this.

The Plan Assumptions Area
Once you enter assumptions into the Quicken Planner, a brief summary of the assumptions appears in the Plan Assumptions area in the Planning tab (see Figure 15-1). To open this window, choose Planning | Lifetime Planner.

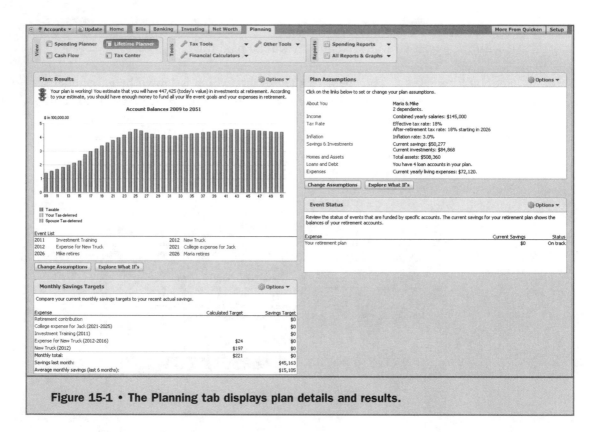

Figure 15-1 • The Planning tab displays plan details and results.

You can click links in the Plan Assumptions area to open the same dialogs discussed earlier in this chapter. Review and change plan assumptions as desired and click Done in the dialog to save them.

The Planning Assumptions Window

A better way to review plan assumptions is in the Planning Assumptions window (see Figure 15-2). To open this window, choose Planning | Lifetime Planner, and click the Change Assumptions button in the Plan: Results area of the Planning tab. You can also choose Change Assumptions from the Options drop-down menu.

You can use links on the left side of the window to navigate quickly from one category of assumption to another. The details appear in the main part of the window. Each category of assumption offers two links:

- **How Is This Used?** explains how the information in that category of assumption is used in the plan.
- **Edit** enables you to edit the assumptions for that category, using the same dialogs discussed earlier in this chapter.

Figure 15-2 • The Planning Assumptions window displays details about your Quicken Plan assumptions.

Saved Plans

Figure 15-1 shows the results of your saved plan, the plan assumptions, and your monthly savings targets. You can use this screen to review your savings plans and change them if you need or want to. Click a link to open the associated planner and change data as desired. Quicken's planners are discussed later in this chapter, in the section "Using Quicken's Planners."

Planners

As I discuss later in this chapter, in the section titled "Using Quicken's Planners," each individual planner can also be used to add assumptions to your plan. Follow the instructions within the planner to enter data, and the data is added to the Quicken Planner's data.

Viewing Plan Results

When Quicken has enough data about your assumptions to calculate plan results, it displays them graphically in the Plan: Results area of the Planning tab (see Figure 15-1).

The top of the Plan: Results area tells you whether your plan is working and how much you should have in investments at retirement. Amounts are in today's dollars; to view them in future dollars, choose Show Amounts In Future Value from the Options pop-up menu at the top right of the area.

The graph beneath this summary shows your taxable and tax-deferred savings. The ideal shape of this graph shows a steady increase until the year you retire and then a gradual decrease. Hover your mouse pointer over a column to show a yellow box with the amount for that year. Double-clicking the column opens a Plan Summary dialog for that year showing income and expenses. You can use the <<Prev Year>> and <<Next Year>> buttons in the dialog to scroll through the years in the graph. This enables you to see the detailed numbers that make up the graph columns—very helpful! Plan results change automatically based on a variety of changes within your Quicken data file:

- When the account balances referred to in the plan change, the plan changes accordingly.
- When you change plan assumptions, the plan changes accordingly.
- When you use Quicken's planners to plan for major purchases, college, retirement, and other events that affect your finances, the plan changes to include these events.
- When you play "what if" with assumptions and save the changes as your plan, the plan changes accordingly. I tell you about playing "what if" a little later in this chapter, in the section "Playing 'What If.'"

Viewing Event Status and Savings Targets

Quicken also keeps track of your progress toward certain events and savings targets. It displays this information in the Planning tab of the Lifetime Planner window (refer to Figure 15-1).

- **Event Status** displays information about events in your plan that are funded with specific accounts.
- **Monthly Savings Targets** displays information about your savings toward events in your plan.

Clicking a link for an expense displays the summary area of the appropriate planner. As discussed next, you can use the planner to review and modify event information.

Using Quicken's Planners

Quicken's planners offer another way to add financial planning information to Quicken. Rather than enter general assumptions, most planners concentrate on specific events or goals, such as buying a home or sending a child to college. Unlike the plan assumptions dialogs discussed earlier in this chapter, the individual planners provide more information about the event or item you are planning for.

In this part of the chapter, I introduce the individual planners and give you an idea of how their interface works. You can then explore each of the planners on your own.

A Look at the Planners

Quicken includes several planners, all of which can be accessed by clicking Planning | Lifetime Planner and then clicking Your Retirement Plan in the Event Status pane. Here are some of the types of planning you can do:

- **Retirement Planner** is the most comprehensive planner. It looks at all of your current financial information, as well as the results of other planners, to help you plan for retirement. It basically reviews all data entered for Quicken Planner assumptions, as discussed earlier in this chapter.
- **College Planner** helps you plan for your children's college education. It gathers the same information you could enter for a new college expense in the College Expenses tab of the Expenses dialog.
- **Home Purchase Planner** helps you plan for the purchase of a new home. It gathers the same information you could enter for a new home in the Planned Assets tab of the Homes And Assets dialog.
- **Debt Reduction Planner** helps you save money while getting out of debt as quickly as possible. I cover this planner in detail in Chapter 17.
- **Special Purchase Planner** helps you plan for special purchases, such as vacations, vehicles, and other large expenditures. It gathers the same information you could enter for major expenditures in the Special Expenses tab of the Expenses dialog.

All of these planners work pretty much the same way. You enter information about your current financial situation or let Quicken enter the information for you based on account balances and category transactions. Then you tell the planner a little about the event you're planning for. For example, the College Planner needs to know how old your children are now and when you expect them to go to college. It also needs to know how much you expect their education to cost. When you enter all this information into Quicken, it performs calculations and shows you results. Planning information is saved within your Quicken data file so you can view or update it at any time.

Adding Plan Details with Quicken's Planners

You can add details to the assumptions of your financial plan by using Quicken's planners to add specific events to the plan. The information you enter into these plans becomes part of your overall financial plan, thus changing the Plan Results. When you use any of these planners to create plans, each individual plan appears in the Event List beneath the graph in the Planning tab. This makes it easy to view and change plans.

Here's a look at four of Quicken's planners; the other one (the Debt Reduction Planner) is covered in Chapter 17.

Retirement Planner

The Retirement Planner enables you to plan for your retirement. It is, by far, the most exhaustive planner, primarily because it requires all the information entered as plan assumptions. In fact, if you have already entered plan assumptions, you can go through the Retirement Planner very quickly; if not, it'll take you about 30 minutes to enter all the information it requires. (That information will be saved for use by other planners.)

To start, choose the Planning tab and then click Your Retirement Plan under the Event Status pane, as shown. The My Retirement Plan window opens (see

Event Status			⚙ Options ▼
Review the status of events that are funded by specific accounts. The current savings for your retirement plan shows the balances of your retirement accounts.			
Expense		Current Savings	Status
Your retirement plan		$0	On track

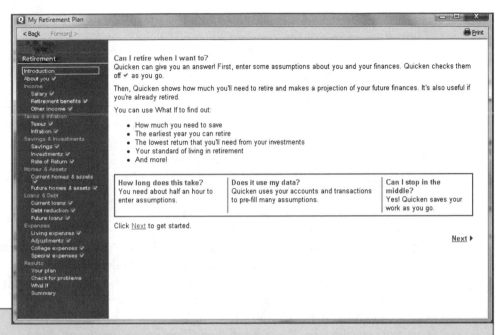

Figure 15-3 • The Retirement Planner can help you determine whether you can retire when you want to.

Figure 15-3). You may need to click the Introduction link in the left navigation bar if you see the summary instead of the introduction. Read the information in the window, and then click the Next link to begin entering information. Follow the prompts that appear to open dialogs and enter data for a number of topics, many of which may already include information from plan assumptions or other planners. The items you complete are checked off in the navigation bar on the left side of the My Retirement Plan window; you can also click links for items there to complete them in any order you like.

When you have finished entering information, the Your Plan screen shows your financial plan. Subsequent windows enable you to check your plan for problems, play "what if" with your plan (as is discussed later in this chapter, in the section "Playing 'What If'"), and view a summary of your plan.

College Planner

The College Planner enables you to plan for a college education. It uses information already entered as plan assumptions, as well as new information you enter about your child's college plans.

To bring up the College Planner, first click Your Retirement Plan under the Event Planner area of the Planning window. Click College Expenses on the left navigation bar, and then click the Can I Afford College? link. Read the information in the introduction screen and click the Next link to get started. Then follow the prompts to add or edit information about a dependent's college education.

When you have finished entering information in the planner windows, the Results screen shows your financial plan with your child's college education included. Subsequent screens offer you a chance to play "what if" with your financial plan, summarize cost and funding information, and allow you to connect to the Internet for other resources, including college and financial aid information.

Home Purchase Planner

The Home Purchase Planner enables you to plan for the purchase of a home—either a primary residence or a vacation home. Like the other planners, it prompts you for information about a specific event, but it also has built-in calculators to help you determine affordability so you can understand how a home would fit into your budget.

To get started, click Your Retirement Plan under the Event Planner area of the Planning window. Click Future Homes And Assets on the left navigation bar, and then click the Can I Afford That House? link. Read the information on the introduction screen and click the Next link. Then follow the prompts to enter information about your finances (see Figure 15-4) and the proposed purchase. In some cases, you can get information from your Quicken data file and from the Internet by clicking links within the window. When you're finished entering information, the planner displays its results. Subsequent screens summarize the information and display a glossary of terms you should know when purchasing a home.

Special Purchase Planner

The Special Purchase Planner enables you to plan for a major purchase, such as a new car or recreational vehicle or a costly vacation. It uses information already entered as plan assumptions, as well as new information you enter about the special purchase.

Choose Your Retirement Plan under the Event Planner area of the Planning window. Click Special Expenses on the left navigation bar, and then click the Can I Afford That Purchase? link. Read the information in the window and follow the prompts that appear to enter all information about the purchase. When you are finished, the Results window shows your financial plan with the planned purchase included. The Resources window provides links to other

Figure 15-4 • **The Home Purchase Planner even helps you determine whether you can afford to buy a home.**

resources within Quicken and on Quicken.com to learn more about purchasing big-ticket items.

Playing "What If"

Once you've entered assumptions, created plans for specific events, and viewed your plan results, you might wonder how a change in one or more assumptions would affect the plan. You can use the "What If" Event Scenarios feature to see how the changes would affect the plan without changing the plan itself.

Here's an example. Say you've been offered a job in another state. The job pays about the same salary that you make now, but you can move to a town where your living expenses would be greatly reduced. You can see how the job change would affect your financial plans for the future by playing "what if" to modify existing assumptions, and then see the old and new plan results side by side.

Setting "What If" Options

Click the Planning tab and click the Explore What If's" button at the bottom of the Plan: Results area. The What If window, which is shown in Figure 15-5, appears. The first time you use it, it displays the account balances shown in your Plan Results.

Choose a goal option from the drop-down list at the top left of the window. Then click appropriate links on the left side of the window to open dialogs to change assumptions.

In our example, you might use the following links:

- Click Current Homes & Assets to add proposed sale information about your current home.

Figure 15-5 • You can use the What If window to play "what if" with your financial plans.

- Click Current Loans to record the proposed payoff of your mortgage when you sell your current home.
- Click Future Homes & Assets to add proposed purchase information about your new home and its associated mortgage.
- Click Adjustments to add a proposed adjustment for the reduced living expenses when you move to your new home.

Get the idea? Each time you make a change, the Plan Comparison chart changes. Here's what it might look like for our example:

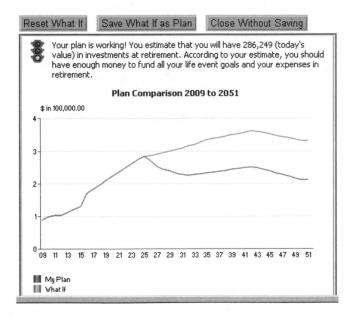

Using "What If" Results

When you've finished changing assumptions and viewing results, you can click one of the three buttons at the top of the What If window:

- **Reset What If** clears all the assumptions you changed while playing "what if." This enables you to start over.
- **Save What If As Plan** saves the assumptions you changed while playing "what if" as your actual financial plan. When the window closes, you'll see the results in the Planning tab change accordingly.
- **Close Without Saving** simply closes the window so you can continue working with Quicken. Your settings are not saved.

Using Financial Calculators

In This Chapter:

- *Financial calculators overview*
- *Retirement Calculator*
- *College Calculator*
- *Refinance Calculator*
- *Investment Savings Calculator*
- *Loan Calculator*

Sometimes, the hardest part about financial planning is making the calculations you need quickly to determine the feasibility of a potential plan. For example, suppose you're thinking about refinancing your home because you can now get an interest rate that's lower than the rate you locked into six years ago. You know your monthly payment can decrease, but you're not sure if you'll save enough money to cover the fees involved in the refinancing. The calculations seem complex, and you're not sure what to do. That's where one of Quicken Personal Finance Software's financial calculators—the Refinance Calculator—can help. It can take raw data about your current mortgage and the one you're considering, and crunch the numbers in a flash to tell you whether it's worthwhile to take the next step.

This chapter tells you about each of Quicken's financial calculators. I'm sure you'll find them handy tools for making the quick calculations you need to start the decision-making process with your financial plans.

Chapter 16

A Look at Quicken's Financial Calculators

Quicken includes five financial calculators you can use to make quick financial calculations: the Retirement Calculator, the College Calculator, the Refinance Calculator, the Investment Savings Calculator, and the Loan Calculator. These calculators make complex calculations simple.

How the Calculators Work

All five of the financial calculators share the same basic interface. But although they are similar in appearance, each is designed for a specific purpose. It's important that you use the correct calculator to get the job done.

In most instances, you begin by telling the calculator what part of the formula you want to calculate. For example, when calculating a loan, you can calculate the loan amount or the periodic payment. Then you enter values and set other options in the calculator's dialog to give Quicken the information it needs to make its calculations. Clicking a Calculate button completes the process. Quicken is fast; the results appear as soon as you click Calculate—if not sooner.

Accessing the Financial Calculators

To view the financial calculators, click the Planning tab and then in the toolbar, click the Financial Calculators down arrow. You will see five options, as shown here:

If the Planning tab is not visible, click View | Tabs To Show | Planning on the menu bar.

Using the Financial Calculators

Ready to give Quicken's financial calculators a try? The rest of this chapter provides some detailed instructions for using each of them.

Retirement Calculator

The Retirement Calculator can help you calculate some of the numbers you need to plan for your retirement. To open it, choose Planning | Financial Calculators | Retirement Calculator. The Retirement Calculator appears:

Select a Calculate For option, and then enter or select values and options throughout the dialog. Most options are pretty straightforward and easy to understand. When you're finished, click the Calculate button to see the results. Click Done when you're finished.

Here's a closer look at the options in the Retirement Calculator.

Retirement Information

Retirement Information options enable you to enter the values Quicken should use in its calculations. The values you must enter vary depending on the Calculate For option you select.

Inflation

Inflation options make complex calculations to account for the effect of inflation on your savings dollars. To use this feature, enter an inflation rate in the Predicted Inflation box, and then toggle check marks for the two options below it.

- **Inflate Contributions** makes calculations assuming that the annual contributions will rise with the inflation rate.
- **Annual Income In Today's $** makes calculations assuming that the Annual Income After Taxes entry is in today's dollars and not inflated.

Calculate For

The Calculate For option affects which value is calculated by Quicken.

- **Current Savings** calculates the amount of money you should currently have saved based on the values you enter.
- **Annual Contribution** calculates the minimum amount you should contribute to a retirement account based on the values you enter.
- **Annual Retirement Income** calculates the annual amount of retirement income you'll have based on the values you enter.

Tax Information

Tax Information options enable you to indicate whether your retirement savings are in a tax-sheltered investment or a non-sheltered investment. If you select the Non-Sheltered Investment option, you can enter your current tax rate and Quicken will automatically calculate the effect of taxes on your investment income. By experimenting with this feature, you can clearly see why it's a good idea to use tax-sheltered or tax-deferred investments whenever possible.

Schedule

Clicking the Schedule button displays a printable list of deposits made and income withdrawn, with a running balance total. Here's what it looks like with the calculations shown earlier.

Deposit Schedule

Print   ? How Do I?

This deposit schedule assumes that your retirement income keeps pace with a 4.0% annual inflation rate. Note that income is in future, pre-tax dollars.

Age	Deposit	Income	Balance
0	0.00	0.00	285,000.00
47	8,000.00	0.00	307,250.00
48	8,000.00	0.00	330,612.50
49	8,000.00	0.00	355,143.13
50	8,000.00	0.00	380,900.28
51	8,000.00	0.00	407,945.30
52	8,000.00	0.00	436,342.56
53	8,000.00	0.00	466,159.69
54	8,000.00	0.00	497,467.67
55	8,000.00	0.00	530,341.06
56	8,000.00	0.00	564,858.11

College Calculator

The College Calculator enables you to calculate savings for the cost of a college education. Choose Planning | Financial Calculators | College. The College Calculator, shown here, appears.

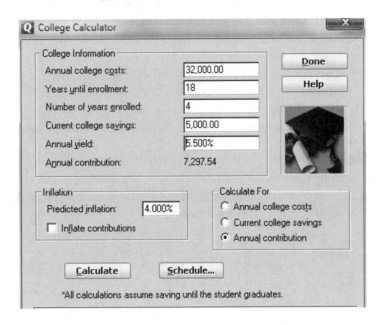

Select a Calculate For option, and then enter or select values and options throughout the dialog. Most options are pretty straightforward and easy to understand. When you click Calculate, Quicken calculates the results. When you are finished, click Done.

Here's a look at the options in the College Calculator.

College Information

The College Information area is where you enter the values Quicken should use in its calculations. The values you must enter vary, depending on the Calculate For option you select.

Inflation

Inflation options make complex calculations to account for the effect of inflation on your savings dollars. To use this feature, enter an inflation rate in the Predicted Inflation box. You can then toggle the Inflate Contributions check box, which makes calculations assuming that the annual contributions will rise with the inflation rate. Quicken automatically inflates the amount of tuition no matter how you set the Inflate Contributions check box.

Calculate For

The Calculate For option affects which value is calculated by Quicken.

- **Annual College Costs** calculates the annual tuition you'll be able to afford based on the values you enter.
- **Current College Savings** calculates the amount of money you should currently have saved based on the values you enter.
- **Annual Contribution** calculates the minimum amount you should contribute to college savings based on the values you enter.

Schedule

Clicking the Schedule button displays a printable list of deposits made and money withdrawn for tuition, with a running balance total. Here's what it looks like with the calculations shown earlier:

Year	Deposit	Tuition	Balance
0	0.00	0.00	5,000.00
2009	7,297.54	0.00	12,572.54
2010	7,297.54	0.00	20,561.57
2011	7,297.54	0.00	28,990.00
2012	7,297.54	0.00	37,881.99
2013	7,297.54	0.00	47,263.04
2014	7,297.54	0.00	57,160.04
2015	7,297.54	0.00	67,601.38
2016	7,297.54	0.00	78,617.00
2017	7,297.54	0.00	90,238.48
2018	7,297.54	0.00	102,499.13

Refinance Calculator

If you own a home and are thinking about refinancing, you can try the Refinance Calculator to see whether refinancing will really save you money and, if so, how much. Choose Planning | Financial Calculators | Refinance Calculator. The Refinance Calculator, shown next, appears.

Enter values for your current mortgage and proposed mortgage in the text boxes to calculate your monthly savings with the new mortgage. When you are finished, click Done. Here's a closer look at the entries.

Existing Mortgage

Existing Mortgage options enable you to enter your current total monthly mortgage payment and the amount of that payment that is applied to property taxes and other escrow items. Quicken automatically calculates the amount of principal and interest for each payment. If you already know the principal and interest amount, you can enter that in the Current Payment box and leave the Impound/Escrow Amount box empty. The result is the same.

Proposed Mortgage

Proposed Mortgage options enable you to enter information about the mortgage that you are considering to replace your current mortgage. The Principal Amount may be the balance on your current mortgage, but it could be more or less depending on whether you want to refinance for more or less money. (Refinancing often offers a good opportunity to exchange equity for cash.)

Break Even Analysis

Break Even Analysis options are optional. If you enter the closing costs and points for the proposed mortgage, Quicken will automatically calculate how long it will take to cover those costs based on your monthly savings. As you can see in the previous illustration, it will take nearly a year for the savings to pay for the closing costs and points on the new mortgage.

Print

Clicking the Print button displays the Print dialog, which you can use to print the results of your calculations.

Investment Savings Calculator

The Investment Savings Calculator enables you to calculate savings annuities—periodic payments to a savings account or investment. Choose Planning | Financial Calculators | Savings Calculator. The Investment Savings Calculator appears, as shown here.

Select a Calculate For option, and then enter or select values and options throughout the dialog. Most options are pretty straightforward and easy to understand. When you click Calculate, Quicken displays the results. When you are finished, click Done.

Here's a closer look at each of the entry options.

Savings Information

Savings Information options enable you to enter values for Quicken to use in its calculations. The option you choose from the Number Of drop-down list will determine how interest is compounded; in most cases, you'll probably set this to Months.

Inflation

Inflation options make complex calculations to account for the effect of inflation on your savings dollars. To use this feature, enter an inflation rate in the Predicted Inflation box, and then toggle check boxes for the two options below it:

- **Inflate Contributions** makes calculations assuming that the annual contributions will rise with the inflation rate.
- **Ending Balance In Today's $** makes calculations assuming that the Ending Savings Balance is in today's dollars and not inflated.

When you click Calculate, Quicken displays the results. You can click the Schedule button to see a printable list of deposits, with a running balance total.

Calculate For

The Calculate For option affects which value is calculated by Quicken.

- **Opening Savings Balance** calculates the amount of money you should currently have saved based on the values you enter.
- **Regular Contribution** calculates the minimum amount you should regularly contribute to savings based on the values you enter.
- **Ending Savings Balance** calculates the total amount saved at the end of the savings period based on the values you enter.

Schedule

Clicking the Schedule button displays a printable list of deposits made, with a running balance total. Here is what it looks like with the calculations shown earlier:

Deposit Schedule

Print   (?) How Do I?

The effect of 4.0% annual inflation over the period of 36 months will make $14,243.19 worth $12,635.10 in terms of today's purchasing power.

Number	Deposit	Total
0	0.00	6,000.00
1	200.00	6,217.50
2	200.00	6,435.63
3	200.00	6,654.40
4	200.00	6,873.81
5	200.00	7,093.86
6	200.00	7,314.55
7	200.00	7,535.09
8	200.00	7,757.87
9	200.00	7,980.49
10	200.00	8,203.77

Loan Calculator

Quicken's Loan Calculator can quickly calculate the principal or periodic payment for a loan. Choose Planning | Financial Calculators | Loan Calculator. The Loan Calculator, which is shown here, appears.

Select one of the Calculate For options, enter information in the remainder of the dialog, and click Calculate. Getting the answer is a lot quicker and easier with the Loan Calculator than using one of those loan books or building an Excel spreadsheet to do the job. When you're finished, click Done.

Here's a look at the Loan Calculator options.

Loan Information

Loan Information options enable you to enter values for Quicken to use in its calculations. The information you must enter varies depending on the Calculate For option you select. Be sure to set the Periods Per Year and Compounding Period options correctly; an incorrect entry will misstate the results.

Calculate For

The Calculate For options determine what Quicken calculates.

- **Loan Amount** enables you to calculate the amount of a loan based on specific periodic payments.
- **Payment Per Period** enables you to calculate the periodic loan payment based on the loan amount.

Schedule

Clicking the Schedule button displays a printable amortization table that lists the payment number, the amount of the principal and interest paid at each payment, and the ending balance for the loan:

Pmt	Principal	Interest	Balance
		7.0%	24,000.00
1	335.23	140.00	23,664.77
2	337.19	138.04	23,327.58
3	339.15	136.08	22,988.43
4	341.13	134.10	22,647.30
5	343.12	132.11	22,304.18
6	345.12	130.11	21,959.06
7	347.14	128.09	21,611.92
8	349.16	126.07	21,262.76
9	351.20	124.03	20,911.56
10	353.25	121.98	20,558.31
11	355.31	119.92	20,203.00
12	357.38	117.85	19,845.62
13	359.46	115.77	19,486.16

Q Approximate Future Payment Schedule

Print — ? How Do I?

Reducing Debt and Saving Money

In This Chapter:

- *Reducing debt*
- *Budgeting and forecasting*
- *Setting up savings goals*

The best way to prepare for life events is to build up your savings. Saving money is an important part of financial management. Savings enable you to take vacations and make major purchases without increasing debt, help your kids through college, handle emergencies, and have a comfortable retirement.

This chapter tells you about saving money and how tools within Quicken Personal Finance Software can help. If you're in debt and can't even think about saving until you dig your way out, this chapter can help you, too. It starts by covering Quicken tools for reducing your debt.

Reducing Your Debt

Consumer credit is a huge industry. It's easy to get credit cards—sometimes too easy. And it's a lot easier to pay for something with a piece of plastic than with cold, hard cash. The "buy now, pay later" attitude has become an acceptable way of life. It's no wonder that many Americans are deeply in debt.

Those credit card bills can add up, however. And paying just the minimum payment on each one only helps the credit card company keep you in debt—and paying interest—as long as possible. I've been there, so I know. Unfortunately, it took two experiences to set me straight. I hope you can learn your lesson the first time.

If you're in debt, don't skip this part of the chapter. It'll help you dig yourself out of debt so you can build a solid financial future.

Take Control

It's not easy to save money if most of your income is spent paying credit card bills and loan payments. If you're heavily in debt, you might even be having trouble keeping up with all your payments. But don't despair. There is hope! Here are a few simple things you can do to dig yourself out of debt.

Breaking the Pattern

Your first step to reducing debt must be to break the pattern of spending that got you where you are. For most people, that means cutting up credit cards. After all, it's tough to use a credit card if you can't hand it to a cashier at the checkout counter.

Before you take out the scissors, however, read this: You don't have to cut up *all* of your credit cards. Leave yourself one or two major credit cards for emergencies, such as car trouble or unexpected visits to the doctor. The cards that should go are the store and gas credit cards. They can increase your debt, but they can be used in only a few places.

Here's the logic behind this strategy. If you have 15 credit cards, each with a credit limit of $2,000, you can get yourself into $30,000 of debt. The minimum monthly payment for each card may be $50. That's $750 a month in minimum credit card payments. If you have only two credit cards, each with a credit limit of $2,000, you can get yourself into only $4,000 of debt. Your monthly minimum payment may be only $100. This reduces your monthly obligation, enabling you to pay more than the minimum so you can further reduce your debt.

Reducing Your Credit Limits

Sure, it's a real temptation to use your credit cards to spend just a little more every month—especially when you're not even close to your credit limit. But high credit limits are a trap. The credit card company or bank flatters you by offering to lend you more money. What they're really doing is setting you up so you'll owe them more—and pay them more in monthly finance and interest fees.

The next time your credit card company tells you they've raised your credit limit, do yourself a favor: Call them up and tell them to reduce it right back to where it was—or lower!

Shopping for Cards with Better Interest Rates

Yes, it's nice to have a credit card with your picture on it. Or one that's gold, platinum, or titanium. Or one with your college, team, club, or association name on it. A friend of mine who breeds horses showed off a new Visa card with a picture of a horse on it. She told me it was her favorite. I asked her what the interest rate was, and she didn't know.

The purpose of a credit card is to purchase things on credit. When you maintain a balance on the account, you pay interest on it. The balance and interest rate determine how much it costs you to have that special picture or name on a plastic card in your wallet. Is it worth 19.8 percent a year? Or 21 percent? Not to me!

Here's a reality-check exercise: Gather together all of your credit card bills for the most recent month. Now add up all the monthly finance fees and interest charges. Multiply that number by 12. The result is an approximation of what you pay in credit card interest each year. Now imagine how nice it would be to have that money in your hands the next time you go on vacation or need a down payment on a new car or home.

Low-interest credit cards are widely available. Sometimes you don't even have to look for them—offers arrive in the mail all the time. They promise low rates—usually under 10 percent a year. But you must read these offers carefully before you apply for one of these cards. Most offer the low rates for a short, introductory period—usually no longer than 6 or 12 months. (I once got one that offered 0 percent for the first 25 days. Big deal.) Some offer the low rate only on new purchases, while others offer the low rate only on balance transfers or cash advances. Be sure to find out what the rate is after the introductory period.

Here are two strategies for using a low-interest card:

* Consolidate your debt by transferring the balances of other credit cards to the new card. For this strategy, select a card that offers a low rate on balance transfers. When you transfer the balances, be sure to cut up the old cards so you don't use them to add more to your debt.
* Make purchases with the low-interest card. Make the new card your emergency credit card. Be sure to cut up your old emergency card so you don't wind up using both of them.

And if you really like that special picture or name on the card in your wallet, call the credit card company and ask if they can give you a better interest rate. In many instances, they can—especially when you tell them you want to close your account.

Consolidating Your Debt

Consolidating your debt is one of the best ways to dig yourself out. By combining balances into one debt, whether through balance transfers to a single credit card or a debt consolidation loan, you're better able to pay off the balances without causing financial hardship. This is sometimes the only option when things have gotten completely out of control and you can't meet your debt obligations.

Although this can be a risky way to handle your debt, if you own a home, you might consider a home equity loan to consolidate your debt. The interest rate is usually lower than any credit card or debt consolidation loan, and the interest may be tax-deductible. I tell you more about home equity loans in Chapter 13.

Using Charge Cards, Not Credit Cards

There's a difference between a credit card and a charge card:

- **Credit cards** enable you to buy things on credit. If each month you pay less than what you owe, you are charged interest on your account balance. Most major "credit cards" are true credit cards. MasterCard, Visa, and Discover are three examples. Most store "charge cards" are also credit cards.
- **Charge cards** enable you to buy things on credit, too. But when the bill comes, you're expected to pay the entire balance. You don't have to pay any interest, but if you don't pay the entire balance on time, you may have to pay late fees and finance charges. American Express is an example of a charge card.

The benefit of charge cards is that they make it impossible to get into serious debt. How can you owe the charge card company money if you must pay the balance in full every month? Using these cards prevents you from overspending. Every time you use the card to make a purchase, a little accountant in the back of your head should be adding the charge to a running total. You should stop spending when that total reaches the limit of your ability to pay.

Chapters 5 and 6 explain how you can use Quicken to track credit and charge card balances manually or online. If you use Quicken to keep track of expenditures, you won't need that little accountant in the back of your head.

If you don't want an American Express card (for whatever reason), use another major credit card as a charge card. Just pay the entire balance each time you get a bill. If you don't carry a balance, you won't be charged interest.

If You Can't Stop Spending, Get Help

Many people who are deeply in debt may have a spending problem. They can't resist buying that fifth pair of running shoes or that trendy new outdoor furniture. They don't *need* the things they buy, but they buy them anyway. There's nothing wrong with that if your income can support your spending habits, but if your net worth is less than $0, it's a real problem—one that might require counseling to resolve.

The next time you make a purchase, stop for a moment and think about what you're buying. Is it something you need? Something you can use? Something you can justify spending the money on? If you can't answer yes to any of these questions, don't buy it. If you have to buy it anyway, it's time to seek professional help.

Living Debt-Free

It is possible to live debt-free—and you don't have to be rich to do it. Just stop relying on credit to make your purchases and spend only what you can afford to spend.

Imagine how great it would feel to be completely debt free. It's worth a try, isn't it?

Using the Debt Reduction Planner

Quicken's Debt Reduction Planner is a tool for helping you reduce your debt. You enter information about your financial situation, and Quicken develops a debt reduction plan for you. The Debt Reduction Planner is thorough, easy to use, and

---

What Does This Mean to You? The Debt Reduction Planner

If you're in serious debt—actually having trouble making ends meet because you can't seem to get any of your debts paid down—a pair of scissors, a telephone, and the Debt Reduction Planner are probably your three best tools for getting things under control.

First, use the scissors to cut up most, if not all, of your credit cards. Next, use the telephone to call your credit card companies and try to get your interest rates reduced. (The worst they can do is say no.) Then use the Debt Reduction Planner to come up with a solid plan for reducing your debt.

Here's what the Debt Reduction Planner can do that you might not be able to do on your own:

- Objectively look at your debts and organize them by interest rate. The debts that cost you the most are the ones that are paid off first, thus saving you money.
- Show you the benefit of using some of your savings to reduce the balances on your most costly debt.
- Help you set up spending limits, with alarms, for the categories on which you spend too much money.
- Create an itemized plan based on real numbers that you can follow to reduce your debt.
- Show you, in dollars and cents, how much money you can save and how quickly you can become debt-free, by following the plan.

Don't dread the daily mail and its package of bills. Use the Debt Reduction Planner to get things under control.

an excellent tool for teaching people how they can get out of debt as quickly as possible, saving hundreds (if not thousands) of dollars in interest charges.

Note that the Debt Reduction Planner works best when you track all of your debt—including credit card debt—using Quicken accounts. That means setting up accounts for your credit cards rather than simply tracking monthly payments as bills paid. I tell you more about the two different ways to track credit cards in Chapters 2 and 5.

To get started, choose Planning |Other Tools | Debt Reduction Planner. If the Planning tab is not visible, select View | Tabs To Show | Planning from the menu bar. If you have explored this feature before, the Debt Reduction window appears with a chart showing the information you previously entered (refer to Figure 17-1, later in this chapter). If you have never used it before, the Debt Reduction dialog, with its Welcome screen as shown here, appears, enabling you to create a new debt reduction plan.

Creating a New Debt Reduction Plan

Insert your Quicken CD in your CD-ROM drive and click Next to continue. An introductory movie plays, telling you what the Debt Reduction Planner can do for you. (If you don't have your Quicken CD-ROM available, you can skip the movie. But I do recommend viewing it the first time you use the Debt Reduction Planner.) When the movie has finished, click Next to begin.

Entering Debt Information

When you click Next after viewing the movie, the Debts tab of the window appears. It should look something like this:

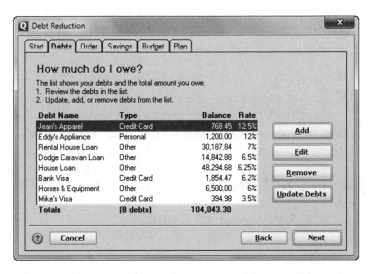

This tab lists all of your current debts, as they are recorded in Quicken. Use the buttons to the right of the list to modify the list:

- If the debt list is not up-to-date or complete, click the Update Debts button to import current debt information from your Quicken data file.

- To add a debt that you do not track in Quicken, click the Add button. The Edit Debt Reduction dialog, shown right, appears. Use it to enter information about the debt, and click OK to add it to the list.

- To modify information about a debt, select it and click the Edit button to display the Edit Debt Reduction dialog shown next. Make changes as desired and click OK to save the changes.

- To remove a debt from the list, select it and click the Remove button. In the confirmation dialog that appears, click Yes. This removes the debt from the Debt Reduction Planner but does not remove it from your Quicken data file. You may want to use this feature to remove a long-term debt, such as a mortgage, so you can concentrate on higher interest, short-term debt, such as credit cards and personal loans.

When the debt list shows all of your debts, click Next to continue.

If required information is missing from one or more debts, Quicken will tell you and then display the Edit Debt Reduction dialog for each debt so you can update the information. You must complete this process before you can continue.

Next, Quicken tells you about your current debt situation, including your total debt, your total monthly payments, and a projection of when you will be debt-free based on the debt information you provided. Click Next to continue.

Setting the Order of Debts

The Order tab of the Debt Reduction dialog begins with some information about the order in which debts are paid off. Quicken puts your debts in the order of cost, with the highest at the top. It might look something like this:

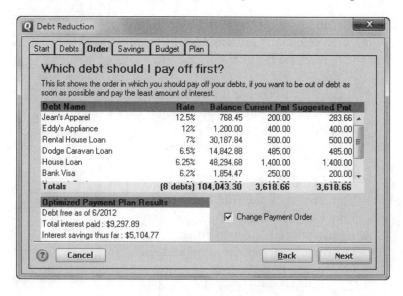

This tab sets the debt payoff order so that the most expensive debt is paid off first, thus saving you interest charges. The Suggested Pmt column offers a suggested payment amount; following the suggestion makes it possible to pay off the debts faster without increasing your total monthly payments. If desired, you can turn on the Change Payment Order check box to change the order in which debts are paid off—this, however, will cost you more and increase the payoff time.

If you turn on the Change Payment Order check box and click the Next button, the dialog changes to enable you to change the order of debts. Click a debt to select it, and then click Move Up or Move Down to change its location in the list. When you've finished, click Next.

Using Savings to Pay Off Debt

The Savings tab begins by playing a movie that tells you why you might want to use savings and investments to pay off your debt. Listen carefully—the movie is full of good information! When the movie is finished, click Next.

Quicken summarizes your current savings and investments, and enables you to specify how much of your savings should be applied to your debt, as shown here.

Enter a value in the text box and click the Recalculate button. The Results area shows the effect of your change. Click Next to continue.

Adjusting Your Budget

The Budget tab offers options for helping you reduce your spending, which can, in turn, help you reduce your debt. It begins by displaying a movie with tips and instructions. When the movie is finished, click Next to continue.

As shown on the next page, Quicken displays a list of your top four expenses, with text boxes for entering the amount by which you can cut back on each one every month.

Enter the amounts by which you can cut back for the categories that appear
or for different categories you select from the drop-down lists. Click Recalculate.
Quicken automatically suggests that you apply the savings to the debt, thus
adjusting the Results area for your entries. Click Next to continue.

Reviewing the Plan

The Plan tab, shown here, displays your custom debt reduction action plan:

Scroll through the debt reduction plan to see what it recommends. Better yet, click the Print This Action Plan button to print a copy you can refer to throughout the coming months. Click Next to continue.

Next, Quicken offers to track your debt reduction plan for you. You can toggle the settings for two different check boxes to enable this feature:

- **Alert Me If I Fall Behind** tells Quicken to alert you if you fall behind on debt reduction and to include your debt in budgeting and forecasting models. (I tell you about Planning Center alerts, budgeting, and forecasting later in this chapter.)
- **Set Up Scheduled Transactions For My Monthly Payments** tells Quicken to schedule transactions for the monthly payments included in your debt reduction plan. This makes it impossible for you to forget about debt reduction payments. (I tell you about scheduling payments in Chapter 7.)

Turn on the check box for each option that you want to enable, and then click Done.

Viewing the Debt Reduction Plan Results

When you click Done in the final screen of the Debt Reduction dialog, the Debt Reduction window appears (see Figure 17-1). It uses a graph to compare debt reduction using your current method (the right line) with that of your new debt reduction plan (the left line).

To see the results of your plan on a month-to-month basis, click the Payment Schedule button at the top of the Debt Reduction window. The Debt Reduction Payment Schedule dialog, shown on the next page, appears. It lists the payments you should make for each month, according to the plan and your account balances at month-end.

Modifying the Plan

Once you have a debt reduction plan, you can modify it in a number of ways:

Debt Reduction Payment Schedule		
Detailed Payment Schedule		
Debt Name	**Payment Amount**	**Ending Balance**
One-time payment:	12,000.00	92,043.30
Monthly Payment for November, 2009		
Rental House Loan	1,508.66	18,765.21
Dodge Caravan Loan	485.00	14,438.28
House Loan	1,400.00	47,146.21
Bank Visa	200.00	1,664.05
Horses & Equipment	150.00	6,382.50
Mike's Visa	200.00	196.13
	Total Balance	**$88,592.38**
Monthly Payment for December, 2009		
Rental House Loan	1,511.96	17,362.71
Dodge Caravan Loan	485.00	14,031.49
House Loan	1,400.00	45,991.76
Bank Visa	200.00	1,472.65
Horses & Equipment	150.00	6,264.41

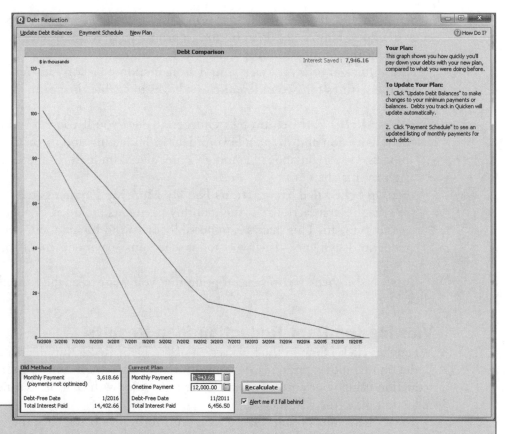

Figure 17-1 • The Debt Reduction Plan window clearly illustrates how quickly you can get out of debt and save interest costs by using Quicken's plan.

- Click the Update Debt Balances button on the button bar to import the current balances of your debt into the Debt Reduction Planner.
- Enter new values in the Current Plan area at the bottom of the Debt Reduction window. Click Recalculate to see how that new value will impact the plan.
- Click the New Plan button on the button bar to create a new plan from scratch. New data entered will replace the existing data for your plan.

No matter which method you choose, Quicken will automatically revise the graph and other information to reflect your changes.

Budgeting and Forecasting

When money is tight or you're interested in meeting financial goals, it's time to create a budget and monitor your spending. But if you're serious about managing your money, you might want to create a budget *before* you need one. While Quicken's categories give you a clear understanding of where money comes from and where it goes, budgets enable you to set up predefined amounts for each category, thus helping you to control spending.

Budgets also make it easier to create forecasts of your future financial position. This makes it possible to see how much cash will be available at a future date—before the holidays, for summer vacation, or for the day you plan to put down a deposit on a new car.

In this part of the chapter, I tell you how to create a budget and use it to monitor your spending habits. I also explain how to create a forecast so you can glimpse your financial future.

Budgeting

The idea behind a budget is to determine expected income amounts and specify maximum amounts for expenditures. This helps prevent you from spending more than you earn. It also enables you to control your spending in certain categories. For example, say you realize that you go out for dinner a lot more often than you should. You can set a budget for the Dining category and track your spending to make sure you don't exceed the budget. You'll eat at home more often and save money.

This section explains how to set up a budget and use it to keep track of your spending. I think you'll agree that budgeting is a great way to keep spending under control.

Organizing Categories into Groups

Budgets are based on transactions recorded for categories and subcategories. (That's why it's important to categorize all your transactions—and not to the Misc category!) Quicken also enables you to organize categories by category groups. Although you don't have to use the Groups feature when creating your budget—it's entirely optional—grouping similar categories together can simplify your budget.

You can see the group to which each category is assigned in the Group column of the Category List window (see Figure 17-2). Choose Banking | Banking Tools | Category List to display the window. If the Group column does not appear in your list, choose Show Category Group from the Options menu at

Figure 17-2 • The Category List window displays all categories and the names of the groups to which they are assigned.

the bottom of the window to display it. At first, you will not have groups assigned to the categories. How to assign groups is explained in "Assigning a Group to a Category," later in this chapter.

The Default Groups   By default, Quicken includes several category groups that it assigns to the categories it creates when you first set up your Quicken data file.

- **Income** is for earned income, such as your salary, and miscellaneous income items, such as interest, dividends, and gifts received.
- **Discretionary** is for expenses you can avoid (or at least minimize), such as entertainment, subscriptions, and vacation.
- **Mandatory Expenses** are expenses you can't avoid, such as fuel for your car, groceries, rent, and insurance.

In addition, if your Quicken data file includes business-related categories, Quicken includes Business Income and Business Expenses groups to track the income and expenses from your business.

Assigning a Group to a Category   You can assign a group to a category when you create or edit the category. In the Category List window (see Figure 17-2), either click New or select an existing category and, from the Action column, click Edit.

The Set Up Category or Edit Category dialog appears. Click the arrow next to the Group box to display the Group drop-down list, which is shown here, and choose a group. When you click OK, the group you chose is assigned to the category.

Assigning Groups to Multiple Categories
You can also assign groups to multiple categories at once. Choose Assign Category Groups from the Options menu at the lower-left corner of the Category List window (refer to Figure 17-2). The Assign Category Groups dialog, shown next, appears. Select a category name

from the Category Name list, select a group name from the Category Group List, and click the Assign Category To Group button. Repeat this process for each category for which you want to assign a group. To assign a group to multiple categories at the same time, you can hold down the ctrl key while clicking each category to select multiple categories; then choose the group and click the Assign Category To Group button. When you are finished, click OK.

Modifying the Category Group List You're not stuck with the group names built into Quicken. You can add new group names, or modify or delete existing group names.

In the Assign Category Groups dialog, click the New, Edit, or Del button beside the Category Group List to add a new group or modify or remove a selected group.

Creating a Budget

Quicken can automatically generate a budget for you based on past transactions. You can edit the budget it creates to meet your needs. Or you can create a budget from scratch.

To start creating a budget, choose Planning | Other Tools | Budget. The Setup tab of the Budget window, which is shown in Figure 17-3, appears.

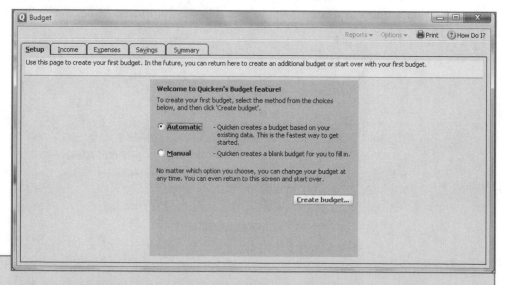

Figure 17-3 • The Setup tab of the Budget window offers options to create a budget.

Creating a Budget Automatically The quickest and easiest way to create a budget is to let Quicken do it for you based on your income and expenditures. For Quicken to create an accurate budget, however, you must have several months' worth of transactions in your Quicken data file. Otherwise, the budget may not reflect all regular income and expenses.

Select the Automatic option in the Setup tab of the Budget window (refer to Figure 17-3) and click Create Budget. The Create Budget: Automatic dialog, which is shown here, appears. Use this dialog to set options for the budget.

In the date range area, enter the starting and ending dates for the transactions on which you want to base the budget. Whenever possible, the date range should be the most recent 12-month period. But if you have less than 12 months' worth of data, enter the date range for the period for which you have data.

Next, select one of the following budget method options:

- **Average Amounts** enters monthly averages based on the period in the date range. If you select this option, choose a frequency from the drop-down list.
- **Monthly Detail** copies the total values for each month to the corresponding month in the budget.
- **Quarterly Detail** copies the total values for each quarter to the corresponding quarter in the budget.

If you're not sure which to select, consider this advice: Select Monthly Detail or Quarterly Detail if you have a full year of transactions (or close to it) and you have seasonal income (such as a teaching job) or expenses (such as a vacation home). Select Average if you have less than six months of transactions or don't have seasonal income or expenses.

Toggle the following check boxes in the Options area as desired:

- **Round Values To Nearest** enables you to round calculated values to the nearest $1, $10, or $100. If you enable this option, choose a value from the drop-down list beside it.
- **Exclude One-Time Transactions** tells Quicken not to consider one-time transactions when creating the budget. For example, suppose you made a single large payment to a furniture company to buy living room furniture. If that transaction is considered for budgeting purposes, Quicken will automatically assume that you make payments like that every year and include it in the budget. (Of course, you can always edit a budget to exclude such items after the budget has been created.)

Clicking the Categories button displays the Choose Categories dialog, shown here. You can use this dialog to select specific categories to budget. You may find this useful if you want to budget only certain categories, such as dining, clothing, and entertainment. Initially, all the categories are selected. You can click Clear All to remove the selections for a fresh start. Click to toggle the check boxes beside each category name. The categories with check marks will be included in the budget when you click OK.

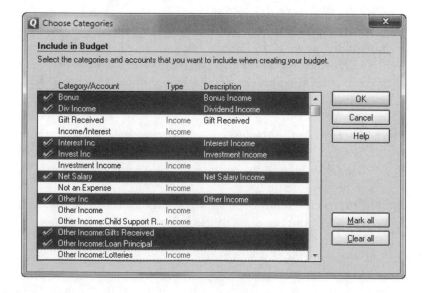

When you click OK in the Create Budget: Automatic dialog, Quicken displays a dialog telling you that the new budget has been created. Click OK to dismiss this dialog. The Income tab of the Budget window appears next.

Creating a Budget Manually   If you prefer, you can create a budget from scratch. This is more time-consuming, but it forces you to look at each category carefully to estimate future expenses.

Select the Manual option in the Setup tab of the Budget window (refer to Figure 17-3) and click Create Budget. A dialog appears with instructions for completing your budget. Click OK to dismiss the dialog. The Income tab of the Budget window appears next.

Completing a Budget

Once you have created a budget, you can fine-tune it to set the categories and amounts that should appear. If you created your budget automatically, this is a matter of reviewing budget income, expense, and savings items, and making changes you deem necessary. If you created a budget manually, however, you must manually add categories and set amounts for each one. You do this in the Income, Expenses, and Savings tabs of the Budget window. Because these windows all look and work pretty much the same way, only one is illustrated: the Expenses tab, which is shown in Figure 17-4.

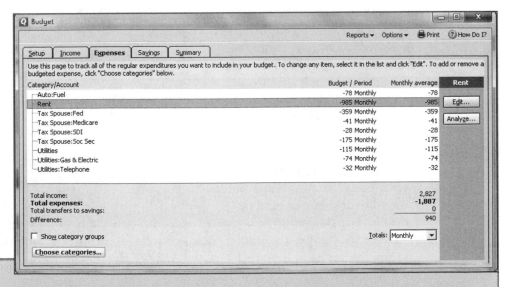

Figure 17-4 • Here's an example of the Expenses tab of the Budget window, with several expense categories entered.

Depending on your monitor settings and the width of the budget window, you may see only the Edit and Analyze buttons, as shown in Figure 17-4, or you may see an expanded right pane. Increase the width of your screen or set your monitor resolution to a higher setting to see the expanded view.

Adding or Removing Categories To add or remove a category from the budget, click the Choose Categories button at the bottom of the Budget window. This displays the Choose Categories dialog shown earlier. Click to place a check mark beside a category you want to include in the budget or to remove a check mark from beside a category you want to exclude from the budget.

By default, when you create a budget automatically, Quicken includes only the categories for which transactions exist. When you create a budget manually, Quicken does not include any categories at all; all categories must be added manually.

Setting a Budget Item's Options

You can modify the budget for a category or other item by modifying its settings using the buttons on the right side of the Budget window. Click the item name in the Budget window to select it, and then click Edit. The Edit Budget dialog, an example of which is shown here, will be displayed. Again, depending on your monitor settings, you may not see the Edit and Analyze buttons, but instead see the dialog shown next right in the budget window You have the following options:

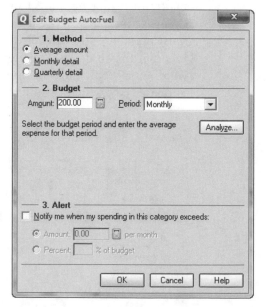

- Change the budget method to enter budget amounts as averages, monthly details, or quarterly details. The Budget options change depending on the method you select.
- Change the budget amount by entering values in each of the amount boxes in the Budget area. If you selected the Average Amount method, you can also choose a frequency from the Period drop-down list.
- Click Analyze to see a chart of your actual expenses for the category selected. This helps you visualize the actual pattern of income, expense, or savings.

- Set up an alert for a category by turning on the Notify Me check box in the Alert area and entering an amount or percent in one of the two text boxes below it. (This option appears for Expense categories only.)

If your monthly spending exceeds the amount you specified, Quicken displays a dialog to tell you.

Adding a Savings Transfer The Savings tab of the Budget window enables you to add budgeted transfers to investment or savings accounts. Click the Choose Accounts button at the bottom of the window and use the dialog that appears to select the accounts you want to transfer money to. Then set Budget options for the account as instructed in the preceding section.

Viewing a Completed Budget

When you're finished setting options in the Income, Expenses, and Savings tabs of the Budget window, click the Summary tab. This displays the budget summary, which is shown in Figure 17-5.

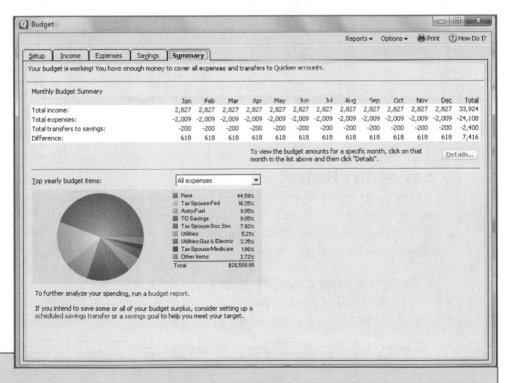

Figure 17-5 • The Summary tab of the Budget window summarizes your budget information.

You can change the graphic display content by clicking the drop-down arrow next to the graph and clicking the content you wish to see.

To view the details of a month's budget, first click the column month name, and then click Details, as shown for the month of April here. You see that month's budget entries listed. When you are done, click Done.

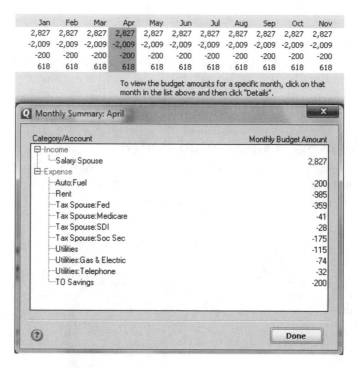

Saving the Budget

You need to save the budget so your work won't be lost. You can always revise it or create a new one from this data, as you'll see in "Working with Budgets."

To save your data, in the upper-right corner of the Budget dialog, click Options | Save Budget.

Changing the Budget View

The Budget dialog has alternative ways you can view your budget. These can be found in the Options menu in the upper-right area of the budget dialog.

- Click Options | Separate to show the Budget dialog as it is displayed in Figure 17-5. This shows all tabs for Setup, Income, Expenses, Savings, and Summary, allowing you to change data as you have been doing.

- Click Options | Income/Expense View to show only the Setup, Income, Expenses, and Summary tabs. You might use this if you have no desire to work with your savings data at this time.
- Click Options | Combined to show only the Setup, Budget, and Summary tabs.

Working with Budgets

Here are a few additional things you might want to do with Quicken's budgeting feature. All of these things can be done from the Setup tab of the Budget window. The following illustrations show what the tab looks like when you've created one budget (left) and when you've created multiple budgets (right):

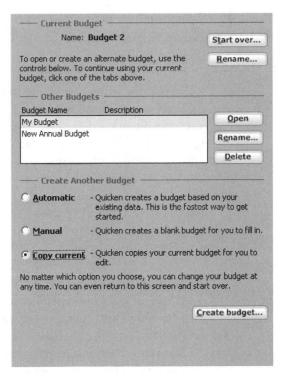

Creating Another Budget Quicken enables you to create more than one budget. In the Setup tab, select the method you want to use to create the new budget and click Create Budget. If you selected Automatic, the Create Budget: Automatic dialog that appears includes a place to enter a name for the budget. If you selected Manual or Copy Current, the Budget Name dialog appears so you can name the budget. Enter the requested information and click OK. Then fine-tune your new budget as discussed earlier in this section.

Opening a Specific Budget To open a specific budget, select the budget name in the middle part of the Setup tab and click Open.

Renaming a Budget To rename the current budget, click the Rename button in the top part of the Setup tab. To rename another budget, select the budget name and click the Rename button in the middle part of the Setup tab. Enter a name and description in the Rename Budget dialog that appears and click OK.

Deleting a Budget To delete a budget, select the budget name and click the Delete button in the middle part of the Setup tab. Click Yes in the confirmation dialog that appears. You cannot delete the currently open budget.

Comparing a Budget to Actual Transactions

Once you have created a budget you can live with, it's a good idea to periodically compare your actual income and expenditures to budgeted amounts. Quicken lets you do this in a number of different ways.

There's one important thing to keep in mind when comparing budgeted amounts to actual results: Make sure your comparison is for the period for which you have recorded data. For example, don't view a year-to-date (YTD) budget report if you began entering data into Quicken in March. Instead, customize the report to show actual transactions beginning in March. I provide details about creating and customizing reports and graphs in Chapter 9.

Budget Reports and Graphs The Reports menu on the button bar in the Budget window offers two reports and one graph for comparing budgeted amounts to actual results:

- **Budget Report** displays actual and budgeted transactions. Figure 17-6 shows a budget report with YTD amounts.
- **Monthly Budget Report** displays the actual and budgeted transactions by month.
- **Monthly Budget Graph** graphically displays the favorable and unfavorable differences between monthly actual and budgeted income amounts.

Budget Comparison Graphs You can display budget graphs in a custom view of the Quicken Home window. This feature enables you to keep an eye on the budget categories and groups that interest you most.

To use this feature, switch to the Home tab and click Main View in the Tool Bar. Use the Customize View dialog as instructed in Appendix B. The following items or snapshots found under Planning provide budget information:

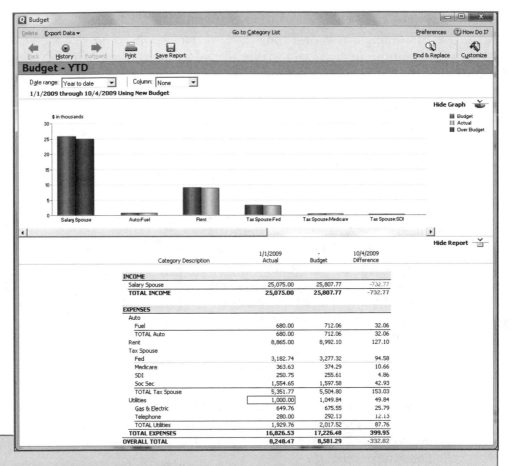

Figure 17-6 • A budget report compares actual to budgeted amounts.

- **Budget** displays a chart that compares your actual to budgeted income and expenses.
- **Budget Goal Progress** tracks spending for a single category's budget. This helps you monitor spending for a specific category that's important to you.
- **Budgeted Categories** compares actual category amounts with your budget.
- **Budgeted Net Income** displays a chart that compares your budgeted to actual net income.
- **Category Group Budget** tracks progress against your budget by category group.

You can customize any of the graphs by right-clicking them and choosing the Customize This Chart or Customize This Graph command from the context menu that appears. I explain how to customize reports and graphs in Chapter 9.

Forecasting

Forecasting uses known and estimated transactions to provide a general overview of your future financial situation. This "crystal ball" can help you spot potential cash flow problems (or surpluses) so you can prepare for them.

Creating a Forecast

A forecast without data is like a crystal ball that's full of fog—it doesn't show you much. To get a clear picture, you need to enter data about future transactions by creating a forecast.

To create a forecast, begin by opening the Cash Flow Forecast window. Choose Planning | Other Tools | Cash Flow Forecast. If you have not yet created a forecast, the Automatically Create Forecast dialog, which is shown here, appears. If you have already created a forecast and want to create a new one, choose Options | Update Forecast on the Cash Flow Forecast window's button bar.

How you proceed depends on the kind of data you use—budget data or register data.

Creating a Forecast with Budget Data To create a forecast with budget data, enter beginning and ending dates for which you have a budget. This will normally be the current year. To start, click Planning | Other Tools | Cash Flow Forecast. In the Cash Flow Forecast window, click Options | Update Forecast. Then click the Advanced button to display the Advanced AutoCreate dialog, shown here. Select Create Both in the top part of the dialog and From Budget Data in the bottom part of the dialog. Click Done

to save your settings, and then click OK in the Automatically Create Forecast dialog to create the forecast. Figure 17-7, shown later in the chapter, illustrates a forecast based on a budget.

Creating a Forecast with Register Data To create a forecast based on register data, enter beginning and ending dates for which you have register data. The time span should cover at least six months; for best results, it should cover a full year. Click Planning | Other Tools | Cash Flow Forecast. On the Cash Flow Forecast dialog, click Options | Update Forecast. Then click the Advanced button to display the Advanced AutoCreate dialog. Select Create Both in the top part of the dialog and From Register Data in the bottom part of the dialog. Click Done to save your settings, and then click OK in the Automatically Create Forecast dialog to create the forecast.

Entering Income and Expense Items

Once you've created a forecast, you can fine-tune it by entering or modifying known or estimated events. Click the Income Items or Expense Items button in the Cash Flow Forecast window (see Figure 17-7). The Forecast Income Items or

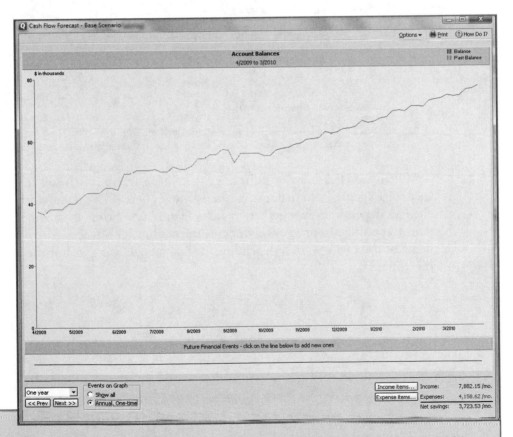

Figure 17-7 • **This forecast was based on budgeted expenditures for the current year with known and estimated items.**

Forecast Expense Items window appears, as shown on the next page; use this window to add, modify, or delete items.

- To display either income or expense items, select one of the Show options.
- To edit an item, click it to select it and enter a new value.
- To add, modify, or remove items, click the New, Edit, or Delete button.

When you click New or Edit, the Create New Income/Expense Item or Edit Income/Expense Item dialog appears, as shown here. (The name of the dialog changes depending on whether you are creating or editing an income or expense item.) Use this dialog to enter or edit information for a forecast item. The exact name of the dialog varies, depending on how you're using it, but the options are the same.

Start by selecting the Income or Expense option to determine the type of item you are creating. Then fill in the remaining fields with information about the item. You can click More to select a category for the item and set the total number of entries for a recurring item (you must first have filled in the Edit Advanced Info dialog). When you're finished, click OK.

A quick way to display the Create New Expense/Income Item is simply to double-click in the empty space immediately above the line over the Income Items button.

Working with Scenarios

When you create a single forecast, you create a forecast for the *base scenario*. Just as you can have multiple budgets, you can also have multiple forecast scenarios.

Creating a New Scenario To create a new scenario, choose Manage Scenarios from the Options menu on the Cash Flow Forecast window's button bar. The Manage Forecast Scenarios dialog, which is shown here, appears. Click New to display a dialog in which you can enter a scenario name and choose to copy the existing scenario. When you click OK, the new scenario's name appears as the selected scenario on the Scenario Data drop-down list.

Changing a Scenario's Display The Display Options in the Manage Forecast Scenarios dialog let you change the display of a selected scenario:

- **Current Scenario Only**, which is the default option, displays only one scenario in the Forecasting window.
- **Show How Forecast Looked On** enables you to update the scenario for the current date. Select this option, and then click the Update button.

- **Compare Current Scenario With** enables you to include two scenarios in the Forecasting window. This makes it easy to see how one differs from the other.

Select the option you want and click Done to apply it.

Saving Money

Remember when you got your first piggy bank? It may not have looked like a pig, but it had a slot for slipping in coins and, if you were lucky, a removable rubber plug on the bottom that made it easy to get the coins out when you needed them. Whoever gave you the bank was trying to teach you your first financial management lesson: Save money.

As an adult, things are a little more complex. This section explains why you should save, provide some saving strategies, and tell you about the types of savings accounts that make your old piggy bank obsolete.

Why Save?

Most people save money so there's money to spend when they need it. Others save for a particular purpose. Still others save because they have so much they can't spend it all. (We should all have such problems!) Here's a closer look at why saving makes sense.

Saving for "Rainy Days"

When people say they are "saving for a rainy day," they probably aren't talking about the weather. They're talking about bad times or emergencies—situations when they'll need extra cash.

For example, suppose the family car needs a new transmission. Or your beloved dog needs eye surgery. Or your daughter manages to break her violin three days before the big recital. In the "rainy day" scheme of things, these might be light drizzles. But your savings can help keep you dry.

Here are a few other examples. Suppose your employer goes bankrupt and closes up shop. Or after a three-martini lunch with a customer, you get back to the office, tell your boss what you really think of him, and quit on the spot. Or, after being poked one too many times in the butt by a bull, you find it impossible to continue your career as a rodeo clown. If your paychecks stop coming, do you have enough savings to support yourself or your family until you can get another source of income? On the "rainy day" scale, this could be a torrential downpour. Your savings can be a good umbrella.

Saving for a Goal

Planning for your future often includes planning for events that affect your life—and your wallet. Saving money for specific events can help make these events memorable for what they are, rather than what they cost.

For example, take a recently engaged couple, Sally and Joe. They plan to marry within a year and buy a house right away. Within five years, they plan to have their first child. That's when Sally will leave her job to start the more demanding job of mother and homemaker. They hope their children will go to college someday, and they want to help cover the expenses. They also want to be able to help pay for their children's weddings. Eventually, they'll retire. And throughout their lives, they want to be able to take annual family vacations, buy a new car every six years or so, and get season tickets for the Arizona Diamondbacks.

All of these things are major events in Sally's and Joe's lives. Saving in advance for each of these events will make them possible—without going into debt.

Saving for Peace of Mind

Some people save money because events in their lives showed them the importance of having savings. Children who lived through the Depression or bad financial times for their families grew up to be adults who understand the value of money and try hard to keep some available. They don't want to repeat the hard times they went through. Having healthy savings accounts gives them peace of mind.

Saving Strategies

There are two main ways to save: when you can or regularly.

Saving When You Can

When money is tight, saving can be difficult. People who are serious about saving, however, will force themselves to save as much as possible when they can. Saving when you can is better than not saving at all.

Saving Regularly

A better way to save money is to save a set amount periodically. For example, save $25 every week or $200 every month. Timing this with your paycheck makes sense; you can make a split deposit for the check. A savings like this is called an *annuity*, and you'd be surprised at how quickly the money can accumulate. Table 17-1 shows some examples based on a 4.5 percent annual interest rate.

Month	Weekly Contributions				Monthly Contributions				
	$25	$50	$75	$100	$50	$100	$200	$300	$400
1	$100	$200	$300	$401	$50	$100	$200	$300	$400
2	$226	$452	$677	$903	$100	$200	$401	$601	$801
3	$327	$653	$980	$1,307	$151	$301	$602	$903	$1,205
4	$428	$856	$1,284	$1,712	$201	$402	$805	$1,207	$1,609
5	$555	$1,110	$1,665	$2,220	$252	$504	$1,008	$1,511	$2,015
6	$657	$1,314	$1,971	$2,628	$303	$606	$1,211	$1,817	$2,423
7	$759	$1,519	$2,278	$3,038	$354	$708	$1,416	$2,124	$2,832
8	$888	$1,776	$2,664	$3,552	$405	$811	$1,621	$2,432	$3,242
9	$991	$1,982	$2,974	$3,965	$457	$914	$1,827	$2,741	$3,654
10	$1,095	$2,190	$3,284	$4,379	$509	$1,017	$2,034	$3,051	$4,068
11	$1,225	$2,449	$3,674	$4,899	$560	$1,121	$2,242	$3,363	$4,483
12	$1,329	$2,658	$3,987	$5,316	$613	$1,225	$2,450	$3,675	$4,900

Table 17-1 • Your Savings Can Grow over Time

Types of Savings Accounts

There are different types of savings accounts, each with its own benefits and drawbacks. Here's a quick look at them.

Keep in mind that all the accounts discussed in this chapter (except where noted) should be insured by the FDIC (Federal Deposit Insurance Corporation). This organization covers savings deposits up to $100,000 per entity (person or company) per bank, thus protecting you from loss in the event of a bank failure.

Standard Savings Accounts All banks offer savings accounts, and most accommodate any balance. Savings accounts pay interest on your balance and allow you to deposit or withdraw funds at any time.

Holiday Clubs A "holiday club" account is a savings account into which you make regular, equal deposits, usually on a weekly basis. Many banks offer these accounts, along with an option to withdraw the deposit funds automatically from your regular savings or checking account. The money stays in the account, earning interest until the club ends in October or November. The idea behind these accounts is to provide you with cash for the holidays, but there are variations on this theme, such as vacation club accounts that end in May or June.

Credit Union Payroll Savings A bank isn't the only place where you can open a savings account. If your company has a credit union, it also offers a number of accounts. These accounts often offer the option of payroll savings deductions. This is a great feature for people who have trouble saving money, because the money comes out of their paychecks before they see (and can spend) it. It's as if the money never existed, when in reality it's accumulating in an interest-bearing account. In case you're wondering, the withdrawn funds are included in your taxable income.

Certificates of Deposit A certificate of deposit, or CD, is an account, normally with a bank, that requires you to keep the money on deposit for a specific length of time. As a reward for your patience, your earnings are based on a higher, fixed-interest rate than what is available for a regular savings account. The longer the term of the deposit and the more money deposited, the higher the rate. At the CD's maturity date, you can "roll over" the deposit to a new account that may have a different interest rate, or you can take back the cash. If you withdraw the money before the CD's maturity date, you pay a penalty, which can sometimes exceed the amount of the interest earned.

Money Market Accounts A money market account is actually a form of investment, but it should be included here because many banks offer it. It has a higher rate of return than a regular savings account but is not insured by the FDIC. It is considered a conservative investment and can be treated just like a savings account for depositing money. There may, however, be restrictions on the number of withdrawals you can make each month.

Interest-Bearing Checking Accounts Many banks offer interest-bearing checking accounts. They usually have minimum balance requirements, however, forcing you to keep a certain amount of money in the account at all times. Although it's nice to earn money on checking account funds, the interest rate is usually so low that it's better to have a regular checking account and keep your savings in a savings account or money market account.

Using Savings Goals

Quicken's Savings Goals feature helps you save money by "hiding" funds in an account. You set up a savings goal and make contributions to it using the Savings Goals window. Although the money never leaves the source bank account, it is deducted in the account register, thus reducing the account balance in Quicken. If you can't see the money in your account, you're less likely to spend it.

What Does This Mean to You? Savings Goals

Kind of sounds silly, doesn't it? Using Quicken to transfer money from your checking account to another account that doesn't even exist.

But don't laugh—the Savings Goals feature really works. I used a technique similar to this with a paper check register years ago, before I started using Quicken. I simply deducted $50 or $100 from the account balance, thus giving the illusion that I had less money in the account than I really did. This helped me save money by making me think twice about writing a check for something I really didn't need. More important, however, is that it prevented me from bouncing checks in the days when I kept a dangerously low checking account balance.

Give it a try and see for yourself!

Getting Started

Open the Savings Goals window by choosing Planning | Other Tools | Savings Goals. Here's what the window looks like with one savings goal already created:

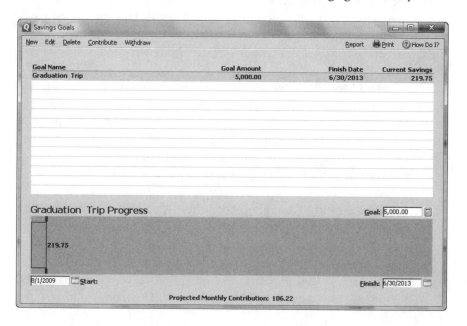

The top half of the Savings Goals window lists the savings goals you have created with Quicken. The bottom half shows the progress for the selected goal. You can use button bar options to work with window contents:

- **New** enables you to create a savings goal.
- **Edit** enables you to modify the selected savings goal.

- **Delete** removes the selected savings goal.
- **Contribute** enables you to contribute funds from a Quicken account to the selected savings goal.
- **Withdraw** enables you to remove funds from a savings goal and return them to a Quicken account.
- **Report** creates a report of the activity for savings goals.
- **Print** prints a report of savings goal details.
- **How Do I?** displays the Quicken Personal Finances Help window with instructions for using the Savings Goals feature.

Creating a Savings Goal

To create a savings goal, click New on the button bar in the Savings Goals window. The Create New Savings Goal dialog, which is shown here, appears.

Enter the information for your savings goal in the text boxes. The name of the savings goal cannot be the same as any Quicken category or account. For the Finish Date, enter the date by which you want to have the money saved. For example, if you're using a savings goal to plan for a vacation, the Finish Date should be shortly before the date you want to start the vacation. When you've finished, click OK to add the savings goal to the list in the Savings Goals window.

Contributing Funds to a Savings Goal

To contribute funds to a savings goal, select the savings goal in the Savings Goals window and click the Contribute button on the button bar. The Contribute To Goal dialog, shown here, appears.

Select the account from which you want to transfer the money from the drop-down list. The balance of the account appears in the bottom of the dialog. Then enter the amount of the transfer in the Amount box. By default, Quicken suggests the projected monthly contribution amount, but you can enter any amount you like. When you've finished, click OK.

As shown in the next illustration, Quicken creates an entry in the account register of the account from which the money was contributed. It also updates the progress bar and information in the Savings Goals dialog.

| 10/5/2009 | Contribution towards goal
[New Computer] | | 300 00 | | 41,454 28 |

When you create a savings goal, Quicken creates an asset account to record the goal's transactions and balance. To automate contributions to the goal, you can create a scheduled transaction to transfer money periodically from one of your bank accounts to the savings goal asset account. I tell you about scheduled transactions in Chapter 7.

Meeting Your Goal

Once you have met your savings goal, you can either withdraw the funds from the savings goal so they appear in a Quicken account or delete the savings goal to put the money back where it came from.

Withdrawing Money   In the Savings Goals window, select the savings goal from which you want to withdraw money. Click the Withdraw button on the button bar. The Withdraw From Goal dialog (shown here), which works much like the Contribute To Goal dialog, appears. Use it to remove funds from the savings goal and put them back into the account from which they were contributed.

Deleting a Savings Goal   In the Savings Goals window, select the savings goal you want to delete and click the Delete button on the button bar. A dialog appears, asking if you want to keep the savings goal account for your records:

- Click Yes to transfer the funds back to the original account(s) and keep the savings goal account.
- Click No to transfer funds back to the original account(s) and delete the savings goal account.

Tax

This part of the book explores the features of Quicken Personal Finance Software's Planning tab's Tax Center and Tax Tools, which can make tax preparation quicker and easier, enable you to plan for tax time, and even help you save money on your income taxes. Its two chapters are:

Chapter 18:   Simplifying Tax Preparation

Chapter 19:   Planning for Tax Time

Part Six

Simplifying Tax Preparation

In This Chapter:

- *Including tax information in accounts and categories*
- *Tax reports*
- *Online tax tools*
- *TurboTax*

Tax time is no fun. It can force you to spend hours sifting through financial records and filling out complex forms. When you're done with the hard part, you may be rewarded with the knowledge that you can expect a refund. But it is more likely that your reward will be the privilege of writing a check to the federal, state, or local government—or worse yet, all three.

Fortunately, Quicken Personal Finance Software can help. Its reporting features can save you time. By using the tax tools that are part of Quicken or available on Quicken.com, the next tax season may be a little less stressful. In this chapter, I show you how.

Tax Information in Accounts and Categories

As discussed briefly in Chapter 3, Quicken accounts and categories can include information that will help you at tax time. In this section, I explain how you can set tax information in accounts and categories.

Including Tax Information in Accounts
You enter an account's tax information in the Tax Schedule Information dialog for the account. Choose Tools | Account List

or press CTRL-A to display the Account List window. Select the name of the account and click the Edit Details button that appears beneath the account name. In the General Information tab of the Account Details dialog that appears, click the Tax Schedule Info button. The Tax Schedule Information dialog, shown here, appears.

Use the Transfers In and Transfers Out drop-down lists to map account activity to specific lines on tax return forms and schedules. If the account has tax-deferred or tax-exempt status, be sure to turn on the Tax-Deferred Or Tax-Exempt Account check box. When you're finished, click OK. Repeat this process for all accounts for which you want to enter tax information.

Keep in mind that if you use the Paycheck Set Up feature to account for all payroll deductions, including retirement plan contributions, you shouldn't have to change the settings for any of your accounts. (That's another good reason to set up your regular paychecks in Quicken.) I explain how to set up a paycheck in Quicken in Chapter 7.

Including Tax Information in Categories

Quicken automatically sets tax information for many of the categories it creates. You can see which categories are tax-related and which tax form lines have been assigned to them in the Category List window (refer to Figure 18-1). (If this information does not appear, choose Show Tax Line Item from the Options menu at the bottom of the window.) Concentrate on the categories without tax assignments; some of these may require tax information, depending on your situation.

You can use the Set Up or Edit Category dialog, shown on the next page, to enter or modify tax information for a category. Choose Tools | Category List to open the Category List window. Select the category for which you want to enter or edit tax information. Then click the Edit button in the Action column to display the Set Up or Edit Category dialog.

What Does This Mean to You? Entering Tax Information in Quicken

I know what you're saying! More entry stuff! Ick!

Stop whining! This is one Quicken setup task that can save you hours of time and maybe even a bunch of money. You see, by including tax information in Quicken accounts and categories, you make it possible for Quicken to do several things for you:

- Prepare tax reports that summarize information by tax category or schedule. You can take these tax reports to your tax preparation guy and make it a lot easier for him to do your taxes. He'll be so appreciative that he'll knock a few bucks off his bill and take you to lunch. (Okay, so he might not take you to lunch, especially during tax time, when he's really busy.)
- Display tax information in the Tax Center window, which shows an up-to-date summary of your tax situation. Knowing how you stand now will help prevent surprises at tax time.
- Save time using the Tax Planner, a Quicken feature that can import information from your Quicken data file based on tax information you enter. Do a little work here and save a bunch of work there. I tell you about the Tax Planner in Chapter 19.
- Distinguish between taxable and nontaxable investments, so you can create accurate reports on capital gains, interest, and dividends. You wouldn't want to include tax-exempt income with taxable income when preparing your tax returns, would you?
- Use TurboTax to prepare your tax return based on information imported right from your Quicken data file. With the money you save on doing your returns yourself, you can buy yourself lunch. I tell you a little more about using TurboTax with Quicken in Chapter 19.

See? By spending a few minutes setting up tax information for your accounts and categories, you can save time and money at tax time, and know your tax situation all year long.

If the category's transactions should be included on your tax return as either income or a deductible expense, turn on the Tax-Related check box. Then use the Tax Line Item drop-down list to choose the form or schedule and line for the item. (You can expand this list by selecting the Extended Line Item List option.) A description of the tax line item you chose appears at the bottom of the dialog. Click OK. Repeat this process for all categories that should be included on your tax return.

Keep in mind that you can also enter tax information when you first create a category. The Set Up Category dialog looks and works much like the Edit Category dialog. I tell you more about the Set Up Category dialog in Chapter 3.

Figure 18-1 • The Category List window shows the tax information provided for each category.

Auditing Your Tax Line Assignments

Quicken can "audit" the tax line information associated with categories and tell you where there may be problems with the assignments. This feature helps ensure that you have properly set up your categories to take advantage of Quicken's tax features.

Open the Planning tab and click Tax Tools | Tax Category Audit in the Tools subtab. Quicken quickly reviews all your categories. If it finds potential problems, it displays them in the Tax Category Audit window (see Figure 18-2).

If the Planning tab is not visible, open the View menu and click Tabs To Show | Planning to display the tab.

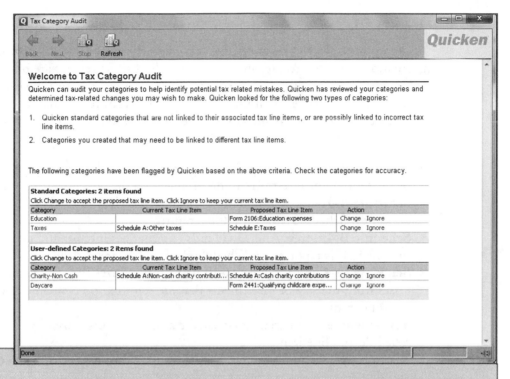

Figure 18-2 • The Tax Category Audit window lists categories that may have incorrect tax
line assignments.

You have three choices for working with the items Quicken finds:

- To accept Quicken's suggested correction for the category, click the Change
  link in the Action column on the category's line. Then click OK in the Edit
  Selected Tax Audit Category dialog that appears. (This dialog looks and
  works just like the Edit Category dialog, shown earlier in this chapter.)
- To ignore the possible problem, click the Ignore link in the Action column
  on the category's line.
- To change the tax line assignment manually, click the category name link
  and make the desired changes in the Edit Selected Tax Audit Category dialog
  that appears, and then click OK. (This dialog looks and works just like the
  Edit Category dialog shown earlier in this chapter.)

If Quicken doesn't find any problems with your categories, it displays a dialog
that tells you so. Keep in mind, however, that this doesn't necessarily mean that
your tax line assignments are error-free. You should review them the old-
fashioned way—by looking them over yourself—before relying on them.

Tax Reports

Quicken offers several tax reports that can make tax time easier by providing the information you need to prepare your taxes. All of these reports are based on the tax information settings for the accounts and categories in your Quicken data file. You can learn more about Quicken's reporting feature in Chapter 9.

To create a report, open any tab but the Bills tab, select All Reports & Graphs | Tax, and choose the name of the report from the submenu:

- **Capital Gains** summarizes gains and losses on the sales of investments, organized by the term of the investment (short or long) and the investment account.
- **Schedule A–Itemized Deductions** summarizes the itemized deductions that appear on Schedule A of a 1040 tax return.
- **Schedule B–Interest And Dividends** summarizes interest and dividends income that is reported on Schedule B of a 1040 tax return.
- **Schedule D–Capital Gains And Losses** summarizes the capital gains and losses from the sale of investments that are reported on Schedule D of a 1040 tax return.
- **Tax Schedule** summarizes tax-related transactions, organized by tax form or schedule and line item.
- **Tax Summary** summarizes tax-related transactions, organized by category and date.

Online Tax Tools

The Online Tax Tools submenu under the Tax Tools menu in the Planning tab's Tools subtab offers access to a number of tax-related features and information sources on the TurboTax.com Web site that can help you with your taxes. All you need to take advantage of these features is an Internet connection.

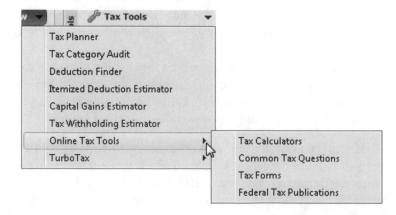

Here's a quick look at the online tax tools. The next time you're thinking about taxes, be sure to check these out.

Tax Calculators   The Tax Calculators option displays the TurboTax Free Tax Calculators And Money Saving Tax Guides page. You can find links to various online tools for making tax and other financial calculations on this page. You can also follow links to get tax tips and learn more about TurboTax.

Common Tax Questions   The Common Tax Questions option also displays the TurboTax Free Tax Calculators and Money Saving Guides page.

Tax Forms   The Tax Forms option displays the Tax Forms For Federal And State Taxes page on TurboTax.com (refer to Figure 18-3), which offers links to various categories of tax forms. Click a link to display additional information and links to forms.

When you click a form link, the form is downloaded as an Acrobat PDF file that appears in either a Web browser window or an Adobe Acrobat Reader

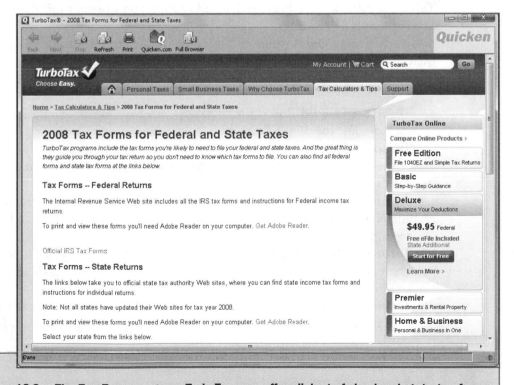

Figure 18-3 • The Tax Forms page on TurboTax.com offers links to federal and state tax forms.

window. (You must have the freely distributed Adobe Acrobat Reader software to open and use these forms.) Print the form to fill it out manually.

Federal Tax Publications The Federal Tax Publications option also displays the Tax Forms For Federal And State Taxes on TurboTax.com.

TurboTax Online

If you're tired of paying a tax preparer to fill out your tax return for you, but you're not quite confident enough about your tax knowledge to prepare your own return manually, it's time to check out TurboTax online tax-preparation software. It's a great way to simplify tax preparation.

TurboTax works almost seamlessly with Quicken to prepare your taxes. Just follow the instructions in this chapter to set up your accounts and categories with tax information. Then import your Quicken data into TurboTax. You can go through an easy interview process to make sure you haven't left anything out—much like the interview you might go through with a paid tax preparer. TurboTax calculates the bottom line and enables you to either print your returns or file them electronically.

Intuit offers several versions of TurboTax Online. You can learn more about them by opening the Planning tab and selecting Tax Tools | Turbo Tax | TurboTax Online.

- **TurboTax Free Edition** is for taxpayers with basic tax preparation needs. It includes just the 1040EZ form.
- **TurboTax Deluxe** can perform tax calculations for taxpayers who own a home, make donations, or have childcare or medical expenses. In other words, most people.
- **TurboTax Premier** offers all of the functionality of TurboTax Deluxe and adds tax calculations for taxpayers who own stocks, bonds, mutual funds, or rental properties.
- **TurboTax Home & Business** offers all of the functionality of TurboTax Premier and adds tax calculations for small businesses, such as sole proprietorships or single-owner LLCs.
- **Turbo Tax Business** provides tax preparation for corporations, partnerships, and multimember LLCs while maximizing business tax deductions. It does not include the means to prepare your personal taxes.

Planning for Tax Time

Chapter 19

In This Chapter:

- *Tax planning basics*
- *Tax Planner*
- *Tax Withholding Estimator*
- *Tax Center*
- *Deduction Finder*
- *Itemized Deduction Estimator*

Surprises can make life interesting. But not all surprises are good ones. Consider the surprise you may get one April when your tax preparer announces that you'll have to write a rather large check to your Uncle Sam and his friends in your state revenue department.

Quicken Personal Finance Software's tax planning features, like the Tax Planner and Tax Withholding Estimator, can help you avoid nasty surprises. Other built-in tax tools, like the Deduction Finder and Itemized Deduction Estimator, can save you money and help you make smarter financial decisions. All of these features can be found in the Tax Tools menu of the Tools subtab in the Planning tab, which is full of options to help you plan and monitor your tax situation. In this chapter, I tell you all about Quicken's tax planning and monitoring features.

Planning to Avoid Surprises

One of the best reasons to think about taxes before tax time is to avoid surprises on April 15. Knowing what you'll owe before you owe it can help ensure that you pay just the right amount of taxes up front—through proper deductions or estimated tax payments—so you don't get hit with a big tax bill or tax refund.

You may think of a big tax refund as a gift from Uncle Sam. Well, it isn't. It's your money that Uncle Sam has been using, interest-free, for months. When you overpay your taxes, you're giving up money that you could be using to reduce interest-bearing debt or earn interest or investment income. Make sure you don't overpay taxes throughout the year so you can keep your money where it'll do *you* the most good.

Quicken offers two built-in tax planning tools that you can use to keep track of your tax situation throughout the year. The Tax Planner helps you estimate your federal income tax bill for the 2009 and 2010 tax years. The Tax Withholding Estimator helps you determine whether your withholding taxes are correctly calculated. Finally, the Tax Center in the View subtab of the Planning tab summarizes your tax situation with a number of useful snapshots. Here's a closer look at each of these features.

Using the Tax Planner

Quicken's Tax Planner includes features from Intuit's TurboTax tax preparation software to help you estimate your federal income tax bill for the 2009 and 2010 tax years. While this can help you avoid surprises, it can also help you see how various changes to income and expenses can affect your estimated tax bill.

Opening the Quicken Tax Planner Window

To open the Tax Planner, open the Planning tab and choose Tax Tools | Tax Planner in the Tools subtab. The first time you open the Tax Planner, it may display a dialog that offers to import TurboTax data into Quicken for tax planning purposes. If you click Yes, follow the instructions that appear onscreen to complete the import. If you click No, or when the import process is complete, the Tax Planner window with introductory information appears. Read this information to get a clear understanding of what the Tax Planner can do for you and how it works.

Viewing the Tax Planner Summary

To see what data is already entered in the Tax Planner, click the Tax Planner Summary link in the navigation bar on the left side of the Tax Planner window. A summary of all data, as well as the calculated tax implications, appears as shown in Figure 19-1.

Entering Tax Planner Data

Data can be entered into the Tax Planner from three different sources:

Figure 19-1 • The Tax Planner Summary screen displays a summary of all information stored in the Tax Planner.

- **TurboTax** data can be imported into Quicken. In the main Quicken application window, from the Planning tab, choose Tax Tools | TurboTax | Import TurboTax File. Then use the dialog that appears to locate and import your TurboTax data. This information can be used to project current-year amounts in the Tax Planner.
- **User Entered** data can override any automatic entries. Use this to enter data that isn't entered any other way or that has not yet been entered into Quicken—such as expected year-end bonuses or tax-deductible expenses.
- **Quicken Data** can be automatically entered into the Tax Planner. This works only if you have properly set up your tax-related Quicken categories with appropriate tax return line items, as discussed in Chapter 18.

Here's how it works. Click a link in the navigation bar on the left side of the Tax Planner window or in the Tax Planner Summary screen (refer to Figure 19-1) to view a specific type of income or expense. Then click a link within the window for a specific item. Details for the item appear in the bottom of the

Figure 19-2 • You can enter additional information into the Tax Planner.

window, as shown in Figure 19-2. (You may have to click a Show Details link to expand the window and show the details.) If desired, change the source option and, if necessary, enter an amount.

The options you can choose from vary depending on whether TurboTax data is available or the item has transactions recorded in Quicken. For example, in Figure 19-2, TurboTax data is not available, but transactions have been entered in Quicken. You can either select the User Entered option and enter a value in the Annual Total column or select the Quicken Data option and enter an adjusting value in the Adjustment column. This makes it easy to manually override any automatic source entries.

Repeat this process for any Tax Planner items you want to check or change. The Tax Planner automatically recalculates the impact of your changes.

To reset values quickly to amounts automatically entered by Quicken, choose Reset To Quicken Default Values from the Reset menu on the Tax Planner's button bar.

Using Scenarios

The Scenarios feature of the Tax Planner enables you to enter data for multiple scenarios—a "what if" capability that you can use to see tax impacts based on various changes in entry data. For example, suppose you're planning to get married and want to see the impact of the additional income and deductions related to your new spouse. You can use a scenario to see the tax impact without changing your Projected scenario.

To use this feature, click the Scenario link in upper section of the navigation bar on the left side of the Tax Planner window (refer to Figure 19-1 or 19-2). The Tax Planner Options screen, which is shown here, appears. Choose a different scenario from the Scenarios drop-down list. If Quicken asks whether you want to copy the current scenario to the scenario you chose, click Yes if that other scenario hasn't been set up yet. Choose options from the Tax Year and Filing Status drop-down lists to set the scenario options. Then click the Next link at the bottom of the window to return to the Tax Planner Summary window. If necessary, change the values in the new scenario.

To compare one scenario to another, click the Compare button in the Tax Planner window's button bar. A Tax Scenario Comparisons dialog like the one shown next appears, showing the results of each scenario's calculations. When you're finished viewing the comparative information, click OK to dismiss the dialog.

	Projected		Scenario 1		Scenario 2		Scenario 3
Filing Status	Married-Joint		Married-Joint		Married-Sep		Head of House
Tax Year	2010		2010		2010		2010
Adjusted Gross Income	76,306		86,306		68,123		68,123
Deductions and Exemptions	22,350		22,350		13,000		15,650
Taxable Income	53,956		63,956		55,123		52,473
Total Tax	10,022		11,522		9,968		7,971
Marginal, Avg. Tax Rates	15.0%	13.1%	15.0%	13.3%	25.0%	14.6%	25.0% 11.7%

OK   Help

Finishing Up

When you're finished using the Tax Planner, click the Close button above the button bar or switch to another window. This saves the information you entered and updates the Projected Tax calculations in the Tax Center. (Learn about the Tax Center later in this chapter, in the section "The Tax Center.")

Tax Withholding Estimator

Quicken's Tax Withholding Estimator feature helps you determine whether your W-4 form has been correctly completed. It does this by comparing your estimated tax bill from the Tax Planner to the amount of withholding tax deducted from your paychecks.

Using the Tax Withholding Estimator Feature

To get started, in the Planning tab, choose Tax Tools | Tax Withholding Estimator in the Tools subtab. The Am I Under Or Over Withholding? window appears, as shown in Figure 19-3.

Read the information and follow the instructions in the middle column of the window. You'll be prompted to enter information related to withholding taxes. The instructions are clear and easy to follow, so I won't repeat them here. Each time you enter data, the Projected Refund Due or Projected Tax Due amount in

Figure 19-3 • Use the Tax Withholding Estimator to determine whether your federal withholding taxes are correct.

the lower-right corner of the window changes. Your goal is to get the amount as close to zero as possible, which you can do by adjusting the number of W-4 allowances and additional withholding per pay period.

(Although I tell you that your goal is to get the Projected Tax Due amount as close to zero as possible, a *Quicken 2002: The Official Guide* reader had a problem with my advice. He pointed out that your goal should be to pay as little taxes as possible throughout the year without getting an underpayment penalty on April 15. His logic is to hold onto your money as long as you can. While his strategy is good and legal—remember, if there's no penalty, you couldn't have done anything wrong—I personally don't like to write a check on April 15, so I aim for zero. It's your choice.)

None of the entries you make in the Tax Withholding Estimator feature will affect your Quicken data or any other tax planning feature within Quicken, so don't be afraid to experiment.

Acting on the Results of Tax Withholding Estimator Calculations

What do you do with this information once you have it? Well, suppose your work with the Tax Withholding Estimator feature tells you that you should change your W-4 allowances from 2 to 3 to avoid overpaying federal withholding taxes. You can act on this information by completing a new W-4 form at work. This will decrease the amount of withholding tax in each paycheck. The result is that you reduce your tax overpayment and potential refund.

Periodically Checking Withholding Calculations

It's a good idea to use the Tax Withholding Estimator feature periodically to make sure actual amounts are in line with projections throughout the year. (I recommend using it once every three months or so.) Whenever possible, use actual values rather than estimates in your calculations. And be sure to act on the results of the calculations by filing a new W-4 form, especially if the amount of your Projected Refund Due or Projected Tax Due is greater than a few hundred dollars.

The Tax Center

Quicken summarizes all information about your tax situation in the Tax Center (see Figure 19-4). Here's a quick look at what you can find in the Tax Center window.

Projected Tax

The Projected Tax snapshot provides a summary of your upcoming projected tax return, including the amount that you'll have to pay or get back as a refund. The information in this snapshot is based on the Tax Planner's Projected scenario, discussed earlier in this chapter.

Tax Calendar

The Tax Calendar lists recent and upcoming events on the IRS tax calendar. You can use the Options menu to set up alerts.

Tax-Related Expenses YTD

The Tax-Related Expenses YTD snapshot summarizes all of your year-to-date tax-related expenses. Quicken automatically calculates this information based on the transactions you enter throughout the year. All expense categories that are marked "tax-related" and have transactions appear in this snapshot.

Taxable Income YTD

The Taxable Income YTD snapshot summarizes all of your year-to-date tax-related income. Quicken calculates these totals based on the transactions you enter throughout the year. All income categories that are marked "tax-related" and have transactions appear in this snapshot.

Figure 19-4 • The Tax Center window is full of snapshots of your tax situation.

Tax Alerts

Tax alerts, which in previous versions of Quicken were displayed at the top of what is now the Tax Center, are only visible in the Alert Center, opened from the Tools menu, Alert Center option. This is also where you go to set alerts related to your tax situation. Quicken offers three tax alerts.

- **Withholding Threshold** (shown on the top of the next page) enables you to set a threshold value to alert you if your payroll withholding is too much or not enough.

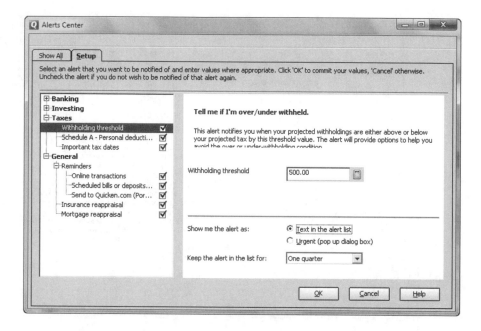

- **Schedule A – Personal Deductions** (Schedule A Reminder) displays information about the types of personal deductions you can claim on Schedule A of your tax return.
- **Important Tax Dates** notifies you in advance of tax calendar events, such as estimated tax due dates and extension deadlines.

Learn more about setting alerts in Chapter 9.

Minimizing Taxes by Maximizing Deductions

One way to minimize taxes is to maximize your deductions. While Quicken can't help you spend money on tax-deductible items—that's up to you—it can help you identify expenses that may be tax-deductible, so you don't forget to include them on your tax returns.

Quicken offers two features to help maximize your deductions. Deduction Finder asks you questions about expenditures to determine whether they may be tax-deductible. Itemized Deduction Estimator helps make sure you don't forget about commonly overlooked itemized deductions.

Deduction Finder

The Deduction Finder uses another TurboTax feature to help you learn which expenses are deductible. Its question-and-answer interface gathers information from you and then provides information about the deductibility of items based on your answers.

Working with the Deduction Finder Window

To open the Deduction Finder, open the Planning tab and choose Tax Tools | Deduction Finder in the Tools subtab. An Introduction dialog may appear. Read its contents to learn more about Deduction Finder and then click OK. Figure 19-5 shows what the Deductions tab of the Deduction Finder window says about the expenses of maintaining a home office.

You can use button bar options to work with the Deduction Finder window:

- **See Introduction** displays the Introduction window, so you can learn more about how Deduction Finder works.
- **Clear Checkmarks** removes the check marks from items for which you have already answered questions.
- **Print** prints a summary of deduction information about all the deductions for which you have answered questions.
- **How Do I?** opens the Quicken Personal Finances Help window, where you can find additional information about using the Deduction Finder.

Finding Deductions

As you can see in Figure 19-5, the Deductions tab of the Deduction Finder window uses clearly numbered steps to walk you through the process of selecting deduction types and deductions, and then answering questions. It's easy to use. You don't have to answer questions about all the deductions—only the deductions you think may apply to you. When you've finished answering questions about a deduction, the result appears near the bottom of the window. You can then move on to another deduction.

The Summary tab of the window, shown here, summarizes the number of deductions available in each category, the number for which you answered

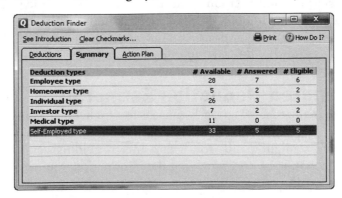

Deduction types	# Available	# Answered	# Eligible
Employee type	28	7	6
Homeowner type	5	2	2
Individual type	26	3	3
Investor type	7	2	2
Medical type	11	0	0
Self-Employed type	33	5	5

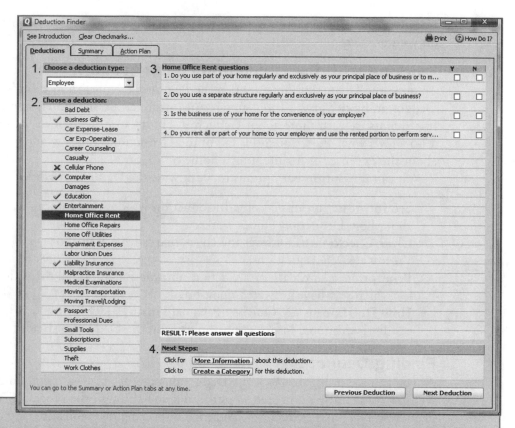

Figure 19-5 • The Deduction Finder helps you identify expenses that may be tax-deductible.

questions, and the number for which you may be eligible to take deductions based on your answers to the questions.

When you've finished answering questions, you can click the Action Plan tab to get more information about the deductions and the things you need to do to claim them. Although you can read the Action Plan information onscreen, if you answered many questions, you may want to use the Print button on the button bar to print the information for reference.

Itemized Deduction Estimator

The Itemized Deduction Estimator feature helps make sure you don't overlook any itemized deductions—the deductions on Schedule A of your tax return—that you might qualify for. It does this by guiding you through a review of deduction ideas and providing the information you need to know whether you may qualify.

To get started, open the Planning tab and choose Tax Tools | Itemized Deduction Estimator in the Tools subtab. The How Can I Maximize My Deductions? window appears, as shown in Figure 19-6.

Read the information and follow the instructions in the middle column of the window. You'll be prompted to enter information related to itemized deductions for medical expenses, taxes paid, interest paid, charitable contributions, and other items. The instructions are clear and easy to follow. Each time you enter information that can change your tax, the Projected Refund Due or Projected Tax Due amount in the lower-right corner of the window changes. Your goal is to get a Projected Refund Due amount as high as possible or a Projected Tax Due amount as low as possible.

Again, none of the entries you make in the Itemized Deduction Estimator feature will affect your Quicken data or any other tax planning feature within Quicken. Experiment as much as you like.

Figure 19-6 • With the Itemized Deduction Estimator, you won't miss out on any Schedule A deductions.

Appendixes

This part of the book provides some additional information you may find helpful when using Quicken Personal Finance Software. These three appendixes explain how to work with Quicken data files and how to customize Quicken.

Part Seven

Managing Quicken Files

In This Appendix:

- *Creating and opening data files*
- *Backing up and restoring data files*
- *Performing other file management tasks*
- *Password-protecting Quicken data*

All the data you enter in Quicken Personal Finance Software is stored in a Quicken data file. This file includes all account and category setup information, transactions, and other data you have entered into Quicken.

Technically speaking, your Quicken data file consists of a single file with the QDF extension. Manipulating these files without using Quicken's built-in file management tools can cause errors.

Commands under Quicken's File menu enable you to perform a number of file management tasks, including creating, opening, backing up, restoring, exporting, renaming, deleting, and password-protecting data files. In this appendix, I cover all of these tasks.

Working with Multiple Data Files

Chances are, you won't need more than one Quicken data file—the one that's created as part of the Quicken Express Setup process, covered in Chapter 2. But just in case you do, here's how you can create and open another one.

Creating a Data File

Start by choosing File | New Quicken File. A dialog appears, asking whether you want to create a new Quicken file or a new Quicken account. (Some users confuse the two and try to use the

File menu's New command to create a new account. I tell you the correct way to create an account in Chapters 2 and 3.) Select New Quicken File and click OK.

A Create Quicken File dialog, like the one shown next, appears. Use it to enter a name for the data file. Although you can also change the default directory location, it's easier to find the data file if it's in the Quicken subdirectory of your Documents (or Documents and Settings) folder with other Quicken data files. It is also easier to find the Quicken file if it is renamed with eight or fewer characters, with no spaces or other special characters. Click OK.

Quicken's Express Setup appears next. It walks you through the process of specifying information about yourself and your finances for a basic Quicken setup. I explain how to use Express Setup in Chapter 2; turn to that chapter if you need help.

Opening a Different Data File

If you have more than one Quicken data file, it's important that you enter transactions into the right one. You can see which data file is currently open by looking at the file name in the application window's title bar.

To open a different data file, choose File | Open Quicken File, or press

CTRL-O, and use the Open Quicken File dialog that appears to select and open a different file. Only one Quicken data file can be open at a time.

Backing Up Your Quicken Data File

Imagine this: You set up Quicken to track all of your finances, and you record transactions regularly so the Quicken data file is always up-to-date. Then one evening, when you start your computer to surf the Net, you find that your hard drive has died. Not only have your plans for the evening been ruined, but your Quicken data file is also a casualty of your hard drive's untimely death.

If you back up your Quicken data as regularly as you update its information, the loss of your Quicken data file would be a minor

> ## What Does This Mean To You?
> ## Quicken Online Backup
>
> By far, the most secure backup file is the one that resides someplace other than near your computer. Why? Well, if your computer is stolen or damaged in a fire or flood, don't you think your backup disks might be lost with it?
>
> Quicken Online Backup can help protect your data by making it easy to back up your data to a secure server far from your computer and other backup files. This service, which starts at just $9.99 per year for 100MB of storage, is fully integrated with Quicken. Just use Quicken's Backup command to back up your data file to an offsite server.
>
> If your Quicken data is important to you, check out this feature. Click the Learn More link in the Quicken Backup window to get the details on this great service.

inconvenience, rather than a catastrophe. In this section, I explain how to back up your Quicken data file and how to restore it if the original file is lost or damaged.

Backing Up to Disk

Quicken makes it difficult to forget backing up. Every third time you exit the Quicken program, it displays the Quicken Backup dialog, shown on the top of the next page, which prompts you to back up your data file. You can change the backup reminder prompt frequency by clicking Edit | Preferences | Quicken Preferences. Click Backup on the left navigation bar, and under Manual Backup Reminder, change the number of times to the frequency you want.

You can begin the backup process by choosing File | Backup And Restore | Backup Quicken Data or by pressing CTRL-B at any time while using Quicken.

This displays the Quicken Backup dialog for the currently open Quicken data file:

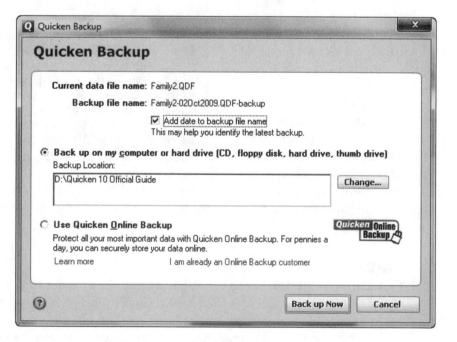

Select one of the backup location options:

- **On My Computer** enables you to back up to another disk, either on your computer or on one that's accessible via a network. If you select this option, you can use the Change button to locate and select a backup disk and directory. As the dialog recommends, it's a good idea to alternate between two disks for backup purposes. This means you'll always have two versions backed up, in case one version is bad. It's a good idea to choose a backup location other than your hard disk, such as a floppy disk (for very small data files) or CD-R disc. (Backing up to your hard disk defeats the purpose of backing up!) If you want to automatically append the current date to the backup file name, select the Add Date To Backup File Name check box. (These instructions assume you have selected On My Computer.) Keep in mind that your computer may not be able to write directly to a CD-R. If you choose to back up to a CD, you might have to back up to your hard disk and then burn the resulting file to disc.

- **Online** enables you to back up to a server on the Internet, using Quicken's Online Backup service, which is available for a nominal fee. You can learn more about this service by selecting Online and then clicking OK to display the Quicken Services window for the Quicken Online Backup service.

After selecting On My Computer and indicating a backup directory in the Quicken Backup dialog, click Backup Now. Your Quicken data file disappears momentarily and a small window tells you that Quicken is backing up your data. When the backup is complete, the data file's windows reappear and a dialog informs you that the file was backed up successfully. Click OK to dismiss the dialog.

If your Quicken data file is too large to fit on the disk you indicated in the Quicken Backup dialog, Quicken will prompt you to insert additional formatted disks until the backup is complete. Follow the instructions that appear onscreen to complete the backup.

Restoring

In the event of loss or damage to your data file, you can restore from the most recent backup. Start Quicken and then choose a backup file from the Restore Backup File submenu under the File menu. This submenu includes all backups you have created with Quicken. It also includes two Browse commands that you can use to browse your computer or online backups for the file you want to restore from.

When you choose the backup file, one of two things may happen:

- If the file has the same name as the Quicken data file currently in use, a dialog appears, asking if you want to overwrite the file in use. To replace the current file with the backup copy, click OK.

- If the file has the same name as another Quicken data file in the Quicken directory in your My Documents folder, a dialog appears, warning you that you will overwrite the existing file. If you're sure you want to restore the backup and overwrite the existing file with the same name, click OK.

Quicken restores the file from the backup copy. It places a copy of the restored file in the Quicken directory in your Documents folder on your hard disk, displaying a status window as it works. When it has finished, it displays a dialog telling you that the file has been restored successfully. Click OK.

Moving a Quicken Data File Between Two Computers

Intuit's Technical Support staff is often asked how to move a Quicken data file from one computer to another. In fact, this question is so common that Intuit asked me to address it in this book.

The best way to move a data file from one computer to another is with the Backup and Restore Backup File commands. Begin by opening the file with Quicken on the computer on which it resides. Then follow the instructions in this appendix to back up the file to removable media, such as a floppy disk or CD-R disc, or to a network drive (preferably one that the other computer is connected to). Then fire up Quicken on the other computer and follow the restoring instructions in this appendix to restore the backup copy. When you're finished, the Quicken data file is ready to use on the new computer.

It's important to remember that once you begin making changes to the file on the new computer, the file on the old computer will no longer be up-to-date. That means that if you want to use the file on the old computer again, you need to complete the backup and restore process to move the file back to that computer. As you can imagine, if you often move the file from one computer to another and back, it can be difficult to keep track of which version of the file is the most up-to-date.

Although you can make your Quicken data file "portable" by keeping it on removable media so you can access it from any computer, neither Intuit nor I recommend doing so. Removable media is more susceptible to data loss and damage than an internal or networked hard disk. Quicken users have reported numerous problems using this technique; don't add your own problems to the list.

Other File Management Tasks

The File Operations submenu under Quicken's File menu enables you to perform several other tasks with Quicken data files. Here's a quick summary of each command, with tips for when you may find them useful.

Copying the Current Data File

The Copy command enables you to copy the current data file to a different disk or save a copy with a different name.

When you choose File | File Operations | Copy, the Copy File dialog, shown here, appears. Use it to enter a pathname for the copy and specify which transactions should be included. Click OK to make the copy.

When the copy is finished, a dialog asks if you want to continue working with the original data file or the new copy. Select the appropriate option and click OK to continue working with Quicken.

Locating Your Current Data File

You can immediately find where your current file is located by choosing File | Show This File On My Computer. When you click this command, Quicken opens a Windows Explorer window showing where the currently open file is located on your computer.

Renaming a Data File

You can rename a file by saving a copy with a new name.

When you choose File | Save A Copy As, the Copy Quicken File dialog, shown on the next page, appears. Use it to select the file you want to rename and enter a new name. When you click OK, Quicken changes the name of the data file you selected.

Checking the Integrity of a Data File

The Validate command enables you to check the integrity of a Quicken data file. This command is particularly useful if you believe that a file has been damaged.

When you choose File | File Operations | Validate, the Validate Quicken File dialog appears. It looks very much like the Copy Quicken File dialog, just illustrated. Use it to locate and select the file you want to validate. When you click OK, Quicken checks the data file's integrity. It then displays a dialog that tells you whether the file has any problems.

Sometimes you can repair a damaged file by simply opening it in Quicken. Use the Open command as discussed near the beginning of this appendix. If Quicken can't open the file, it tells you. That's when it's time to reach for that backup file. You *did* make one recently, didn't you?

Making a Year-End Copy of a Data File

The Year-End Copy command creates two special copies of your data file. Choose File | File Operations | Year-End Copy to display the Create A Year End Copy dialog, shown on the next page, and set options for the two files.

Current Data File

The Current Data File section allows you to set options for the file you will continue working with in Quicken:

Do Nothing. My Current Data File Will Remain Unchanged. This option simply saves a copy of the current data file as is.

I Only Want Transactions In My Current Data File Starting With This Date. This option enables you to enter a starting date for the files in the data file you will continue to use. For example, if you enter 1/1/2008, all transactions prior to that date will be removed from the data file. This option reduces the size of your data file, which makes it easier to back up and may help Quicken operate quicker and more efficiently.

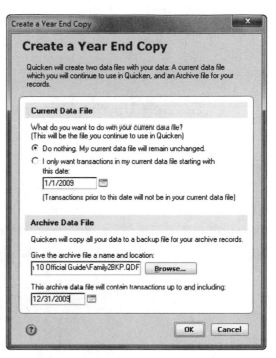

Archive Data File

The Archive Data File section allows you to set options for creating an archive copy of the file. An *archive* is a copy of older transactions saved in a separate file. You can set two options:

- Enter a complete path (or use the Browse button to enter a path) for the archive file.
- Enter the date for the last transaction to be included in the file. For example, if you enter 12/31/2010, the archive file will include all transactions in the current file, up to and including those transactions dated 12/31/2010.

Creating the Files

When you click OK in the Create A Year End Copy dialog, Quicken creates the two files. It then displays a dialog that enables you to select the file you want to work with: the Current file or the Archive file. Select the appropriate option (normally Current File) and click OK to continue working with Quicken.

Password-Protecting Quicken Data

Quicken offers two types of password protection for your data: file passwords and transaction passwords. In this section, I tell you how these options work.

Protecting a Data File

When you password-protect a data file, the file cannot be opened without the password. This is the ultimate in protection—it prevents unauthorized users from even seeing your data.

Setting Up the Password

Choose File | Set Password For This Data File to display the Quicken File Password dialog, which is shown here. Enter the same password in each text box and click OK.

Opening a Password-Protected Data File

When you open a data file that is password-protected, the Quicken Password dialog, which is shown here, appears. You must enter your password correctly and then click OK to open the file.

Changing or Removing a Password

Choose File | Set Password For This Data File to display the Quicken File Password dialog. Enter the current password in the Old Password box, and then enter the same new password in the two boxes beneath it. (To remove a password, leave the two bottom boxes empty.) Click OK.

Protecting Existing Transactions

When you password-protect existing transactions, the transactions cannot be modified unless the password is properly entered. This prevents unauthorized or accidental alterations to data.

Setting Up the Password

Choose File | Set Password To Modify Transactions to display the Password To Modify Existing Transactions dialog, shown here. Enter the same password in the top two text boxes. Then enter a date before which the transactions cannot be modified and click OK.

Modifying a Password-Protected Transaction

When you attempt to modify a transaction that is protected with a password, the Quicken Password dialog, shown here, appears. You must enter your password correctly and then click OK to modify the transaction.

Changing or Removing a Password

Choose File | Set Password To Modify Transactions to display the Change Transaction Password dialog. Enter the current password in the Old Password box, and then enter the same new password in the two boxes beneath it. (To remove a password, leave the two bottom boxes empty.) Click OK.

Password Tips

Here are a few things to keep in mind when working with passwords:

- Passwords can be up to 16 characters in length and can contain any character, including a space.
- Passwords are case-sensitive. That means, for example, that *PassWord* is not the same as *password*.

- If you forget your password, you will not be able to access the data file. Write your password down and keep it in a safe place—but not on a sticky note attached to your computer monitor.

Your data file is only as secure as you make it. Quicken's password protection can help prevent unauthorized access to your Quicken data files.

Customizing Quicken

In This Appendix:

- *Creating custom Home tab views*
- *Customizing the toolbar*
- *Setting Quicken preferences*

Once you've worked with Quicken Personal Finance Software for a while, you may want to fine-tune the way it looks and works to best suit your needs. Some customization options—like selecting securities for online quotes and selecting accounts to synchronize with Quicken.com—are an integral part of using Quicken. Most of these options are discussed elsewhere in this book. Other customization options—like customizing the toolbar and setting Web Connect preferences—are less commonly used. This appendix will explain all the customization options available for Quicken and provide cross-references to other chapters in the book where you can learn more about the features they work with.

Customizing Quicken's Interface

Quicken offers a number of ways to customize its interface to best meet your needs. This part of the appendix explains how to customize the Home tab and the Quicken toolbar.

Creating Custom Home Tab Views

As discussed in Chapter 1, the Home tab offers customizable views of your Quicken data. You can use this tab to create multiple Home tab views, each of which show the "snapshots" of summarized financial information that you want to display. Figure B-1 shows an example.

Figure B-1 • An example of the Main View of the Home tab, with some snapshots added.

The Home tab was known as My Pages in some previous versions of Quicken. If you've upgraded to Quicken 2010 from a previous version, you may already have custom views of the Quicken Home page set up in your Quicken data file. You'll get access to these views on the Home tab, where you can switch from one to another, modify them, and delete them as discussed in this section.

Displaying the Home Tab Views

To get started, click the Home tab near the top of the Quicken window. Quicken displays the View and Reports subtabs. Before you customize this view, it displays three snapshots: See Where Your Money Goes, Stay On Top Of Monthly Bills, and Set Spending Goals To Save Money. Once you've customized it, it displays the snapshots you added to it (refer to Figure B-1.)

Modifying the Current View

You can modify the current view with the Customize View dialog, which is shown next. Choose Customize This View from the Main Views pop-up menu in the View subtab (refer to Figure B-1). Make changes as desired and click OK to save them.

Adding an Item Items are organized by type in the Available Items list, making it easy to find the one you want. To add an item to the view, select it in the Available Items list and click Add. Its name appears in the Chosen Items list. You can include up to 16 items in the view.

Removing an Item To remove an item from the view, select it in the Chosen Items list and click Remove.

Rearranging Items To rearrange the order of items in the Chosen Items list, select an item and click Move Up or Move Down. Repeat this process until the items appear in the order you want.

Creating a New View

By creating multiple views, you can make several versions of the Home tab window, each with a specific set of information. You can then quickly switch from one view to another to see the information you want.

In the Home tab window, choose Add A Custom View from the Main View pop-up menu in the View subtab (refer to Figure B-1). The Customize View dialog, which is shown earlier, appears.

Enter a name for the view in the View Name box. Then follow the instructions in the previous section to add items to the view and click OK. A new Quicken Home tab window view is created to your specifications and appears onscreen.

Switching from One View to Another

If you have created more than one view for the Quicken Home window, each view has its own menu in the View subtab at the top of the Home tab window, as shown here. To switch from one view to another, simply click its button.

Deleting a View

To delete a view, open the pop-up menu for the view you want to delete. Then choose Delete This View from the menu. Click Yes in the confirmation dialog that appears. The view is deleted. You cannot delete the Main View.

Customizing the Toolbar

The toolbar is an optional row of buttons along the top of the screen, just beneath the menu bar. These buttons offer quick access to Quicken features.

You can customize the toolbar by adding, removing, or rearranging buttons, or by changing the display options for toolbar buttons. You can do all this with the Customize Toolbar dialog, which is shown on the top of the next page. To open this dialog, open the View menu and click Show Tool Bar. With the toolbar displayed, right-click it and choose Customize Tool Bar.

To customize the toolbar, make changes in this dialog and click OK. The toolbar is redrawn to your specifications.

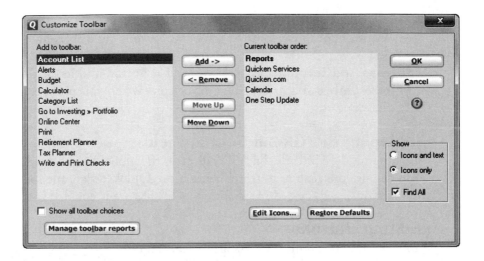

Adding Buttons

To add a button, select it in the Add To Toolbar list and click Add. Its name appears in the Current Toolbar Order list. If you want more items to choose from, turn on the Show All Toolbar Choices check box. The list expands to show approximately three times as many items.

You can include as many buttons as you like on the toolbar. If the toolbar includes more buttons than can fit within the Quicken application window, a More button (the green down arrow) appears on the toolbar. Click this button to display a menu of buttons; choose the name of the button you want.

Adding Saved Reports to the Toolbar

To add a saved report to the toolbar, click the Manage Toolbar Reports button. Then turn on the In Toolbar check box beside each saved report you want to add to the toolbar. Click OK to save your changes. Learn more about the Manage Toolbar Reports dialog in Chapter 9.

Removing Buttons

To remove a button, select it in the Current Toolbar Order list and click Remove. Its name is removed from the list.

Rearranging Buttons

You can rearrange the order of buttons in the toolbar by changing their order in the Current Toolbar Order list. Simply select a button that you want to move and click Move Up or Move Down to change its position in the list.

Changing the Appearance of Buttons

Two Show options determine how toolbar buttons are displayed:

- **Icons And Text** displays both the toolbar button and its label.
- **Icons Only** displays just the toolbar icon. When you point to an icon, its label appears.

Including the Global Search Field

Turning on the Find All check box displays the global Search field in the toolbar. You can use this feature to search your entire Quicken data file for specific transactions, as discussed in Chapter 5. This feature is enabled by default.

Editing Buttons

You can modify a button to change its label and assign a keyboard shortcut. Click the Edit Icons button to display the Edit Toolbar Button dialog, which is shown here. Then change the label or shortcut key for the toolbar button's command. Click OK to save your change. The label change does not appear in the Current Toolbar Order list, but it does appear on the toolbar when you save your customization settings.

Restoring the Default Toolbar

To restore the toolbar back to its "factory settings," click the Restore Defaults button in the Customize Toolbar dialog. Then click OK in the confirmation dialog that appears. The buttons return to the way they appear when Quicken is first installed.

Setting Preferences

The Preferences submenu under the Edit menu gives you access to dialogs for changing Quicken preference settings. In this section, I review all of the options you can change and tell you where you can learn more about the features they control.

Quicken Preferences

As the name suggests, Quicken Preferences control Quicken's general appearance and operations. To access these options, open the Edit menu and choose

Preferences | Quicken Preferences. The Quicken Preferences dialog appears, as shown next. It lists a variety of preference categories, each of which is discussed next.

Startup

Startup preferences enable you to specify what should appear when you start Quicken. Use the drop-down list to select Home (the default setting), one of the tabs (Home, Bills, Banking, and so on), or one of the views within the tabs. You can choose what you want Quicken to do when it starts, such as download transactions, and also choose one of the predefined color schemes for the Quicken program: blue (the default), green, purple, or tan.

Navigation Startup Navigation allows you to choose how you want to get around Quicken.

- **Main Navigation** lets you choose to use the Classic Menus (those used prior to 2010) and what to show in those menus.
- **Optional Navigation** lets you select where to place the Account Bar, whether to show the toolbar, and whether to dock the side bar.

```
┌─────────────────────────────────────────────────────────┐
│ Navigation preferences                                    │
│ ┌─Main Navigation──────────────────────────────────────┐ │
│ │ ☐ Use Classic Menus                                  │ │
│ │    ◉ Show Tabs and Action Bar                        │ │
│ │    ○ Show Action Bar only                            │ │
│ │    ○ No Tabs or Action Bar                           │ │
│ └──────────────────────────────────────────────────────┘ │
│ ┌─Optional Navigation──────────────────────────────────┐ │
│ │ ☑ Show Account Bar on:    ◉ Left Side   ○ Right Side │ │
│ │    ☐ Dock Account Bar                                │ │
│ │ ☑ Show Quicken Tool Bar                             │ │
│ │ ☐ Dock Side Bar (for wide screens only)             │ │
│ └──────────────────────────────────────────────────────┘ │
└─────────────────────────────────────────────────────────┘
```

Setup

Setup options, which are illustrated next, control basic Quicken operations such as:

```
┌─────────────────────────────────────────────────────────┐
│              Setup preferences                            │
│                                                           │
│                                                           │
│              Use Ctrl-Z/X/C/V for:                        │
│                 ○ Quicken standard                        │
│                 ◉ Windows standard (Undo/Cut/Copy/Paste)  │
│                                                           │
│              ☑ Turn on Quicken Sounds                     │
│              ☑ Turn on Animation                          │
│              ☐ Automatically Minimize Pop-up Windows      │
│                                                           │
└─────────────────────────────────────────────────────────┘
```

- **Keyboard Mappings** enables you to change what certain standard Windows keyboard shortcuts do. In most Windows programs, the CTRL-Z, CTRL-X, CTRL-C, and CTRL-V shortcut keys perform commands on the Edit menu. Because these commands have limited use within Quicken, you can map several Quicken-specific commands to these keys. Select the option as shown in Table B-1 for the mapping you want.
- **Turn On Quicken Sounds** turns on Quicken sound effects. You may want to turn this check box off if you use Quicken in an environment where its sounds might annoy the people around you.
- **Turn On Animation** turns on Quicken animation effects that appear when you complete certain actions.

Keystroke	Quicken Standard	Undo/Cut/Copy/Paste (Windows Standard)
CTRL-Z	QuickZoom a report amount	Edit | Undo
CTRL-X	Edit | Transaction | Go To Matching Transfer	Edit | Cut
CTRL-C	Tools | Category List	Edit | Copy
CTRL-V	Edit | Transaction | Void Transaction	Edit | Paste

Table B-1 • Keyboard Mapping Options

- **Automatically Minimize Popup Windows** automatically minimizes a Quicken window—such as a report window or the Category List window—to the Quicken task bar when you click outside that window. (This is the window behavior in some older versions of Quicken.) With this option turned off, you can have multiple Quicken windows open at once and can manually minimize each one. Learn more about Quicken's windows in Chapter 1.

Calendar and Currency The folks at Intuit realize that not everyone manages their finances on a calendar year basis or in U.S. dollars alone. The Calendar And Currency options, which are shown next, enable you to customize these settings for the way you use Quicken:

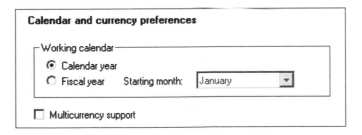

- **Working Calendar** enables you to choose between two options: Calendar Year is a 12-month year beginning with January, and Fiscal Year is a 12-month year beginning with the month you choose from the drop-down list.
- **Multicurrency Support** assigns a "home" currency to all of your current data, placing a currency symbol beside every amount. You can then enter amounts in other currencies by entering the appropriate currency symbol. You can confirm the default currency in the Windows Regional Settings control panel. It is not necessary to set this option unless you plan to work with multiple currencies in one Quicken data file.

Backup   The Backup options, illustrated next, enable you to customize the way Quicken's Backup feature works. Beginning with Quicken 2010, you can now choose to have Quicken automatically do backups on your computer's hard drive and choose to be reminded to do manual backups on any drive you want. Besides allowing you to turn these two forms of backup on or off, you also have these settings:

- **Back Up After Running Quicken *NN* Times** tells Quicken to automatically back up (make a copy) of your Quicken data on your normal hard drive after you have run Quicken NN times.
- **Maximum Number Of Backup Copies** is the number of backup copies Quicken should automatically keep. The higher the value in this text box, the more backup copies of your Quicken data are saved. This enables you to go back further if you discover a problem with your current Quicken data file. I tell you more about backing up data in Appendix A.
- **Remind After Running Quicken *NN* Times** enables you to specify when you want to be reminded to manually back up your Quicken data file. If you also have automatic backups turned on, this allows you to back up your data on another drive other than your normal drive. Learn how to back up your data in Appendix A.

Web Connect The Web Connect options, shown next, enable you to customize the way Quicken's Web Connect feature works. Web Connect, as discussed in Chapter 6, is a method for downloading transaction information from your financial institution into your Quicken data file.

Web Connect preferences

☐ Give me the option of saving to a file whenever I download Web Connect data.

☑ Keep Quicken open after Web Connect completes.

- **Give Me The Option Of Saving To A File Whenever I Download Web Connect Data** displays a dialog that enables you to save the downloaded Web Connect information to a file on disk. Normally, the data is imported directly into the appropriate account in your Quicken data file.
- **Keep Quicken Open After Web Connect Completes** tells Quicken to keep running after Web Connect completes a download from the Web.

Alerts

Alerts preferences enable you to set the lead time for calendar notes to appear in Alerts snapshots. This does not affect the lead time for scheduled transactions or Billminder. Select a lead time period from the drop-down list; timing options range from Last Week to Next 14 Days. Learn about alerts in Chapter 9.

Investment Transactions

Investment Transactions options (shown here) let you customize the way the Investment Transaction list looks and works. Learn about the Investment Transaction list in Chapter 10.

Investment transaction list preferences

List display: One Line
Sort choice: Oldest First
☐ Show hidden transactions
☑ Show Attach button

- **List Display** determines whether transactions should appear with one or two lines in the list.
- **Sort Choice** determines whether transactions should be sorted in ascending or descending order by date.
- **Show Hidden Transactions** displays hidden transactions in the list.
- **Show Attach Button** displays the Attach button beside the Enter, Edit, and Delete buttons for the current transaction. You may want to turn off this check box if you do not use the Image Attachment feature. Chapter 5 explains how to attach images to transactions.

Register

Register preferences enable you to fine-tune the way the account register works. Four groups of settings appear. Account register windows are discussed throughout this book, but details for using them are provided in Chapter 5.

Register   Register options, shown next, affect the way the transactions you enter appear in the account register window.

- **Show Date In First Column** displays the transaction date in the first column of the register.
- **Show Memo Before Category** displays the Memo field to the left of the Category field.
- **Show Tag Field** displays the Tag field in the register form.
- **Show TurboTax Icon** displays an icon beside any transaction for which the category is tax-related. Learn how to set tax options for categories in Chapter 18.
- **Automatically Enter Split Data** turns the OK button in the Split Transaction window into an Enter button for entering the transaction.
- **Use Automatic Categorization** uses the Automatic Categorization feature to "guess" which category should be assigned to a transaction based on a database of company names and keywords stored within Quicken.

- **Automatically Place Decimal Point** automatically enters a decimal point two places to the left when using Quicken's built-in calculator. For example, if you enter **1543** in the calculator, Quicken enters 15.43.
- **Show Transaction Toolbar** adds the Enter, Edit, and Split buttons to the currently selected transaction.
- **Show Attach Button** displays the attachment button, which looks like a paper clip.
- **Gray Reconciled Transactions** displays all reconciled transactions with gray characters rather than black characters.
- **Remember Register Filters After Quicken Closes** remembers any register filter settings you may have made when you close Quicken so those settings are in place the next time you start Quicken.
- **Use Pop-Up Registers** opens registers in separate windows, allowing you to have several windows with various information open at the same time.
- **Fonts** displays a dialog you can use to select the font and size for register windows.
- **Colors** displays a dialog you can use to select colors for register windows.

QuickFill QuickFill options, which are shown next, allow you to fine-tune the way Quicken's QuickFill feature works. Learn more about QuickFill in Chapter 7.

- **Use Enter Key To Move Between Fields** enables you to use both the ENTER and TAB keys to move from field to field when entering data.

- **Complete Fields Using Previous Entries** enters transaction information using the information from previous entries.
- **Recall Memorized Payees** uses memorized payees to fill in QuickFill entries. This option is not available if the Complete Fields Using Previous Entries option is disabled.
- **Provide Drop-Down Lists On Field Entry** automatically displays the drop-down list when you advance to a field with a list.
- **Capitalize Payees And Categories** automatically makes the first letter of each word in a payee name or category uppercase.
- **Show Buttons On QuickFill Fields** displays drop-down list buttons on fields for which you can use QuickFill.
- **Automatically Memorize New Payees** tells Quicken to automatically enter all transactions for a new payee to the Memorized Transaction list.
- **Automatically Memorize To The Calendar List** tells Quicken to automatically add memorized transactions to the Memorized Transaction list in the Calendar window. This option is turned on by default. The Financial Calendar is covered in Chapter 7; you can display the Memorized Transaction list by choosing Show Memorized Transaction List from the Options menu on the Calendar's button bar.
- **Add Address Book QuickFill Group Items To Memorized Payee List** tells Quicken to add entries from the Financial Address Book to the Memorized Payee list so they automatically fill in address fields when writing checks.
- **Remove Memorized Payees Not Used In Last *NN* Months** tells Quicken to remove memorized transactions that have not been used within the number of months you specify. By default, this feature is turned off; as a result, Quicken remembers the first 2,000 transactions you enter and then stops remembering transactions. By selecting this check box and entering a value of **6** (for example), Quicken memorizes only the transactions you entered in the past six months, thus keeping the Memorized Transaction list manageable. Using this feature with a lower value (for example, **3**) can weed one-time transactions out of the Memorized Transaction list. Changing this option does not affect transactions that have already been entered. Chapter 7 discusses memorized transactions.

Notify Notify options, shown on the top of the next page, affect the way you are notified about problems when you enter transactions in the register:

- **When Entering Out-Of-Date Transactions** warns you when you try to record a transaction for a date more than a year from the current date.

```
┌─────────────────────────────────────────────────────────┐
│ Notify preferences                                        │
│                                                           │
│  ┌─ Notify ────────────────────────────────────────────┐ │
│  │  ☑  When entering out-of-date transactions          │ │
│  │  ☑  Before changing existing transactions           │ │
│  │  ☑  When entering uncategorized transactions        │ │
│  │  ☑  To run a reconcile report after reconcile       │ │
│  │  ☑  Warn if a check number is re-used                │ │
│  └─────────────────────────────────────────────────────┘ │
└─────────────────────────────────────────────────────────┘
```

- **Before Changing Existing Transactions** warns you when you try to modify a previously entered transaction.
- **When Entering Uncategorized Transactions** warns you when you try to record a transaction without assigning a category to it.
- **To Run A Reconcile Report After Reconcile** asks if you want to display a Reconcile report when you complete an account reconciliation.
- **Warn If A Check Number Is Re-used** warns you if you assign a check number that was already assigned in another transaction.

Write Checks   Write Checks options, shown here, affect the way the checks you enter with the Write Checks window appear when printed:

```
┌─────────────────────────────────────────────────────────┐
│ Write Checks preferences                                  │
│                                                           │
│  ┌─ Printed date style ────────────────────────────────┐ │
│  │  ⦿  4-digit year                                     │ │
│  │  ○  2-digit year                                     │ │
│  └─────────────────────────────────────────────────────┘ │
│                                                           │
│  ┌─ Check settings ────────────────────────────────────┐ │
│  │  ☐  Spell currency units                            │ │
│  │  ☐  Allow entry of extra message on check           │ │
│  │  ☑  Print categories on voucher checks              │ │
│  │  ☐  Change date of checks to date when printed      │ │
│  └─────────────────────────────────────────────────────┘ │
└─────────────────────────────────────────────────────────┘
```

- **Printed Date Style** enables you to select a four-digit or two-digit date style.
- **Spell Currency Units** tells Quicken to spell out the currency amount in the second Amount field.
- **Allow Entry Of Extra Message On Check** displays an additional text box for a message in the Write Checks window. The message you enter is printed on the check in a place where it cannot be seen if the check is mailed in a window envelope.

- **Print Categories On Voucher Checks** prints category information, including splits and classes, on the voucher part of voucher checks. This option affects only voucher-style checks.
- **Change Date Of Checks To Date When Printed** automatically prints the print date, rather than the transaction date, on each check.

Downloaded Transactions Downloaded Transactions options, which are shown next, control the way Quicken handles transactions downloaded into Quicken from your financial institution. I tell you more about downloading transactions into Quicken in Chapter 6.

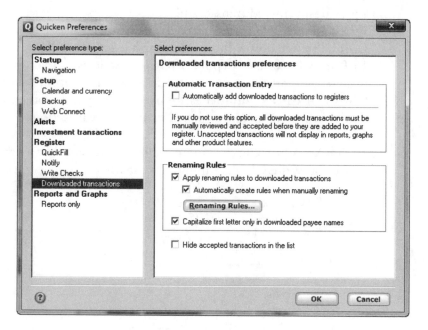

- **Automatically Add Downloaded Transactions To Registers** saves manually reviewing and accepting each transaction and possibly leaving an unaccepted transaction out of Quicken reports and graphs.
- **Apply Renaming Rules To Downloaded Transactions** turns on Quicken's renaming feature, which is discussed in Chapter 6.
- **Automatically Create Rules When Manually Renaming** tells Quicken to create renaming rules automatically based on transactions you rename manually.
- **Renaming Rules** displays the Renaming Rules For Downloaded Transactions dialog, which you can use to create, modify, and remove renaming rules.

- **Capitalize First Letter Only In Downloaded Payee Names** capitalizes just the first letter of a payee name for a downloaded transaction.
- **Hide Accepted Transactions In The List** does not display transactions that have already been accepted in the Downloaded Transactions list.

Reports and Graphs

Reports And Graphs preferences include two categories of options for creating reports and graphs. Creating reports and graphs is discussed in Chapter 9.

Reports And Graphs Preferences Reports And Graphs options, shown next, enable you to set default options for creating reports and graphs:

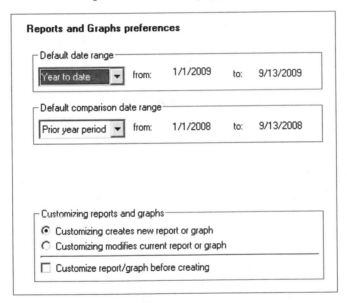

- **Default Date Range** and **Default Comparison Date Range** enable you to specify a default range for regular and comparison reports. Choose an option from each drop-down list. If you choose Custom, you can enter exact dates.
- **Customizing Reports And Graphs** options determine how reports and graphs are customized and what happens when they are. Customizing Creates New Report Or Graph, which is the default setting, creates a subreport based on the report you customize. Customizing Modifies Current Report Or Graph changes the report you customize without creating a subreport.
- **Customize Report/Graph Before Creating** tells Quicken to offer to customize a report or graph when you choose one.

Reports Only This group of options, which is shown next, applies only to reports:

```
┌─────────────────────────────────────────────────────┐
│ Report only preferences                               │
│ ┌─Account display──────────────────────────────────┐ │
│ │  ○ Description                                    │ │
│ │  ◉ Name                                           │ │
│ │  ○ Both                                           │ │
│ └──────────────────────────────────────────────────┘ │
│ ┌─Category display─────────────────────────────────┐ │
│ │  ○ Description                                    │ │
│ │  ◉ Name                                           │ │
│ │  ○ Both                                           │ │
│ └──────────────────────────────────────────────────┘ │
│  ☑ Use color in report                               │
│  ☑ QuickZoom to investment forms                     │
│  ☐ Remind me to save reports                         │
│  Decimal places for prices and shares:  [3]  (0-6)   │
└─────────────────────────────────────────────────────┘
```

- **Account Display** and **Category Display** enable you to set what you want to display for each account or category listed in the report: Description, Name, or Both.
- **Use Color In Report** tells Quicken to use color when displaying report titles and negative numbers.
- **QuickZoom To Investment Forms** tells Quicken to display the investment form for a specific investment when you double-click it in an investment report. With this check box turned off, Quicken displays the investment register transaction entry instead.
- **Remind Me To Save Reports** tells Quicken to ask whether you want to save a customized report when you close the report window.
- **Decimal Places For Prices And Shares** enables you to specify the number of decimal places to display for per-share security prices and number of shares in investment reports.

Customize Online Update Options

You can customize One Step Update options in the Connection tab of the Customize Online Updates dialog, shown next. (Other options in this dialog are covered in Chapter 11.) Open the Edit menu and choose Preferences | Customize Online Updates and click the Connection tab.

- **Send Anonymous Product Usage Data During One Step Update** sends information about the way you use Quicken to the product development team at Intuit. This helps them understand how users like you utilize Quicken's features so they can improve Quicken.
- **Run One Step Update When Starting Quicken** automatically starts the One Step Update procedure when you start Quicken. You might find this feature useful if you always run One Step Update as part of a Quicken work session.
- **Change My Quicken.com Member ID And Password The Next Time I Run One Step Update** instructs Quicken to display the Quicken.com login screen when you connect to Quicken.com. With this option turned off, Quicken can automatically enter your saved login information if, when you registered with Quicken.com, you selected the option to save your login information and are connecting with the same computer. This check box is disabled until you set up a Quicken.com login by registering your copy of Quicken online. Learn about registering Quicken in Chapter 1.

Internet Connection Setup

Under most circumstances, the Internet connection used by Quicken to download transactions, update Quicken, and connect to Quicken.com is the default connection established in Windows for your computer. Quicken, however, gives you the option of using a different established connection or setting up an Internet connection.

If you want to change the Internet connection you will use with Quicken or begin the setup of an Internet connection from within Quicken, open the Edit menu and choose Preferences | Internet Connection Setup. The Internet Connection Setup dialog will open, as shown the next, with the default to use the computer's Internet connection selected.

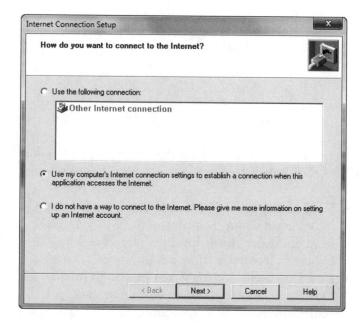

If you have multiple Internet connections, or if you want to select one at the time of connecting to the Internet, click Use The Following Connection, choose the connection you want to use or Other Internet Connection to choose at the time of connecting, and click Next. If you selected Other Internet Connection, you will be told you must make a manual connection each time you connect to the Internet. Click Done. If you selected another established Internet connection, click Done.

If you select to get information about a way to connect to the Internet, click Next. You will be told to find and sign up with an Internet service provider (ISP). Then click Done. Talk to your neighbors, associates at work, or your friends about ISPs that they recommend. Your telephone and cable TV companies can probably provide Internet service.

Converting from Microsoft Money

Welcome to Quicken, Microsoft Money user! This document will help explain some of the similarities and a few differences as you start using Quicken. I will talk about what you are used to seeing in Microsoft Money and what the same process looks like on your Quicken screen. Along the way, I think you'll learn to appreciate the many features that Quicken offers.

Converting Your Data Files from Money To Quicken

As you prepare to convert your Money data files to Quicken, there are a few things you can do in Money to make the conversion easier. Review your files as shown below, and ensure that all of your Money records are complete and up to date.

 If you are converting Money data files to versions of Quicken prior to Quicken 2010, see the information Intuit has available at http://quicken.intuit.com/support/articles/getting-started/upgrading-and-conversion/5521.html.

Before You Start Your Conversion

To ensure a smooth transition, first review your Money data files. Each of these actions will improve the chances of a good conversion:

- Clean up your Payee list to ensure there are no duplicate names because of mistyping. It's a lot easier to do this *before* you convert than to take the time afterwards.
- Review your Category list and remove any that are unused.
- Review your online recurring payments and calendar to ensure you have stopped them. You'll be setting them up again in Quicken.
- Check that your financial institution can download into Quicken (most can) and how that download is accomplished.

A quick way to check is to use the Setup tab in Quicken to set up a new (dummy) account in a new Quicken file, and enter the name of your financial institution.

Delete the dummy account before you start your conversion to ensure an empty file for your conversion.

- Reconcile all of your accounts prior to converting.
- Ensure that all of your downloaded transactions are complete and up to date
- Review your account names in Money to ensure they are less than the Quicken maximum character length (40 characters) and change them if necessary.

Your Money category names, payee names, and notes and memos do not have this same 40-character limit and the Quicken file converter will truncate file names if needed.

Both Quicken and Money are, by default, installed in the Program Files folder on your main hard drive (usually the "C" drive). However, you can keep your data files in whatever folder you choose as discussed in Chapter 1. After you have installed Quicken, it is time to convert your files (those with the file extension .mny) from Microsoft Money to Quicken.

In order to convert your .mny files, you must have installed both Quicken and Microsoft Money on the same computer.

You should have no problem converting all of your bank transactions, your checking, savings, and credit card accounts. Likewise, your category and other name information should also convert cleanly after you have made any necessary changes to the number of characters in each name. Remember that any recurring payments you have set up in Money, such as monthly insurance payments, will have to be canceled in Money and reset in Quicken.

Converting Your Money Files

Quicken 2010 can convert Microsoft Money 2007 and 2008 files. If you have an earlier version, you can download a trial version of Money Plus (2008) from these websites:

- **Deluxe:** http://www.microsoft.com/downloads/details.aspx?displaylang= en&FamilyID=d7e321d1-3965-46aa-87e2-8f4259e63b63
- **Home & Business:** http://www.microsoft.com/downloads/details.aspx? displaylang=en&FamilyID=ede8403f-a5dd-461b-a9d6-0fd9969824d7

Convert your old Money data files to Money 2008 files and convert from the 2008 files into Quicken. Before you start your conversion, verify the balances in each of your Money accounts. Print a list of these balances to compare with your Quicken balances after the conversion. To print the list:

- In Money, click **Account List**. Ensure that each of your accounts is displayed.
- Click **File | Print** to print the report.

Then, check these account balances after the conversion to ensure the information has come across cleanly.

Begin the Conversion

To begin converting your .mny files:

- Install and launch Quicken. The Welcome to Quicken window appears as seen in Figure C-1.

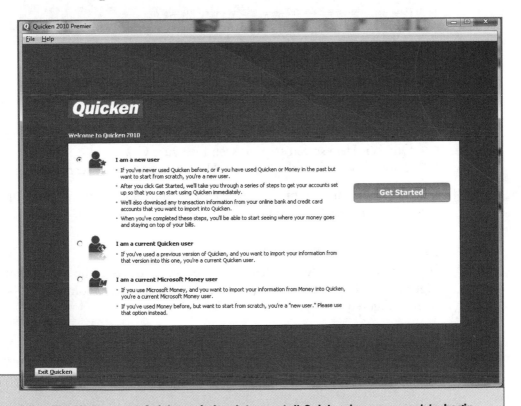

Figure C-1 • The Welcome to Quicken window lets you tell Quicken how you want to begin.

- As seen in Figure C-1, you have three choices. If you want to start from scratch, click **I Am A New User** and then the **Get Started** button to follow the onscreen directions. See "Starting From Scratch" later in this chapter.
- If you want to convert your Money files right away, click **I Am A Current Microsoft Money User.** and click the **Get Started** button.
- If you use a password to protect your Microsoft Money data file, you are prompted to enter it.
- You may also be asked for your Windows Live ID password. A progress bar appears showing the progress of your conversion. If your file is quite large, this may take many minutes.
- When the conversion has completed successfully, the message box shown here is displayed. If your conversion has errors, a dialog appears that allows you to view a log that explains where the errors occurred.

- Click Read Next Steps to continue. Review the suggestions shown in the Quicken Help screen steps as seen in Figure C-2.
- If you choose Skip, the Quicken Home page opens as seen in Figure C-3.

Check this web site for more information: http://quicken.intuit.com/support/articles/getting-started/upgrading-and-conversion/7468.html.

Starting From Scratch

If you choose the "I Am A New User" option at the welcome screen shown in Figure C-1, click Get Started to begin. A blank Quicken Home page opens as seen in Figure C-4.

- Click File | File Import | Microsoft Money File as seen here.
- Locate your .mny files and click Open as seen in Figure C-5.

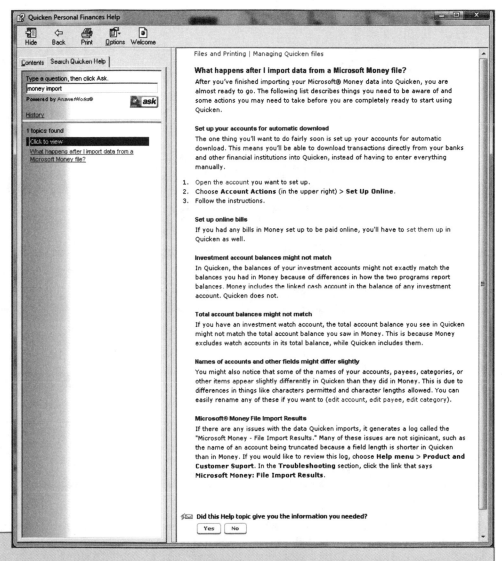

Figure C-2 • You can follow the Quicken Help steps to ensure a smooth conversion from Microsoft Money.

- Click OK. A message box appears showing the progress of the file being imported.
- After the files have been converted, you see a message box telling you that your Microsoft Money data file has been imported as seen above. Click Read Next Steps to see a list of steps you may take to ensure a smooth conversion.

Figure C-3 • The Quicken Home page is your starting point in Quicken.

You import your Money data files into a new, empty Quicken file. Do *not* try to convert Money data files into an existing Quicken file with data in it. If you try to do this, you will see this warning message.

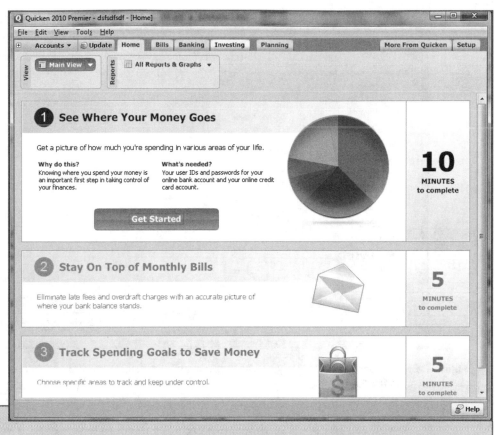

Figure C-4 • From a blank Quicken Home page, you can manually import your Microsoft Money data file.

If you see warning or error messages during the conversion process such as the ones shown here, click Help | Quicken Support from the Quicken menu bar or choose Help | Quicken Live Community to see if there is a known issue about your error. You can also visit http://quicken.intuit.com/support/articles/getting-started/upgrading-and-conversion/7416.html.

- WARNING: One or more accounts in Money is in the middle of a reconciliation.
- WARNING: Account bank name truncated to: ...
- WARNING: Transaction memo truncated to: ...
- WARNING: Payee memo truncated to: ...
- WARNING: Address notes truncated to: ...

Figure C-5 • Choose the .mny file you want to convert and select Open to tell Quicken which data file to import.

As you can see, some of these errors refer to issues that you fixed if you followed the "Before You Get Started" tips provided earlier in this chapter.

Your converted file opens to the Home page as shown in Figure C-3.

Your New Quicken Home Page

Your new Quicken Home Page has some similarities to your familiar Microsoft Money Home Page as well as some noticeable differences as seen in Table C-1 below.

Quicken Comparisons

Description	Quicken	Money
Files	Collection of accounts Click File | New Quicken File from Menu bar	Collection of accounts Click File | New | New File from Menu bar
Account Bar	Lists all of your accounts in a file. By default, always is displayed on the left of the open window.	Click Home | My Money | Account List OR Banking | Account List
Action Bar	Available under each tab in Quicken, allowing quick access to tools and reports for that section. Also, no need to switch between settings. Complete information is available from one window.	Each task has a separate tab or menu which can vary between Essential and Advanced settings.
Edit an Account	Click Edit Account to change information on the account itself to open the Account Details dialog. No need to click two or three menu items to accomplish these tasks!	In Money, you edit an account by clicking Home | Account List | Change Account Details or Banking, right-mouse click on the account name and click Rename.

Table C-1 • Quicken Makes Much of Your Important Information Available with One Click

To show both the Payee and the Category lines in your register, click Account Actions and click Two-line Display as shown here.

Bills Tab

The Bills tab in Quicken provides all of your bill information in one location. All of the bills you have scheduled appear on the list and you can add new Reminders with a simple click.

Table C-2 gives some comparisons to what you see in Microsoft Money.

Description	Quicken	Money
Calendar	Click Bills | Calendar to see a colorful and a complete calendar. Simply double-click or right-click a bill to enter the transaction into an account.	Click Bills | Bills Summary | Show Calendar | Enter in Register to open the Record Payment window
Recurring Payments	In Quicken, recurring payments are called Reminders. To set up a new reminder, simply right-click on a transaction and click the Schedule Bill or Deposit to open the Add Transaction Reminder dialog, as discussed earlier in this book. You can also click the Add Reminder sub-tab in the Bills tab Action Bar.	Switch to Advanced Bills and click the Bills tab. From the Bills Summary page, click New | *transaction type*. Complete the Create a Recurring Bill dialog and click OK.
Printing Checks	Make the transaction's payment method Print Check. Click File | Print Checks to open the Select Checks To Print dialog and enter the information as covered in Part Two of this book.	Click Banking | Account List | *account name*. Right-click in the Num field | Print This Transaction | Enter. Click File | Print Checks.
Online Payments	Set up online payments through your bank or Quicken Bill Pay service. Click Setup | *account name* | Activate Bill Pay. See Chapter 6 for more information about setting up online payments.	Set up through either your bank, MSN Bill Pay or other bill paying service. Click Banking | Account List | Common Tasks | Manage Online Services

Table C-2 • Reviewing and Paying Bills is Easy in Quicken

Banking Tab

The Account Actions button under the Banking tab allows you to enter and print transactions, write checks, transfer funds from one account to another, run reports, and change your register views as shown in Table C-3.

View

The View sub-tab in the Banking tab lets you see a list of all of your accounts; Spending (usually your checking and cash accounts), Savings, and Credit Card Accounts. Just as you would do in Microsoft Money, simply click on any of the account names to open the register. The Quicken account list shows the financial

Description	Quicken	Money
Move through the account register	Press Tab	Press Tab
Enter Key	If you are entering a transaction and inadvertently hit Enter, the transaction will be automatically entered into the register, even if you have not completed the entry. To return to the transaction, simply click on it to make any necessary changes.	If you press Enter without completing the transaction, a dialog appears asking you to complete the information or press OK to enter the transaction as is. To return to the transaction, double-click to open the transaction form dialog from which you can make changes, additions, or deletions.

Table C-2 • Banking Transactions Are Straightforward

institution where the account is held (if you choose), what you have set as the minimum balance, (useful if your institutions offers free checking if you maintain a minimum balance), the interest rate for the account if there is one, and the Ending Balance in the account. The Ending Balance includes all future transactions if they have been entered into the account. For example, if you have ordered a product that will not be shipped for several weeks, and have entered that order into your credit card account, the Ending Balance of that credit card will show the future transaction as part of its total.

Reports

Quicken includes robust reporting capabilities. You can create a report for any period, using any information you choose. If you are used to using the Advanced Reports from Microsoft Money, you'll feel very comfortable with Quicken reports. Each tab in Quicken has a Reports sub-tab as shown here.

You can also see a menu for all Quicken reports by choosing View | Classic Menus. Choose Reports to open the drop-down menu as seen on the top of the next page. These reports are the same ones available in each sub-tab.

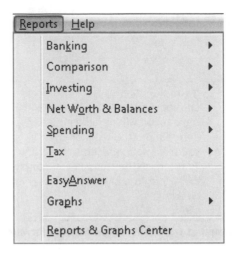

The Reports and Graph Center gives you a number of options for colorful graphs that are sometimes easier to read than a report full of numbers. Figure C-6 shows one example.

Figure C-6 • Quicken's graphs and charts make understanding your financial information easy.

Planning Tab

The Quicken Planning tab places all of your budget and forecasting tools in one location. This tab is a combination of the Planning, Budget, and Tax tabs you used in Microsoft Money. In one screen you access all of the tools, calculators, and reports that help you plan your financial life. For example, in the Cash Flow view, you see how much you spent, how much you earned and can display your daily balances in one or more banking accounts as seen in Figure C-7.

Figure C-7 • Quicken makes understanding your finances simple—with graphs, reports, and lists—all accessible in one place.

Along with your budget tools, the Planning Tab includes a number of tax tools as shown here. These include online tax calculators and links to common tax questions.

Investing Tab

The Quicken Investing tab displays all of your investing information as seen in Table C-4.

Description	Quicken	Money
Retirement Accounts	Does not allow linked cash accounts with retirement accounts. They are shown separately.	Allows linked cash accounts.
Investing Information	Click the Investing tab | View | Account Overview to see the current standing of your investing and retirement accounts.	Click Investing tab | My Investing Tools | Portfolio Manager to view just your account information.
Investing Tools	In the Investing center's Action Bar, click Tools to open a menu as shown here.	The Investing tab opens a window with Investing Tips; the Investing Advisor and several other tools. You see other information by clicking on the Investing bar at the left of the window.

Table C-4 • From the Investing Tab, You Can See All of Your Investing Activities

How Quicken Backup Procedures Differ From Money

As discussed in Appendix A, Table C-5 describes the backup procedures in Quicken compared to how you backed up in Microsoft Money.

It is always a good idea to save your backup data to someplace other than your main hard drive. Choose an external hard drive, a flash (thumb) drive, a recordable CD or DVD, or an online backup service such as Quicken Online Backup.

Quicken	Money
From the Menu bar, click File | Backup and Restore. Choose Back Up Quicken File *or* from anyplace in Quicken Hold down CTRL and press B.	From the menu bar, click File | Backup and type a name for the backup file.
Either accept the default location for your backed up file or select a new one. You can even enter today's date to distinguish this file from others in the same location.	Click Save.
Click Back Up Now. The backed up file is saved in your selected location. A message box appears telling you the file has been backed up successfully.	The backed up file is saved in the selected folder.

Table C-5 • Backing Up Your Files Using Quicken's Backup Procedures Is an Easy Task

These are just some of Quicken screens, windows, and dialogs with which you'll be working as you transition from Microsoft Money. As you continue to work with Quicken, you'll find that it is intuitive and helpful. Again, welcome to Quicken!

Index

523